"Bob Dylan .... blues singers of western world; ancient art, on-the-spot improvisation, mind quickness, endless variation, classical formulae, prophetic vision, mighty wind-horse. Paul Williams's *BOB DYLAN: Performing Artist* historicises Dylan's genius of American tongue."

— Allen Ginsberg

"Anything Paul Williams writes about Bob Dylan — and always in his wonderfully unpretentious, conversational, and heartfelt manner — is worth reading. *BOB DYLAN: Performing Artist* immediately enters the canon as one of the few necessary books on Bob Dylan." — Jonathan Cott, contributing editor, *Rolling Stone*

About Paul Williams:

"*The* pioneer of modern rock journalism."   — *Twilight Zone*

"A major talent."   — *Publishers Weekly*

"The best writer around today whose subject is rock and roll."
— *Rolling Stone*

Library Journal calls Paul Williams "one of the architects of serious rock criticism". He is the author of eighteen books, including *Dylan — What Happened?*, and the founder of *Crawdaddy!*, the first American rock music magazine.

Bob Dylan

Performing Artist

1974 ★ 1986

The Middle Years

by Paul Williams

Exclusive Distributors
Music Sales Limited,
8/9 Frith Street,
London W1D 3JB, UK.

Music Sales Corporation,
257 Park Avenue South,
New York, NY 10010, USA.

Macmillan Distribution Services,
53 Park West Drive,
Derrimut, Vic 3030,
Australia.

To the Music Trade only:
Music Sales Limited,
8/9 Frith Street,
London W1D 3JB, UK.

Every effort has been made to trace the copyright holders of the photographs in
this book but one or two were unreachable. We would be grateful if the
photographers concerned would contact us.

Printed by: Cox & Wyman Ltd, Reading.

A catalogue record for this book is available from the British Library.

Visit Omnibus Press on the web at www.omnibuspress.com.

*this book is for the ones
who walk on stage
and open their mouths
and sing*

Contents

Bob Dylan

Performing Artist

1974 ★ 1986

The Middle Years

by Paul Williams

OMNIBUS PRESS
LONDON · NEW YORK · SYDNEY

Preface

This is the second of two books about Bob Dylan in performance. They are intended as a survey of the entire output of this prolific artist, on stage and in the recording studio, from the beginning of his career in 1960 up to the end of his 1986 tour, the cut-off point for this volume.

I see Dylan as first and foremost a performing artist, as opposed to a composer or songwriter. He *is* a songwriter, of course, and a very good one; but in my view (and apparently Dylan's as well, according to comments he has made to interviewers throughout his career) his songwriting is best understood as an activity directed by and in service to the needs of the performer.

A performer cannot be pigeon-holed as neatly as an author or a recording artist, whose complete works may be put on a shelf or stored in a record cabinet. Our era is one that likes to think of works of art as objects, to be placed in museums and evaluated in terms of money if possible, so many millions of dollars per Van Gogh canvas. Performance, an older art form than composition (though both have ancient roots, and neither exists entirely apart from the other), has been until this century an ephemeral art, leaving no trace of itself except in the memory of the observer. This ephemeral quality is closely linked to the spiritual value that has always been associated with music and with the dramatic arts. Spiritual as opposed to rational meaning is most often communicated in a moment of transitory comprehension. The moment does not last, but its effects most certainly do.

My appreciation of the work of this great living artist, almost my contemporary (I'm seven years younger), has required me to explore some methods of talking about music and songs and performances that are perhaps a little different from art criticism as we have known it. The idea of "explaining" a performance is, in a real sense, absurd. What we can attempt to examine, however, is the experience of the observer, the listener, the person who is moved by the performance. If this can be described, however imperfectly, then we may have the beginnings of a common reference point for discussion of Bob Dylan's work, his artistic oeuvre.

Elsewhere in this volume I attempt to address the question of to what extent an audiotape or videotape "recording" of a performance can be considered equivalent to the performance itself. For now it is sufficient to say that many persons, including myself, have found tremendous satisfaction and whatever other rewards are associated with enjoyment of an artist's creations by listening to Bob Dylan's concerts on tape as well as by attending them in person. The existence of an enduring and accessible body of work in the form of these tapes of live performances makes possible this present volume, which argues that much of the artist's finest work has been done in the 1970s and the 1980s, and outside of the confines of the recording studio.

The book begins at the moment of Bob Dylan's return to the stage, after a seven and a half year hiatus during which he did not tour and in fact only performed one complete concert. Dylan was 32 years old. His creative life could well have been behind him, as it was for so many of his contemporaries. Instead he succeeded, by tremendous efforts of will and through a demanding process of self-honesty, in finding a new and continuing creative ground for himself, not unrelated to but finally not imprisoned by any expectations or concepts placed upon him by the outside world. His is the rare story of an artist who overcame and continues to overcome the obstacle of great public attention in order to keep on with his real work.

I need to acknowledge that this book is itself a sort of performance, heavily rewritten as it goes along but for the most part not tampered with much once each section is completed to my satisfaction. The emphasis placed on certain songs and performances from each period represents an attempt to be true to my own impressions and enthusiasms at the time of writing, and so it would be awkward and perhaps misleading for me to go back and rewrite these chapters at a later date based on new material that has become available or come to my attention. This issue comes up particularly in regard to Columbia Records' release in spring 1991 of *The Bootleg Series, Volumes 1–3*, a remarkable collection of 58 Bob Dylan performances not previously released to the public.

Many of these were circulating privately among Dylan fans, and therefore were available to me as I wrote these pages. But other songs and performances were new to me, and so I've had to decide whether to go back and rework my discussions of *Blood on the Tracks* and *Desire*, for example, to include consideration of such fascinating performances as "Call Letter Blues" and "Catfish" and the incomparable "Golden Loom." I've chosen not to, and instead have included a few footnotes to indicate that songs that were unreleased or even unheard when I was writing about a particular period are now available to all of us. On the other hand, I have referred to material from *The Bootleg Series* in my chapter on *Infidels* and in subsequent chapters, because they were written after that collection was released.

More and more unreleased work by this prolific artist will be made available as the years go by, and so the story will continue to change. As I wrote in Volume One, "it is my hope that . . . this book may serve as a kind of catalog, the merest beginnings of a guide, to the story of Bob Dylan that he himself has told and is still telling, every time he sings, every time he steps up to a microphone."

Paul Williams
March 1992

I. Hero

January 1974 - February 1974

"Well, it wasn't planned ... I saw daylight; I took off."
—Bob Dylan, January 1974

1.

Bob Dylan and the Band performed forty concerts in forty-three days in January and February of 1974. Their itinerary ran through twenty-one cities in the United States and Canada, starting in Chicago and ending in Los Angeles. After trying out a number of different songs and switching things around somewhat in the first few shows, Dylan let the concerts settle into a fairly fixed format. The typical show featured eighteen Dylan performances (thirteen backed by the Band, five Dylan solo on acoustic guitar), plus ten songs by the Band alone.

In June 1974, Dylan released *Before the Flood*, the first live album of his career. It includes three acoustic performances by Dylan; ten songs by Dylan with the Band; and eight by the Band alone. The resulting two-record album is an excellent representation of the tour, given the time limits of an lp record. Still, one misses the songs that were left out. And although the Band's songs are first-rate, and their inclusion here appropriate, they don't sustain this listener's interest the way the Dylan/Band and Dylan solo performances do. The ideal *Before the Flood*, for me, would be four sides of Dylan (with the Band songs on a separate album).

The performances on *Before the Flood* are from the last three concerts of the tour, in Los Angeles, except for "Knockin' on Heaven's Door" (NYC 1/30) and "Highway 61 Revisited" (Seattle 2/9). The recording quality is excellent—generally speaking the sound on the album is probably better than it was in most parts of the indoor sports arenas (typically seating 14,000 to 15,000 people) where these concerts were held. There's a lot to be said for the excitement and immediacy of being present at a concert; but if you end up, as I did at the one show I attended, in the distant recesses of a large stadium, your inability to see anything or to hear the music clearly tends to diminish the experience.

(I admit I was intimidated by the much-publicized information that five million paid mail orders were sent in for the 650,000 seats actually available on the tour, making this the biggest Event and most sought-after ticket thus far in rock and roll history. So I accepted my poor seats with gratitude and never thought of trying to see another show. But I learned something about commitment and trust from my friend Heckel, who flew in from Tokyo with no concert tickets and managed to attend all five of the New York area shows, often in very good seats, buying his tickets from scalpers at little more than face value five or ten minutes after each show began. And here I was not even willing to go from Manhattan to Long Island unless I already had a ticket in my hand! What we get from the music depends on what we're willing to put into it, no question about it.)

The producer who put together *Biograph*, Jeff Rosen, astutely chose the two most electrifying tracks from *Before the Flood* to represent Tour '74: "Most Likely You Go Your Way" and "All Along the Watchtower." Ironically, while these fierce, biting, totally engaging performances are playing on the stereo, the listener can read Dylan in the *Biograph* booklet saying, "I think I was just playing a role on that tour ... It was all sort of mindless ... We were cleaning up but it was an emotionless trip ... The greatest praise we got on that tour was 'incredible energy, man,' it would make me want to puke."

In the context of the longer tirade these comments are culled from, it's clear that what Dylan is remembering is his own discomfort and dissatisfaction at being hemmed in by the expectations of his audience. That, of course, was one of the things that kept him off the road for so long: he was waiting for expectations to fall, for the hysteria to be muted by the passage of time, so he could just go out and be an ordinary performer again. Instead, no matter how long he stayed away and how many disappointing albums he released, his legend and the expectations directed at him kept growing.

Finally he resolved the situation by leading with his chin, throwing himself aggressively (and courageously) back into the arena. On *Before the Flood*, and on the tapes of the 1974 tour, Dylan is in a sense singing and performing in a straightjacket, and it is the brilliance with which he adapts to the situation, his success at putting forward his music and his feelings in spite of all obstacles, that gives these performances their power. "Incredible energy," indeed – it took a lot of inner strength for Dylan to play the role of "Bob Dylan" in 1974 and still be true to his present-moment self-awareness. And he did it. Listening to "Most Likely You Go Your Way," the presence of Bob Dylan 1974 (as distinct from Dylan the imagined legend) is unmistakable. The performer has found a way to transcend his circumstances. His spirit is biting through.

For his 1974 tour, Dylan put together a selection of songs that is carefully balanced to represent all of his best-loved work (the only albums left out are the first – though he did do "Song to Woody" a few times – and, significantly, *Self Portrait* and *New Morning*). The basic sequence went like this, sometimes with one or two variations (usually in the acoustic set):

1. Dylan & Band: "Most Likely You Go Your Way (and I'll Go Mine)," "Lay Lady Lay," "Just Like Tom Thumb's Blues," "Rainy Day Women," "It Ain't Me Babe," "Ballad of a Thin Man."
2. Six songs by the Band alone.
3. Dylan & Band: "All Along the Watchtower," "Ballad of Hollis Brown," "Knockin' on Heaven's Door."
4. Dylan solo acoustic (after a fifteen-minute intermission): "The Times They Are A-Changin'," "Don't Think Twice, It's All Right," "Gates of Eden," "Just Like a Woman," "It's Alright, Ma."
5. Four songs by the Band alone.
6. Dylan & Band: "Forever Young," "Something There Is About You" (first 26 shows) *or* "Highway 61 Revisited" (last 14 shows), "Like a Rolling Stone," and finally the encore, usually a repeat of "Most Likely You Go Your Way," sometimes followed by a second encore, typically "Blowin' in the Wind."

Other songs performed included (electric, with the Band): "I Don't Believe You" (8 shows), "Leopard-Skin Pill-Box Hat" (6 shows), "Maggie's Farm" (4), "Tough Mama" (3), "Hero Blues" (2), and "One Too Many Mornings," "It Takes a Lot to Laugh," "As I Went Out One Morning," and "Mr. Tambourine Man" (once each).

The list of alternate acoustic performances is longer: "Wedding Song" (9 shows), "Except You" (8 shows), "She Belongs to Me" (6), "The Lonesome Death of Hattie Carroll" (5), "It's All Over Now, Baby Blue" (4), "Love Minus Zero/No Limit" (4), "Blowin' in the Wind" (2), "Girl from the North Country" (2), "Song to Woody" (2), and "A Hard Rain's A-Gonna Fall," "Desolation Row," "Visions of Johanna," "4th Time Around," "To Ramona," "Mama, You Been on My Mind," and "Mr. Tambourine Man" (once each).

While the performances of most of the songs sound quite different from their original recordings, the arrangements for the most part are not greatly changed (except as necessary when a song previously done solo acoustic is now performed electric with a band, i.e. "Lay Lady Lay," "It Ain't Me Babe," and, most dramatically, "Ballad of Hollis Brown"). Dylan may have been perfectly happy with this choice of material and these arrangements — but there can be no question that he was setting out not to challenge expectations, this one time, but to satisfy them as well as possible. The mood of his performances, as well as his later comments, suggest that the primary reason for this was that he felt he had no choice.

In hindsight, at least, Tour '74 was Dylan's opening gambit in a whole new stage of his career. On one level, he was scared, and so he protected himself by playing his surest hand. (Maybe, just maybe, if he gave them everything they could possibly want from him, they'd let him escape with his life.) And on another level, he knew without thinking about it that it takes jacks or better to open. He had to use every resource he had going for him up to this point (greatest hits, rock and roll, solo acoustic, frizzed-up hair), if he was going to have a chance at getting back into the game.

Because what he had going against him was the audience's heartfelt conviction that he could walk on water, write our innermost feelings across the sky at the drop of a hat, bring down governments, and usher in the Millennium. We were ready to forgive him for the fact that our personal and collective world had not become everything his presence in it seemed to promise us nine years earlier ... as long as he was willing to get out there and start making up for lost time. Let the concert begin!

By way of ironic commentary, Dylan opened the first two shows with the obscure "Hero Blues" from 1963, singing some of the original lyrics ("The gal I got, I swear she's the screaming end/She wants me to be a hero so she can tell all her friends") plus some new ones that seem relevant to his immediate situation: "Running down the highway, just as fast as I can go"; and "Don't you remember, I told you long ago/... just ain't gonna work around here no more"; and finally something about what "you can write on my tombstone." Powerful stuff; one wishes he'd felt free to do more improvising.

Ten days later he told a reporter, "Back then it was the scene. Greenwich Village. Gerde's. There wasn't any audience and performer. It was all one. [This is an inaccurate and highly romanticized recollection, but quite revealing.] I wasn't a hero. I wasn't giving those young people anything to focus on back then. It was just something I was articulating that a whole bunch of us felt. But now there's a lot of ambiguity out there in the audience ... the younger kids, [I'm] just not sure why they're here." "Hero Blues" expresses the same feelings more directly: "You need a different kind of man, babe – you need Napoleon Bonaparte!"

At the third show Dylan dropped "Hero Blues" and tried starting with "Ballad of Hollis Brown." The next three shows he opened with "Rainy Day Women," and then on January 10 in Toronto he settled on "Most Likely You Go Your Way," which had been the encore for some of the early shows, as his opener. The next night he went a step further and used it as both opener and encore ("it completes a circle in some way," he told Ben Fong-Torres), and stayed with that structure for most of the remaining concerts.

In the context of starting and ending the 1974 concerts, "Most Likely You Go Your Way (and I'll Go Mine)" is a declaration of non-relationship, as if to say, "I want to make it clear that you [audience] and I really have no connection with each other, and as long as we remember this we can have a good time here tonight." The "message" of the song is all in the title phrase (although "you say my kisses are not like his" could be heard as a cute comment on being judged in comparison to your remembered past self) and in the way Dylan sings the song – not as sly or as nasty as on *Blonde on*

Blonde, but much more assertive, sung in the manner of a hustler who has grabbed your lapel in one hand, has his face up inches from yours, and is jabbing the air with the forefinger of his other hand just in case you might miss the point.

"You say you love me/And you're thinking of me/But you know you could be WRONG!" Dylan screams good-naturedly at the expectant audience, and then, true to his double nature, he turns around and woos them (aggressively) with his next selection: "Stay, lady, stay/Stay while the night is still ahead." The next two numbers are drug songs: "Just Like Tom Thumb's Blues" ("... take another shot") and "Rainy Day Women" ("... must get stoned"). They could also be called "outsider" songs (indeed one of the changes between 1966 and 1974 was that drugs and political positions and sexual attitudes that were once part of outlaw culture had become mass culture – and an underlying and perhaps unresolvable challenge for Dylan on this tour was how to sing his consummate expressions of outsiderhood as a conquering hero before an uncritical mass audience). And let's note, as we look at the relationship between singer, audience, and subject matter, that these two songs have the paradoxical ability to make the listener feel like an insider, a member of the outsider community. ("Tom Thumb" does this through intimacy, the implicit camaraderie of the wasted, whereas "Rainy Day Women" is direct and impersonal, "I would not feel so all alone," an anthem.)

"It Ain't Me Babe" is always to some extent Dylan's disclaimer to his audience ("it ain't me you're looking for") – on this tour it takes on a surprising joyfulness, it's become a song of not just personal but collective freedom. "Ballad of a Thin Man" is another outsider/insider, them-and-us song; Dylan plays piano on this one. If the song has less punch than it did in 1966, it's probably because the times have changed; and also because Dylan loves it so much he's forgotten to re-create it, to make it new.

Before the Flood offers versions of most of these songs as good as any I've heard on tapes of the 1974 shows. "You Go Your Way" is phenomenal; I can listen to it over and over and over and still hear more in it. Every member of the Band outdoes himself on this one. That guitar solo! The drumming! The sound these six musicians create here is different from and just as memorable as the studio sound achieved on *Bringing It All Back Home* or *Highway 61 Revisited* or *Blonde on Blonde*.

It's obviously not a coincidence that Dylan as singer/song-writer/frontman has again and again inspired different sets of musicians to jointly create such wonders. How does he do it? Certainly not by writing out charts or even by saying, "I'd like the bass to play this chord sequence and then have the piano come in here." He does it instead by trust, by insinuation, by power of personality, by enthusiasm, and by projecting a musical presence through his voice and his sense of rhythm that weaves these musicians together into one consciousness while inspiring each of them separately to put more of himself (feelings, imagination, spirit) into this than he's ever been able to express through music before. Dylan again and again has brought groups of musicians to this point — the proof of this is in his recordings — and however he does it, the process may be correctly described as part of the act of performing. He carries others with him, and is inspired by them, and feeds his own enthusiasm back into the group effort. What results is great music, great art ... not songs or compositions but performances. February 14, 1974, Los Angeles, California, Bob Dylan and the Band kicked off the final show of their tour with a rousing rendition of their standard opener, and in the process created a sound not quite like anything ever heard before, and a performance that people will listen to and enjoy and be moved by for centuries to come.

I'm also very fond of the performance of "Lay Lady Lay" included on *Before the Flood*. What a great guitar player Robbie Robertson can be! So much is said between the words in this performance, it's like Dylan's singing (the way he stretches the word "brass," for example) is percussive accompaniment for the lead guitar.

"Rainy Day Women" is notable for its fine groove (credit piano and rhythm section) and the wonderful solos (guitar, organ) between the verses. Like "It Ain't Me Babe," this is happy music, celebratory, full of life. The latter song in particular hints at a new direction for Dylan, a way of performing that couldn't be explored further within the limits of this tour but might provide a reason for Dylan to try a different kind of tour in the future. (I recommend St. Louis, February 4, afternoon show, for a particularly free and joyous 1974 "It Ain't Me Babe.")

Of the tapes I've heard, Toronto, 1/10/74, strikes me as having the finest first set overall, including unusually good versions of "I

Don't Believe You," "Just Like Tom Thumb's Blues," and "Ballad of A Thin Man." This Toronto set also features one of the high points of the tour, a rare and marvelous performance of "As I Went Out One Morning." The Band play martial music and Dylan responds with a new and eerie variation on his Tour '74 emphatic vocal style. Great spontaneous performance art, and an example of what keeps the blood flowing through tape collectors' veins.

The second Dylan set (he rejoins the Band onstage after they've played a set on their own) is short and powerful: a hard rock "All Along the Watchtower," "Ballad of Hollis Brown" as an up-tempo electric blues, and finally (last song before intermission) the wonderfully apocalyptic recent hit single (proof of Dylan's return to action) "Knockin' on Heaven's Door."

Dylan acknowledges in the *Biograph* notes that his live 1974 version of "All Along the Watchtower" is partially based on Jimi Hendrix's performance of the song (a top 20 hit in the U.S. in fall 1968), and says, "when I sing it I always feel it's a tribute to him in some way." Interesting, because Dylan's singing on the *Before the Flood* version is solid but unremarkable; it primarily serves as a jumping-off place for the soaring lyricism of the Band's performance, especially Robertson's guitar playing. The tribute, then, is in that part of the performance that Dylan "sings" through Robertson. On this track, as on so many of the Tour '74 performances, Dylan's vocal sounds hemmed in (appropriate for this song), as if the size and nature of the crowd and Dylan's feelings about them and about returning to the live stage (scene of his greatest triumphs and horrors) all serve to restrict his vocal sphere of motion, he is constrained, he doesn't feel free to move around or won't give himself that freedom, he's found a place he can successfully sing from and he's not going to risk budging from this spot until this tour, this ordeal, is history. Fortunately though, he has his musical alter ego, J. R. Robertson, genius of Tour '66 and the Basement Tapes, by his side to read the colors in Dylan's mind and show them, spectacularly, to the audience.

There is also a suggestion, in Dylan's comments about Hendrix, that he is performing his own song as if it were a cover, a song written by and associated with someone else. This is a liberating idea, and it suggests to me, as it may have suggested to Dylan at the time, the idea of approaching all of his older songs as if they were created by someone he admires who is dead now. He doesn't have to play the role of Bob Dylan, in other words – he can play the role of a guy on stage who is performing Bob Dylan songs. The audience won't know the difference, but the performer (and, more importantly, the performances) will be set free.

"Ballad of Hollis Brown" (not included on *Before the Flood*) points up the limitations of this tour. When Dylan and the Band opened their show with this song in Philadelphia, January 6, it was an interesting performance and a great concept – take a grim, uncompromising, relatively unfamiliar song from Dylan's topical songwriter period and give it the full electric treatment. Thirty-seven performances later, closing night, Dylan's growls and Robertson's guitar clichés are as forceful as ever and rather more polished, but the song hasn't grown in any way – it's a set piece, it hasn't taken on a life or meaning of its own.

"Knockin' on Heaven's Door," on the other hand, reveals itself as a great fluid vehicle for live performance. Dylan's voice here is an open door to his feelings: the sibilants especially ("trace," "see," "shoot") have an urgent, piercing quality that bond listener to singer. The way he says "I" in "I can't shoot them" is unforgettable. I'm referring here to the *Before the Flood* version, which is from January 30; the performance from the last show, February 14, is quite different (more forceful in the chorus, different emphases within the verses) but just as good. The song breathes; at each performance it speaks, without premeditation, the truth of its moment.

The solo set, which follows an intermission and therefore begins the second half of the concert, implicitly promises Dylan at his most naked, and, since the very sight of Dylan alone on stage with acoustic guitar and harmonica would send audiences into reveries of nostalgia (this continues to be true even in the late 1980s), the tension within Dylan regarding what people wanted from him and what he was willing to give them must have been most pronounced during this part of the show.

In 1965 Dylan wanted to quit performing because his solo concerts had become so limiting for him, so predictable, such a drag. In 1966 he split his shows between a solo first half and an electric second half, and used a combination of drugs and artistic ambition to cut through the implicit restrictions of a solo set and produce intimate, daring, soul-searing music. In 1974 Dylan's solo set was an island within a larger electric presentation. I don't think

Dylan's sense of himself changed from one segment of the 1974 show to another – he continued to sing from the one perspective that worked for him on this tour (like a window he could stick his head out of), whether the Band was playing with him or not.

He was determined, in any case, not to just go through the motions of singing his songs. Instead he built his (necessary) defenses into his style of performing, and found ways to sing from his heart not in spite of but with the aid of his belligerent, aggressive stance. The performances that resulted are not among the best of his career, but they are frequently very moving and represent a crucial transition: Dylan's reclaiming of the stage after a long and stifling silence, his rediscovery and reassertion of himself as a performing artist.

Before the Flood offers us three songs from the solo set: "Don't Think Twice," "Just Like a Woman," and "It's Alright, Ma." The latter provoked more audience reaction, night after night, than any other song except "Rolling Stone," partly because it lent itself so well to Dylan's current "attack and conquer" singing style, and partly because of the stunning appropriateness in early 1974 (as the Watergate revelations and the siege of the Nixon presidency dominated public consciousness) of Dylan's 1965 lyric "even the president of the United States sometimes must have to stand naked." Dylan's status as prophet was confirmed; and the passionately-performed song became an anthem of the moment, the embodiment of what the audience had come here hoping to experience: Dylan as hero, songwriter/performer as truthteller and fiery-tongued spokesperson for a generation.

Here more than at any other moment during the concert, Dylan is "playing a role." He does it well, he gives the audience their money's worth – and not, I think, in a cynical fashion; "It's Alright, Ma" is a great song, full of truth, and he sings it like he's proud of having written it – but the unavoidable falseness of the situation necessarily comes into focus here. What started as truthsaying has become spectacle. Dylan is singing in a sports arena to an adoring audience with a preconceived and unshakeable picture of who he is; he has become part of the mass culture that the song warns against. Each performance of the song is as energetic and fiery as the one the night before; each performance is an orgasmic fulfillment for the audience and a carved notch for the performer's ego but a dead end for the performer as artist, because there's nowhere he can go with this. Paradoxically, I think Dylan's awareness of this dilemma helps give the performance its edge—breathes life into it. "It is not he or she or them or it that you belong to." Indeed.

"Don't Think Twice" on *Before the Flood* is a particularly rewarding performance. There is a beauty in the sound of Dylan's voice here that is more striking to me each time I listen to it. One becomes fascinated with an artist's body of work, I think, precisely because there is no way to quantify (analyze, describe, explain) the richness one experiences in each new work encountered or each previously-seen or -heard work encountered again. Oh that harmonica solo before the last verse! What sets this performance apart from other versions of the same song from other years is, superficially, the breakneck speed at which it's played and sung, and yet that's not the important thing. The important thing is the depth of feeling this unique work of music evokes, which has to do with the tempo but has just as much to do with the way particular words ("twice," "heart," "mind," "right") are enunciated, and the vocal timbre, and the way the various elements of the performance work together. The performer gives and the listener receives. We could also say the listener gives the gift of his listening, and the performer, in some mysterious way, receives this gift, and responds.

There are moments on the tour when Dylan seems particularly inspired. The acoustic set from the first show in St. Louis (February 4) is a high point, not only for the songs he was moved to share for the first and only time on this tour ("Hard Rain" and "Desolation Row") but also for the regularly-performed songs ("The Times They Are A-Changin'," "Don't Think Twice," "Just Like a Woman"), which sound especially magical on this tape, as though the performer feels himself especially well-listened-to on this day, or for some other reason is in a very giving, creative mood. "Gates of Eden" from Nassau, January 29, is another exceptional performance. It is as though he is more inside the songs on these occasions, and the songs are bigger and more expressive, more compelling, as a result. There are also simple changes in mood. "Just Like a Woman" from *Before the Flood* sounds like a description of a very different person from the one he sings about in St. Louis.

Dylan introduced one new song during the 1974 tour, "Except You" (the official title, in *Lyrics*, is "Nobody 'Cept You," but that sounds all wrong to me, so just this once I'm going to take the law into my own hands). Dylan apparently made a tape, possibly an early start on *Planet Waves*, in July 1973, of "Except You," "Forever Young," and "Never Say Goodbye." "Except You," which Dylan performed in his solo set for the first six shows of 1974, then twice more in the week that followed, is a love song, a Dylan classic, one of those perfect meetings of melody and lyrics that establishes its emotional territory and pierces the listener's heart in its opening line: "There's nothing 'round here that I believe in/Except you."

The song (all the performances are moving, but my favorite is from Chicago, January 4) is fresh evidence of Dylan's extraordinary natural talent as a songwriter. It sounds like it just flowed out of him, and quite possibly it did ("Sometimes that's what you're given"), born whole like Athena from the forehead of Zeus, with all its subtle chord changes and structural shifts, its precise, inspired lyrical weaving of memory, spiritual feelings, love, loss, boredom, attachment and detachment, all effortlessly turned back to the central point: you make life meaningful, your presence awakens me when everything else is a fog. In a handful of words (and with the power of the music, and his voice) Dylan shares large chunks of his experience of reality: "everybody wants my attention/Everybody's got something to sell"—and then adds that tagline: "except you." The song is a sequel to and every bit as powerful as "Love Minus Zero/No Limit." The bridging verse starts as reminiscence and becomes a remarkable, compact essay on time and aging:

> Used to run in the cemetery
> Laugh and sing and play when I was a child
> And it never seemed strange
> Now I just pass mournfully
> By that place where the bones of life are piled
> I know something has changed
> I'm a stranger here, and no one sees me
> Except you
> Nothing anymore seems to please me ...

This is genius. And very hummable. It runs through the mind. It challenges, and lifts, the heart.

Maybe someday it will be released to the public.*

The last segment of the 1974 concerts features three more songs by Dylan with the Band, plus one or two encores. "Forever Young," not included on *Before the Flood*, sounds a lot like the slower *Planet Waves* version most nights, another song that suffered from the limitations Dylan labored under for the duration of the tour. And yet, within those limitations (by which I mean a sense of having to do things a certain way, night after night, no room for structural improvisation), the song could still occasionally become the basis for a soaring, magical performance. This occurred in Toronto, January 10—what comes across (surprisingly) is great love, as though Dylan for whatever reason found himself flooded with affection for his audience, and it just radiated out as he sang. The rapport between Dylan and the Band here is unusually keen. The harmonica playing, and the crystalline sound achieved by the Band as a whole, are exquisite.

"Something There Is About You" is a fine song that doesn't stand out for me on the concert tapes because, again, it wasn't allowed to develop and take on a life of its own in live performance. For the last few weeks of the tour it was replaced by "Highway 61 Revisited"—the hotter-than-a-crotch performance of this song included on *Before the Flood* is a delight. It jumps, it really jumps.

On the 1974 tour Dylan was playing with the same band he'd toured with in 1965-66, the same band he'd played with at the Isle of Wight, the only band he'd ever played with publicly (with the exception of a few songs at Newport and at the Bangladesh concerts). They'd built a considerable reputation of their own since 1966, and were now the Band and shared billing with Dylan; but at times it must have seemed to them and Dylan as if no real time had passed. "All right, let's go out and do our act again." In 1966 their set together consisted of eight songs; three of these songs remained as standard numbers in 1974, and two others were performed

---

*In 1991, a studio take of "Except You"/"Nobody 'cept You" was included on the Columbia Records Dylan compilation *The Bootleg Series, Volumes 1–3*. It's a lackluster and unsatisfying version, proving my comments above wrong: the song didn't flow out of Dylan perfectly formed, or if it did it occurred on stage in January and not in the studio the previous November. In any case, the superb song/performance I'm talking about has yet to be released to the public.

often in the early shows. The arrangements of the songs, the approach of singer and musicians to the material, are about the same in 1974 as 1966. And both concerts were structured to build to the same inevitable climax: "Like a Rolling Stone."

The *Before the Flood* performance of "Like a Rolling Stone" is the last of forty in a row, which sets up a nice comparison with the Manchester 1966 performance, near the end of at least seventy in a row. The 1966 version has the edge, no question about it, but there's a lot to be said for 1974 as well. Both performances are totally fresh, as though the song (famous though it may be) had just been created earlier the same day, and this is the first and final run-through, the one that matters.

It's hard to imagine, listening to the 1974 version, that Dylan hasn't always sung the song *just like this*, shouting the chorus and the last few words of each line, biting into each syllable of almost every word and forcing it out from the diaphragm, leading the music forward like a crazed general running ahead of his cavalry ... hard to imagine that that punchy organ figure that separates and emphasizes every line of the chorus hasn't always been part of the song, isn't the hook that made it so memorable in the first place. I'm speaking now of how the 1974 version, by its power and its commitment to this moment of performance, can temporarily obliterate the memory of the original studio recording whose triumph is being celebrated here (and celebration is what this 1974 performance of "Like a Rolling Stone" is about: celebration of the song, the singer, the audience, the band, this whole exultant home-coming, our collective victory over every sort of personal and public repression, real or imagined)...not because it's better but because it's all-absorbing, it gives and demands full attention, as a great performance must.

It's interesting to note how different the equally entrancing 1966 live performance is: Dylan seldom shouts, he sounds weary, totally into the truth of the song and on top of the performance but much more worldly-wise than energetic. The passion of the 1966 performance is implicit in Dylan's held-back vocal, but it finds its release in the manic drumming and overwhelming organ and guitar lines that surge forward with a force appropriate to an all-out assault on the fortress of the gods. Rock and roll—live electric ensemble music—reaches a kind of apotheosis here. The 1974 version, by contrast, is merely hysterical, almost a pastiche—

except that it has its own sense of purpose, its own reason for existence, expressed so powerfully that again memories of past triumphs become moot in the face of what is right this moment being achieved.

Before the Flood ends with another anthem (one pounding on top of the next until mind and spirit reel), an electric version of "Blowin' in the Wind." This was used as a second encore at many of the later concerts. It seems as though most of the songs on this tour were performed in some variation of a marching rhythm, and here's another. It's actually quite a good presentation of a difficult song—especially Robertson's melodic guitar solo. Dylan continues to explore the possibilities of the particular style of enunciation he adopted for Tour '74, sometimes seeming to lose the meanings of the words altogether (*"how* many *times musta* man look *up"*) but perhaps arriving at something more interesting than meaning in the process. He has a way of flexing his lips and moving language into an entirely abstract plane.

The tour ended in Los Angeles, and Dylan presumably went home to Malibu. He walked offstage and the hero disappeared; but from what little we know of his private life, he had a hard time resuming his life as a husband. By spring he was in New York City, studying art on the eleventh floor of Carnegie Hall with a 73-year-old painter named Norman Raeben.

II. Poet

"I hope that you can hear
Hear me singin' through these tears."
—Bob Dylan, summer 1974

2.

On my short list of Dylan's masterpieces in Volume One—purposely very short because unless such a distinction is used to call attention to a few quintessentially bright moments it loses all effectiveness—I did not name any albums. Many of his albums are masterful, momentous achievements; and what they achieve is exactly what the word "momentous" implies—they convey a great deal about the moment (personal, collective) in which the album was recorded, and thereby also speak powerfully to the moment the listener happens to be listening in. If any of Dylan's record albums deserves to be singled out as a "masterpiece" (and I've avoided this because how can one leave out *Blonde on Blonde*? *Highway 61 Revisited*? *Hard Rain*?), it is the one that most successfully combines conscious, deliberate creation (composition) with spontaneous expression (performance)—1974's *Blood on the Tracks*.

Between the February 14th concerts that ended Tour '74 and the mid-September recording sessions for *Blood on the Tracks*, the only recorded Dylan performance is the few songs he sang at the "Friends of Chile" benefit concert in New York on May 9, 1974, one of his best-documented and more extreme instances of public drunkenness (there are some rather charming photos of him waving the wine bottle around, but the audiotape is horrifying). But this "lost weekend" aspect of his separation from Sara is balanced by another fragment of biographical information, which is that his spring in New York was followed by a summer in Minnesota as a single father with at least three of his children. He bought a farm (an investment and summer retreat), and worked on writing a kind of song cycle. In late July he played eight or nine new songs for musicians Tim Drummond and Stephen Stills as they passed through St. Paul on a concert tour. There is good reason to believe these were essentially the songs Dylan recorded two months later for his new album.

The new album grew out of *Planet Waves* (which was a door-opener for Dylan in a number of ways), it grew out of the tour and whatever accounts it may have settled or new questions it may have raised (for him), it grew out of his tremendous need to speak to and about his wife and marriage, at least one song grew out of his movie experience in Mexico, but most of all the album seems to have been inspired by Dylan's studies with a person he recognized as a teacher for him: "I had the good fortune to meet a man in New York City who taught me how to see. He put my mind and my hand and my eye together in a way that allowed me to do consciously what I unconsciously felt."

This man was an art teacher, Norman Raeben, son of the great Yiddish storyteller Sholem Aleichem (I am indebted to Bert Cartwright for his well-researched articles in *The Telegraph* on Dylan's "mysterious man called Norman"). He was 73 in 1974, and he had been conducting art classes for 40 years. Dylan was apparently first attracted to him sometime before 1974 when friends of Dylan's wife shared with him Raeben's definitions for "truth" and "love" and "beauty" — "all these words I had heard for years, and they had 'em all defined. I couldn't believe it." In late April of 1974 Dylan began attending Raeben's classes, which involved individual instruction in a group situation. "All the students would overhear what the teacher was saying to each individual, and thus advice that was personally directed often allowed moments of insight for all," says Cartwright, who interviewed Raeben's widow in 1986.

Dylan in a series of interviews in 1978 gave his two months of study with Raeben ("Five days a week I used to go up there, and I'd just think about it the other two days") responsibility for "changing" him so much "my wife never did understand me since that day," for influencing "a lot of the ideas I have," and specifically for guiding him to a new "technique" that allowed him to create the album *Blood on the Tracks* and the film *Renaldo & Clara*. Dylan was attracted by the teacher's philosophy, and applied himself in class to the practice of painting and drawing; but what he came away with was a major breakthrough in his primary calling, the art and practice of songwriting and performing.

Dylan speaks of *Blood on the Tracks*, in the context of talking about what he learned from Raeben, as the first time he was able to do consciously what he once did unconsciously, for example when he wrote *Highway 61 Revisited*. In the *Biograph* notes Cameron Crowe, drawing on his 1985 conversation with Dylan, says of *Blood on the Tracks*, "Reportedly inspired by the breakup of his marriage, the album derived more of its style from Dylan's renewed interest in painting. The songs cut deep and their sense of perspective and reality was always changing."

Perspective and reality. Dylan speaks in the interviews of "no time"; the word I find myself using to describe the special world many of his songs and performances evoke is "timelessness." And the first few words of the *Blood on the Tracks* suite (we could call it, "Concerto for a Breaking and Opening Heart") are the very essence of timelessness, evocation of the past as a universal, omnipresent now:

> Early one morning the sun was shining
> I was laying in bed
> Wondering if she'd changed at all
> If her hair was still red.

"I guess I was just trying to make it like a painting," says Dylan in the *Biograph* notes, "where you can see the different parts but then you also see the whole of it." And, thanks largely to the tone of his voice as he sings these words, he succeeded beyond wildest imaginings.

There are ten songs on *Blood on the Tracks*. Initially, Dylan recorded them in New York in mid-September, 1974. The album was ready for release, and in fact some promotional copies had already circulated, when Dylan decided he wasn't satisfied with some of the performances. He was visiting Minneapolis, and he asked his brother to get some musicians together for a recording session. Thus the versions of "Tangled Up in Blue," "Idiot Wind," "If You See Her, Say Hello," "Lily, Rosemary and the Jack of Hearts," and "You're a Big Girl Now" included on *Blood on the Tracks* were recorded three months later (December 27 and 30, 1974) than the other five songs on the album. Since Dylan sings always about what he's feeling at the moment, this adds significantly and intangibly to the emotional complexity and richness of the album. It is a cycle of songs written together but performed in two separate, intense bursts.

It is perhaps fortunate that when Dylan's teacher spoke to him about mind, hand, and eye, he never mentioned voice. The brilliant, detached, finely-wrought self-consciousness of this album's composition (Dylan speaks of it in terms of "technique," and "a code") provides a perfect springboard for some of Dylan's most spine-tingling, least self-conscious singing on record. In fairness, this is exactly what Raeben directed Dylan towards. He showed him a technique by which he could consciously, deliberately, bring himself to that elusive locus of freedom, intention, and abandon where great art is created—a place where words and voice flow freely into charming, unexpected forms, where one can sing totally from the heart. The technique has a lot to do with being aware of one's perspective or point of view as one is drawing and/or telling a story, which also means being aware of and therefore to some extent free of the power of time, the force that links things together in their normal order.

Dylan put it this way to Jonathan Cott in 1978: "[*Renaldo & Clara*] creates and holds the time. That's what it should do—it should hold that time, breathe in that time and stop time in doing that." He told Karen Hughes in another interview that he once had an opportunity to spend two months drawing every day (i.e, the class with Raeben) and "it locked me into the present time more than anything else I ever did. More than any experiences I've ever had, any enlightenment I've ever had. Because I was constantly being intermingled with myself, and all the different selves that were in there, until this one left, then that one left, and I finally got down to the one that I was familiar with."

In other words, a sort of no-self in no-time who is instantly recognizable as real-self, the person we can hear singing in, for example, "If You See Her, Say Hello." This (the album version) is

one of Dylan's greatest vocal performances, and it makes me remember Dylan telling Nat Hentoff in 1963, in reference to "Don't
Think Twice" being a hard song to sing, that he doesn't yet carry
himself "the way that Big Joe Williams, Woody Guthrie, Leadbelly
and Lightnin' Hopkins have carried themselves. I hope to be able to
someday, but they're older people. I sometimes am able to do it ..."

Blood on the Tracks begins with "Tangled Up in Blue" and ends
with "Buckets of Rain." "Tangled Up in Blue" is so beguiling in its
language and story-technique, and so richly and lovingly sung, we
may find ourselves overlooking another aspect of its power: its
extraordinary rhythmic core. This song pulses. Its six minutes pass
in a flash and you want to hear it again. As an album-opener, it
propels us forward into the rest of the music. It is a love song, and
a song about how it feels to have a personal history (the story of the
story of our lives), but it is also a great road song, filled with the
essential energy of the American highway. The Minnesota musicians Dylan performs with here achieve an unforgettable groove,
bass and drums and acoustic guitars (one a twelve-string, it sounds
almost like a harpsichord at times) totally blended into a new and
different wild mercury sound.

I need to say again that Dylan performs a song not only with
his voice but also through the musicians around him; the brilliant
success of these Minnesota recordings (and the New York sessions,
including most of the discarded tracks, are equally wonderful) is
proof again that the power of his presence as a performer can
transform whoever is playing with him into a perfect extension of
his instincts and his unconscious will. Dylan short-circuits any
intellectual approach to music and conducts his bands from his gut,
his solar plexus, invisibly, intuitively, trusting the music to find its
way into existence if they (he and the band) will just lean into it
enough, press through their own limits and surrender to the
sound that's trying to happen.

Tracing road images through the song we catch a glimpse of
Dylan's "technique" in action: first verse starts in bed but also "on
the side of the road," second verse "we drove that car as far as we
could," third "I drifted down to" (aimlessness) and "the past was
close behind" (pursuit), fourth verse she catches him as he's about
to move on, sixth verse the image of a fixed address turns quickly
into death of spirit, withdrawal and time to move again "like a bird
that flew"; last verse "I'm still on the road, heading for another

joint." And geography flies by: heading for the East Coast (i.e. from the midwest), driving from eastern shore to West, then north woods to New Orleans, Delacroix, Montague Street (Brooklyn), and finally "now I'm goin' back again" (where? to her—another sweep across internal and external continent, and a closing or reopening of the circle).

One example of what Dylan might mean by "doing consciously what I used to do unconsciously" is his shifting use of personal pronouns in "Tangled Up in Blue." I've called attention to this in discussing the early songs—for instance, "When the Ship Comes In" is third person for the first five verses, then a second person element ("your weary toes") is introduced in verse six, and finally in the last verse the first person involvement that has been suggested from the start becomes explicit ("we'll shout from the bow"). It seems fair to say that the song just turned out this way; Dylan probably didn't think about when to withhold or insert first or second person pronouns while he was doing the writing.

It seems equally clear that the ambiguity between "she" in the first two verses of "Tangled Up in Blue" and "she" in the fourth and fifth verses is something Dylan was fully aware of as he worked on this song. The version of "Tangled"—the very word suggests the way close interpersonal contact can blur the lines between "you" and "me" and "he" or between the various "she"s in one's life—included on *Blood on the Tracks* is fairly straightforward, first person narrative all the way (except maybe for the mysterious intrusion of "them" and "he" in verse six). But the potential for identity switching is constantly present right under the surface of the song's structure, and in the original (New York) recording Dylan sang "he" (was laying in bed, was standing by the road etc.) for the first three verses, suddenly switching to first person in the fourth. In later live performances the pronouns jump all over the place, Dylan having fun with the song's fluidity (and occasionally getting totally lost within it).

So this time he knows what he's doing. But the breakthrough is not Dylan being aware of his use of such techniques (he was talking about this sort of thing at least as far back as 1968) but rather his ability to be conscious of what he's doing and still have it come out as magical and mysterious and pregnant as it did when he was an unconscious arrogant whiz kid who never even thought about looking back.

There's a point, in other words, in a creator's life, where one can no longer pretend not to know certain things; and this knowledge or awareness becomes an insurmountable burden to new creation unless one learns methods for completely accepting and assimilating it (going through self-consciousness back to unself-consciousness) and thereby regaining freedom.

"Simple Twist of Fate" is another absolutely extraordinary performance. Where "Tangled Up in Blue" is bright, bouncy, jangly, "Simple Twist of Fate" is soft and warm and mournful. The edges of Dylan's voice are sharp (in a wonderfully sweet way) in the former song, but gentle and rounded in the latter. The first conjures the smell of the air on an early spring morning; the second is hot summer night. Dylan on this album has become a master of textures. "Simple Twist of Fate" unmistakably creates the time, holds it, breathes it in, and stops it; the tools it uses to accomplish this are storytelling, imagery, phrasing, timing, vocal texture, rhyme, melody, and ensemble sound. The bass playing (content, timing, attack) is revelatory. The harmonica solos sum up the song's essence and push it out to the furthest corners of the universe.

The rhyming sequence and meter of the song/poem are truly elegant. Each verse rhymes AAABBCC, with the third A and second B both internal rhymes (five-line verses). The C rhyme is always the same. As on *Highway 61 Revisited*, the songs on *Blood on the Tracks* tend to end each verse with their titles (in lieu of choruses): "tangled up in blue"; "simple twist of fate," "shelter from the storm"; "the Jack of Hearts." In this song, because the verses are short, this creates a rhyming resonance between the verses as well as within them. And the song's meter puts a little burst of emphasis on each rhyming word, in a pleasing, very lightly humorous fashion, as if to say, "hey, we're singing *poetry* here."

I want to take a quick look at Dylan's vocal technique, as illustrated by his singing on the first verse of "Simple Twist of Fate." But first I have to say that attention to technique should not blind us to the fact that something very natural is occurring here: a man is singing a song and, because he feels so much as he's singing it, we feel a lot as we listen to him. We are moved by his presence, his passion. Technique is not the cause of presence but its byproduct. Dylan's passion spurs his inventiveness—he cares about the words and tune he's written and the story they tell, the feelings they unleash; this caring makes him more aware and present as he sings, so he's able to put more of himself into the mouthing of each word, the delivery and shaping of each note. The results are spectacular. The danger, however, is that we may (like Greil Marcus and other critics of Dylan's later work) be deafened to other great Dylan performances because we are waiting to hear him sing "like he did on *Blood on the Tracks*." We start waiting for a remembered form of greatness instead of opening ourselves to greatness itself.

So, remembering that the critter's tracks are not the critter, let's examine this first verse. What I notice is a subtle emphasis on the meter in the first line ("to-geth-er"), as if to establish the tempo (once it's established, Dylan is free to work against it), and the way the last word, "park," has a slightly breathy quality. Dylan is almost speaking (rather than singing) the lyrics, and then "park" hits a note that brings together the words and the beautiful, poignant melody established in the instrumental prologue. In the second line ("evening sky") I become aware of the huskiness in his voice, somehow central to establishing the mood and viewpoint of the story (cool and detached, but filled with intimations of shivering regret). "Dark" echoes "park" and is trumped by "spark," which becomes a springboard for the marvelous, characteristic twist in Dylan's voice as he sings "tingle to his bones" (once we would have considered this part of his "accent"; now we can see that his accent always served as an intuitive framework for expressive phrasing). While we've got the microscope out, note that there are two distinct emphases within this short phrase, cute on "tingle" and then decidedly eerie on "bones."

"Tingle to his bones" represents a mini-release from the tension established by the repeating, loping melody of the three opening lines (the ones ending in "ark"). The real breakthrough comes at the end of the fourth line, the word "straight" (not overlooking the expressiveness with which Dylan sings "alone" earlier in the same line). The sonic hook that links together the verses (and gives the song its powerful cyclical effect) is this wonderful series of stressed "ate" words at the end of every line four ("straight," "freight," "gate," "relate," "wait," "late") as much as it is the deliciously anticlimactic "simple twist of fate" cleverly reintroduced in each line five. Notice also the impact of Dylan's phrasing of the verbs "wished" and "watched out."

And the song just gets better (how about the way he sings "heat of the night" in verse two? the word "cup" in verse three? "again" in verse five?).I love the resonance and dissonance between "Tangled Up in Blue" and "Simple Twist of Fate" as the first two songs on the album. The titles sound similar (four words, one a preposition, and "twist" mimics "tangled"), both are acoustic-based ensemble performances, both narratives of love affairs. They sound like they could have the same protagonist (on a fairly simple level, we always believe the song is about the person singing it). And there's even an outrageous (accidental?) situational echo which turns out (or purports) to be a kind of pun when we read the lyrics: "hunts her down by the waterfront docks" in "Twist" naturally follows "[We] split up on the docks that night" in "Tangled," which is the way I always heard it (and I know I'm not alone), till I read in the lyrics book that it's "[We] split up on a dark sad night." Oh.

But the songs are so different, too. In particular, although there are some sneaky pronouns, "Simple Twist" as written is an unambiguous narrative, and instead of being about the character's whole life is about a single (12-hour) incident, albeit one that has come to dominate his life since. The pronouns (all "he" and "she" and "they" except for a stray "I" in verse two and full first person in verse six) can even be accounted for: "Simple Twist" is consciously presented as a song in which the narrator is projecting his own experience into a story told in the third person; he acknowledges this in passing in verse two and then deals with it directly at the end of the song ("I still believe she was my twin," what a great playful — and sincere — line for Dylan to throw at his audience!). It must be noted, however, since this is done so consciously, that we can't claim to know the narrator *is* Dylan; rather, he's a created character who is telling a story about himself, like say Ishmael in *Moby Dick*.

There is, in *Blood on the Tracks*, a very careful balance between songs in which the artist speaks directly to people in his life and of things that are happening to him, and songs set up as fictions to explore issues related to what's been happening in his life. "Lily, Rosemary, and the Jack of Hearts" is obviously a fiction, and so (less obviously) are "Tangled Up in Blue" and "Simple Twist of Fate." "Shelter from the Storm" is the same sort of fiction, but with moments where it crosses over into very immediate language: "Now there's a wall between us, something there's been lost/I took too much for granted, I got my signals crossed." The songs that are most obviously immediate, with the fiction (narrative) aspects receding into the background, are "If You See Her, Say Hello," "You're a Big Girl Now," and "Idiot Wind." "Idiot Wind" stirs the soup in a different direction, because transparently fictional material is impeccably mixed into what is unavoidably and primarily first person direct address. No, Dylan didn't shoot a man named Gray; but yes it is certainly Dylan and not some character he's created who says, "I kissed goodbye the howling beast on the borderline which separated you from me." The triumph of the album (one of many triumphs, but this is the one that pulls together all the others) is its success at blending the totally personal and the totally fictional so thoroughly and with such originality that the end result is a tale told by and for Everyman (or woman), speaking from and to a timeless place where it all happened a million years ago and is also all going on unresolved right now, these songs themselves being vital and unpredictable factors in whatever may come to pass.

So, returning to the resonance and dissonance between "Tangled Up in Blue" and "Simple Twist of Fate," we notice that in both songs the narrator (male) is essentially passive, and the woman initiates sexual contact (says hello, takes him home, seduces him with dope and poetry in the first song; looks at him, loves him, and leaves him in the second). But in the first song the protagonist ultimately seems in charge of his own life, and—perhaps just because of the tone of the performance—in a mood to celebrate and feel good about whatever's happened. In the second song, the man has fallen in love with a woman who appeared out of and disappeared back into the night; he has lost his freedom, become obsessed. Yet there's an implication that he treasures his broken heart, that despite his real regrets it's the best thing that ever happened to him. If we project "Simple Twist of Fate" onto the known context of Dylan's broken marriage (come on, how can we help it?), we find a supremely romantic message in a bottle: I live for the day I meet up with you again. Its very indirectness adds to its impact. And there's a fascinating resonance here with a song that will appear on his next album: "I married Isis on the fifth day of May/But I could not hold on to her very long." Maybe she'll pick him out again? In "Isis" she does—but that's another album, another story.

When Dylan is really hot, he creates a new sound not just with every album but with every performance on the album. "You're a

Big Girl Now" is startling in the originality of its musical structure
as well as in the raw power of Dylan's lyrics and the way he sings
them. Each verse of this song is a separate monolog, as if Dylan
were an actor stepping to the back of the stage and then coming
forward again as he thinks of something else he wants to say to the
lady. Dylan complains in the *Biograph* notes about "stupid and
misleading jerks" (i.e. critics) who have suggested this song is
"about my wife." Let's say, then, that it's a song sung by an imaginary person whose present relationship with the person he's singing
to is not altogether unlike the performer's relationship with his
own estranged spouse (which perhaps is why the performer can
throw himself into the song so passionately). Likewise "Shelter
from the Storm" is about another invented character who once had
a woman do for him something not unlike what Sara Lowndes did
for Robert Zimmerman back in 1965 or so. And in a typical clever
Dylan inversion, "Shelter" comes along much later in the album
sequence, although the first verse of "Big Girl" ("I'm back in the
rain") establishes it clearly as a sequel to "Shelter from the Storm."

   Dylan's harmonica solo at the end of "You're a Big Girl Now"
is a fine example of how effective his shoot-from-the-hip, primitive,
ballsy approach to music-making can be. He and the band reach
for and brilliantly achieve something that could never have been
described if he'd tried to tell them or himself beforehand what he
had in mind.

   If "You're a Big Girl Now" is startling, "Idiot Wind" is shock
treatment. The voice that had been so gentle in "Simple Twist" now
is right in your face, one moment reasonable and remarkably lucid,
the next moment filled with fury. Lyrically there's something here
for everybody, a great grab bag of image and language and insight,
reminiscent of major Dylan songs of the past like "Desolation Row,"
"Hard Rain," and "Visions of Johanna," but, surprisingly, less
linear in structure—on the page there are four long verses (ten
lines each, plus a five-line chorus), rhyming couplets, all neat and
orderly, but the performed song doesn't come across like that at all.
The lyrics have more unexpected transitions, more new beginnings and shots from the blue than you can shake a stick at, no
matter how many times I hear it it still comes at me from a dozen
directions and I have trouble being sure what verse this is or which
fragment comes up next. Dylan more than ever shows himself
master of juxtapositions, connections, quick dissolves and timeless

freeze frames. For once the words he's singing are as astonishing as the way he sings them: "Down the highway, down the tracks, down the road to ecstacy." "People see me all the time, and they just can't remember how to act" (I had that experience in 1975, when he was sitting in the booth next to mine at the Other End). "There's a lone soldier on the cross, smoke pouring out of a boxcar door." And, getting a little personal but oh so universal (I notice if you read these lyrics without hearing the music, the melody, the chords that go with 'em, it's not the same; music and words *have to* be experienced together): "You'll never know the hurt I suffer, nor the pain I rise above/And I'll never know the same about you, your holiness or your kind of love/And it makes me feel so sorry." (For myself, and for what I've done, both at once, and also for nothing, just pure inarticulate screaming feeling for its own sake.)

(Norman Raeben's widow acknowledged to Bert Cartwright that "idiot" was one of his favorite words. "According to Raeben's observation of life, there is an idiot wind blowing and blinding all human existence." A fellow student reports that Raeben called Dylan an idiot all the time.)

And how smoothly the album slips from this orgy of marital upchuck into the lightest, most innocent, most enticing love song of the whole batch, a throwaway which on closer inspection seems quite as brilliant (in composition and performance) as anything else here: "You're Gonna Make Me Lonesome When You Go." So clever, so perfect, to have a song that puts any separation squarely in the future, instead of present, near past, or distant past. Listen to the way he says, "You're gonna make me give myself a good talkin' to." Sure as we've all been in love, been loved, we've all had the experience of being in someone's eyes this charming, this much fun—and isn't it amazing? Dylan's sense of humor is evident everywhere on *Blood on the Tracks*, and nowhere more than in this song. "It always has hit me from below," indeed!

"Meet Me in the Morning" is a sweet, bluesy interlude, serving almost to rest the listener's attention before the bright, seductive intensity of "Lily, Rosemary and the Jack of Hearts." "Lily" offers the most dramatic evidence imaginable of the power of a good performance. By all rights this should be a tiresome song—nine minutes long, three simple chords (D G A), the same melody over and over without change for fifteen verses. And in fact, the early (New York) recording of the song can only be described as tedious;

Dylan's vocal has its moments, but overall his performance is so listless I honestly believe it would have made most listeners reluctant to play side two of the album more than once or twice, thus sabotaging the entire project.

Enter the Minnesota miracle. The take of "Lily, Rosemary, and the Jack of Hearts" that does appear on *Blood on the Tracks* is a completely different animal, lilting, energetic, so much fun it's irresistible; I find myself thinking about skipping over it because of its length, and then as soon as I hear a few lines I'm drawn in again, following the story, watching the movie, delighting in the subtle ways the music and words and singing interconnect, all the elements of the story and the performance constantly recombining to form new images, new insights, new pleasures for me the listener. The masterstroke seems to have been the speeding up of the tempo, and the replacement of strummed guitar with electric bass and (understated) organ and drums. Dylan's voice responds to these instruments totally differently from the way it responded to the sound of the guitar. A dynamic is created. The song ends, and I want to hear it again. A great performance.

I have written down elsewhere (*Dylan – What Happened?*, 1979) the thought that perhaps what seduced Dylan away from his marriage (he tells us what *drove* him away from it in "Idiot Wind") was the perceived opportunity to play the part of the Jack of Hearts, a brilliant synthesis of Dylan's Alias and Peckinpah/Kristofferson's Billy the Kid: silent, cool, a natural leader, lucky, clever, and on the side of the angels. And all the girls saying, "I'm glad to see you're still alive, you're looking like a saint." Mm. It's a great role. He plays it right here on this album in a number of places, for example "You're Gonna Make Me Lonesome When You Go" and "Buckets of Rain." Then again what seduced him away if anything might be nothing more complex than another woman (sung to openly on this album and also referred to in a code as subtle as the one Picasso used in *Still Life on a Pedestal Table*). But that could be the same thing, if it's true that what most attracts us to a lover is the image of oneself as seen through the other's eyes.

"I still *believe* she was my twin" (emphasis mine). In the same manner do we recognize nemesis: "'I know I've seen that face somewhere,' Big Jim was thinking to himself." Jack is certainly a dance-away lover, but that's also his appeal. And Rosemary, well, I like to think her motherly instincts were aroused when she and Jim found Lily and Jack in flagrante. Maybe not. But that's the beauty of the song: you can make of it what you will. Like a tuning fork you can strike it anywhere, and it will give off a pure, ringing note.

I have spoken before of Dylan being inspired to write because he couldn't find the kind of song he wanted to sing—his need to sing driving him to create stories worth sharing—and, later, of how his singing itself was inspired to new levels by the linguistic and aural and intellectual richness of his writing. *Blood on the Tracks* is another instance (in the tradition of *Blonde on Blonde, The Basement Tapes, John Wesley Harding*) of something unique and extraordinary coming into existence out of this cross-fertilization between voice and language, writer and singer each inspiring the other to new heights. This is in the ancient tradition of the bard or minstrel—storyteller as musical performer—a calling that long precedes novelist or biographer.

Dylan, at this moment in his life, had a story to tell. He certainly had an audience (a very personal one—or more than one—as well as a large public one). He wanted to find a vehicle—like a script, a play—by which he could express his feelings in a public performance. So he wrote the ten songs on this album, plus a couple of others, and brought them into the studio. The studio must be understood as a stage: it is a place to bring your material when you're ready to perform it. Through the mechanisms of recording and playback, the studio is a stage where you can stand in front of possibly millions of people at one moment. What comes out of your mouth and heart in that moment is what your audience (distant though they may be in space and time) will hear. So you prepare yourself as well as you can (including pretending that no preparation is necessary), and then you step forward and sing.

And, once or twice or a handful of times in a lifetime, what results is something like "If You See Her, Say Hello." The words tell the story so perfectly they actually disappear, and the listener is left alone with the performer, the sound of his voice and what comes through it, as each verse builds to a fierce intensity of confessed, shared, feeling. The music surrounds the listener like trees and breeze and light in a forest. The overall effect is of overwhelming beauty, not at a distance but so immediate as to be inside the listener, just as the subject of the song is inside the singer—"we've never been apart." The singer's depth of feeling and commitment to the truth become the listener's self-awareness (how I feel in this world full of beauty, pain, love, separation, and longing) through a process of direct transmission.

About "Shelter from the Storm" not much more needs to be said, except to point again to the delicious humor in Dylan's lyrics and delivery, throughout *Blood on the Tracks*. Apparently pain *does* bring out the best in people, sometimes. And "Buckets of Rain" is almost the flip of the same coin—a bit of humorous nonsense sung and played with such sweetness it actually hurts. It's a song about being in love, and it projects a steadiness to precisely counterbalance the restlessness of "Tangled Up in Blue": "If you want me, honey baby, I'll be here." Is this the real Dylan? Is there a real Dylan on this album? Yes, in every contradictory word and every playful, heartfelt note from his guitar, his harmonica, his voice, his band. The last words sum it up nicely:

> You do what you must do, and you do it well
> I do it for you, honey baby, can't you tell?

There are six known outtakes from *Blood on the Tracks*, the five unused New York takes that were on the promotional version of the album plus the song "Up to Me," unreleased until its inclusion on *Biograph*. In addition I've seen lyrics for a song entitled "Call Letter Blues," which, based on its copyright date, is probably from this same period.

The New York alternate takes, with the exception of "Lily," are classic Dylan performances, very much deserving of release (the alternate of "You're a Big Girl Now" is already available, also on *Biograph*), even though I believe in each case Dylan was right to choose the later versions, because of the way they contribute to the sound and impact of the album taken as a whole. Our experience of Dylan's art is made richer by our being able to listen to both takes of "Big Girl," not just because of what we can learn through the comparison (fascinating the evolution of "mm mm" to "oh oh," and the way the earlier take articulates the second "mm mm" in each verse—for example, after "you are on dry land"—whereas the later version simply implies it, so powerfully that the absence of the vocal shudders through the listener's body every time he doesn't hear it), but because of how much the unchosen take communicates as a performance, how much it gives that is uniquely its own, not to be recaptured at any other moment. If a great artist singing a great song results in a precious work of art once, why not twice, or as many times as inspiration and accident allow? "I hope that you can hear ..." Dylan has a lot to say in this song. And whoever else he may think he's talking to, he *is* singing just for me when I'm the one listening.

There are significant lyric variations between New York and Minnesota versions. A small one on "If You See Her, Say Hello" could have been important enough to motivate the second session by itself, because the earlier line "if you're making love to her" is rude, condescending, even though it probably wasn't intended to be — not an acceptable phrase in an album meant to be an olive branch, and an act of courtship. (But does this mean I think "you're an idiot" *is* acceptable? Yes, though I won't try to explain why. And for what it's worth, we do know Dylan and his wife got together again — perhaps even before the album was released, but certainly by March of 1975, when photos show her with him during his guest appearance at a benefit concert in San Francisco.)

The lyric changes between versions of "Idiot Wind" are massive — fully a third of the song has been rewritten — but the really striking change is in the tone of the performance. The earlier "Idiot Wind" is folk rather than rock in its overall sound; Dylan's singing is gentle throughout, which somehow serves to make the song more vicious than the later, louder version. Softspoken anger can be more threatening, more self-righteous, than uninhibited hollering. It's interesting (on both versions) how the object of Dylan's anger shifts (again, an old trick now employed consciously) — often it seems to be his wife, but in other places he's referring to someone else, maybe the press or whoever is gossiping about him, maybe his former manager (a good candidate for "your corrupt ways had finally made you blind"), and certainly at times the "you" is, as much as anyone else, himself. Is it perhaps some destructive alter-ego that he wishes dead ("flies buzzing around your eyes")? That verse, surely, couldn't be addressed to the woman he loves. Or could it? The gloves are off in this song; Dylan dares everything, which is part of the song's appeal. "We pushed each other a little too far," he says in the early take, "And one day it just jumped into a raging storm." So now, perhaps, he needed shelter from the storm his marriage, his shelter, had become. The harmonica solo that closes the New York version of "Idiot Wind" is particularly poignant, and deserves a mention here.

There's another great harmonica solo at the end of the early "Tangled Up in Blue." It's a delightful performance, with quite a different flavor to it, like a painting found underneath a later painting. The major lyrical difference (other than the fact that the first three verses are in the third person, as previously mentioned) is in the transitional, "Montague Street" verse, which previously read:

> He was always in a hurry
> Too busy or too stoned
> And everything that she ever planned
> Just had to be postponed.
> She thought they were successful
> He thought they were blessed
> With objects and material things
> But I never was impressed ...

This—and the more oblique "dealing with slaves" in the later version—is about as close as Dylan ever gets to acknowledging that he had some substance abuse problems and that they might have been a factor in his marital difficulties.

Dylan throws glimpses at us throughout these songs, quick pictures from inside of relationships and lives that seem obviously real and obviously invented, both at once. Sometimes these pictures add up and form a story within a given song; other songs sound like half a dozen stories mixed together, playfully pretending to be a single narrative. "Shelter from the Storm" falls into this latter category, and so does the wonderful *Blood on the Tracks* outtake included on *Biograph*, "Up to Me." ("Call Letter Blues," the other outtake, looks like an extremely powerful song—"Children cry for mother, I tell them mother took a trip/I walk on pins and needles, I hope my tongue don't slip"—and we can only hope it will be released one of these years.*)

The voice with which Dylan sings "Up to Me" is utterly remarkable. Norman Raeben, according to Cartwright, liked to bring

---

*"Call Letter Blues" was included on *The Bootleg Series* in 1991 and turns out to be an earlier (and very different) set of lyrics for "Meet Me in the Morning." Alternate takes of "Idiot Wind," "Tangled Up in Blue," and "If You See Her, Say Hello" are also included in the same collection; all three are slightly different takes from the alternate takes of these songs discussed above.

a book to class and read to his students: "he would read a description of a character and raise a question as to the author's personal attitude toward that character." This as an exercise to help them link up mind, hand and eye. Let us notice, then, that Dylan has assumed a persona to sing/write/speak this song; and let us ask ourselves, what is Dylan's personal attitude toward this character?

I don't know the answer; but I think if I could contemplate the question long enough, listen carefully enough to this voice, all of *Blood on the Tracks'* mysteries would open to me and fall neatly into place. Meanwhile, I'll simply note that here Dylan has detached himself from, and placed himself inside, not only the character called "Dylan the lover," but also a character called "Dylan the public figure, the performer, the artist." This boastful but lovable character describes his relationship with his work and his audience in (consciously) irresistible terms: "If I'd-a paid attention to what others were thinkin', the heart inside me would've died." "The harmonica around my neck, I blew it for you free." "Somebody's got to tell the tale, I guess it must be up to me." The song could be taken as terminally clever. But the beauty of the singing opens the door to another way of hearing it: Dylan is accepting responsibility for everything on *Blood on the Tracks*, overt or covert, contrived or genuine. In the end, he admits, it all comes from him.

Dylan makes reference, in "Tangled Up in Blue," to the power of poetry ("pouring off of every page, like it was written in my soul"); in "You're Gonna Make Me Lonesome" he identifies himself with two outlaw poets of an earlier era ("relationships have ended bad/mine have been like Verlaine and Rimbaud's"). The *Blood on the Tracks* songs, written at the height of Dylan's self-consciousness of himself as a poet/composer, have the added or balancing virtue that they are performed with tremendous passion and immediacy, poetry not of the academy but of the marketplace, the street. Dylan at this point seemed to have truly found his voice and his native medium, as a popular artist. But, characteristically, he had no interest in holding onto what he'd developed or found. As soon as the album was released, it was behind him; and he was back on the road, moving on.

3.

In mid-January, 1975, *Blood on the Tracks* was released. In March Dylan taped a radio interview with Mary Travers, and appeared at a benefit concert in San Francisco. He sang and played with Neil Young and members of the Band; two songs from the concert ("I Want You" and "Knockin' on Heaven's Door," the latter reborn as "Knockin' on the Dragon's Door") feature Dylan on lead vocals, but his singing is almost inaudible on the circulating tape due to a microphone problem. Also around this time Dylan made the decision to have *The Basement Tapes* released as a double album, eight years after the songs had been recorded (and bootlegged). The album came out in late June, and was surprisingly successful; Dylan agreed to release it at least partly to bring some extra income and attention to his friends in the Band.

Dylan spent much of the spring of 1975 vagabonding in the south of France (Savoie, Marseille, Corsica) with David Oppenheim, a French painter who had done the drawing on the back of *Blood on the Tracks*. Oppenheim describes Dylan at the time as: "completely despairing, isolated, lost ... he was having problems with his wife. She was supposed to have come with him, but she hadn't arrived. He phoned her every day. He also talked to his accountant about cash problems concerning the two of them.

"We lived an adventurous life. No complications. We screwed women, we drank, we ate. Nothing else. At first he was really surprised at it all, but soon it seemed that he liked it. ... Pathetic and superb at the same time, Dylan is a bloke who invents everything. He's the most egotistical person I know. That's what makes him an incredible person, his amazing self-confidence. ... He stripped me of all my ideas of wealth, of fame, of romanticism and love."

At the end of June, 1975, Dylan reappeared in Greenwich Village, New York City, ready to kick up some dust. Sara and the children were in Malibu; Dylan was living alone in a borrowed loft on Houston Street, socializing, drinking, making music. He attended club appearances by Muddy Waters, Patti Smith, Ramblin' Jack Elliott, and frequently got up on stage to jam or share a new song of his own. He started hanging out with some old pals, notably Bobby Neuwirth, who had accompanied him as friend, helper, and scene-maker in the Village and on the road in the mid-1960s. And he found new friends with whom he could write, record, perform, create—in particular Jacques Levy, Rob Stoner, and Scarlet Rivera.

I've noted before Dylan's knack for serendipity. The story of how he met Scarlet Rivera, whose violin playing would dominate his next album and play an important part in the sound of his next tour, should be apocryphal but is mere truth: he spotted this striking, sexy woman walking on an East Village street carrying a violin case, pulled his car over and (using the other woman in the car as an intermediary) eventually convinced her to get in the car with them. He said they were gypsies from Hungary; she asked for a ride uptown; he took her downtown to his loft and played her a new song he was working on called "One More Cup of Coffee." Rivera: "I added some violin to it which brought a smile to his face, so we played it a couple more times and it sounded better and better each time." Then Dylan and Sheena (the percussionist he'd been driving with) and Rivera and another friend who'd dropped by went over to the Other End on Bleecker Street and Dylan introduced Rivera to everyone he knew there: "She's in my band, she's gonna be in my band."

Jacques Levy, an off-Broadway director who'd collaborated with Roger McGuinn on some songs, was another person Dylan

bumped into on the street that week — Dylan played him the beginning of a song he'd been thinking about called "Isis" and suddenly
they were staying up all night writing lyrics together. Rob Stoner
got roped into being part of Bob Neuwirth's impromptu house
band at the Other End when he walked into the club one day; soon
he too was playing with Dylan, electric bass, de facto leader of the
band for what turned out to be the *Desire* album and the Rolling
Thunder tour.

On July 3, little more than a week after coming into town,
Dylan visited a Ramblin' Jack Elliott gig at the Other End and, after
backing Jack on Guthrie's "Pretty Boy Floyd" and Carr's "How
Long Blues," nudged him aside to play an extraordinary new song
that we now know as "Abandoned Love." A tape survives: Dylan's
performance is delightful, and there are some notable lyric differences from the studio version recorded a month later — "I can't
play the game no more, I can't abide/By the stupid rules which
kept us sick inside/That are made by men who've given up the
search..." and "Send out for St. John the Evangelist/All my friends
are drunk, they can be dismissed."

Levy and Dylan spent several weeks in mid-July holed up in
East Hampton, Long Island, writing a dozen new songs. Then
Dylan was back in New York, ready to record. Monday, July 28, in
a studio jammed with people who had no idea what was expected
of them (and Dylan wasn't about to tell them), Dylan tried out songs
and musicians, listening to see what might come together. "Romance
in Durango" was recorded that night, with a somewhat baffled Eric
Clapton on lead guitar. Clapton and most of the other musicians
disappeared into the aether, Stoner brought in his friend Howie
Wyeth to play drums, Rivera played her fiddle, Sheena played
congas and bells, and country singer EmmyLou Harris (who'd
never worked with Dylan before) sang harmony, and on Wednesday
July 30 most of the album was completed in a long, inspired session.
(An accordion player and a bellzouki player were brought in for
one song, "Joey.") The next day Dylan's wife Sara was at the studio,
and Dylan recorded "Abandoned Love" (not on *Desire*; it was first
released in 1985, on *Biograph*) and "Sara." The album was done,
except that a potentially libelous factual error in the song "Hurricane" required it to be rerecorded with new lyrics; that session took
place on October 24. "Hurricane," the single, was released in early
November; *Desire*, the album, was released in mid-January, 1976.

Of the performances recorded at the *Desire* sessions, eleven have been released (the nine on *Desire*, plus "Abandoned Love" and "Rita May" – the latter was released as a single at the end of 1976, and is included on the Japanese lp *Masterpieces*). One other circulates among collectors: the July 30 recording of "Hurricane." In addition, the following unheard songs are believed to have been recorded at the July sessions: "Catfish," "Money Blues," "Wiretappin'," and "Golden Loom." A complete set of recordings would also include alternate takes of those songs that were performed more than once, and the various songs Dylan sang (especially at the October session) to warm up before a demanding performance or to unwind afterward.*

Out of this set of recorded performances, someone, presumably Dylan, selected the nine tracks included on *Desire*, and devised a sequence for them. The result is the album as we know it. Once it's in our hands, we naturally think of a record album as a finished product, the creative work towards which the artist was directing his efforts. But when the artist is primarily a performer, an album is more likely to be a snapshot of an ongoing artistic process, taken at the flood if we're lucky, or else recorded either prematurely or past its peak.

All of the songs from the *Desire* sessions are collaborations between Dylan (words and music) and Levy (words), with the exception of "Sara," "Abandoned Love," "One More Cup of Coffee," and "Golden Loom," all written by Dylan alone. It is of course uncharacteristic of Dylan to work with another writer – this marks only the first or second time he ever shared credit for the lyrics of a song, and still stands as his most extensive collaboration with another songwriter. The performances of these songs are also collaborative to a greater-than-usual degree: for the first time Dylan shares vocals with a harmony singer throughout a song and throughout an album (he sang with Baez, but only on stage; Danko and other Bandmembers had sung with him on recordings, but usually just in the chorus of a song). And Dylan collaborates generously and effectively with Scarlet Rivera's violin-playing as they (he is represented by his voice, and sometimes his harmonica) jointly

---

*"Catfish" and "Golden Loom" from the *Desire* sessions are included on *The Bootleg Series, Volumes 1–3*.

create mood, sound, and melody in these songs. It is as though on the one hand he is humble enough at this moment in his life to accept help, to be able to work collaboratively with other bright spirits, and on the other hand he is so self-confident that he can give away control of his work and still be certain it will come out exactly right, will indeed be enriched and enlivened as a result. He relies not on explaining or directing but on the divine power of timing and the temporal power of his own presence, his confidence, his infectious enthusiasm for music and for the act of collective creation.

The result is a sound and a set of songs unlike anything Dylan or anyone else has ever done before. My private cassette of "the best of *Desire*" puts the four love/mystery songs together ("Sara," then "Oh Sister," "Abandoned Love," and "One More Cup of Coffee") as if on one side of an ordinary-length lp – the other side leads off with "Isis" and ends with "Hurricane," with silly sexy "Rita May" stuck between them as a breather. What I'd like to do now, if you'll humor my odd impulse, is discuss these four "love/mystery" songs as if it were Dylan and not me who stuck them together, as if they were somehow one performance, one communication, blending and melting into itself from all directions, four movements of a seamless, no-time symphony.

Allen Ginsberg, in his liner notes to *Desire*, speaks of the "Semitic mode" of "Sara" and "One More Cup of Coffee" ("voice lifts in Hebraic cantillation never heard before in U.S. song, ancient blood singing" and refers repeatedly to "now lets loose his long-vowel yowls and yaps" ("Isis"), "that long-vowelled voice in heroic ecstacy triumphant" ("Like a Rolling Stone"), "singer to open his whole body for Inspiration to breathe out a long mad vowel to nail down the word into everyone's heart" ("Romance in Durango").

To me Dylan's long vowels are present not only directly in the four songs of which I speak ("mysteriously saaaaved" "daddy he's an outlaaaaw"), but symphonically in the harmonica, the violin, and in the chords and colors of every moment of these performances – so that I feel a unity of color and sound between "Oh Sister" and "Sara" and "One More Cup of Coffee," though I couldn't say in words what the name of that color/sound is. I've never heard a cantor singing in a synagogue but I'm sure Ginsberg's right on the money, a certain low vibratory note and unique melodic and vocal sound brought back from Jewish/gypsy Old

World vagabonding is intuitively put over here, a sound of loneli-
ness and self-knowledge, separation from and acknowledgement of
God, sexual/spiritual longing, and a sense of the odd power of
verbal clarity and openness to evoke mystery even more than old
reliable techniques like obfuscation and allusion. And "Abandoned
Love," with its related but dissimilar sound (not so basso mournful,
all that trebly acoustic guitar stronger for once than the violin
keening), weaves magnificently in and out of these other three
lyrically, tying up all threads and opening every end:

> I can see the turning of the key.
> I've been deceived by the clown inside of me.
> I thought that he was righteous but he's vain
> Oh something's telling me, I wear the ball and chain.

Isn't this amazing? Precisely the self-insight and self-indictment
of "Like a Rolling Stone," but so calm, straightforward, mockingly
humorous, painfully honest. There's anger in the song, and we can
hear it in the "Other End" version, but in the studio, with Sara
present, Dylan deadpans brilliantly, pushing through to a level of
bitter, loving self-awareness (and relationship awareness) beyond
irony, beyond anger, resting finally on nothing more than the reality
of the two opposing concepts side by side: love and abandonment.
How it is possible to walk away but still feel it, how it is possible to feel
it but still walk away. And not only possible, necessary.

And then, if Larry Sloman's account is accurate and if the
song he calls "Love Copy" is indeed "Abandoned Love," Dylan
went ahead ("This is for you," he told her, and we're reminded of
his introduction to "Oh Sister" when he taped the "The World of
John Hammond" in September) and sang "Sara." One take. Rivera
and Stoner and Wyeth learning the song as they played it. "Don't
ever leave me, don't ever go." "Let me feel your love one more time
before I abandon it." Here are the contradictions of "Wedding
Song" and "Going, Going, Gone" taken to their aesthetic ultimate.
And what the outcome of all this honesty will be is no longer even
imaginable. All he can do is sing the truth, or anyway sing the
words and the tune that he's written. All he can do, all he wants to
do, is perform.

The lyrics of "Sara" and "Abandoned Love" (and, for that
matter, of "Isis" and "Hurricane") could not be more perfect, but

overall the triumph of *Desire* is musical, so much so that one realizes how much the need to write and sing lyrics limits Dylan as an artist (the way a painter, inspired to share light and color, may be limited at times by his need to paint images and forms). The "lesser" songs on the album (in my opinion, "Mozambique," "Joey," "Romance in Durango," "Black Diamond Bay") point to this—they are wonderful, inventive, pleasure-giving musical performances that don't achieve the unity of purpose and the intensity of most of the other songs because the stories they tell are a little too vague, too clever, too distanced to serve as full force vehicles for the singer's and listener's identification and passion.

"Joey" is marvelous, but it's hard not to get caught in mind chatter about the story being told, ambivalent ethical questions, ultimately I don't identify with Joey or with the person singing about him, whereas I identify fiercely with Hurricane and, particularly, with the narrator of Hurricane's story, every time I hear that song. It has immediacy. "Joey" by contrast is a set piece, albeit a brilliant one. I love to listen to it and would hardly kick it out of my collection, but I don't want to hear it as often or give it the same degree of attention as "Sara." And "Black Diamond Bay" is fun but my inability to care about characters or narrator/character again makes it a different order-of-experience from the major works on this album. "Romance in Durango" comes closest—so well-crafted as a story, excellent language, but ultimately the (first person) protagonist is such an unconscious jerk that neither singer nor listener can invest in him the amount of feeling that the song demands and its music deserves. Later, in live performance, Dylan manages to go beyond the limitations of the lyrics and makes us hear what he feels rather than what he says, and of course the song benefits greatly as a result.

Of all the Levy/Dylan story songs, only "Isis" and "Hurricane" are stories that matter enough to Dylan to pull greatness out of him and his co-lyricist. Good *music*, on the other hand, is just pouring out of Dylan at this moment in his life, and one easily imagines the sounds and structures and musical ideas in all these songs ready to rise to any occasion, any level of communicative brilliance demanded by the story being told. But I am not regretting that "Black Diamond Bay," for example, is not more ambitious. Rather, I am grateful that Levy was there with Dylan and that they had fun fooling around with this, and could churn it out and complete it, otherwise we wouldn't have its unique, charming music at all. Without words and stories, even less-than-transcendent ones, the music and sounds inside Dylan's head can't be released, the performer has nothing to perform. Far better then to be quick and careless with words (when the musical urge is there) than slow and careful and empty-handed. And besides, some of what is quick and careless is also (and I do understand that genuine hard work goes into it) unmistakable genius.

Desire, listened to as a musical work, is a phenomenal album, rewarding from start to finish, over and over again. Amazing the process that created this. EmmyLou Harris: "I'd never heard the songs before and we did most of them in one or two takes. There were no overdubs, we sang live. His phrasing changes a lot ... I just watched his mouth and watched what he was saying. There were times when I didn't even know I was supposed to come in and had to jump fast ... The very first time I'd sung 'One More Cup of Coffee,' it was recorded." Eric Clapton: "He'll just start playing something his way and when he starts to play, especially if you're recording, he'll say, This is the way it goes [Eric demonstrates a few strums on an imaginary guitar] ... if you didn't get it then that's the end of the song. You've got to be very quick. I was just watching his hands, because I didn't know what he was going to play. I didn't know the chord sequences or anything. I was just listening to his voice and watching his hands. ... He was dynamite. Very good. Very cynical, but very good. [Interviewer: why cynical?] Because he didn't seem to care whether anyone was listening to him or watching him or anything. He'd turn his back on you just as soon as look at you."

Having said that the need for lyrics can limit Dylan, I need to reemphasize that it also is what makes his work possible. Words and music cannot be separated, for a singer — you can't sing words alone, you can't sing music alone (although one of the singers Dylan most admires, the Egyptian Om Khalsoum, comes close). Dylan's chosen form is the song, specifically the performed (as opposed to written) song; he is a performer who makes music with and around his voice. Without songs, without words, he just messes around musically — he can't get focused. Without words, stories, verbal material he cares about (even if it's just nonsense), he doesn't put his heart into his singing, isn't inspired to draw on his extraordinary musical inventiveness and depth of feeling. The words are like a door he can walk through to get to his feelings. And when he really cares about something – his feelings about marriage, for example, in 1965–66 and again in 1973–75 – words and song ideas flow out of him, and music flows to be with the words, and performance follows in a white heat of creativity. Like certain baseball sluggers, he's a natural. That pure, easy, mind-reading swing. Born with it. Working always just to stay out of his own way.

Coming back from Europe, arriving in New York (probably by way of California, but I don't know), Dylan had with him most of "One More Cup of Coffee" and little else – possibly an idea in the direction of "Isis," possibly a few other vague starts that might or might not ever become something (he wanted to write a song about Marseille; that could have been the origin of "Mozambique"). And he had a yearning. Desire. Stopping his car for a woman on the street. A woman with a violin. Maybe he could hear the violin in its case, feel the music it would make with him, as he drove by. Someone had sent him a book, *The Sixteenth Round*, autobiography of a black boxer who was in prison doing time for murder on (he said) trumped-up charges, politics. Dylan read the book and the first thing he did when he got to New York was go to New Jersey to meet the man, Rubin "Hurricane" Carter, to find out who he was and how he could help. Not because Dylan normally did this sort of thing – but because it caught him at the right moment, he felt it, and he was looking for something. Community. A cause. A certain violin sound. How could he know what it was, until he found it? So he met Rubin, and then found himself with the sort of overt challenge he very seldom takes on. He had a song to write, a song with a purpose, an adaptation in fact from book to 45 rpm record, the Hurricane story.

Larry Sloman: "Rubin's plight became of such paramount importance to Dylan that at first it seemed that Bob was having difficulty writing the song about Hurricane because he was too emotionally involved in the situation." Jacques Levy: "He was just filled with all these feelings about Hurricane. He couldn't make the first step." Dylan (to Sloman): "I wrote that song because it was tops in my mind, it had priority. There's an injustice that has been done and … the fact is that it can happen to anybody. We have to be confronted with that."

A month after arriving in New York, Dylan was recording songs and living in a community brought into existence by the powerful yearning emptiness he'd come into town with. *Desire*, indeed. July 30, he recorded "Hurricane" (only adequately, in my opinion). September 10, for a television program, he performed it passionately. October 24, back in the studio, he and his musicians recorded the song, uncharacteristically, eleven times, starting over because of mistakes (by Dylan), trying to get it right. One of those takes became the official record, released as a single a quick two weeks later. It is one of the most powerful recordings Bob Dylan has ever made.

Reader, please know that Author realizes that all an essay on aesthetics (which this book is) can be, at best, is a sort of exercise in finger-pointing (there! that's greatness!), dressed up in (one hopes) stimulating language. My purpose today is to point, first, to "Hurricane" as a generally underrated work. It is as much a cornerstone of Dylan's oeuvre as "Desolation Row" or "Gates of Eden" or "Sad-Eyed Lady of the Lowlands," as well-executed and vital a statement as anything he has undertaken, and as rewarding to hear and experience.

Beyond this, or as an extension of it, I feel called on to point, if I can, to some of the elements within Dylan's performance of "Hurricane" that contribute to its greatness. "What rewards, Author?", asks Reader, maybe skeptical, maybe in full agreement but curious to see how I'll answer.

Watch my finger, then: I'll point first to my heel pounding the floor as I sit listening to "Hurricane" over and over with ever-increasing pleasure, my head bobbing rhythmically, emphatically, and, listen, there I am suddenly shouting out the words of the song along with the singer, excited, full of feeling, enraptured. Next, let me point to the power of the violin silence/conga "solo" during the fifth and sixth lines of each verse, and the way Dylan sings into it and with it ("You'll be doing so-ci-e-ty a *fa*vor"). Which leads naturally to our noticing the precision and energy and awareness with which Dylan mouths every syllable of the song (Ginsberg: "every consonant sneered out with lips risen over teeth to pronounce them exactly to a T in microphone"), and the incredible solidity the song achieves as a result, every relatively plain-spoken, understated phrase ("obviously framed") has a scream inside it, a scream the listener feels and wants to unleash even as the singer holds back, calmly continuing the story, letting go only on the last vowel of each verse, a long controlled moan punctuated by exactly four drumbeats, music (between-verse break) exploding on the fifth.

"Hurricane" the performance is an expression of love for life, love for freedom, love for justice. It is a cry of pain at the existence of injustice, an acknowledgement of the imperfection of our nation, and at the same time a ringing affirmation of personal power, via the singer's evident conviction that his telling of this story will have an effect, that "testifying" to truth will ultimately dethrone falsehood.

Dylan throws away all artifice for this song, all irony, all assumed distance. This is another, quite different example of Dylan seeking to do consciously what he once did unconsciously — he needs to write a "Hattie Carroll," more complicated story this time with many more details that must be included, and it has to be just as agile and aesthetically satisfying while promoting a much more specific and immediate response (instead of "burying the rag," the job this time is to "clear his name and give him back the time he's done") ... and, you see, if "Hattie Carroll" hadn't come together Dylan would have put the draft aside and gone on to something else, but this time he's made a commitment to himself and to Carter that leaves him much less free to go with the flow of his own creative process.

So he and Levy have, in essence, allowed nothing to stop them. They invent brilliant new techniques of storytelling in telescoped, song format, on the one hand; and on the other hand break rules that even Dylan would have bent to in less desperate circumstances — break 'em and make 'em work better broken. The rhyme scheme here varies widely from verse to verse, even though the verses are otherwise regular in length and structure. Sometimes the last word is a rhyme, sometimes it isn't, and either way it seems to gain power as a result. More surprising is Dylan's success in moving back and forth between present and past tense as he tells the story.

He starts out in present tense ("Pistols shots ring out"), difficult and very effective, nicely worked into an opening that sounds like stage directions, not a film this time but a play unfolding in gloriously dramatic terms before your eyes/ears. The problem with present tense is staying in it without sounding ridiculous. In the third verse Dylan slips into past tense in the fourth line, more or less in the middle of a thought, like a dream transition. And somehow, as in a dream, it seems to work.

He goes back to present tense in the first line of the fifth verse (although, perhaps by mistake, he backslides briefly in the second line as performed), staying there till the start of the seventh when, again in mid-scene, we're suddenly in the past. Present reemerges in the last (eleventh) verse. What's strangest about this is that it is so effective. My sense of it is that the songwriters tried to fix up the verbs and just couldn't do it; finally, the song being more important than their ideas of how language should go, they let it be, let the story tell itself in its own chosen fashion.

The great success of the vocal is totally dependent on and inseparable from the success of the instrumental performance. The instruments walk on one by one in the intro: bass, acoustic guitar, congas, violin, drums, and finally the voice: "Pistol shots—!" Dylan never sings a note that is not linked with, sung against, the beat of Howie Wyeth's drums, and the timbre of his voice is constantly tuned to, reaching towards, the melodic drone of Scarlet Rivera's violin (true even when drums and violin step aside for the conga and a sort of vocal "change-up" in the middle of each verse). Here is an artistry possibly beyond the comprehension of those who believe that musical (or any sort of) artistry depends on premeditation. For Dylan, this is the place where music originates—first, in the interaction between lyrics and piano sound or guitar sound or memory sound during songwriting, and second in the interaction between voice and instruments during live performance, whether on stage or in the studio. "Hurricane," even though it is an uncharacteristic fifth or sixth take (I surmise) at a second or third recording session, is being created musically even as we hear it; this groove, this dynamic, never existed before; sparks are flying; a song is coming to life. At least as much is said between the verses (even between the words) of the song as in its verbal text. And all of it is directed, finally, by the passion in Dylan's heart, by his determination to bear witness to what has occurred. He succeeds.

By way of postscript, this information: the murders occurred in June 1966. Carter and his friend John Artis were arrested in October 1966 (they'd been questioned but released the night of the crime, as the song reports—"he ain't the guy!") on the strength of Alfred Bello's statement (later recanted) placing them at the murder scene. They were convicted in May 1967. March 1976, four months after Dylan's single was released, their convictions were overturned because the prosecution had withheld evidence favorable to the defense. In December 1976 they were convicted again, at a second trial, and sent back to prison.

Artis was released on parole in 1981. In November 1985 the second trial convictions were overturned by a federal court, because they were based on "racism rather than reason." The state appealed; Carter was released on bail, after 19 years in prison. In January 1988 the U.S. Supreme Court denied the state's appeal. In February 1988 the Passaic County Prosecutor's Office announced they would not seek a third trial, and indictments were dismissed. Federal Judge Lee Sarokin, November 1985: "I cannot in the face of the conclusions reached in my opinion and the injustices found, permit Mr. Carter to spend another day or even an hour in prison..."

"Hurricane (Part 1)", the shortened single, made it to #33 on the U.S. national charts at the beginning of 1976. There have been other rock and roll hit singles in which the hook, the dominant riff, is played on a violin, but not many, and certainly none that rock as hard as this.

"Isis" is the most talked-about song on *Desire*. Levy: "We finished 'Isis' that one night ... we went down to the Other End and Bob read the lyrics to a bunch of people sitting around the bar, just read them, and everybody responded to the thing because everyone gets hooked in that story, apparently. The two of us didn't know that at that time, I mean we were getting hooked."

Exactly. Myth is not created but discovered; storyteller suddenly finds himself hooked into something bigger and deeper than his own imagination or conscious awareness. "Isis" is not a retelling of an Egyptian legend (Levy: "the only thing it has to do with the Egyptian goddess is that at some point we threw in the pyramids instead of the Grand Teton Mountains, which is probably really what it's about, going up into the hills in Wyoming or something"). The song has its origins partly in a western ballad Dylan learned from Woody Guthrie, "The Trail of the Buffalo." The choice of "Isis" as the woman's and song's name was inspired — two syllables, four letters, like "Joey," like "Sara" — and it sets in motion all sorts of associations and resonances.

And certainly the story told, in its basic form, is not unrelated to Dylan's recent journeying in France. The man leaves, goes out on an intense but seemingly pointless excursion, and comes back, but now he "looks different" to the woman — because, as John Bauldie points out, he has "the sun in his eyes," the fire in his spirit that had gone out has been rekindled. His desire for her, and her insistence that he be worthy of/attractive to her, has broken through his self-satisfaction and forced him out on a quest of self-discovery and renewal.

Interesting that Dylan read the lyrics to the people sitting around the bar, because "Isis" is less a song and more a minstrel's poem (to be read aloud, preferably but not necessarily accompanied by music). The magic is in the story and the language, and the musical accompaniment is ornamention (very different from "Hurricane," which must be heard as song, as music, or it loses all impact). Dylan plays piano on the album version, with harmonica/violin improvisations after each verse.

The live version on *Biograph* (from fall 1975) is almost two minutes shorter—Dylan sings every verse, but he sings 'em faster, and the band comes in only after every second or third verse. I like both versions, a lot—but it was a shock to hear the slowed-down album version after being introduced to the song through Dylan's exuberant live performance of it on the Rolling Thunder tour. Never before or since has he so consciously and successfully played the part of an actor on stage. He even—and this is unique in his career up to this point, I believe—sang the song without a musical instrument, guitar or piano, in front of him. Hands open and visible. Astonishing. Unforgettable.

Open and visible. *Desire* is an extraordinary album, and never more so than when Dylan shares himself, unambiguously, in "Sara." These lyrics, as poetry on a page, probably wouldn't be publishable in any but the hungriest college literary magazine, yet combined with melody and rhythm and sung from the heart by a great singer, they are profound art. How song differs from poetry! And yet the distinction is simple. To be poetry, these words would have to sing on the page. They don't. But so also a great poem will usually fail completely the requirements of performed song—regularity, clarity, simplicity, roundness, whatever it is that lets words music rhythm and voice work together successfully as a gestalt.

Sound is the essence in both poetry and song, but a different sort of sound depending on the medium. How shall we explain to the page poet that the power of these lyrics lies in their ability to suspend themselves modestly between the bookends of the harmonica solos, and to nestle into the landscape created by the primary vocalizations, the repeated word/sound/melody (cantillation) "Sara!" as harmonized with the violin? That the musical color of the words is as important as the images they evoke, images/colors of intimacy, family life, friendship, female beauty, and always holy mystery? That awkwardness of language is not necessarily a pitfall and may even be helpful at times to keep listener and singer from floating away?

Sound of voice, sound of voice is everything; words are secondary to song and song itself is secondary to performance, the final unit of artistry. This performance—slow drums, 6/8 time, exquisite tune, and always and so simply the voice, not just Dylan's voice but uniquely Dylan's voice singing this song "Sara"—is so ... open and visible. Translucent. Sincere. Finally it doesn't matter that Dylan has a wife named Sara. She and the person singing to her could be imaginary, and this would still be the same classic love song. Our knowledge of and relationship with the singer gives the song a special edge and immediacy, and the singer knows it, but it is the sound of this voice singing this name that will endure, beyond context, beyond time, beyond language. When these words no longer have meaning, there will still be sound.

"Oh Sister" "Abandoned Love" (that tune taps at my brain constantly, always brings a smile to my face) "One More Cup of Coffee"—three very different flavors of glorious more-of-the-same. Dylan later reports that he met a dying King of the Gypsies in the south of France whose family situation (Dylan probably just imagining himself the daughter's lover, as in "Spanish Harlem Incident") helped inspire "One More Cup of Coffee." Awareness of mortality is a conscious thread that weaves through these songs, as though Dylan has rediscovered Death as a companion, life-enricher, old friend.

Beginning of August, album recorded and mixed, Dylan's phenomenal energy turned to putting together a tour (let's take this show on the road!) and filming a movie. Those stories will be told in the next few chapters. But one more recorded performance must be mentioned here, as poet prepared to transform himself into troubadour: a Chicago public television station was taping a salute to John Hammond, the legendary producer who had signed Dylan to his first record contract, and Dylan agreed to be on the program. He brought Stoner, Wyeth, and Rivera with him, and they played "Hurricane," "Oh Sister," and "Simple Twist of Fate."

The taping was September 10, 1975; the show aired in mid-December. Good quality audio and videotapes survive and circulate among collectors. Dylan gives an excellent performance, and is surprisingly unselfconscious about the camera—he looks uncomfortable at the start of each song (he scowls, grimaces, casts suspicious glances in various directions) but it is a functional discomfort, which evolves into a purposeful seriousness, clearly a surface expression of his concentration, his intensity, his intent. One gets the feeling (as he raises his eyebrows, closes his eyes, makes small meaningful gestures with his face, head, and body) that this is how he looks also when he's singing into a mike with no camera on him, on stage (most folks in a concert audience can't see the expressions on his face) or in a recording studio. This is Dylan performing, not to be watched but to be *heard*, and the various comments he makes with his face as he sings are to himself or an imaginary companion, and help him be present with and put across his song.

What comes across unmistakably is the man's strength, his commitment to his own vision of reality, his self-confidence, and the power of his presence. He performs "Hurricane" and "Oh Sister" publicly for the first time (also his first public appearance with the core of what will be the Rolling Thunder tour band), and then unleashes a rewritten "Simple Twist of Fate." It is as though he is declaring his independence even from his recent past, his unwillingness to be chained to his own songbook and his insistence on being related to always as the artist he is at this moment. The new lyrics are good—something is gained here, lost there, but overall the story of the song stays the same. The mood, the spirit of it are different, but that seems a function more of the moment of performance (the sound, the attack, the phrasing) than of the changes in the words.

The taping ran late, and Dylan and his band, scheduled last, didn't come on till two a.m. Dylan can be seen wiping sleep from his eyes at one point. But then when we see those eyes they're filled with fire. Dylan, after that long fallow period when he had little interest in or heart for performing, writing, sharing his essence with the world, has now completely reclaimed his reputation, his creativity, and his personal energy. His presence burns from the video screen. His music bursts with aliveness. Anyone can see he's being driven by some kind of primal force.

Ironically, by the time the TV taping hit the airwaves, that force had already been unleashed, had roared across the countryside, had spent itself fully and gloriously. It is as though this little TV appearance served simultaneously (outside of time) as both invocation and benediction. In between fell that remarkable expression of Dylan's expansive, visionary restlessness known as the Rolling Thunder Revue.

III. Troubador

October 1975 - May 1976

"We'd go out at night and run into people and we'd just invite them to come with us, you know."
— Lou Kemp, tour manager, Rolling Thunder Revue

4.

The Rolling Thunder Revue had its debut on October 30, 1975, at the War Memorial Auditorium in Plymouth, Massachusetts, in front of a sold-out audience of 1800 people. The Revue band – Rob Stoner, Howie Wyeth, Bob Neuwirth, Steven Soles, Mick Ronson, T-Bone Burnett, Luther Rix, David Mansfield, and Ronee Blakley – opened the show with ten songs sung variously by Neuwirth, Soles, Stoner, Ronson, Burnett, and Blakley. Ramblin' Jack Elliott followed with four songs. Then Dylan came on and started his set, as he did every night of the tour, with "When I Paint My Masterpiece," sung as a duet with Neuwirth, backed by the full band, Dylan wearing (and singing through) a transparent Richard Nixon mask. Later he'd take off the mask to reveal a face heavily daubed with white face-paint. He was playing the minstrel, the entertainer, troupe leader, troubador.

Four more songs by Dylan and band completed the first half of the show (with Scarlet Rivera joining on violin). After intermission, Dylan and Joan Baez sang four songs together (backed by the band on three), then Baez did six songs (starting with "Diamonds and Rust," her beautiful, very evocative then-and-now love song to

Dylan), Roger McGuinn did one, and Baez did one more; and then Dylan came back to do one solo song and five backed by the band, followed by a show-closing (no encore) performance by the whole troupe, Woody Guthrie's "This Land Is Your Land."

The 31st and final show of the 1975 tour took place at Madison Square Garden in New York City on December 8th. Dylan by now was performing 22 songs instead of 16. But the essential structure of his performance had remained the same, and almost all the songs he started out with were still in the show. Six of these songs—the core of the performance—were from his forthcoming album, *Desire*. Several other songs were covers. This was not a greatest hits tour. Dylan only sang "Like a Rolling Stone" once during the entire six weeks.

Dylan's sets on December 8th went as follows:

1. "When I Paint My Masterpiece" "It Ain't Me Babe" "The Lonesome Death of Hattie Carroll" "Tonight I'll Be Staying Here with You" "It Takes a Lot to Laugh, It Takes a Train to Cry" "Romance in Durango" "Isis."
2. (with Baez) "The Times They Are A-Changin'" "Dark as a Dungeon" "Mama, You Been on My Mind" "Never Let Me Go" "I Dreamed I Saw St. Augustine" "I Shall Be Released."
3. "Love Minus Zero/No Limit" "Simple Twist of Fate" (these first two songs solo acoustic) "Oh Sister" "Hurricane" "One More Cup of Coffee" "Sara" "Just Like a Woman" "Knockin' on Heaven's Door" "This Land Is Your Land" (last two songs sung by the whole troupe).

Other songs performed during the tour included "Hard Rain" (at about half the shows, during the first set); "Blowin' in the Wind" "The Water Is Wide" "Wild Mountain Thyme" (all with Baez); "I Don't Believe You" "Tangled Up in Blue" "Mr. Tambourine Man" "It's All Over Now, Baby Blue" "Fourth Time Around" "With God on Our Side" "It's Alright, Ma" (these took turns in the solo acoustic slot starting the third set); and (once) "Like a Rolling Stone."

The primary thrust of the Revue (presumably in response to Dylan's dissatisfaction with the rock-and-roll-star tour, as he experienced it in 1974) was to create an alternative form of musical tour, spontaneous barnstorming carried forward by the energy and camaraderie of a community of performers and support people, "let's go out together and play music in the countryside."

Another major undertaking was to create something theatrical: more visual, more dramatic, more conscious of sequence and timing than your ordinary concert. Jacques Levy was the prime mover here; he designed the set and the lighting (the entire stage was lit up, like a living room instead of rockstar spotlight stuff), and devised the sequence of performances. This theatricality was consistent with the music Dylan wanted to do and the musicians he was working with—"Isis" and "Hurricane," songs he'd written with Levy, were visual, dramatic works, and a band that included and encouraged the outrageous gestures of Neuwirth and the startling visual impact of Scarlet Rivera on fiddle cried out to be showcased (the other musicians were also striking to look at, powerful contrasting archetypes, and of course much was made of the audience's sense of drama at seeing Dylan and Baez together again on stage, lips almost touching as they leaned in to sing at the same microphone).

The third major factor influencing the shape and character of the Revue was Dylan's decision that the time had come to shoot the movie he'd been wanting to make ever since he and Howard Alk edited together *Eat the Document* out of scrap 1966 tour footage (on and offstage). So the Revue and its rich cast of performers rolled from town to town, from Plymouth to Niagara Falls to Montreal to Manhattan, and between shows and during them the cameras were rolling, a nonstop festival of creativity and craziness. All the footage for the film that became *Renaldo & Clara* was shot during this part of the tour, October to December, 1975.

Renaldo & Clara is the primary document, therefore, of Dylan's fall 1975 performances; much has been written about the Rolling Thunder Revue (notably Larry Sloman's *On the Road with Bob Dylan* and Sam Shepard's *Rolling Thunder Logbook*), but the only publicly released Rolling Thunder performances are those included in the film. Twelve of these feature Dylan (there are also many excellent soundtrack fragments, in which we hear but do not see the performers); solo performances by Baez, McGuinn, Elliott, and Blakley can also be seen in the film. One of the Dylan segments, an acoustic performance of "Tangled Up in Blue" shot in tight close-up of Dylan's face, his startling blue eyes playing peekaboo with the shadow of his broad-rimmed blue hat, was released as a promotional video for *Biograph*. That performance is not on *Biograph* but two other Revue songs are, both from the film, both recorded in Montreal December 4, 1975: "Romance in

Durango" and "Isis." The same "Isis" was also included on a promotional record, *4 Songs from Renaldo & Clara*, that CBS sent to radio stations in January 1978, at the time of the film's release. The other three songs are "Never Let Me Go" (with Baez, 12/4/75), "It Ain't Me Babe" (Cambridge, Mass., 11/20/75), and "People Get Ready" (heard but not seen in the film; probably recorded during tour rehearsals in October 1975).

We come now to the real reason I started writing these books — to celebrate, defend, and call attention to a major body of work by one of the great artists of the twentieth century: Bob Dylan's performances, particularly his live performances, and particularly those from 1975 to the present.

The stature of Bob Dylan's body of work in the 1960s — his songs, his records, and the groundbreaking performances on those records — is well established now. Even some of Dylan's live performances from the '60s (particularly the Manchester '66 concert) are widely accepted as legendary works that in recorded form constitute some sort of enduring artistic triumph, sure to be listened to and applauded for decades and centuries to come.

Dylan's subsequent work, with the exception of *Blood on the Tracks*, is virtually unappreciated by the public and vastly underrated by most critics and commentators. I would like, in this book, to set the record straight. If Dylan's art is seen for what it is, the recorded output of a great spontaneous performer ("yes. well i could use some help in getting this wall in the plane"), it is easier to get a sense of how much he has accomplished since his legend days, and to recognize him as a hardworking artist who has continually carved out new musical ground, first as songwriter and album-maker in 1962–1966, and then as a performer on stage, in 1966, in 1974, and from 1975 through to the present.

1975 is significant because it marks the moment of Dylan facing one of his greatest challenges as a creator: learning to do consciously what he had previously done unconsciously (as Norman taught), not in relation to his writing this time but on stage, in the spotlight. Learning how to find that place where sincerity and power and originality come from, and how to keep coming back to that place while creating, while performing. Learning to be a mature artist. Learning that he could no longer count on the situation, the world around him, to stir things up; if he wanted intensity, he'd have to bring it with him. The Rolling Thunder

Revue is a remarkable response to the threat of having to repeat Tour '74, with its triumphs, its imprisonments, and ultimately its tedium, for the rest of one's life.

Dylan didn't stop at changing the external form of his concerts in a truly radical manner. He also (as we shall see by examining the radio sampler *4 Songs from Renaldo & Clara*, a superb distillation of Dylan's creative output as a Revue member) attacked his own and the world's assumptions about the inner rules that determine what a song is and how it must be performed. Most important, as he innovated, he continually produced individual works, specific performances, of truly memorable beauty and power.

The first track on *4 Songs* is "People Get Ready," a 1965 gospel-based r&b hit by the Impressions ("People get ready, there's a train a-comin'/Don't need no baggage, you just get on board/All you need is faith..."). Dylan sings and plays the piano, with bass and drums accompaniment in a party atmosphere (various conversations can be heard going on around him); clearly this is a one-off performance from a string of old songs, typical loosening-up stuff at a rehearsal or soundcheck (at the end of the track, Dylan starts pounding out a new set of piano chords and can be heard saying to the other musicians, "Remember this one?").

"People Get Ready" is a gem. It's a great song, first of all, and even though he can only half-remember the words, Dylan is completely successful at expressing and communicating his love for the song, his respect for its tempo, its message, its magic. This comes through in his voice (and in his enthusiastic, rhythmic piano playing, itself a sort of second voice). And mysteriously, levels within levels, something else comes through: it's as if his open mouthing of the chords, words, and rhythms of love opens a door to the feelings behind the love, perhaps (one can only speculate) feelings that were touched when the musician as listener first heard and felt the song.

Something emerges. It is a feeling of wonder, of smoothness, of personality, of spiritual contact. Beauty is another aspect of it, that odd, intense sort of beauty that requires disorder, imperfection, randomness, a sense that something exquisite and short-lived is occurring and we are observing it only by accident, by rare good fortune. People who've attended Dylan recording sessions or concert rehearsals often speak of such performances with awe. Here is one that Dylan himself has recorded and included on his movie's soundtrack and even released to radio stations. In the movie the song accompanies and gives character to footage of an American Indian gathering, and to an astonishing sequence in which we watch a truck rolling along a highway and then suddenly the truck recedes in the distance, not in the direction it's going but sideways, and we realize we've been watching it, filming it, from a train which is now moving away from, at a tangent to, the truck and the highway. Whew. The observer becomes aware of his own motion, his own role in the experience, becomes aware of the person telling and the person listening to the story. And the timing, in relation to the music and in relation to the images, colors, and textures of the scene (visual words, chords, rhythms), is so wonderful. And the point is…

The point is that the movie *Renaldo & Clara* and the Rolling Thunder tour and Dylan's performances during the tour reflect and express an aesthetic that starts, perhaps, with the ability to appreciate "People Get Ready." Here is a performance full of garbled, slurred and forgotten words, a performance joined in progress by drums, bass, and eventually guitar (and just as the guitar player gets into something, the singer/pianist drops the song, leaves him hanging). A recording almost drowned out by chatter at the beginning, focused on a vocal that comes on with astonishing power for a few words and then dies away. What is this shit?

This shit is Dylan's idea of what great music is and where it comes from, and I celebrate him and his movie and the music he made on this tour because my experience is, he's right.

Dylan believes in spontaneity, believes in striking two stones together to get sparks, and knows how easy it is to fall into a sleepwalking groove, as he did on the road in early '65, as his band did at times in '74. So he invented a way to create a dynamic relationship between himself and the song that he's singing, one that can change each time depending on the mood or spirit of the moment, but at the same time is structured and familiar enough so it doesn't have to be thought about, there are no decisions to be made. He created, as it were, a new place for the singer to stand in relation to the song; and along with it, a bizarre and powerful new place for singer to stand in relation to his band, the people making music with him.

Returning for a moment to "People Get Ready," its triumph is the mood it evokes, like a single note reached for and achieved — Dylan picks up the song, tries it on, and discards it, but something incredible and quite complete has occurred during the moment of his wearing it. If we want to speak of the experience in terms of emotional/intellectual content, what the performance evokes gains added poignance in hindsight—more than three years before his "conversion," here is Dylan showing with his heart how real, how tangible to him is this slow train coming. It's in his blood. That's pure delight in his voice when he sings, "All you need is faith to hear those diesels humming" (surely he can hear them; surely that's what he's unconsciously sharing here); and unshakable conviction and great boozy sweetness when he sings, "Don't need no ticket, you just *thank the Lord*."

How did he know? Because he himself heard this message from other gospel voices, and felt, not from the words but from the voices, that it was true. This is not a religious matter I'm talking about. I'm talking about how we receive, retain, and express information through music, on a level more real to us than any thoughts thunk by our minds.

Small minds might deny that there is any meaning in a performance other than what the songwriter and performer consciously put there (have to be awfully small, though). Small minds might also say that a performance on which the singer forgets or botches the words can't be worth releasing or listening to. Small minds would probably also insist (and they often have) that Bob Dylan could be so much better a singer if he would just make the effort to sing on tune and in time, and to let the musicians he's working with know what he's going to do.

Of course, small minds have always nipped at the heels of great art. Bob Spitz, in his careless and sometimes mean-spirited *Dylan: A Biography* (published 1988), dismisses Howard Alk as a "hack" and Scarlet Rivera as "mediocre," and quotes Rob Stoner on singing harmony with Dylan: "It's an incredibly tough maneuver. You try to hear which note's coming and then nail whatever ones are left ... It becomes a constant game of cat-and-mouse that ultimately detracts from the show." One can't blame Stoner for his frustration (as bass player and bandleader he was as much as anyone responsible for the musical success of the Rolling Thunder tours; no doubt he took a lot of abuse from Dylan and received relatively little compensation or acknowledgement in return), but it's unfortunate that Spitz manages to leave the impression that Dylan's "duels" with Joan Baez on stage were, in the end, detrimental to the music. No doubt there were lots of (seemingly unnecessary) bad moments, but they are forever eclipsed by the triumphs produced by Dylan's bizarre, playful, arbitrary, even just plain mean approach to "harmonizing" — he attacks like a martial arts teacher, requiring the other to respond unflinchingly or be annihilated — triumphs epitomized by the magnificent "Never Let Me Go" included on *4 Songs from Renaldo & Clara*.

Roland Penrose, in his biography of Picasso, speaks of Picasso's images (in this case, surprisingly, in reference to a poem by the artist rather than a painting) as "a direct transcription of his thoughts, inspired equally by the sensations gathered from his immediate surroundings and memories often going far back into the past ... [an] automatic flow of sensation from the subsconscious freely transmitted in words." This is painter or poet as performer, intuitively expressing the immediate and the long-remembered both at once, spitting it out with all attention focused on avoiding premeditation. If we know the language of poetry, we know how important meter is, beat and lack of beat recurring in regular (but, sometimes, freely violated) patterns, like waves rolling in and breaking on the shore. Meter in a poem serves as a channel through which the pent-up energy of the words, the forces stringing these syllables together into sentences (laments, furies), can be released. Imagine, then, the opportunity of the singer on stage to use the rhythm of the music in sync with the rhythm of the language (even adding movements of body and face — dance — to the overall impact) as a means of stimulating and transmitting an "automatic flow of sensation." This is done in large part consciously, with the song (and its words and music) chosen and even rehearsed, arranged, ahead of time ... yet in the end the ability of the singer to be present as he performs, to be open to creating a brand-new relationship with the song as of this moment, is the key to his success at sharing his deepest feelings. This doesn't mean that Dylan invents a new way to sing the song every night. It simply means that on December 4, 1975, in Montreal, during "Never Let Me Go," he and Baez sing the word "million" as if they were meeting it for the first time.

And I've still got it wrong, because it isn't about how any one word is sung. It's about the way every syllable of the song is driven in as if with a hammer, and the way the guitars and rhythm section wrap themselves around and support and repeat and augment the singers' phrasing, so that each word and note of the tune impresses itself on the listener's consciousness, finally causing him to cry out involuntarily, shouting the words of the song like they contain everything he's ever felt that's still inside him at this moment (and they do). Here is Dylan taking a song that is essentially pre-rock-and-roll (an r&b hit for Johnny Ace in 1953, written by Joseph C. Scott) and not adding to it in any way but rather stripping it down to uncover its rock and roll heart. The songwriting is masterful: the expressiveness and simplicity and subtlety of the lyrics, the power of the melody, the cleverness of the rhymes, the perfect release in the bridging verse. A classic. A great song needs a great performer; here it benefits from six or seven of them, at least one of whom is certifiably a genius. Under his leadership and in response to his challenge, the others discover and reveal their own extraordinary gifts.

"I think marriage is the hottest furnace of the spirit today," Leonard Cohen announced in an interview at the end of 1974. A year later, in Montreal, Bob Dylan and his band conjured up the *sound* of that furnace with an intensity worthy of Jimi Hendrix or the Who at their live best. Dylan, in a rare word to the audience, introduces the tune: "Here's a song about marriage; this is called 'Isis.'" Drums, guitars, violin crash in, and Dylan, with his usual impeccable timing, waits a few measures before shouting over the din, "This is for Leonard, if he's still here."

"Isis" is about marriage because the narrator's marriage to Isis frames his adventure, is indeed the very environment in which the adventure takes place. Material greed is a secondary motivation, but mostly the hero is "thinkin' about Isis, how she thought I was so reckless." When the tomb turns out to be empty, his first response is to feel cheated; then he acknowledges his own part in things: "When I took up his offer, I must have been mad." Finally, at the end of the song, after his triumphant reunion with the woman he married, he identifies the source of his madness: "What drives me to you is what drives me insane." No marriage, no conflict; also, in the end, no adventure, and so no hero. This little slab of modern myth is, if you will, a celebration of being driven; and Dylan (with a lot of help from the band) gives one of his most driven performances, for once consciously putting on a hero's mask instead of just walking out there the hero the audience already thinks he is.

One of the things that needs to be said about the Rolling Thunder tour is that Dylan at least initially conceived of it as something that could exist without him. He imagined, in his cups, that he and his friends were setting up a whole new form of musical tour, one that could move freely through the countryside, self-sufficient enough (book the halls ourselves, do our own publicity, sell our own tickets) to be spontaneous, something flowing and creative rather than rigid and prestructured — and he saw himself, as headliner, able to go home and rest for six weeks when he wanted or needed to, with someone else (he mentioned Eric Clapton as an example) taking his place as headline attraction. The Rolling Thunder Revue, in other words, was not simply a Bob Dylan show. Having Joan Baez on the bill also supported this idea. I'm not suggesting that this was an expression of humility on Dylan's part — on the contrary, the problem with not being part of a community, from Dylan's point of view, was that you had no one to compete with. The audience was yours before the show started. How much more satisfying to be challenged to prove yourself every night as the brightest star in a galaxy of fabulous talent! Far from being a casting off of ego, it was a way of making something risky and meaningful out of what had become safe and meaningless (performing as a superstar), with one payoff being a chance for the ego to get strokes for its glorious accomplishments this evening, instead of always being in the shadow of the great moves you made way back when.

And "Isis," on the Rolling Thunder tour, was (each night) Bob Dylan's biggest risk and greatest triumph. Invariably the closing song of Dylan's first set (Act One finale), it was the moment at which he had to make good on the promise of the whiteface, and prove that he was indeed an actor or clown or mime and not just a songster with pretensions. By taking off the guitar that *always* had stood between him and his audience (the notable exception being that other moment of great risk, reciting "Last Thoughts on Woody Guthrie" at Town Hall in '63), he rises to the challenge, announces his vulnerability like a magician stripping to his underwear and getting handcuffed before he's locked in the trunk.

And if there were justice in the world, the white heat of Dylan's "Isis" performance would have been enough to free him forever from his "legendary-Sixties-songwriter-with-guitar-and-harmonica" straightjacket. I heard this song for the first time at a Rolling

Thunder Revue show in New Haven, and for weeks after was haunted by the sound of Dylan shouting "Yes!" at the end of the penultimate verse. A recording, even a film, is of course not the same as being present at a live performance, but the recording of "Isis" from Montreal is unusually vibrant and lifelike (better on vinyl than compact disc—the latter loses punch by separating out the instruments too much—best of all is listening to it on 45, as the B-side of the 1984 "Jokerman" single). The filmed footage of "Isis" as seen in *Renaldo & Clara* is also riveting: what sticks in my mind are the images of Bobby Neuwirth flickering his tongue like a snake, and Dylan holding up his crossed wrists as though trying to ward off a vampire ("I picked up his body..."). And always, over and through all the images of singer and band and ice pyramids and Isis in the meadow, supporting and transcending the majestic cacophony of stuttering rhythm guitars and soaring lead notes, keening fiddle and crashing snares and fiery dart vocal explosions, there's the implacable steady one-two-three-four punctuating every line, which I guess is performed by bass guitar and bass drum together but which anyway is the total key to the power of the performance, bam (pause) bam (pause) bam (pause) bam over and over, with never a word of the song landing right on the bam, so the beat of the lyric is never confused with this whole other force against which the rest of the drama—lyric and melodic—is played out. Bam ... bam ... bam ... bam. He never will remember all the best things she said, but we at least can play the record again and be thankful.

So on this little sampler from *Renaldo & Clara*, Dylan's look back at his 1975 tour from the perspective of late 1977, we have an interesting variety of selections: something old ("It Ain't Me Babe"), something new ("Isis"), something borrowed ("Never Let Me Go"), and something blue ("People Get Ready" is blue in the sense that Billie Holiday sang the blues even though most of the tunes she did were pop songs until she wrapped her voice around them—Dylan's vocal on this track is just exquisitely blue: sweet, scary, and timeless).

Wedding songs? "Never Let Me Go" fits nicely; "It Ain't Me Babe" is its antithesis, the opposite, or polar, emotion. In the actual listening, "Never Let Me Go" is very much about audience, performer, and performance: "Just let me love you tonight/Forget about tomorrow..." The primary thrust of "It Ain't Me Babe" is quite different, but equally clear; this arrangement, and specifically this performance (Harvard Square Theater, November 20, 1975), is an unselfconsciously ecstatic celebration of freedom.

There are many kinds of freedom; this song has often had a particular edge of "freedom from"—and a bite to it, a bitterness along with the humor, suggesting that the freedom is an uncertain one, still being fought for. This is not the case in the 1975 performances. The 1975 song is about spiritual freedom, that is, freedom that is not "from" or "of" any person or thing, but rather a freedom spontaneously experienced from within, a sense or sensation of the breath of the divine and of the unlimited possibilities that exist within the limits of the immediate situation. What I hear expressed in this performance, quite simply, is Dylan's joy at playing music. It is the band, the other people he's playing with, who most immediately make this possible; and so he and they are here celebrating the freedom they give each other.

No one is playing charts. No one is playing it safe. Everyone is creating at the very edge of his or her individual abilities and imagination, as part of a difficult collective undertaking, and they love it. And what they are producing together is, in my opinion, a work of art: a gestalt created of their skill and their interaction and their joy, that in turn brings joy and some kind of profound, enduring nourishment to its listeners, this evening and, thanks to the magic of recording, maybe forever.

This kind of ensemble creativity is not improvisation in the jazz sense; listening to a number of different performances of "It Ain't Me Babe" from the 1975 tour I hear the various musicians playing approximately the same musical phrases at the same times and for similar durations at each performance; clearly they're playing something that was worked out in detail in rehearsals before the tour. And yet each performance is truly different from the others. A simple mechanical concept of "performance" might lead us to think that if the form of the piece doesn't change, but the sound and character of it does, the only variable must be how well the musicians execute the work on a given evening.

This mechanical model fails, however, when I listen to "It Ain't Me Babe" from New Haven, 2nd show, 11/13/75, and from Bangor, 11/27/75, and find that both performances lack some of the elements I most love in the 11/20/75 one—and yet both are very good on their own terms, and different enough in their nature that something would be lost by choosing only to listen to 11/20 because

it's the "best." There is, in other words, a substantial difference in
content between these various performances, rather than a technical difference involving quality of execution (or a cosmetic difference involving changes in the vocal or instrumental flourishes) ...
substantial enough that I assert that they are separate works of art,
not necessarily of equal value but definitely valuable, and far from
interchangeable.

No doubt the same issues arise when one compares performances of a classical piece by different orchestras, conductors,
soloists (and perhaps even by the same orchestra on different
nights). In any case, the underlying questions go to the heart of
what performance means, in aesthetic terms. Solo performance,
certainly, is a matter of personal expression; and it satisfies me to
say that I'm sure the moving quality of Dylan's acoustic performance of "I Don't Believe You" on 11/27/75 is a function of what
he was feeling as he sang and played the song, and of unknowable
circumstances that allowed and stimulated him to transmit so
freely from his heart or from the subsconscious at this particular
moment and through this particular song. But the magic of "It
Ain't Me Babe" 11/20/75 is not simply a matter of Dylan's singing,
and therefore the image of one man's momentary inspired "automatic flow of sensation" is not sufficient here. I know I've suggested in the past that Dylan can sometimes play his musicians
like he plays the harmonica, but that's only one side of the truth,
and not the right description for this tour. Instead, let me suggest
that sometimes all the musicians, including Dylan, get into a
groove or fall under a collective spell, inspired by, expressed
through, and held together by a kind of musical grace. They hear
it together, they reach for it together, and they don't fail. Dylan as
singer and focal point becomes the vehicle for the expression of
the group heart. He speaks for all of them (not them for him),
and so they speak as one.

But what audible characteristics can I point to that distinguish
the 11/20/75 performance of "It Ain't Me Babe" from its aforemen-
tioned Rolling Thunder brethren? Well, right from the start, the
lead guitar intro sounds different all three times, and so does
Dylan's voice when it comes in. Mick Ronson (lead guitar) may
actually be in a different key at least one of the times, and certainly
there's a variation in the little melodic figure he plays, as though
he's got a framework in mind but within that framework he's

totally free to improvise, and in fact he's expected to come up with a slightly different twist each time. On the other hand the difference in the lead guitar once the singing starts sounds more like it has to do with the sound mix — I think he's playing the same riff, but one time it's dominant (11/20) and another time you can hardly hear it. And doesn't it seem likely, in this kind of freewheeling performance, that that in itself could help set the mood of the performance, musicians and singer taking off on different tangents depending on how much leadership the lead guitarist takes, which in turn may depend not only on his mood but on the acoustics of the hall or the stage monitors or the vagaries of the mixing board? And Dylan's voice: Bangor, Maine, he sounds hoarse, and so he holds himself and his voice differently, applying just as much energy and imagination and soul to the song but putting it in different places, making the best use of what he's got to work with (also in Bangor he sings, "*I told you* I'm not the one you need," the extra words seeming to reflect a particular experience he's just had or a way he's feeling, like a cue or clue to himself and the musicians to push the song forward along a new, unique angle of attack).

Stoner's bass playing also sounds different to me each time; my mind says he must be playing roughly the same part, but on 11/20 there's a magical energy to it, skipping, lyrical, whereas in New Haven he's right there but not leaning into it with the same adventurousness, and in Bangor he sounds laid back, almost lugubrious (it's weird, and it works). The climactic lead guitar solo that dominates the fourth verse of the song (three verses with words and then one that's pure music) is like a connect-the-dots puzzle that's done in the same order each time but the lines are fatter or thinner and twist in odd directions between dots and so the three pictures end up looking radically different. When I'm comparing these solos to try to understand 11/20, the others sound tentative and inadequate, but when I listen to them for themselves each has a character and power and charm of its own, entirely appropriate to the performance it grows out of. So there is improvisation, and accident, and personal expression which instantly becomes group expression, and infinite variation within fixed form, and finally, and above all, this collective commitment to a felt purpose, a cause, a fugue, an unspoken awareness that something is present here between us and we have this one fleeting opportunity to catch it if we can.

I'm sure I've listened to 11/20 (IAMB) a hundred times in the last few days, and I can't seem to exhaust it, can't wear it out. Is that T-Bone Burnett on second electric—sounds like amplified slide—guitar? The man's a crazed modest lilting romantic *phenomenon*. The sound of this performance is nothing like the sound of "Isis" or "Never Let Me Go," though all three are solid rockers. I've never felt these particular rhythms anywhere else in the universe, and I can't get enough of them. Mick Ronson achieves immortality (group effort though this may be) with this evening's guitar solo, not just what he's playing but (like Stoner on bass) the *way* he's playing it, something about the energy of fingers (or pick) impacting strings, personal and inventive as your lover's touch, the music rises to crescendo and descends (just as energetically) just far enough to be embraced by Burnett and company and turned into ever-widening ripples of blissful circular sound, joined in new crescendo by Dylan's harp (provoking the audience into wild applause that should be for the guitar solos but isn't), and settling gracefully and raucously back to earth. Whew. And that's just the second song of the set. (They go into a "Hattie Carroll" that's almost as good.)

Angle of incidence. The performance has an angle of incidence and an inner momentum that are all its own, and without which the universe would be a far poorer place.

"Romance in Durango" (12/4/75) on *Biograph* is not an exceptional performance, but it serves as a good example of the loose, raucous, intense spirit of the Rolling Thunder Revue. Dylan seems a thousand miles away from the constraints he wrestled with during the 1974 tour. He's back—briefly—where he belongs, creating a myth (blue-hatted minstrel, and champion of the could-have-beens) instead of trying to live up to one.

Listening to the tapes of individual concerts from this tour, there's a whole lot to appreciate. "Hard Rain," redone as a blistering folk-rock song with a Muddy Waters/Bo Diddley beat (invention is king on this tour), is a delight. "Tonight I'll Be Staying Here with You" is another boisterous mix of musical styles, an ode to the fun of touring with appropriate ironic dashes of ennui and melancholy thrown in. Dylan constantly finds new places to go with his voice. Other songs stand out for the intense beauty of sound they achieve on good nights: the violin sweetness of "Oh Sister," aching forthright vocals on "Sara," the bell-like symphonic instrumental breaks on "Knockin' on Heaven's Door" (salute to a band with six guitarists, most of 'em playing rhythm or counterpoint), haunting Baez/Dylan harmonies on "The Water Is Wide" and "Dark As a Dungeon," hypnotic ensemble work supporting great heartfelt singing on "Hattie Carroll" (with a dominant slow rhythmic figure overriding everything, as in "Isis," but three beats to a line instead of four).

The last show of the 1975 tour, New York, December 8, was "The Night of the Hurricane," a benefit concert for the imprisoned boxer, with appearances by Roberta Flack and Muhammad Ali. In hindsight it looks like everything was building up to this (and indeed it was a powerful show, not better or worse than most of the others but with its own special quality of hysterical exhausted earnestness, Dylan magically finding ways to reach deeper into himself and push the band still further into wild unknown places as if to compensate for the general sloppiness of the evening)...but in fact the whole idea of the tour was that it would be everlasting and all-encompassing, not building up to anything but just rolling steady (ragged but steady), on and on.

Didn't work out that way. Dylan announced a Christmas break, and the band and assorted Revue headliners headed home to wait for their phones to ring. The next Revue show (after 31 concerts in 40 days) was a poorly-planned benefit concert in Houston in late January; and after that another three months went by before the thunder started rolling again.

5.

In the movie *Rain Man* Dustin Hoffman offers us one of the more striking performances of his exceptional career. The pulse of the performance, the rhythm of the actor's presence, is so strong that one leaves the theater feeling the presence of the autistic Raymond Babbit inside one's own skin — the moviegoer becomes the character to some extent, or rather identifies with the character, thus discovering unexpectedly the autistic side, the *Rain Man* side, of himself. This occurs viscerally, not intellectually; it is as though Hoffman's performance reaches past the moviegoer's mind to speak directly to his body, his senses, his nervous system.

How, ultimately, can we speak of great performances in the language of mind, when, by the nature of performing, their greatness lies in their ability to communicate synergistically, to supersede the intellect and impact the entire person of the recipient? Dance, theater, music — all the performing arts — have the power to create a link between living beings that is too immediate, too alive, too complex to be codified in linear, rational, primarily thought-based terms.

This is not to suggest that fiction, poetry, painting, sculpture, are essentially static arts that lack this power to create a bridge between souls. Rather, it is the intrinsic mental bias of criticism and of art history, because they are by nature word-based, intellectual forms, that I call attention to here. In my opinion the most useful criticism is that which is aware of, and which seeks, however imperfectly, to address, the poem or painting as a performance, in terms both of how it is created and of how it is received. The bias towards composition, by which I mean towards a theory of art that relates to the artist as someone who consciously controls and chooses all the elements of his or her work (a theory which implicitly minimizes not only the true nature of inspiration, but also the vital creative role of the audience, the reader viewer listener), has led to an increasingly limited view of art, one in which great visceral communicators like Shakespeare or Beethoven are praised primarily for those aspects of their work that can be analyzed, intellectualized, academicized, explained.

This limitation of criticism becomes transferred, in our media-dominated culture, to the audience at large, and so we tend to think of Bob Dylan as a brilliant songwriter (composer) whose songs contain important messages, and whose job on stage is to recreate those songs somewhat in the manner (as Dylan once sardonically suggested) of a Western Union messenger reading a telegram. This very limited view is applied to the music as well as the lyrics: because critics and journalists lack a language in which they can effectively address performance as a creative medium, they find it all the easier to fall in with the human tendency to want an artist to constantly reenact his original triumph rather than go on with his work. Essentially nostalgic experimentation (Rolling Thunder Revue part one, taken as a whole, as a concept) appeals to them, but radical creativity from an already-established artist is generally viewed unsympathetically (often with smug disdain). The resultant critical and journalistic condemnation supports the natural conservatism of a mass audience (that is, of all of us — when we first hear something truly new from an old friend, our normal response is disappointment; we want him to be like he was). The true artist goes ahead and does what he has to do anyway — may even be stimulated or granted freedom by the misunderstanding. But the public's idea that (in this case) Bob Dylan "lost it" somewhere along the way does not go away easily, especially since few of us really want to make the effort to listen carefully to a larger body of work than the one we're already familiar with.

It is an interesting historical fact that Dylan did not lose his mass audience with *Self Portrait* and six years of largely mediocre albums and no touring. Instead he lost it or began to lose it immediately after three consecutive #1 albums (*Planet Waves, Blood on the Tracks,* and *Desire,* the first and only #1 records of his career) and two hugely successful tours. And this loss occurred, ironically, as the artist was reaching the height of his powers. His spring 1976 performances, and the live album and one-hour television show (both called *Hard Rain*) that made those performances available to a broader audience, were unpopular with the public and (at best) ignored by critics and commentators, but they contain some of the very finest performed art Bob Dylan has ever produced.

After ending the 1975 tour on December 8, Dylan and the Rolling Thunder Revue (but without Baez) played a concert at the Houston Astrodome on January 25, 1976. The stadium was half-empty, the acoustics were awful, and Dylan sang only fourteen songs—but the concert is historically interesting because Dylan added a number of songs he hadn't been performing on the fall tour, and these songs ("Maggie's Farm," "One Too Many Mornings," "Lay, Lady, Lay," "I Threw It All Away") with their dramatic new arrangements became key elements in the new, very different Rolling Thunder concerts of April and May.

Sometime in late March Dylan joined Eric Clapton in a Malibu recording studio, and they recorded a new Dylan composition ("Sign Language") for inclusion on Clapton's next album. By mid-April Dylan was in Florida with the Rolling Thunder Revue band (same personnel, except Ronee Blakley was gone and Gary Burke replaced Luther Rix on congas), rehearsing for the next leg of the tour. The tour started April 18 in Lakeland, Florida; it wandered through Florida, Alabama, Mississippi, Louisiana, and Texas, and ended with one show each in Oklahoma, Kansas, Colorado, and Utah. The 25th and last show of the tour was in Salt Lake City on May 25. Two days earlier, on the eve of Dylan's 35th birthday, the show at Colorado State University in Fort Collins was taped for television. There had been earlier television tapings (Clearwater, April 22, afternoon and evening); an hour-long program was put together but Dylan decided not to release it and brought in another camera crew instead. Following the Salt Lake show, Dylan returned to California, and the Rolling Thunder Revue was not heard from again. Dylan's only other 1976 performance was with his old comrades the Band at their "Last Waltz" concert in November in San Francisco.

The first concert of the tour, Lakeland, April 18, was and is most remarkable. Dylan opened the first set of his new tour with a courageous and generous gesture: "Visions of Johanna," solo—a song he had only sung in concert on one other occasion since 1966, and the first time since 1966 that Dylan had begun a concert from the vulnerable position of the solo acoustic performance. (He continued to open his concerts with a couple of solo songs—usually "Mr. Tambourine Man" was first—throughout the spring 1976 tour.)

It's a well-sung, deeply felt, marvelously opaque rendering of "Johanna," Dylan singing the song as song rather than personal story (he seems to be making an offering to the audience, I'll give you what I think you most want to hear, and after that please listen while I sing what *I* need to sing tonight), yet sharing more and more of his person and personality as he gets into the act of singing. You can hear in his voice (and, at the end, his harmonica) the sound of his heart opening to the audience, to the blessed release of being on stage again, of having a purpose in life and knowing who he is, again, if only for a moment.

And then, with an ease I find terrifying, Dylan moves into one of the most nakedly personal performances of his career (something like "Sad Eyed Lady of the Lowlands," but inverted, and without the gloss of riddle and mystery): the 1976 version of "If You See Her, Say Hello."

In fall 1975 Dylan began performing a radically reworked "Simple Twist of Fate," but although the words were different, the character of the song stayed similar to what it had been. On his spring 1976 tour he takes this same concept of re-creating a song by rewriting its lyrics, and uses it (with intention to shock the audience, certainly, among other motives) to transform "Lay Lady Lay" and "If You See Her," among others. "Lay Lady Lay" moves from being a sweet sexy song of courtship to a purposely crude (and joyous) assertion of male sexuality: "Forget this dance/Let's go upstairs!/Let's take a chance/Who really cares?" Some nights— notably at this Lakeland show—Dylan improvises lyrics directed to (or seemingly directed to) a particular person, someone he's angry at ("You can have your cake/But just try to eat it!"). Sexual desire and sexual hostility, the woman he's reaching for and the one he's running from, are all mixed up with each other ... and somewhere

in there Dylan as performing artist succeeds in putting his listener
inside the skin of this angry lover who Dylan clearly is but whom he
also is portraying.

"If You See Her, Say Hello," in the shocking Lakeland version, becomes a song spoken from that deep sudden urgent place
where pain and anger are indistinguishable and their expression
seems a violent necessity. Dylan's 90% new words are humorously
contemptuous ("She left here in a hurry/I don't know what she
was on") and yet the honest, even humble, pain of the earlier
versions is also here, and as affecting as ever ("For me time's
standing still/I've never gotten over her/I don't think I ever will").
No one listening can doubt this is a man talking about his own
wife and something that's going on between the two of them at
this very moment, and one blushes in morbid fascination (and
shame-faced identification) as the character in the song snarls to
an imagined rival, "If you're making love to her/Watch it from the
rear/You never know when I'll be back/Or liable to appear." The
horror, the humor, the beauty of Dylan's voice and of his commitment to self-expression (however screwed-up and alcohol- or
ego-distorted his perception of reality may be), and the amazing
intimacy woven between performer and audience at this moment
all come together in the last lines: "Whether she'll be back some-
day/Of that there is no doubt/And when that moment comes,
Lord/Give me the strength to keep her out."

Phew.

Of the 21 songs Dylan sings at Lakeland, only three ("Blowin'
in the Wind," "Wild Mountain Thyme," and "Knockin' on Heaven's
Door") are carryovers from the fall tour. Many of them he's performing live for the first time ever: "Mozambique," "Idiot Wind,"
"Shelter from the Storm" (with Dylan on slide guitar), "Seven Days"
(a powerful new Dylan composition; he played it at the next three
shows but never quite got comfortable with the arrangement)*,
"Going, Going, Gone" (rewritten), "Railroad Boy" (traditional, sung
with Baez), "Gotta Travel On" (group finale, a rockabilly hit from
1959), "Vincent Van Gogh" and "Weary Blues from Waiting" (both
sung with Neuwirth; the former is a bit of silliness, a vocal warm-up,

---

*The Bootleg Series includes a live performance of "Seven Days" from Tampa,
Florida, April 21, 1976.

repeated every night of the tour, the latter a wonderful sweet version of a Hank Williams tune, never to be heard again). "I'll Be Your Baby Tonight" and "I Pity the Poor Immigrant" are sung for the first time since 1969.

Dylan is challenging himself and his band, looking to create an entirely new show and new sound to reflect the new moment he finds himself in, emotionally and creatively. Among the other noises crowding him from within and without, Dylan had the recent (April 9) suicide of Phil Ochs to contend with: Ochs, a tortured and sometimes violently crazed man during his last sad months, had an obsessive, competitive love/hate relationship with Dylan (largely in his own mind, though Dylan was not above twisting the knife in public, responding to Ochs' goading with cool, vicious putdowns) going back to the Sixties and the Village folk scene. Ochs told friends that not being included in the Rolling Thunder Revue was the final blow for him, thus setting Dylan up as "responsible" for his death (though Ochs was in no condition to be included on anyone's tour). Dylan's long slow break-up with Sara had obviously reached the fire and brimstone stage, and, according to Spitz, he was juggling wife, family, and new girlfriend and going through at least a fifth of bourbon a day. "Right now I've got not much to lose," he sings in the Lakeland "If You See Her," and that seems a pretty good summation of the place Dylan was performing from each night of this 1976 tour.

The results in aesthetic terms are mixed. Alcohol, moodiness, and a lack of leadership definitely take their toll on the quality of many of the performances. Lakeland as a whole is not a great tape, despite its boldness and a number of superb individual performances. Songs like "Railroad Boy" and "I Pity the Poor Immigrant" and "Shelter from the Storm" sound feeble compared to the brilliant versions that will come along later in the tour. In fall 1975, Dylan seemed to care passionately about each night's performance, in terms of giving the audience everything they could want and more, while staying true to his own fiercely personal vision. The shows that resulted were wonderful; the 1976 shows are much sloppier, up and down, very uneven, and yet because of this willingness to risk all (and often fail), the 1976 shows finally go further creatively and cut deeper than the more accessible, more classically beautiful and accomplished performances of 1975. Comparison is pointless, and certainly we the listeners are hugely enriched by the existence of both Rolling Thunders; yet it is necessary to understand that in addition to whatever personal and emotional and chemical factors may have been at work, the spring 1976 Rolling Thunder tour represents an artist's response to the potential trap created by his own mastery, even his own very-recent, just-perfected mastery. He must reject that perfection, destroy what he has just completed, if he is to go on with the work of telling the truth and attempting to release the music inside him.

This is not necessarily done heroically; it may just as well stem from anger, self-hatred, boredom, despair. The personal pain involved is certainly regrettable. But it's also none of our business. We, the audience, have our own work to do. We are continually faced with a choice of running away from, deafening ourselves to, the beauty and power of this new art, or of allowing ourselves to hear it, allowing our own pain and anger and hunger and confusion to be touched, restimulated, acknowledged, set free, not in some safe packaged superficial way but to the bone, to the heart, unpredictable, uncontrollable. We may never be the same. That's great art, but is it really what we're ready for tonight, what we had in mind when we bought this ticket? "Forget this dance, let's go upstairs!" I don't know, I don't like that thing he's wearing on his head, there's something scary about his voice, his eyes. I know we had a date tonight, but this is too weird, you're not the guy I remember from high school.

The 1976 shows continued to change considerably night to night, but the rough pattern of them goes like this: 12 songs by various Revue members, then Dylan starts his set with two solo performances ("Mr. Tambourine Man," followed by "It Ain't Me Babe" or "It's Alright, Ma" or "Tangled Up in Blue" or "Simple Twist of Fate" or "Just Like a Woman" or "Love Minus Zero/No Limit" or "It's All Over Now, Baby Blue" or "Gates of Eden"). Dylan and Neuwirth duet on "Vincent Van Gogh," and then Dylan does four songs backed by the full band: usually "Maggie's Farm," "One Too Many Mornings," "Mozambique," and "Isis." In the early part of the tour, "Mozambique" was omitted and Dylan and band did "I'll Be Your Baby Tonight" before "Maggie's Farm." "Isis," a throwback to fall 1975 but sounding very different, took the place of "Seven Days."

The second half of the show opens with sets by McGuinn and Baez, followed by two or three duets by Dylan and Baez ("Railroad Boy," "Blowin' in the Wind," "Deportees" or "Wild

Mountain Thyme," once "Dink's Song," once "I Shall Be Released," and once—tantalizingly, because no tape of this show has surfaced—"Lily, Rosemary, and the Jack of Hearts") and then "I Pity the Poor Immigrant" with Dylan, Baez, and full band. Then roughly ten songs by Dylan and band (with a T-Bone Burnett song thrown in in the middle so Dylan can catch his breath). Typically these are "Shelter from the Storm," "I Threw It All Away," "Stuck Inside of Mobile with the Memphis Blues Again," "You're a Big Girl Now," "Oh Sister," "You're Gonna Make Me Lonesome When You Go," "Lay Lady Lay," "Going, Going, Gone," "Idiot Wind," "Knockin' on Heaven's Door," and "Gotta Travel On." Other tunes heard once or twice include "Rita May," "Just Like Tom Thumb's Blues," "Romance in Durango," "It Takes a Lot to Laugh," "One of Us Must Know," "Just Like a Woman," "Tonight I'll Be Staying Here with You," "One More Cup of Coffee," "Tangled Up in Blue," "I Want You," and "Leopard-Skin Pillbox Hat."

(I include these lists from each tour because the songs the artist chose to sing—even once—can tell us a lot about who he was or how he saw himself at the time. For Dylan, with his huge songbook, the songs or groups of songs he chooses to work with are something like the colors or materials a visual artist favors at different periods in his or her career. They both determine and reflect the character of the creative moment.)

Dylan's album *Hard Rain*, released in September 1976 to coincide with the airing of the TV special from Fort Collins, consists of five songs recorded at Fort Collins May 23, and four from a concert a week earlier in Fort Worth, Texas. The TV special "Hard Rain" offers 10 complete songs from Fort Collins (four of which are on the album), plus part of an 11th, "Knockin' on Heaven's Door." Baez is featured with Dylan on five of the TV tracks, but is not on the album at all; this suggests that for contractual reasons, or perhaps because Dylan wasn't willing to share royalties, the tracks with Baez were not available for the live album, which may be why it differs so much from the TV show.

In any case, the selection and sequencing of songs on the album is masterful. There's a consistent mood in the performances, the lyric content of the nine songs seems almost consciously designed to tell a story, and the songs chosen effectively highlight the tour's musical inventiveness, showcasing the startling and important new musical ideas worked out on the road by Dylan and his band (Stoner, Ronson, Wyeth, Burnett, Soles, Mansfield, Neuwirth, Rivera and Burke).

The album is open-ended and capable of expressing many themes, depending to some extent on the listener. One obvious theme is the state of Dylan's marriage. "I ain't gonna work on Maggie's Farm no more!" sets the tone; this assertive, energetic hymn to separation and independence is followed by the more introspective "One Too Many Mornings," which is conciliatory ("You're right from your side and I'm right from mine"), but firm in its assessment ("I've no right to be here," go the new lyrics, "If you've no right to stay/Until we're both one too many mornings/And a thousand miles away." I can't explain what that means, but listening to it, the feeling comes across unmistakably). "Memphis Blues Again" has always been about the pain (and pleasures?) of displacement; here the thread that holds it most closely to the theme at hand is the recurring question, "Oh, Mama, can this really be the end?" "Oh Sister" follows, a beautiful performance, with an almost hysterical intensity on "We grew up together from the cradle to the grave!" The song is to women, including the one he's estranged from and the ones he hopes will soothe him; momentarily all are one person, lover/ mother/antagonist/friend. "Lay Lady Lay" expresses the expansive (and awkward) sexuality of the newly or not-quite single 35-year-old male.

All this simply sets the stage – introduces the elements – for the extraordinarily complex emotional cross-currents, climax, and resolution that make up side two. It's *Blood on the Tracks*, Take Three, as Dylan rearranges and re-performs the marriage songs from that album, with "I Threw It All Away" thrown in to say that he knows all too well what he's giving up and how much he'll regret it. All four of these songs – "Shelter from the Storm," "You're a Big Girl Now," "I Threw It All Away," "Idiot Wind" – are not only about marriage, they're about the singer/narrator confronting and spending time with his own feelings regarding his marriage, his spouse, and the various positions they find themselves in in relation to each other. Nothing is taken for granted, everything is taken for exactly the unsolvable, unfathomable mystery it is, which is why it all is still alive and more intense than ever for this third or thirtieth go-round.

The man is not singing about some old maze he found his way out of years ago; he's singing about the web of confusion he sees around and inside him at this very moment.

But the mood of the album, of the performances, is not confusion. It is strength, resilience, clarity, renewal in the face of adversity. There's something extremely solid in the singer's voice on every song here, not a forced confidence but an ease and power that seem completely natural. Perhaps this is an outgrowth of having not much left to lose. Whatever it is, the voice we hear on this record is that of a born leader, and we hear it unhesitatingly leading an orchestra of instrumental voices into previously unexplored territory, inspiring them to breathtakingly courageous, unflinching forays into the unknown.

There is very little precedent for what this album accomplishes; perhaps John Coltrane's *Impressions* or the Velvet Underground's first album or Dylan's own *Highway 61 Revisited* are comparable in their sudden, spontaneous opening of whole new realms of musical language, not through some sort of cleverness but as a byproduct of the musicians finding themselves in an unexpected, wondrous place, making a new kind of music together. Unexpected except perhaps for Dylan or Coltrane, the visionary leaders who sensed something out there and reached for it, awkwardly, stubbornly, shrugging off skepticism and misunderstanding, trusting the new sound (new approach to sound!) to emerge. And not for the sake of newness and innovation, but simply because what the artist needed to say could not be expressed in existing language and forms. Necessity is the mother; the breakthrough works, like those I just mentioned, are never simply clever and inventive — without exception, they are filled with the dramatic power and wholeness of a great inner need finally finding expression and release.

When we open our ears — and it may take a dozen listenings before we stop hearing this album in terms of what we expect these songs to sound like, or, for the fans, in terms of the performances we think should have been included — the rewards and surprises of *Hard Rain* are nearly inexhaustible. (I've listened to it as much over the past 13 years as I've ever listened to any recording, and it still sounds fresh to me.) There is an elasticity in this music, a new and liberating approach to time, to rhythm, to the relationship between voice and melodic instrument and rhythmic instrument. Somehow the normal elements of song, of rock and roll, of singer/guitars/ bass/drums performance, have been put together differently here, with one of the more-easily-pointed-to results being a transcending of the usual laws of momentum. This music pauses, halts, falls apart, starts again, and nothing is lost—it has a pulse that is internal rather than external, and it continues even when the musicians are silent. The melodic element of the music also reaches outside normal confines, so that the tuning up before "Maggie's Farm" and the scales that lead into "Oh Sister" become as melodic and meaningful and satisfying to the ears as any other part of the song; something in this band's technique transforms every sound into a grace note. It's like they're playing the space around the music rather than the music itself.

Say what? Well, listen. Listen to Dylan's moan at the end of the fourth verse of "Maggie's Farm" ("... says she's 24, whoa-oo-ohh-ohhh-ahhh ...") and the way it's extended and released and then tickled a little by the guitarists simultaneous with the universe grinding to a halt and starting again (Dylan can be heard muttering to someone as if he's lost his train of thought), just in time for the thundering return of the vocal: "Said I ain't gonna work for Maggie's ma no more!" Listen to the subtle, gonzo, thoroughly brilliant instrumentation on "One Too Many Mornings," noting for example the series of little crescendoes after the second line vocal in the first verse, and the way the same bit works after the second line of the second verse (this time Dylan extends the last word across three-quarters of the instrumental break, "love and I have lai-ai-ai-ai-ai-aid", and the band soars with him). Listen to the guitar riff on "Shelter from the Storm," how it's held back during the verses, and then bursts forth between them, so full of personality that after a while it seems the guitar riffs are the words to the song, and the vocal is the instrumental fill.

The arrangements of these songs, some of which had already been worked out for the Astrodome concert in January, are like new songs in themselves: major creative efforts by Dylan, whether or not he reworked the lyrics while changing the musical shape and texture of the song. The arrangements were created with this band in mind, its looseness, its willingness to improvise, its abundance of guitarists able to play in and around and across each other, Stoner's free melodic bass playing, Wyeth's flexibility on drums, everyone's willingness to watch Dylan and zig when he zigs, their ability to turn mistakes into inventions, to allow discord and create a space around it that transforms it into a new kind of harmony.

"Lay Lady Lay" on *Hard Rain* shows the crystallization of this exciting, risky approach to song-making. The emphatic singing style is perfectly matched by the punchy sweetness of the rhythmic and melodic accompaniment. The music stumbles like a clown lurching around the stage with perfect timing (holding a cup of coffee, say, oops, almost fell over to the left, oops, to the right this time), complete control. A musical texture is created, rich, complex, uneven, full of the colors and flavors and rhythms of real life. There's more here, a lot more, than the familiar techniques of voice and accompaniment can accomplish. Dylan hears a crazy orchestra in his head, and the band reads his mind out loud, with flourishes, with gusto, on the stadium stage. This kind of music will never be created with synthesizers. It can't be written out beforehand. Instead the musicians have to rely on the sound of Dylan's voice and the movement of his hands and their accumulated experience of working with him and with each other, so that finally it's 80% intuition, and on a good night you get in a groove, mutual trust, mutual mind-reading, mutual inspiration, combined with personal expression and abandon (listen to those bass lines of Stoner's, on "Memphis Blues Again," on "Idiot Wind," and just about every other song), and that's it, something worth living for, communion, the sharing of truth through music. Truth on the edge, driven in part by booze and cocaine and road-weariness and more than a little desperation, maybe you look back and you never want to do it again — the Band never really did it again after the 1966 tour — but you still have to be proud and more than a little amazed about the places you got to. And what is it about Dylan that he'd throw away wife and family and shelter just to return to this crazy edge, even throw away career and popularity if they'd force him to paint within the lines? I don't know. But if there's an answer, it's on this album somewhere.

The last three songs on the album ("You're a Big Girl Now," "I Threw It All Away," and "Idiot Wind") are as powerful and exciting as anything Dylan has done (comparable, for instance, to the May 1966 versions of "Ballad of a Thin Man" and "Like a Rolling Stone"). As phenomenal as every aspect of each of these performances is, the unique orchestration of guitars, keyboards, violin, drums and voice on "Big Girl" must be singled out for particular praise. Stoner's bass-playing while Dylan sings "Down the highway, down the tracks, down the road to ecstacy" on "Idiot Wind" will have a special place in my heart as long as I live.

It rained on May 23, 1976, during the outdoor concert at Fort Collins, drenching the audience, which is why Dylan and the band played "A Hard Rain's A-Gonna Fall" as a final encore (the only time they played the song on the spring tour, and it's *not* the fall 1975 arrangement) and where the name for the TV show came from (the album has the same name, but doesn't include the song, just to keep things reasonably confusing). Anyway, as if the album weren't enough, we also have (would have, if Dylan's office would make it available as a commercial videotape) this superb video recording from one of Dylan's more memorable concerts.

The last shall be first, and so the show starts with the "Hard Rain" encore. It's a wonderful performance. But I need to acknowledge that there's something paradoxical about video recordings of musical artists. A good one, which this is, is fascinating to watch, and at first very nourishing of our relationship with the artist—seeing his face and his movements as he sings and performs, we are opened to a deeper understanding and appreciation of his art. But this art is not primarily visual; what we take in through our eyes when we can see him on stage is powerful and affecting, it deepens our experience and heightens our awareness and receptivity, but it is not, if I may make a distinction, the art itself. As a result, watching a video recording over and over is not equivalent to or better than listening to an audio recording again and again. After a while, the visual aspects become distracting, and finally lessen our awareness of and receptivity to the music.

Performed art, in other words, does not necessarily mean visual art. To fully appreciate this, we must have some awareness of the power of a person's presence, and realize that visual perception is only one of the media through which that presence reaches us. In a live musical performance, it is the power of shared presence (musicians and audience aware of each other, present together at the moment of creation) that is vital to the experience—the ability to see the artist performing is secondary, although it certainly contributes greatly to our ability to feel present.

I mention these things because otherwise we might automatically assume that audio plus video recording is "better" or truer than audio alone, and also because if we fail to appreciate the role of shared presence in performing, our minds may convince us that watching and hearing a videotape is actually equal to or better than being there at the concert. This argument, seductive though it is, is ultimately equivalent to the (false) idea that a controlled studio recording (where mistakes can be corrected and improvements can be added) is naturally going to be better than a live recording. The mind has a tendency to want to believe that everything can be reduced to dots and dashes.

But art is not information. It has an intangible, living, sexual quality about it always—a quality which video (in relation to music) enhances, at first, but later deadens. Audio is the less limited medium. So I recommend, wholeheartedly, the "Hard Rain" video, if it is ever released—but I caution you that the music on it is so good you'll want to have it in audio form too, so you can appreciate it fully.

Following "A Hard Rain's A-Gonna Fall," the TV show (which has no narration, just pure concert footage) segues to Dylan's set with Baez, beginning with "Blowin' in the Wind" and continuing through "Railroad Boy," Woody Guthrie's "Deportees," and (conscious, ironic sequence) "I Pity the Poor Immigrant." This segment ends with "Shelter from the Storm" (also on the album); then comes another segment of continuous footage with "Maggie's Farm," "One Too Many Mornings," and "Mozambique" (the first two are on the album); and the last complete song is "Idiot Wind," which is the other performance included on both album and TV show.

It's all great—"Mozambique" is the only performance that is anything less than utterly riveting; all the rest keep me right on the edge of my chair, drinking in each note, each gesture—and while I love "Railroad Boy" (especially the extended word in the last line, that seems to glide out over the continent, and Baez's brilliant ringing guitar figure, so keenly tuned to the sound of the voices and the drama of the story), and have already raved about "Idiot Wind" and "One Too Many Mornings" and "Shelter from the Storm" and "Maggie's Farm," still, if there's a high point, a moment in the video that calls out for special attention, it has to be "I Pity the Poor Immigrant."

Howie Wyeth totally steals the show with his piano playing on this one. ("Okay," he seems to be saying to Dylan, "You want uninhibited music? You want to go over the edge more than a little? You want to let the *drummer* loose at the piano keys? All right, boss ...") He takes Dylan's Rolling-Thunder-era musical ideas and pushes them right past their limit, off the canvas and straight out to blue sky. The look on his face as he completes a musical phrase is priceless.

Dylan rises to the challenge with a masterful vocal performance (Baez gamely foiling his assaults with good-humored warrior harmonies), climaxing when he interpolates "ha ha!" after "fills
his mouth with laughing" (a spooky, unforgettable moment). The
way he then sings "shat. terred. like. the. glaaaaaaassssss" is mind-
altering. What a song. And what an amazing reading it gets here.
Minutes like these are what a performing artist lives for, and rightly
so. This is fulfillment. This is the love-play at the heart of the bond
between man and music.

The documents we have from this tour are full of treasures:
Baez and Dylan harmonizing on "Dink's Song" in Gainesville, the
astonishing "hard rock" version of "Tangled Up in Blue" from Fort
Collins (more wild momentum experimentation, and an incredible
vocal performance in response; classic stuff), "It Ain't Me Babe"
solo in Fort Worth, "Like a Rolling Stone" from the aborted (Clearwater) TV special. The release of professional quality recordings of
more (why not all?) of these shows from the archives would be a
great boon to lovers of Dylan's music.

The troupe that was meant to stay together (and in motion)
forever, and that surely would have revolutionized modern music
if they'd kept at it and if anyone was really listening, played its last
show May 25, 1976, in Salt Lake City. Poor ticket sales was one of
the factors that brought the tour to an early close; the drawbacks of
amateurism on the booking and business end of things had caught
up with the Revue, as had a loss of sense of community (the idea
had gotten old, Dylan wasn't running with it anymore, and you can
bet no new spiritual leader came along to try to challenge his turf).
Time to fade into history.

Not much is known of the details of Dylan's life during the rest
of 1976. The man and his wife were apparently still together, after
their fashion, though they couldn't have been enjoying it much. If
Dylan was writing or recording music, no trace of it has yet surfaced. What we do know is that sometime in 1976 or early 1977,
back in Malibu, Dylan (with Howard Alk) began reviewing footage
in preparation for editing his movie.

IV. Alchemist

June 1976 - December 1977

"The highest purpose of art is to inspire. What else can you do? What else can you do for anyone but inspire them?"
—Bob Dylan, 1977

6.

After the dissolution of the Rolling Thunder Revue, Dylan went into a kind of retreat; his only public performance in the next 20 months was as a guest star at the Band's "Last Waltz" concert in San Francisco, November 25, 1976. With the Band backing him for the first time since the 1974 tour (and the last time ever), Dylan sings "Baby Let Me Follow You Down" (twice), "Hazel," "I Don't Believe You," "Forever Young," and "I Shall Be Released" (the latter a superstar finale, with everyone from Neil Diamond to Ringo Starr on stage to help Dylan and Richard Manuel sing their song). Three of the six performances are included in the film *The Last Waltz*; five are on the record album. Dylan is in good form but not remarkable.

In March 1977, Sara Dylan filed for divorce; the end of Bob and Sara's 11-year marriage had come at last. Money matters (involving many millions of dollars) were apparently settled fairly readily, but child custody struggles continued throughout the year. Dylan retained the Malibu mansion as his primary home.

During this difficult year 1977 Dylan (with the help and companionship of Howard Alk) spent much of his time editing down approximately 100 hours of footage shot in fall 1975 into a three hour and fifty-two minute film called *Renaldo & Clara*. The movie was completed in November 1977, and first shown to the public in January 1978.

"True perfection seems imperfect, yet it is perfectly itself." This line, from Stephen Mitchell's translation of the *Tao Te Ching*, points us in the right direction for a discussion of Bob Dylan's misunderstood masterpiece, *Renaldo & Clara*.

Dylan was an amateur filmmaker when he directed and edited this movie, and so the impulse of many reviewers to dismiss *Renaldo & Clara* as an expensive home movie is understandable. The description is not inaccurate. But the dismissal is deeply regrettable, because Dylan's film is truly radical and visionary, and a great success on its own ambitious and exacting terms.

"It is perfectly itself." This, in a nutshell, describes the essential triumph of "A Hard Rain's A-Gonna Fall" or "Mr. Tambourine Man." The song (composition and performance) is not great because of its fulfillment or transcendence of a preexisting set of standards. Neither song could even be said to fall into any category that existed prior to the song's creation. Each song is radically new — a new way of communicating, a new way of using the music/words/performance form — and what it fulfills and transcends (for these are great works, no question about it) is its own newly-invented form, concept, set of possibilities.

Similarly, *Renaldo & Clara* reinvents film, the pictures/dialogue/sound/drama/music form, gives it a whole new purpose and self-concept. What Dylan wants out of the medium is different from what other filmmakers have gone after; it can't be summarized in a sentence or two, but one aspect of it is that the experience of being alive is to a large extent a function of sensory transitions and juxtapositions, auditory, visual, sensual (touch or the suggestion of touch), and olfactory. In musical terms, we can experience this in the colors (as it were) and textures of an album like *Blonde on Blonde*, where the relationship between voice and percussion is central to Dylan's intention (very keen, purposeful intention; he really has *something to say* here) — easily as important as the dance of language or the specific verbal content of the songs.

Dylan is trying to show us, share with us, how life looks to him, not to him as a singer or star but him as a person. That is, he is trying to express *how it feels*, necessarily assuming, hoping, making the artist's basic leap of faith, that what I feel you also feel, if we could only find common language in which to share our experiences. The (excuse me) simple-minded critic complains that if one wishes to communicate, one must use the already established formats and codes, or else your work will be self-indulgent, impenetrable, in no way a bridge to the other's awareness and perception. This is almost the opposite of the truth, which is that the more one is able to stand apart from the influence of existing forms (neither following them nor attempting to avoid them), the better one's chances of expressing through one's art the audience's previously unacknowledged, unshared (because no one knows how to express them) feelings and perceptions.

Artistic courage and a sort of blindness to "the way things should be done" can lead, if one's talent and will power are great enough, to real breakthroughs in communication, affirmations of previously unvoiced aspects of individual and collective reality. Dylan achieved this (for a mass audience, as it turned out) in his songs and performances circa 1962-66. It is my contention that he achieved it again at other times in his career, but not always to the same degree of public or critical acclaim, because various obstacles got in the way of the audience's receptivity to his art. Or, putting it a different way, certain external (situational, "generational") conditions combined to create a rare public receptivity during the years mentioned above, and later more normal conditions of public and critical impatience and indifference returned, thereby reducing the size or anyway receptivity of the artist's audience.

And, clearly, it is my contention that in *Renaldo & Clara* Dylan again achieved an extraordinary breakthrough in terms of communication and self-expression; a breakthrough that he was, however, very insecure about (in contrast to his past cockiness, self-confidence), so that the negative responses of public and critics (and they were very negative indeed; few praised the movie, and almost no one went to see it or booked it into their theaters) led quickly to a breakdown in which a discouraged Dylan basically withdrew the film from circulation before more than a few thousand people (literally) had a chance to see it. (Later it did get shown on television several times in Europe, as a result of which good quality taped copies began circulating among "the faithful." But no commercial videotape of the movie has been released by Dylan as of this writing.)

So, while it may be unlikely (for reasons that have partly to do with the differences between music and film; the former is accessible in much more radical forms than the latter, since our experience of film is alas conditioned to be very linear) that *Renaldo & Clara* would ever have been a popular film in the sense that Dylan's albums have been popular, still the sad fact is it has never gotten the chance. And while Dylan's early songs, inaccessible to a mass audience because of the radical nature of his singing, were called to the public's attention through recordings of them by other performers, there was and is no equivalent path for Dylan's film to call to its potential viewers through some temporary and more palatable mask.

Dylan did try, in desperation, chopping the movie down to two hours so as to get wider distribution, but to no avail; he tried to sell out, as it were, and still no one was buying. So he put it all aside, not without some heartbreak and lasting bitterness. He had, after all, been spoiled as a young man; up until 1976 everything good he'd ever done had ultimately (and usually rather quickly) been embraced by a fair-sized audience, usually showing up his critics as pathetic old fogies in the process. This scenario of virtue rewarded (from Dylan's point of view, anyway) and the villains defeated did not replay itself in the case of *Renaldo & Clara*.

But the movie's commercial and critical failure and its impact on Dylan is not the primary focus of this chapter. What I want to discuss here is the wondrous success, in artistic terms, of Dylan's 1975–1977 excursion into the moving picture medium.

There were three stages to Dylan's filmmaking process. The first was gestation, which started at least at the time of *Eat the Document* (1966) and probably much earlier, and continued as some kind of smoldering in the back of Dylan's consciousness until it burst into flame in the summer of 1975 and Dylan convinced not only his friends but himself (old pinch-penny himself) that the moment for making the movie had arrived.

The second stage was shooting the movie: October to December 1975. Dylan chose to work without a script, although he did experiment with having writers (Allen Ginsberg, Sam Shepard) around to generate ideas and write scenes during and as part of the process of shooting. Like musicians trying to back Dylan on stage (but more so) these writers, and the professional actors who were brought in (Harry Dean Stanton, Helena Kallianiotes, Ruth Tyrangiel), had no idea what was expected of them. That was because Dylan himself, the director, didn't know; rather, he intuited, and his intuition said try this, try that, and see how you feel about it while it's being shot, and again when you're looking at the rushes. Most of the dialogue and dramatic situations in the film are improvised, with perhaps a little guidance beforehand (i.e., I want you to be a rock and roller trying to convince this girl to be your companion for a six-week tour; and I want *you* to insist that he should come live with you on the farm instead, and anyway you can't go without Daddy's approval; say whatever you want but be sure to mention the following things: God, marriage, Daddy, rock and roll, good times, and the end of the world). A lot of the footage is musical, shot during Rolling Thunder concerts for the most part; and some of it is semi-documentary footage or moving objects (I want shots of trains, trucks, roadies setting up the stage, sky, these statuettes, performers putting on makeup, etc).

The third stage was editing the footage into a movie; it all led up to this. The process in this sense was not at all analogous to Dylan making a recording; there the performance is the moment of creation, and the mixdown is almost an afterthought. But here performance (acting) was a means to an end—what was driving Dylan throughout the time of shooting was his vague but passionate desire to have enough of the right materials at hand at that future moment when he would be at work in the editing room. In 1966 he had become very excited with the possibilities of building something, a new kind of film, out of fragments of images, scenes, sounds, and musical performances, but he was extremely frustrated at the footage he had to work with. He vowed to do it again someday, and do it right.

He was editing film, but he was also editing sound (something he didn't do with his records). Since his concern was not exclusively dramatic (in the linear, acting-out-a-story sense), he had and made use of an unusual freedom: he could superimpose music and dialogue and other sounds (Anne Waldman and Allen Ginsberg reading their poems) over footage that could either be silent or could include its own soundtrack, so that two people would be talking and a song would start, trail off, get louder, softer, while they went on talking. In some cases conversations are very hard to hear because of noise in the room, and it's clearly part of the filmmaker's intention, and it works. Other times people are drowned out by sounds (usually music, not always) that aren't part of the scene but have been put there by the editor, the filmmaker. We are trained very early in the film to accept this as part of the form of what we're watching, hearing, experiencing. We are also informed early that what we see is not necessarily in time sequence (two people have a conversation on a train; later we see them getting on the train, or buying their tickets). This is not flashback, but rather a timelessness that can't be explained, must instead be accepted, as we necessarily accept dream logic as long as we're in the dream.

Transitions and juxtapositions. The real drama of our lives. People trying to decipher the "message" of a Dylan song assume a linearity of purpose that isn't there. Unfortunately Dylan himself fell into this trap during his interviews to promote *Renaldo & Clara* (making one glad that he has largely avoided talking about the "meaning"s of his songs over the years). "What this movie does is create a battle between reality and illusion," he told the *New York Times*. "It's about man's basic nature being duality—between darkness and light, between freedom and oppression." This is bullshit, just as it would be if Dylan or anyone else talked this way about "Just Like a Woman" or "Like a Rolling Stone." The greatest misdirection (arising from Dylan's defensiveness; he gets caught in defending his film, something he almost never does in relation to his music) is the idea that the movie is "about" something. Dylan told *Rolling Stone* that the movie "is mostly about identity." This isn't bullshit—"identity" is a good word for a major thematic area that can be stimulated in the viewer by the scenes, sounds and juxtapositions in *Renaldo & Clara*—but again it's damaging because it encourages people to think that there's a message the filmmaker is trying to put across. Elsewhere in the same interview Dylan says, "What we did was cut up reality and make it more real," which I think is accurate. Even better: "I'll tell you what the film reveals: this film reveals that there's a whole lot to reveal beneath the surface of the soul, but it's unthinkable.... It reveals the depths that there are to reveal. And that's the most you can ask, because things are really very invisible. You can't reveal the invisible." This is very good, but its impact is destroyed and people are conditioned to misunderstand the movie when Dylan indulges in chatter like, "Renaldo is oppressed. He's oppressed because he's born." (Renaldo in the film doesn't seem particularly oppressed to me.) "My film is about naked alienation of the inner self against the outer self—alienation taken to the extreme." Oh, spare us. Actually it's about the way Mama Maria Frasca smiles at Joan Baez, and Joan's smile in response, and Dylan knows this, and knows that he had nothing to do with it except to have the cameras rolling and to have the sense to include the moment in his collage. He knows this, but he's insecure in these interviews and his ego takes over (as it never did in the editing room), and one result is that critics and public alike are primed to misunderstand and dislike the film before they ever see it.

Allen Ginsberg visited Dylan while he was editing the film, saw an early cut, and discussed the film with Dylan at some length. In November 1978 Ginsberg spoke informally with some college students, describing how Dylan edited *Renaldo & Clara*:

> It's built in a very interesting way. You would have to study it like *Finnegan's Wake*, or Cezanne, to discern the texture, to discern the composition of the tapestry. It's like a tapestry. What he did was, he shot about 110 hours of film, or more, and he looked at it all. Then he put it all on index cards, according to some preconceptions he had when he was directing the shooting. Namely, themes: God, rock 'n' roll, art, poetry, marriage, women, sex, Bob Dylan, poets, death — maybe 18 or 20 thematic preoccupations. Then he also put on index cards all the different characters, all the scenes. He also marked on index cards the dominant color — blue or red — and certain other images that go through the movie, like the rose and the hat, and American Indians ... so that he finally had an index of all of that. And then he went through it all again and began composing it, thematically, weaving in and out those specific compositional references. So it's compositional, and the idea was not to have a plot, but to have a composition of those themes.

Ginsberg comments on the reviewers' reaction (the *Village Voice* ran four separate reviews, all four reviling the film and attacking Dylan as an insufferable egotist): "It was like being upset at Van Gogh. It's a painter's film, and was composed like that. I've seen it about four times, and each time I see it, it becomes more and more logical — not rational, but logical. The logic in the composition is more and more explicit."

My experience concurs with Ginsberg's. I've seen the film perhaps a dozen times; it still surprises, delights, stimulates, holds my attention, and the more I see it the more it holds together, the more sense it makes, whereas with most films I lose interest after a couple of viewings. In this way the movie is more closely related to music, the pleasures of listening over and over to a musical performance or composition, than to most of what we think of as film art.

In 1980 Dylan described to me the methodology he followed in putting together *Renaldo & Clara*, and how it evolved from his work on *Eat the Document*; I didn't take notes or record the conversation, but my recollection of it is similar to and consistent with what Ginsberg reports. In the case of *Eat the Document* the index cards had numbers (if I understood Dylan correctly), and Dylan and Howard Alk engaged in something like William Burroughs's cut-up technique, except that there was a system, not a rational one but one having to do with relationships between numbers, something simultaneously related to playing the lottery, religious mysticism, and classical music composition. Definitely a kind of mad bop poetry.

But in addition to a mathematical magician (alchemist) manipulating the elements of film as one would the elements of a musical performance, Dylan also saw himself (while he was working on the film) as a painter, as Ginsberg suggests. Dylan's most frequent references in his descriptions of the film just after it was finished are to Cezanne. In *Rolling Stone*: "The movie creates and holds the time. That's what it should do – it should hold that time, breathe in that time and stop time in doing that. It's like if you look at a painting by Cezanne, you get lost in that painting for that period of time. And you breathe – yet time is going by and you wouldn't know it, you're spellbound."

Dylan is fascinated by timelessness. And in *Renaldo & Clara*, as in many of his songs, from "Restless Farewell" to "Lily, Rosemary and the Jack of Hearts," he specifically works at conveying to the listener his experience of timelessness, how it feels to him. And he succeeds. Certainly this will be one of the characteristics he will be most remembered for, as an artist: how he expresses our feelings about the out-of-time incidents, moments, segments, in our lives.

One way to talk about *Renaldo & Clara* is simply to list scenes, and transitions between scenes, with whatever comments arise:

• The scene in which Rodeo (Sam Shepard) is talking with, breaking up with, his girlfriend Clara (Sara Dylan). Both actors are radiant. Shepard's Rodeo manages to be both glib and inarticulate. He's cocky, vulnerable, stubborn, self-absorbed, while she's patient, nervous, loving, disappointed, determined, and somehow the words that come out of both their mouths are sheer music to the camera's ear. Dylan underlays the scene with a recording of himself singing "One Too Many Mornings," it should be heavy-handed but instead it blends in beautifully; various edits and little rhythmic jumps in the action serve to remind us this is a filmed scene (the edits seem timed to the music), and this contributes to the richness of the experience, like we're getting to eavesdrop on these two as they pretend to be pretending, while all the while we know and the explicitly present director knows that in fact this is real, this is true feeling, not that there's something going on between Sara and Sam but that she's speaking to all the men in her life (or the one man) and he to all and the one woman. And it is so much a painting, no other word for how the music and poetry of their conversation, words, eyes, faces, body movements (shrugs, fidgets), flow together as in a tapestry, a concerto, a visual, verbal landscape, seen in pieces yet all at once. They are embedded in the scene and situation like elegant insects in amber; finally she breaks it off and goes to make a phone call; incongruously the phone rings in the office of Dylan's record producer, he answers the phone, is startled, carries on a conversation — which we know isn't with her, and that discordancy is just right for the moment (Rodeo wasn't really talking to her either, was he?; not that this is the point, but rather that the harmonics and counterpoints are such that all sorts of reverberations are created). Dylan is in the room (and so, obviously, is the camera). Back in the phone booth Clara hangs up and walks off into the night, Rodeo or his ghost moving past her saying, "All I can say is that this has been a big mistake ... Where are you going?" It all rings like music, like song, but different; first time through perhaps what we remember is the man (who seems a stand-in for Dylan) telling the woman, "I need you to perform certain magical things with me" — she looks for a moment as though perhaps he's surprised her and said something loving, but immediately she realizes he's talking about his superstition, his mama-stuff, his fear of riding a bull or going out on stage without her incantations, protection, blessing. Next time through, this moment is as intriguing as the first time, or more so, but other moments or just the sounds of words (or the sound of the song playing against the dialog) stand out more, are particularly moving. It shifts, it changes, it's so full, we want more. In a theater the fact that you can't replay the scene (except in your mind), that you have to go back and see the whole movie again to get another glimpse of it, is also perfect, powerful, effective. In theory any movie could be like this, but in practice even the best of them seem contrived compared to what Dylan — with his naivete, his willfulness, his vision — has achieved. There is a freshness (born not just of the scene or its editing but also of the courage it took to include it, to spotlight it, turning towards the truth just when the impulse must be strongest to turn away) here that points to a huge new canvas, wide open western spaces, on which to create. Like Picasso's assemblages, newspapers, paste, nails, sand: the obvious is revolutionary, changing forever the space that before belonged only to brush and oils, but what is so moving is that the painter doesn't seem concerned with his innovation, his naughtiness, but only with capturing the fragility and beauty and transcendent ordinariness of this apartment universe that has his Eva in it. If he must reinvent painting to do the job, so be it.

- Five or six scenes in which David Blue (a singer-songwriter friend of Dylan's, he didn't perform on the Rolling Thunder tour but hung out with the caravan anyway) is playing pinball in a hotel beside an indoor pool and reminiscing into the camera about the old days in Greenwich Village, how the poets would read aloud in coffeehouses and pass the basket and work the audiences, how he met Dylan and the night "Blowin' in the Wind" was first performed ... The camera barely moves, sometimes the monolog goes on for five minutes at a time, it's so odd and so beautiful, the guy's obviously coked up but it doesn't matter, he's giving an exquisite performance, full of nuance, personality, humor, life (a master storyteller) — the man's smile, his weird verbal mannerisms, his hip (jaded) innocence and enthusiasm, are utterly infectious. The fact that he's playing pinball while he's talking is so great — the sound, the visual effect, the shifting of the speaker's attention to or from the game, the way he includes us in, the rhythm of the rap, it's a classic set of scenes which just for themselves will probably be famous centuries from now, and the way they work in the movie is wonderful: as exposition, history, background narrative, David Blue is narrating the movie, the other scenes are all happening in other rooms in the hotel, and then we come back to this grinning good-natured tale-teller, ding!, face a death-mask, moving while he's talking, the hipster, glad you could make it, This was your life, Bob Dylan. Among other things, the David Blue scenes are Dylan's essay on and celebration of performing. He lets us watch a master at work, the kind of genius who's never quite the same on record or even on stage. You have to catch him backstairs, with the gang —

- The movement of the rose or carnation (always the same red flower, anyway) from character to character and scene to scene, you feel that if you could only make a chart of its progress the movie's secret would be revealed, Clara picks it up when Helena leaves, Scarlet brings it to Dylan, The Woman in White brings it with her to the apartment, and Renaldo doesn't want her to leave without it, it's like a symbol of a symbol, always richly significant and connective, so we know there's a mind at work behind these scenes, but elusive too, Dylan has made dumb remarks about what the rose in the film stands for but the truth is he doesn't know either, who's he kidding? The movie's triumph is that it allows spirit, not some thinking filmmaker, to be in control, and a (still life) portrait of spirit in motion is what results. The same with Renaldo's blue hat, symbol of performance ("who's Dylan?" "he's the one with the hat"), moving through the scenes (so nice the dissolve from Phil Ochs putting it on his head — "the hat, Bobbie!" — to hat on table in Yetnikoff's office, one feels the camera following the hat and understands therefore how we got here), sometimes the flower's on the hat —
- All of the transitions to and away from the concert segments, Dylan in whiteface on stage with the troupe, the timing (in the deli: "She said, 'Tell him I love him anyway!'" bam! we cut to "It Ain't Me Babe") (in the coffee shop: Clara: "Are you sure we can trust you?" Truckdriver: "Don't I have an honest face?" He leers, there's a beat, and we join Dylan singing "Isis," starting *in medias res* with the verse that says, "When I took up his offer I must have been mad." One scene comments on the other, and we see how spirit suggested to editor to end this scene here and move into this song, but we also can see, as editor did, a thousand other resonances, marveling at spirit's cleverness, its sure hand with these transitions) (for transition out of a concert clip, how about the eerie moment when character comments on existence in the reel world, Dylan's just been singing "Romance in Durango" and Rodeo, his rival, says to Clara, "I keep hearing that guy's voice,

you know." "What guy?" eyes innocent. "You know what guy").
Most famous transition, the three lovers in the apartment, Clara
looks at Joan and asks Renaldo, "Who is she?" and Dylan on
stage starts singing "Sara..." But I like the non-cognitive transitions, pure message of rock and roll sound blasting in, just as
well, like the segues to Stoner & troupe playing "Catfish" during
the same sequence. No obvious role for the words of the song,
but oh that riff!

I could go on, probably for years. The scenes in the film most
obviously full of meaning are between a man and a woman – the
already-mentioned-one between Rodeo and Clara, the dialogs between Stoner as the Musician and Tyrangiel as the Girlfriend (some
of which play in audio in Stoner's mind as he's walking towards the
stage), the great scene in the bathroom between Steven Soles and
Ronee Blakley ("I know who you've been fucking"), Dylan and Baez
at the bar ("I haven't changed that much – have you?"), Dylan and
Blakley at the same bar, screaming moment of Tyrangiel as crazed
female fan assaulting Dylan, Renaldo and Clara and the Woman in
White in the apartment (certainly a triangle, but also two manifestations of the same woman), the actors and characters change yet we
understand clearly that in some sense it's always Renaldo and always
Clara, and that the movie is about ("about") the hero's relationship
with his female soul-mate superimposed on and in conflict with his
relationship with his art, his music, the world, the stage. Simple,
really. The triangle is you, me, and that guy singing who might look
like me if you took off his greasepaint and his hat. The whorehouse
sequences especially are eternal no-time, like backstage, but idealized, the Muslim paradise filled with strong beautiful female spirits,
not archetypes but real individuals, "four and twenty windows and a
woman's face in every one." There are also the parties, the roadies
setting up the stage (great sounds in that scene, *musique concrete*),
trains and busses, walking about and down and around the back
areas of the auditorium, Dylan's world but only for the most obvious
of reasons: I paint what I see. Plus the "movie" stuff, expressions of
romanticism and longing, Clara assists in a jailbreak, Renaldo
strums his guitar for the lady while trading a hot T-bird for a fast
bike, later trades the lady (another lady?) for a horse, Jack Elliott the
cowboy is outraged (to him only the horse has value) but Stanton
(the escaped con) modestly and joyously welcomes the love that's
come his way. And there's lots more. The "documentary" stuff (as if

he's taken all the forms of film that have touched him and borrowed their techniques for his collage): great stop-frame interviews in Harlem about Rubin Carter (the faces, Dylan like Sergio Leone understands that great faces and good music and a proper interplay between music and the camera's motion are the best things this medium has to offer; just let that camera linger on those faces), those preachers in downtown Metropolis ("Whatever you say to a man of God, you say direct to God!", segue straight into "A Hard Rain's A-Gonna Fall," fantastic performance, truly great cinema), the wonderful conversations in the deli among Dylan's fans, the audience, the experts, dominated by the Greek counterman ("the Realist"), Ginsberg and Dylan visit Kerouac's grave, talk to the schoolchildren about God, at once a parody of the documentary form (camera presuming to be able to look into the poet's life) and an example of it at its best.

And like music, you just let it all wash over you. Finally you're not able to experience it any other way. Dylan wants us to notice the scenes at the end (Renaldo lying on the carpet, college boys asked if they remember what they dreamt last night, cabaret guy singing "In the Morning") and the way they suggest this was all Renaldo's dream, I like the scenes but we don't need the explanation, we've been walking through this movie like dreamers from the beginning anyway, how else could we relate to characters who change names and faces but continue to be the same people, and footage edited in reverse or sideways sequence (Elliott comes in and says "You just traded your horse for that woman," goes out, comes in and says it again, Baez and Stanton smooching, and then Baez and Dylan arrive and the trade takes place)? Don't try to explain it, Bob. The movie's not a dream, not a document, not a story, nor even all of the above. What you've created is bigger, and more perfectly itself, than your understanding or explanation of it could ever be. Call it an entertainment. "Welcome, willkommen, bienvenu – to Cabaret, yes Cabaret, oh Cabaret."

Ronee Blakley's performance of "Need a New Sun Rising" is worth the price of admission, not to mention 15 seconds of Dylan and Stoner in a hotel room screaming "House of the Rising Sun." And I love Jack Elliott's sweet "South Coast." A great movie. Sara Dylan and Joan Baez in particular are amazing, they give spectacular performances throughout. There's so much here, so much; and better than that is the way it all works together.

Perfectly itself. Twentieth century boy goes to the movies (Dylan's uncle owned a theater downtown) and aspires to that level of creation, even as children we already know the smells and sounds and sights and touch of life and are thrilled by the wonder of it, and want to recreate it, hero worship, we want to be like the Creator, and making music and making movies sure seems like the way to go. And if you're Dylan, and have the talent and will power and perseverance and integrity, you actually do it, and do it in a way no one else but you would ever have thought of or attempted or succeeded at.

It's scary. You work harder than you've ever worked on anything in your life, and in the end you hold your masterpiece in your hands, and look at all the money you've spent, and wonder if your work is going to be accepted, appreciated, recognized. Your act is you don't care about any of that, but it isn't true. You have a lot invested in this.

You try to act cool, but it doesn't work; the critics smell your fear, they've been waiting for this (unconsciously, perhaps; they're not monsters, just a wolf pack), and they tear you limb from limb.

And the public, well, maybe this film is over their heads, maybe it isn't, but they never even take the chance of finding out. They're fickle. Somehow five million ticket requests in 1974 and a string of bestselling albums and fifteen years of phenomenal press coverage doesn't translate into even one half-full theater in the film's first week of release (January 1978) in New York, Los Angeles, San Francisco. Go figure.

Which is something Dylan hadn't experienced before—you produce a masterpiece and no one applauds, no one boos (not like 1965, not like a public *reaction*), no one copies it, steals it, or sends you money. Nothing. Some nastiness in the press the first week of release and after that, silence.

You don't even know how to feel about it. Fortunately, you already have a world tour scheduled, a chance to get back on stage, do some performing, make some money.

Dylan left his brother with the impossible task (impossible for an amateur no matter what the movie is) of distributing *Renaldo & Clara*, and turned his attention to touring. Rehearsals began in December. Dylan gave some interviews to promote the movie, and then left for Japan and Australia shortly after the film was released.

V. Entertainer

December 1977 - December 1978

"When your environment changes, you change. You've got to go on, and you find new friends. Turn around one day and you're on a different stage, with a new set of characters."
—Bob Dylan, 1978

7.

Over a ten-day period at the end of November and start of December, 1977, journalist Ron Rosenbaum recorded an extensive interview with Dylan for *Playboy* magazine. It's a lovely performance — Dylan rapping in short, careful bursts that suddenly blossom into inspired lyrical language and imagery, as the man on the hot seat finds a truth he's willing to share & a fun way to express it — and possibly the single most enlightening introduction to who Dylan is ever published.

Dylan manages to romanticize himself, disguise himself, and reveal great chunks of his essence, all at once, live, unrehearsed, before an audience of one (and millions): "I had some amazing projections when I was a kid, but not since then ... I grew up in a place so foreign that you had to be there to picture it ... In the winter everything was still, nothing moved. Eight months of that. You can put it together. You can have some amazing hallucinogenic experiences doing nothing but looking out your window."

At one point in the interview, talking about his film, Dylan says, "Renaldo's needs are few. He doesn't know it, though, at that particular time." Rosenbaum asks, "What are his needs?" Dylan: "A good guitar and a dark street." Rosenbaum: "The guitar because he loves music, but why the dark street?" Dylan: "Mostly because he needs to hide." Rosenbaum: "From whom?" Dylan: "From the demon within. [*Pause*] But what we all know is that you can't hide on a dark street from the demon within. And there's our movie."

Tour 1978 seems to have been Dylan's effort to hide on a very bright street indeed. He played 115 concerts in 32 states and 10 countries. In May 1977 he'd signed a contract with Jerry Weintraub's management company, which also represented such mainstream show business figures as Frank Sinatra, John Denver, and Neil Diamond; the 1978 tour, his first since Rolling Thunder, was clearly planned by Dylan as a very professional affair, an opportunity to mature, to settle into the role of entertainer. Presumably this was his strategy for protecting himself from the burdensome responsibility and over-the-edge craziness of the 1975-76 tours, and of distancing himself from the public identity imposed on him during the 1974 tour—that of mythic hero, savior, musical embodiment of a vanishing era.

He knew what he didn't want to be. And what he did want was simple enough: in December 1977 he told Jonathan Cott, "I have to get back to playing music, because unless I do, I don't really feel alive ... I have to play in front of the people just to keep going."

Who am I?, he seems to be asking himself—an appropriate question for a 36-year-old man who has recently lost his wife and family, and who knows that he isn't the person the public and the press and most of the people around him expect him to be. And he comes up with a very reasonable answer: I'm the person who wrote these songs, who goes out and sings them on stage with a band and gets paid for doing so.

So Dylan assembled a new band (new and different: 11 people, including three back-up singers and a saxophone player), worked out startling new arrangements for 50 or more songs from throughout his career (a showcase, a retrospective), rehearsed for at least six weeks, and on February 20, 1978, opened his world tour with a 28-song performance (well over two hours in length) in Tokyo, Japan. He and his band played a total of 24 shows on this first leg of their tour, in Japan, New Zealand, and Australia, finishing in Sydney on April 1. Two of the Tokyo shows were recorded by Dylan's Japanese record company, edited into a two-disc album and released under the title *Bob Dylan at Budokan*.

Unfortunately, the 1978 tour was a slow starter, and the *Budokan* album represents it poorly. I don't think it would be possible to put together a really first-rate album from any of the early shows, but these particular performances, from February 28 and March 1, catch Dylan and his band at a low ebb. Steve Douglas, whose sax and flute-playing dominate the record, sounds as though he's just had his creativity squelched by his boss and decided to get back at him by playing the most hackneyed, irritating little riffs he could come up with. Dylan, who normally draws much of his power in performance from the intense, intimate interaction between his voice and the sound of his band, seems oddly detached on many of these songs, and so the band is reduced to doodling mindlessly, following the game-plan of the boss's arrangements but unable (presumably because the singer, their leader, is sleepwalk-ing) to breathe much life into them.

It would be easy, given the questionable artistry of many of the shows on this first leg of the tour, to blame the arrangements and the concept: Dylan was described in his own tour booklet as an "entertainer," and the shows, arguably, were intended only as entertainment. This idea — Bob Dylan marketing himself like a Las Vegas crooner, packaged music and showmanship for the mentally middle-aged — is so repellent to the average Dylan fan that the critical and public backlash that resulted is not surprising, and one wonders at Dylan's failure to anticipate it. But in fact the arrange-ments, radical and deconstructive though they are, and the mis-guided showmanship (flashy white suit, friendly, insincere patter between songs), were not the problem — rather they were expres-sions of a problem that would have been there in any case. The real issue is that a performer, as an artist, lives and dies on presence (what Dylan, in another interview, calls "will power"); when he has it, and can project it, the most absurd trappings become part of the fun, part of the miracle. And when he doesn't have it, everything falls flat, no matter how well thought out beforehand.

What happened? The artist was scared, insecure, he'd lost his family, and now his masterwork (*Renaldo & Clara*) was being soundly rejected by public and critics alike. But by themselves fear and insecurity don't have to interfere with great art, or with a performer's presence — indeed, increased vulnerability is likely to improve a performance, it opens the artist's receptivity and there-fore his expressiveness as well.

My own sense of it is that Dylan, as a performer, was in a dazed state for much of 1978. He described himself in mid-tour interviews as a conscious artist, someone who had learned to create consciously what he once produced unconsciously. I have already acknowledged the usefulness of this insight, as a clue to the source and nature of Dylan's surge of creativity between 1974 and 1977. Now, as we reach the time when Dylan himself began talking about "conscious artistry," it's necessary to point to the dangers, the negative power, of this way of looking at the creative process. Seeing oneself as a conscious artist can lead to a sort of tyranny of the ego, in which receptivity and spontaneity are diminished, and self-serving concepts are given all too free a rein. This is particularly a danger if one has just suffered a loss, in which case the urge to avoid openness and vulnerability may be quite strong (and at the same time well-disguised; one of our best defenses is to keep ourselves unaware of what we're really feeling). Under such circumstances, an infatuation with one's own power and sensitivity becomes a vehicle for closing down, and may cause one to become cut off from inspiration, from the creative spirit.

But not completely. If there was a force driving Dylan to be unconscious (here I am the beloved entertainer in my white suit, singing that old favorite "Girl from the North Country"), a force ironically located in my opinion right in his very pride at being such a conscious artist, there was another force in opposition to it, a force waking him up, a force that would cause his performances over the course of the year to get better and livelier almost in spite of themselves, the same seemingly ill-advised arrangements and carefully distanced vocals turning into powerful expressions of a whole new side of the artist.

And the Far East shows are not bad. Dylan, after all, is a born performer, and each of his tours has carved out its own unique musical territory, in the face of quite a variety of externally and internally generated obstacles. If no other tape of 1978 existed but the March 12 concert in Brisbane (one of the better Australian performances), I know I'd play it over and over, learning to love its nuances more each time — especially in the second half of the show, when Dylan shakes off some of his tentativeness. (The big band version of "One of Us Must Know" is a real kick.) But the shows from later in the year seem to me brighter, more alive, more consistently rewarding.

Dylan apparently recorded many of his rehearsals with the 1978 band, and a number of these tapes have fallen into the hands of collectors. The rehearsals from January and February contain some moving performances (with more dynamic interaction between singer and band than can be heard on tapes of the early concerts), among them "You're a Big Girl Now," "Repossession Blues" (a Billy Lee Riley song, growled with surprising conviction), and a waltz version of "If You See Her, Say Hello" which like so many of these variations sounds flippant and soulless at first but ends up insinuating its way into the listener's mind and heart. There's also an interesting, disturbing take of "Tomorrow Is a Long Time" – Dylan sings a phrase or two of each verse with real feeling and then starts shouting the lyrics, turning them into melodrama, as if to fictionalize and deny the emotions he's just expressed.

Three holdovers from the Rolling Thunder tour were hired for the 1978 band: Rob Stoner on bass, David Mansfield on violin and mandolin, and Steven Soles on acoustic rhythm guitar and vocals. Stoner left after the Far East leg, and was replaced by Jerry Scheff. The rest of the band: Alan Pasqua on keyboards, Billy Cross on lead guitar, Bobbye Hall on congas, Ian Wallace on drums, Steve Douglas on saxophone, and Helena Springs, Jo Ann Harris, and Debbie Dye on backing vocals. Dye was replaced in April by Carolyn Dennis.

One rehearsal tape from April circulates: it includes particularly sweet performances of "Simple Twist of Fate," "Ballad of a Thin Man," and "To Ramona," along with a moving fragment of a new song, one of several written by Dylan in collaboration with Helena Springs, "Coming from the Heart." The richness of Dylan's vocal on this tape is striking – he hasn't backed off his new way of singing (it didn't even sound like a new way of singing to me at first, just an awkwardness, a stiffness), but has patiently (stubbornly) stood by his original impulse, pushed forward with it to the point where it is starting to be a versatile and expressive instrument.

Shortly after this practice session, Dylan and his tour band recorded a new album of nine songs (one of which they'd been performing live, "Is Your Love in Vain?") at Rundown Studios, a rehearsal space Dylan had recently rented near the ocean in Santa Monica, California. It was Dylan's first studio album since *Desire*, recorded three years earlier; and the first batch of songs

Dylan had written alone and then recorded since the *Blood on the Tracks* songs in 1974.

Street-Legal is a tremendous tease. There is a story about Picasso in which an art dealer asks him to go through a stack of "Picasso" canvases he's been offered and tell him which are real and which are forgeries. As Picasso is adding one of the pictures to the "fake" pile, the dealer says, "Wait a minute, Pablo. That's no forgery. I was visiting you the weekend you painted it." "No matter," Picasso replies calmly; "I can fake a Picasso as well as any thief in Europe."

Writing about *New Morning*, I suggested (based on what I hear when listening to the record) that something, some fear, stopped Dylan from sharing what he was really feeling, and as a result all the effort that went into writing the songs and making the album came up empty, the commitment or risk or presence that authenticate a Dylan album and give it its power just aren't there. In the case of *Street-Legal*, something a little different is happening: there's an amazing presence or power here, but it is blocked, denied, kept out of reach, as though the power that suppresses ("that enemy within") is locked in an unresolvable struggle with the power that creates and risks.

I don't mean to be so psychological. The album comes up short, that's all. But it is *so* tantalizing! "Changing of the Guards," on first listen, sounds like a classic Dylan anthem—the title is brilliant, as is the phrase that leads into it ("Or else your hearts must have the courage for the changing of the guards"). The rhythm and melody are original and powerful; and Dylan's use of the back-up singers to echo his words at strategic moments throughout each verse is a marvelous device, effective and haunting. The fade-in at the start, followed by the first words of the song—"Sixteen years," intriguing in any case and neatly self-referential to those listeners who know how many years it's been since Dylan's first album came out, since he started his public journey—promises something really special; the storytelling structure of the song, mixing political and romantic intrigue, rich imagery, and fascinating setting, singer slipping neatly between first and third person narrative, seems more than adequate to deliver on the promise. Surely we have another classic-in-the-making here.

That's on first listen. A hundred spins later, the song sounds as promising as ever ... and the listener is still waiting, breathlessly, for the payoff. The song sounds good, it's fun to listen to, you catch yourself singing along in places, but it's not "Mr. Tambourine Man" or "Desolation Row" or even "Shelter from the Storm." It doesn't satisfy, doesn't resolve, just never quite comes together. If you sit down and read the lyrics, the reason for this failure becomes apparent: the song's a fraud, these images and bits of narrative don't have anything to do with each other, they're just thrown together to give the appearance of meaning, of story. Very clever. And rather cynical. This is not what we've come to expect from Dylan.

More importantly, perhaps, it's not what Dylan expects of himself. He's always recorded his albums quickly, and often the songwriting has been done at the last minute. But there's ample evidence that under the pressure of this kind of quick work, combined with his love for his songs, his earnestness about whatever he feels to communicate at a particular moment, and his facility for language and music, Dylan has worked miracles of editing: rewriting and changing and re-forming songs urgently and energetically to get them to live up to their potential. (And tossing them aside if he's still not satisfied.)

But something (and I really don't believe it was haste) stopped him from doing justice to the *Street-Legal* material. "Senor" is a wonderful song, and the vocal and instrumental performances on the album are masterful—what a mood they set!—and yet song and performance are undercut by careless songwriting. The five short verses that start and end with the word "senor" are brilliant, inspired. ("Let's overturn these tables, disconnect these cables, this place don't make sense to me no more"—God, he could have become poet laureate of a whole new generation with lines like that.) But there are also two bridging verses whose lyrics range from mediocre to laughable, and they take the edge off the mood and prevent the song from reaching the heights it could have achieved. The shortfall here is the responsibility of the performer as well as the songwriter. If he truly cared about the song, if he were fully present in his performance, he wouldn't be willing (or able) to weaken it by singing lines of imitation Dylan like "there's a marching band still playing in that vacant lot" and "...that trainload of fools bogged down in a magnetic field." Unworthy. Unconscious. Unfortunate.

Weird, fascinating album. I find "Baby Stop Crying" a particularly moving performance. Dylan's anguish comes through very directly, in spite of the arrogant, off-the-wall lyrics: "I don't have to be no doctor, babe/To see that you're madly in love." "Go get me my pistol, babe/Honey, I can't tell right from wrong." The fact that the "story" doesn't hold together or make any sense is not such a problem here, since the song is not primarily narrative; the dissonance of the emotional content of the lyrics *is* a problem (I'm supposed to identify with this guy?), but in a strange and probably unintended way it does fit with what the song primarily expresses. Dylan, or the person speaking, imagines he's comforting the woman the song's addressed to; in fact, he's the one in need of comfort. "*Please* stop crying/Cause it's tearing up my mind." It is indeed, and maybe that's why he's babbling about "bad men" and "going down to the river" and seeing that she's madly in love. What is clear is that he wants her to stop for his sake, not hers; that he doesn't know why she's crying (which is why he keeps bragging about how much he knows about it); and that he doesn't want to know and is certainly not going to ask. He just wants to shut off the noise. This is, um, kind of an unusual love song. But the pain and confusion it expresses are anything but phony.

The least ambitious song on the album is the most successful ("We Better Talk This Over"—it's got humor, it's got magnificent resonance between lyrics and music, it's even got some love in it, and some genuine humility); and the most ambitious—"No Time to Think"—is the least successful. What's fascinating about "No Time to Think" is that it actually works better as a poem on the page than it does as a performance. The writing's uneven but unlike "Changing of the Guards" it has something to say and it gets it across—and what it has to say is from the heart. It's also pretty grim, and if we accept the idea that there's an enemy within working overtime on this album to prevent too much truth from escaping, then it's not surprising that the arrangement of this song renders it almost unlistenable. Which is not to say it's a bad arrangement—it's really very clever—it's just that it doesn't work. The worst aspects of the song are pushed forward and the best aspects are buried.

Then there's "New Pony," an excellent performance of a song that gives me the creeps. Dylan clearly enjoys getting in some digs at a former lady friend, but surely his current lover couldn't have found these lyrics very flattering?

I love the sound of "Is Your Love in Vain?" (and "Baby Stop Crying" and "Senor" and "Changing of the Guards" and "Where

Are You Tonight?" and "We Better Talk This Over"—there's a lot of very attractive music and some excellent musical performances on this record), and I even think I know what the song's trying to say … it comes through in the vocal. The words, however, send an opposite message: they speak of nothing but the speaker's vanity. Nasty twin strikes again.

"Where Are You Tonight?" is another song that promises a tremendous amount and, like "Senor," partially delivers. I'm very fond of this song, I can listen to it a lot, it gives me much pleasure … and it frustrates me, because I have to swallow its phoniness with its honesty. The arrangement, the ensemble performance, is wonderful. (So's the tune.) This is where Dylan sings "I fought with my twin/That enemy within/Till both of us fell by the way." He also says (it's possible to hear a lot of regret for his lost soulmate on this album, if one chooses to; and impossible to know whether that's what one actually is hearing), "I couldn't tell her/What my private thoughts were/But she had some way of finding them out." And maybe, just maybe, the last words of *Street-Legal* are its secret message, a secret especially (or only?) from its creator: "I can't believe it, I can't believe I'm alive/But without you it doesn't seem right/Oh, where are you tonight?"

8.

Part two of the 1978 tour began with a week of shows at the
Universal Amphitheater in Los Angeles, June 1–7. Dylan then flew
to Europe, where he played six shows at Earl's Court in London
(June 15–20), five shows at the Pavillon de Paris (July 3–8), plus
four concerts in West Germany, two in Sweden, one in the Netherlands, and one more in England, in front of 200,000 people at the
Blackbushe Aerodrome in Surrey. This last performance (July 15,
1978) was a triumph, as was the entire European tour (in terms of
showmanship, popular enthusiasm, and critical acclaim); but the
high point of the tour (and probably one of the great moments of
the artist's life) was performing before a crowd of 75,000 people on
July 1 in Nuremberg at the Zeppelinfeld, an open-air stadium built
by Adolf Hitler and used for massive rallies during the Nazi era.

The European tour was followed by another two-month break,
and then an extraordinary three solid months of American concerts, beginning September 15 in Augusta, Maine, and continuing
through the Northeast, the Midwest, the West Coast, and the
South, ending December 16 in Hollywood, Florida. (During the
summer break, Dylan had edited down *Renaldo & Clara* to create a

two-hour version, in hopes of getting the film distributed to theaters that were unwilling to take on a four-hour movie. This drastic effort was not rewarded by any greater commercial or public acceptance of the movie, which soon disappeared entirely from public view, at least in the United States, where it has been unavailable for rental by movie theaters or anyone else from 1979 to the present. While it seems reasonable to consider the four-hour version to be the film Dylan intended to make, there is a certain inspired flair to his further edit as well; I remember enjoying it very much the one time I watched it, in the fall of 1978.)

Dylan's tireless barnstorming of the world during 1978 has left behind a legacy of more than 275 hours of recorded performances (unreleased except for the *Budokan* album, and unavailable except in the form of privately circulated tapes made by members of the audience, and some bootleg records excerpted from those tapes). This is an enormous amount of material, and there is no easy way for listener or commentator to begin to assimilate it. It would be convenient to imagine that he played roughly the same concert through the course of the 115 shows (and speaking simply in terms of the script—the songlist and basic arrangements—there's some truth to that), and that the primary variable was in the quality of his performance (poor, good, excellent), in which case a single excellent concert could be considered a fairly good representation of the entire tour. The problem, however, is equivalent to that of studying a year of performances of *King Lear* by an accomplished actor; the best of these performances will differ from each other in significant ways, even though the playwright's words don't change ... they differ because of the malleability of the performer's art, its ability to take on new characteristics each evening. One night's interpretation or inspiration or mood is not necessarily better than another night's—rather, all are expressions of the actor's spirit, the ever-changing challenges (internal and external) that he faces and his ongoing effort to respond to them and share his (changing) vision, his truth. There are of course mediocre performances (even from great actors), and sometimes a sameness in that mediocrity, but the good performances are good in a wild profusion of subtle and unexpected ways, adding up to a body of work that neither performer nor observer can ever fully appreciate. There's just too much of it, and anyway each past performance is partially and necessarily forgotten as we focus in on tonight's show.

In the same way the singer-musician is alive on stage each night, and never wholly repeats himself, even when the external form of what he (or she) does is unvarying. This is more true (or more easily true) of a singer working with a band than of a singer alone, because the interaction with other musicians constantly generates opportunities for spontaneity—the singer working with a band has more to respond to, and may feel more free to invent responses. He is constantly stimulated (surprised), and he is also supported, anchored, counter-balanced, which gives him more leeway to take risks, to push to the edge of the music, whatever edge happens to present itself to him on this particular evening.

Dylan's 1978 concerts all followed the same basic structure: an instrumental overture by the band (based on "Hard Rain" at the start of the tour, then later "My Back Pages," Dylan's subtle announcement that this show will be a retrospective), an old blues song as Dylan's vocal opener ("Love Her with a Feeling" or "She's Love Crazy"—both by Tampa Red—or "I'm Ready" by Willie Dixon), then 10 or 11 Dylan songs, followed by an intermission. "Going, Going, Gone" (from *Planet Waves*, but rewritten with some lyrics borrowed from delta blues singers) was usually the closing song for the first act, although towards the end of the year he replaced it with "Senor." Included in this first act almost every night were "Mr. Tambourine Man," "Shelter from the Storm," "Love Minus Zero/ No Limit" (or "It's All Over Now, Baby Blue"), "Girl from the North Country" (or "Tangled Up in Blue"), "Ballad of a Thin Man," "Maggie's Farm," "I Don't Believe You," "Like a Rolling Stone," and "I Shall Be Released." Other songs that found their way in more than once were "I Threw It All Away" (at the earlier shows), "Baby Stop Crying," and "Is Your Love in Vain?"

In the Far East the second half of the show would begin with "One of Us Must Know." In June and July this was preceded by an instrumental version of "Rainy Day Women." The fall tour went back to "One of Us" as second act opener, alternating with "True Love Tends to Forget"; both were replaced in October by "The Times They Are A-Changin'." In November "Rainy Day Women" returned, now featuring vocals by the three back-up singers. It followed "The Times." The next song in the second set, starting in July, was Dylan's only solo acoustic performance of the evening (there was no solo slot at all prior to the July shows): "Gates of

Eden" in Europe, "It Ain't Me Babe" back in the States. This second set varied a little more in the course of the year than the first set; from October on, it generally consisted of (after "It Ain't Me Babe"): "You Treat Me Like a Stepchild" (a new Dylan song), "One More Cup of Coffee," "Blowin' in the Wind," "Girl from the North Country," "Where Are You Tonight?" (or "We Better Talk This Over"), "Masters of War," "Just Like a Woman," "To Ramona," "All Along the Watchtower," "All I Really Want to Do," "It's Alright, Ma," and "Forever Young." (Other songs that would occasionally or regularly turn up earlier in the tour included "I Want You," "The Man in Me," "Don't Think Twice," "Oh Sister," "You're a Big Girl Now," "Tomorrow Is a Long Time," "Knockin' on Heaven's Door," and "Simple Twist of Fate." There were also a few songs Dylan only sang once, those little surprises that make tape collectors' lives meaningful.)

Dylan always performed an encore. For the first two parts of the tour it was "The Times They Are A-Changin'," alone or with "Knockin' on Heaven's Door" or "I'll Be Your Baby Tonight" or "Changing of the Guards." On the U.S. leg, "Changing of the Guards" was the invariable encore, with "I'll Be Your Baby Tonight" as a rare second encore. The shows were about 2¼ to 2½ hours long, with Dylan singing 25 or 26 songs. A generous helping.

By way of generalization, the shows in the first part of the tour tended to be a little stiff, Dylan not yet fully at home with the band or the material or the audience or himself. The shows from the middle segment were the most professional, with some wonderful performances almost every night as well as some stretches where the passion was lacking. The third segment, in the U.S., was uneven, and as Dylan's voice started to fail him under the stress of all this touring he started shouting more of the songs; but the third segment was also the most lively and spirited, Dylan enjoying himself a lot on stage (when he wasn't suffering from exhaustion), and the performances as a whole had more personality, less professionalism, more spontaneity.

Starting in June, Dylan included two or three songs from *Street-Legal* in each show (six at Blackbushe), but unlike the 1975 Rolling Thunder tour Dylan didn't seem to regard the new songs as strong enough to build a show around (or they weren't as important to him as "Isis" and "Hurricane" and "One More Cup of Coffee" and "Sara" were in 1975).

Dylan's purpose in 1978 seems to have been to redo the '74 tour (the great Bob Dylan retrospective) and do it right. He set out to play the songs that people wanted to hear—there were a significant number of "greatest hits" represented—but despite his entertainer stance he wasn't interested in just granting his audience whatever they might wish from him. The inclusion of only one acoustic song—pointedly, "It Ain't Me Babe"—made this very clear. The songs had new arrangements because he believed in them as living creations, he was celebrating their elasticity and universality, and he also was insisting that he be allowed to sing them as the person he was at the moment. It wasn't so much that the new arrangements were more representative of who he was now than the old ones—it was that he had had to consciously strip the songs of their nostalgic value in order to be able to freely perform them as a singer, a living artist, rather than as some kind of phonograph.

The best performances of the 1978 tour are somewhat overshadowed, in my estimation, by the extraordinary achievements of the two tours that precede and follow it in Dylan's chronology: Rolling Thunder II in spring 1976, and the first "gospel" shows, fall 1979. These are among the performances that make Dylan a great artist, right up there with his work on *Highway 61 Revisited* and *Blood on the Tracks* and live with the Hawks in spring 1966. Even the very best of 1978 falls a little short of these standards of inspiration, content, and commitment; and alas most of the 1978 performances slide off into the "good but not great" category.

Having said that, one has to say also that 1978 was a bold (and, under the circumstances, resourceful) experiment, and that its inventions and achievements add significantly to Dylan's body of work, in particular by acknowledging and displaying the durability and flexibility of so many of Dylan's songs. And finally, the happy fact is that the finest performances of 1978, when one can root them out from among the 275 hours of shows available, are wonderful indeed, and quite delightfully distinct from anything else Dylan has ever done.

At the St. Louis Checkerdome on October 29, my very favorite of all the 1978 concert tapes, Dylan's band starts with an unusually spirited, richly-textured reading of "My Back Pages," just brimming with life, suggesting that it might have been the band's brightness that inspired Dylan to give so much this particular evening. He walks on stage near the end of the instrumental (we hear the audience's response) and seconds later Dylan and band launch into a great version of "She's Love Crazy" — there's a special lilt in Dylan's voice and the other musicians (particularly the saxophone and the back-up singers) tune themselves to it perfectly, just as he perfectly hooks into the fine rhythmic groove the band has going, and for two minutes we're rocking in blues heaven.

This could go on all night and I wouldn't mind, but instead Dylan makes a quick and remarkable musical shift into the first (and most radical) of his song transformations: "Mr. Tambourine Man," sung with hypnotic slowness, as though a capella. The performance is a duet with keyboardist Alan Pasqua, and he and Dylan create a mood that is powerfully evocative and totally fresh. Four-fifths of the way through, the full band enters, playing the uptempo arrangement Dylan had used for the song earlier in the tour; the sense of release this brings is exquisite. Dylan sings a chorus in this style to complete the performance, and one is left with the impression of having been to a far-off, exotic, deeply beautiful island, a dream-space. In this version, the song becomes a sort of brilliantly compact concerto for voice and keyboard, forerunner of a new music yet to be invented, thrown together by Dylan because he wanted a fresh, shocking, transformed "Mr. Tambourine Man," and he wasn't satisfied with what he'd been doing, or else just got inspired to take it in a new direction. The new arrangement reaches its peak in St. Louis, I think; Dylan sings it with so much feeling, such great timing. A powerful and moving performance; and arguably a more significant new work than any of the newly-written songs Dylan debuted in 1978.

The vulnerability and sensitivity of this "Tambourine Man" are not at all typical of the 1978 tour. Certainly this was a function of Dylan's emotional state (consider for contrast the spring 1976 performances, when the artist's angers, fears, and desires seemed to pour out in every song), but the distanced professionalism of the shows was also dictated, as in 1974, by the size of the audience and the environment where the performances took place. 1978 was a stadium tour, one basketball arena after another. I was less than halfway back from the stage at the shows I saw, in the Oakland Coliseum, November 13 and 14, but even so I wished I had a pair of binoculars to help me see the man who was singing to me. The sensitivity of the new "Mr. Tambourine Man" was lost in that environment; I remember thinking, both nights, that it was weird, and theorizing that Dylan's tentativeness was because it was the start of the show and he was still warming up, trying to get loose. (My reaction also hints at the difficulty of what Dylan was doing—offering radically new and "unDylanish" arrangements of familiar songs to an audience that had very fixed ideas about how he and his songs should sound.) What was actually true, I think, was that it took *me* a while to warm up, both nights, to what the performer was doing. I did enjoy the shows, very much—and the songs that made the strongest impression on me at the time were all loud, uptempo numbers whose musical ideas were bold and clear and easy to grasp at a distance: "(You Treat Me Like a) Stepchild," "One More Cup of Coffee," "Masters of War," and "All Along the Watchtower." The quieter, more intimate performances were harder to focus in on.

Certainly Dylan's 1978 concerts were extremely well-paced. The "Shelter from the Storm" that follows "Mr. Tambourine Man" on the St. Louis tape is an easy return to a rocking, full band sound, and again it's an outstanding performance (though hardly an intimate one). The chorus—back-up vocalists singing "From the storm ... from the storm"—is charming, and offers some insight into what Dylan was up to when he added "the girls" (three black female back-up vocalists; the identity of the singers changed over the years, but the trio—occasionally a quartet—would be a standard feature of his live and recorded performances for the next nine years) to his band, his orchestra, his sound.

In effect, Dylan hears an echo, and here he sets out to express that echo in his music vocally as well as instrumentally, and to incorporate its subtleties and reverberations into the structure and arrangements of his songs. He's done this before (the "no more!" chorus added to "Maggie's Farm" at the Isle of Wight, Danko's and Stoner's echoing vocals at Carnegie Hall in 1968 and on certain Rolling Thunder songs); now he institutionalizes it, adding female voices to his basic performing unit, as he had added bass and drums and lead guitar in 1965.

"Shelter from the Storm" on *Blood on the Tracks* is a beautiful performance—and a very intimate one, relying on the closeness of the studio microphone (picking up subtleties of guitar playing as well as voice) and the passionate commitment of the singer to create a delicate framework of call and response around a tune that would otherwise be rather monotonous in terms of melodic and

verbal structure. Such a performance cannot be reliably transferred to the stage—even granted an intimate enough setting, the
song's success or failure in live performance would rest too directly
on the singer's ability to be totally inside it and to feel it as something fresh and new each time (his technical proficiency as a guitar
player would also be constantly on the line). This is not a realistic
expectation in terms of live performance, and has something to do
with why Dylan has not done solo acoustic concerts since 1965—the
format doesn't fit his identity as a performer, it calls for perfection-
ism and technical virtuosity and a kind of uninterrupted intimacy
or illusion of intimacy with the audience that he finds very drain-
ing—it takes away a certain freedom that is central to his ability to
express himself as a performing artist.

Adding "the girls" can be seen as an attempt (sometimes
successful, sometimes unsuccessful) to externalize something that
had always been present in his music as he heard it in his mind,
something that found other vehicles for expression when the back-
up singers weren't there but which he has now chosen to incorporate as an overt part of his compositions and performances. In
print (in *Lyrics*), "Shelter from the Storm" has no chorus. On *Blood
on the Tracks* it has a delightful, subtle chorus, a playful duet between guitar and bass, echoing and underscoring the melodic and
emotional issues raised in the verses (or pairs of verses). On stage
in 1978, Dylan used Steve Douglas's saxophone as the focal point of
a musical chorus in the spring and summer performances of the
song. I don't care for the execution of this, the performance as
opposed to the arrangement, on the *Budokan* album; and indeed all
year long this was the sort of song that singer and band could easily
fall asleep on, and they often did.

But at its best—June 5 in Los Angeles is a good example—the
spring/summer version of "Shelter from the Storm" is excellent
Dylan: biting, meaningful, unsettling, inspiring. The chorus, though,
is the weak point—it works well when guitar, sax, and the girls'
moaning voices work together as equals, but it still lacks punch as a
follow-up to Dylan's fierce vocalizing. The new fall arrangement,
with its verbalized chorus, transforms the whole structure of the
song—fierceness is lost, or is no longer the issue, but the song as a
song comes together as it never has before; this version is not as
beautiful as the one on *Blood on the Tracks* but it is far more per-
formable, to the point that one can imagine singers other than

Dylan doing it effectively. What was an internal power, relying entirely on the ability and willingness of the singer/guitar player to bare his heart at the moment of performance, has been successfully externalized. At its best (St. Louis), the result is a great ensemble performance, a joyous celebration of the storminess of life and the ways we deal with it.

The next song (#6, starting with the instrumental) is one of Dylan's "singer's choice" slots—two songs with similar arrangements and identical intros, so the singer can decide which song he'll do after the band has started playing. On the St. Louis tape, the song is "Love Minus Zero/No Limit"—a spirited performance, but I find the arrangement bland and superficial. This is not one of Dylan's more elastic songs; if it isn't approached with a certain tenderness it loses its charm. By contrast, "It's All Over Now, Baby Blue," the alternate song in this slot, is almost indestructible. On a good night (July 3, Paris, for example) the silly dit-dit arrangement is ennobled as the singer tears into the song, breathing a momentum into it that immediately catches up both band and listener. This is possible because there is an inherent dramatic structure in both the melody and the lyrics that is just made to be performed. Song, story, and tune build and build in every verse, with a release in the repeated title line that sets up the instrumental break, pulling together everything that's been said and rolling it like a snowball into the next verse. Compare the obligatory harmonica break in "Love Minus Zero" (St. Louis) with the impassioned harmonica of Paris's "Baby Blue." The latter is on fire, because the song, in this or any arrangement, has something to say; the former is a set piece.

Whichever song he sang in this slot at his 1978 shows, Dylan would perform it without his guitar (no object between him and his audience). I recently saw some audience footage of Dylan singing "Baby Blue" without guitar in Cleveland, October 20; it's very moving. And yet the gesture is a calculated one, somehow quite different from the courageous and purposeful theatricality of Dylan performing "Isis" sans guitar in 1975.

"Tangled Up in Blue" in 1978 (like "Girl from the North Country," which occupied this #7 slot in the spring and later started showing up in the second half of the concert) was performed as a torch song, a slow dramatic reading (stylized rather than vulnerable), accompanied only by keyboards and saxophone.

Another interesting experiment, often sleep-inducing in the case of "Girl from the North Country" but strangely effective for "Tangled Up in Blue."

This is Dylan as crooner, but not quite. He isn't trying to be something he's not; rather, he's exploring a new side of his voice, perhaps somewhat as he did on *Nashville Skyline* but this is limited to one or two songs per concert, and is more consciously experimental. "Girl from the North Country" doesn't work that well; it is occasionally *very* pretty, but most of the time it drowns in sentimentality, and the accompaniment sounds like bad cocktail music. "Tangled Up in Blue," on the other hand, is a real story, and Dylan leans into it, gets into the telling and the vocalizing. He sings to fill the room, to create something, to project this little movie before your eyes; the story is in the words, but the colors and textures and moods of the film are all in the sound of his voice. And what is fascinating is that the sound of his voice is different every night, on every tape! It isn't a mechanical difference, as in changing the words or the arrangement (although he does do that, in subtle ways—Clinton Heylin cites one performance where "his vocals taper upwards towards the end of each line"); it's a qualitative difference, like the difference in sunlight at various moments in the late afternoon.

The St. Louis performance of "Tangled Up in Blue" is excellent. My other favorite is from Los Angeles, June 2, the second time he performed this version in public. June 2 is chillingly emphatic in places, Dylan's voice strong and sharp and rich—not in nuance as on *Blood on the Tracks* but in texture. It's a dramatic reading, but the rising and falling is musical and rhythmic, not melodramatic. The story and song have a pulse in them and it seems to drive the performance. This is true each night, but the pulse is never quite the same, never calls forth the same expression. Dylan's voice on October 29 (St. Louis) has softer edges, individual lines and images do jump out but not as strongly; the force of the performance is spread more evenly, though in no way diminished. What comes across this time is the beauty of the musical situation. "Written in my soul ... from me to you ... tangled up in *blue*." The pulse and colors of the performance are oceanic and (once you open yourself to them) irresistible.

The next song is "Ballad of a Thin Man" and it's a quick trip from the sublime to the ridiculous if you're sitting close enough to watch Dylan vamping around the stage (again without his guitar), leaning back against his lead guitarist, pretending to be a 1970s rock and roll star in a most inauthentic and bizarre manner. What is he up to with these bits of business, and with his canned chatter that he hauls out on cue between certain songs? There may be a touch of weird humor or put-on here somewhere, but mostly I think these are just misguided manifestations of his dazed state. Road-weariness, perhaps cocaine-and-alcohol-weariness ... and a certain cynicism, a degree of life-weariness as well. Some of the performances—individual songs and entire shows—also reflect this weariness and this isolation from and mistrust of the world. "Ballad of a Thin Man," in fact, is often such a performance; he's done it too many times, he believes in it so much ("This is a song I wrote about fifteen years ago, but it's just like I wrote it the other day—for me, anyway") he doesn't realize he's lost sight of it, and is singing it on automatic pilot. The band follows him dutifully, according to instructions, and nothing much of interest results.

The six songs starting with "Ballad of a Thin Man" and continuing to the intermission may be joyous for members of the audience who've been waiting to see Dylan on stage singing exactly these songs ... but on tape, most of the time, they tend to drag. I love the bass-riff that dominates the 1978 arrangement of "Maggie's Farm"—but I can't find a performance of the song that really satisfies me. The riff is right but there's something missing, what could be a great heavy metal rave-up loses its energy and focus partway through and turns into aimless hard rock chug-chugging. (Of the shows I've heard, Seattle, November 10, comes closest to the 1978 "Maggie's Farm" I'd like to hear.) "Like a Rolling Stone" is given a very creditable performance most evenings; the arrangement, with the back-up singers joining in at the end of each line ("... used to it!"), is straightforward and effective. Clearly Dylan gave some thought to the placement of this one; it was the show-closer in 1966 and 1974, crowd-pleaser, national anthem, rousing climax; in 1975–76 he declared his own independence by eliminating it altogether. Here he reintroduces it, in effect, as just another song—number ten of thirteen tunes in the first part of the show. It's a good decision. And now and then the song really comes alive: Los Angeles, June 5, is a great example.

June 5 is also the source of a particularly wonderful "Going, Going, Gone." The new arrangement is more muscular and uni-

versal than the version on *Planet Waves*; on June 5 it's delightfully
sloppy, it twists in some refreshingly unexpected directions, and all
in all is very expressive of the performer's enthusiasm for his work.

"I Don't Believe You" and "I Shall Be Released" are quite
forgettable, most nights. Dylan's voice is at times very appealing on
the former (I like the lascivious way he stretches out the last word
of "her mouth was watery and wet"); the latter is the victim of a bad
arrangement. This is the sort of song Dylan holds in front of
himself like a wooden mask. The fact that he's singing the song is
the extent of the message, all he wishes to communicate.

The classical violin-based arrangement (introduced October
18) of "The Times They Are A-Changin'" that opens the second
part of the show is quite beautiful, a nice example of a new anthem
born from the ashes of an old one. This was followed by "It Ain't
Me Babe," a moving performance in context — suddenly the big
band steps aside and there's the old Bob Dylan, with his folk guitar
and harmonica, serenading us. His voice sounds sweet, but at St.
Louis and on the other tapes I've heard Dylan sings the song like
an object — here's my de facto acoustic number — rather than as an
opportunity for communication.

"Gates of Eden," on the other hand, as performed solo acoustic in Paris July 6, is stunning. I think a case could be made that it's
even better — more sensitive, more heartfelt, more evocative — than
the original album version. A definitive rendition of a great song.

Why? Why does he open his mouth on a particular night in
Paris and out comes a performance that sounds like he wrote the
song yesterday and it sums up everything he's ever felt about a
certain side of life and all he wants to do now is share it, sing it,
get it across? On seventy other nights he opens his mouth to sing
a solo acoustic song and what comes out is very pleasant but
nothing special — why? It's possible to make feeble guesses: that
this was only the second time he sang "Gates of Eden" in 1978
and the first time had caught him by surprise, got him really
excited about the song, hearing it a new way; or that something
about being in Paris, a non-English-speaking cultural center, fed
his ambitions and set him free of his resistance, both at once, and
he found himself reaching for greatness while letting go of his
self-consciousness, and this was the result. Or that there was
something stopping him from naked free expression in the solo
spot in 1978, and it just happened that this one night (and maybe

a few others, I haven't heard them all) that something got distracted and the performing artist was set free.

And an even tougher question: what is it I'm hearing? How do I know it's so good?

The truthful answer is, I feel it in my body. I play this performance, and then I play a dozen others, and I do it again, and each time when I play this one my skin tingles, and my heart fills with longing, and my hand reaches out to turn up the volume. This is not very scientific, but it seems to work. I believe most of you, listening to the same performance, would also immediately (and inexplicably) recognize its rare power and beauty.

The next song, that night in Paris, is only slightly less wonderful: a full band performance of "The Man in Me," a song I never cared for before, now rewritten and newly arranged and utterly delightful. We can list this right after October's "Mr. Tambourine Man" as best new songs of the year.

The hits keep coming—"One More Cup of Coffee," the brilliant conga drum & saxophone 1978 arrangement, performed masterfully on July 6 (and almost as well October 29 and November 13 and many many other nights; this was not one Dylan fell asleep on). It doesn't replace the *Desire* version but certainly deserves to be placed alongside it in the permanent archives.

Backing up for a moment, "The Man in Me" slot was filled in fall 1978 by "(You Treat Me Like a) Stepchild," an electric blues newly written by Dylan. The lyrics are simple (and a little surprising from a man who had a stepdaughter for eleven years), sometimes funny, sometimes disturbing ("I want to turn and walk all over you"); Dylan's blues vocal and the back-up singing and the combo sound achieved by keyboards, bass, drums and harmonica are terrific (Oakland, November 13, is recommended—and it's worth having more than one version of this one).

A gospel version of "Blowin' in the Wind" is a clever idea, and Dylan's arrangement, though a bit overblown, is not without merit. The problem is, he doesn't really believe in what he's saying, or if he does he doesn't succeed in convincing me. Some of the rearrangements in the course of the tour are quite intriguing—notably November 11 in Vancouver, a very different song from what he and the girls and Pasqua were doing a few weeks earlier. This one does convince me, at least a little bit. Parts of it are lovely.

"Blowin' in the Wind" and the two songs that follow it ("I Want You" and "Senor" in the summer, often "Girl from the North Country" and "Where Are You Tonight?" in the fall) make up another slow spot in the show most nights; but just when you think you might want to slip out early and avoid the traffic, Dylan and band let loose with a firecracker string of anthems, great showmanship and a lot of very good music too, starting with the 1978 remake (hard rock version) of "Masters of War."

Most of Dylan's topical "protest" songs of the early '60s dated quickly or else became so universal they lost their political edge. Bringing back "Masters of War," a song too bitterly true to go out of date and too outspoken to be made into any kind of pablum, was a good idea (and a courageous one, given the supposed "naivete" of the song's sentiments). Rearranging it into the hardest rocker of the night was inspired. Billy Cross is outstanding on lead guitar, and Dylan sings it like he means it. There are many memorable performances of this one, but for obvious reasons the keeper has to be from Nuremberg, July 1. Dylan tells the crowd, over the fierce rhythms of the song's opening chords, "It gives me great pleasure to sing [this song] in this place."

"Just Like a Woman," as performed in Los Angeles June 5, 1978, is a huge favorite of mine, a classic example of a song coming into existence not when it is written but at the moment when it is performed. There already was a song called "Just Like a Woman," and there already was a superb new arrangement of it, rehearsed by Dylan with this band and performed already at more than twenty-five concerts—the June 3 performance in Los Angeles is every bit as exquisite as this one, and so is October 29, St. Louis—but something is communicated in this particular performance as unique as the look on a lover's face at a particular never-to-be-repeated moment in your lives together.

It starts with the first chords, little descending loops, a bit of music unique to this arrangement, and a quality in the sound of these chords—and in the sound of Dylan's voice as he comes in with the word "Nobody"—unique to this performance of this arrangement. Listen enough, as I have, and the delicate melodic rhythms of these chords and the mood of the voice when it joins them will play in your mind, calling to you like a painting that demands to be seen again ... and you will find it no other place. Every moment of this performance has that kind of richness for me. If I'm to cite favorite instants, there's the instrumental fill after the words "... came in here" in the bridge, and the climax-and-transition contained in Dylan's vocalization of the word *"clear!"* (each of the other two exquisite variants I mentioned, June 3, October 29, handles this moment very differently from this one, and from each other), and the sax solo after the last verse, and the epiphanous eruption of the harmonica out of that sax solo, accompanied by scattered fragments of vocal phrases painted onto the swirling music by the back-up singers as if overdubbing live. This is what performing art is about. You just have to be fortunate enough to be there at the perfect moment, paying attention, in the right receptive mood. (Or, if you're lucky, maybe someone will have made a tape.)

The new arrangement of "Don't Think Twice" is very distinctive — it has been called "reggae," which is not quite right, but since there is no actual name for the rhythmic structure Dylan has created here it'll have to do. The emphatic cross-rhythms during the second half of each verse are astonishing. "I ain't saying/You treated me unkind" — these words become a whole new kind of poetry in their 1978 incarnation, Dylan and his organist and drummer and conga player and rhythm guitarist interpolating a dozen new stresses into the cracks of these ten syllables. At least they do in the excellent June 5 version; most other nights Dylan's performance on this one is sloppy.

"To Ramona," the alternate song in this slot, is well performed (notably June 3), and again the ability of Dylan's lyrics to sound perfectly at home after a radical shift in emphasis is impressive. But I find the lugubrious waltz-figure that dominates this arrangement oppressive, so much so that I can't enjoy the song.

"All Along the Watchtower," with David Mansfield's frenzied fiddling, is a dramatic high point of the evening, a real crowd-rouser. The June 3 and October 29 performances are especially manic, and highly recommended.

The brilliant uptempo honky-tonk version of "All I Really Want to Do" on June 5 offers us Dylan the entertainer at his most delightful, and demonstrates once again the plasticity and depth of so many of his songs, ready always to be bent and reshaped into fresh wonders. (The version on *Budokan* is similar but characterless, it's still in transition, unformed; the June 5 performance is a whole new song, new creation, new art, a breakthrough.)

Finally it's time for the introduction of the band. Already in the Far East Dylan was introducing Jo Ann Harris as his "childhood sweetheart"; later he seems to be challenging himself to say something untrue about every band member, a charming, bizarre exercise. This segues into the climax of the night, a satisfyingly explosive "It's Alright, Ma," followed by "Forever Young" as curtain-closer. Both performances tend to be overbearing on repeated listenings. Dylan comes back to do "Changing of the Guards" as an energetic but somehow perfunctory encore, and then it's time to pack everything up and drive all night to the next city and start over again.

It was a very long tour. At a 1979 San Diego show Dylan recalled an incident that happened in the same city a year earlier, November 17, 1978:

> Towards the end of the show, someone out in the crowd, they knew I wasn't feeling too well. I think they could see that. And they threw a silver cross on the stage. Usually I don't pick things up in front of the stage, but … I put it in my pocket. I brought it with me to the next town. I was feeling even worse than I'd felt when I was in San Diego. I said, well, I need something tonight. I didn't know what it was. I was used to all kinds of things. And I looked in my pocket and I had this cross.

On November 24, 1978, at a Fort Worth, Texas concert, Dylan could be seen wearing a large metal cross around his neck.

And in Houston, November 26, he made a lyric change in "Tangled Up in Blue"; the book of poems the woman shared with him was no longer the work of an Italian poet from the 13th century. Instead: "She opened up the Bible, and started quoting it to me/The Gospel according to Matthew, Verse 3, Chapter 33."

There is no such chapter, and the next night he changed it to Jeremiah, but the Bible stayed in the song right up through the last show of the tour, Hollywood, Florida, December 16, later immortalized in "Caribbean Wind" ("I was playing a show in Miami in the Theater of Divine Comedy").

A change was in the air.

VI. Disciple

December 1978 - October 1979

*"I truly had a born-again experience, if you want to call it that.
It's an overused term, but it's something that people can relate to.
It happened in 1978."*
—Bob Dylan, 1980

9.

Ishmael in Melville's *Moby Dick* says of a fellow sailor, "I looked with sympathetic awe and fearfulness upon the man, who in mid-winter just landed from a four years' dangerous voyage, could so unrestingly push off again for still another tempestuous term. The land seemed scorching to his feet."

Bob Dylan in mid-December 1978 had just completed a long period of intensive touring, 115 concerts in ten months, an exhausting schedule comparable only to the 1965–66 tour that climaxed in (or was interrupted by) his motorcycle accident. One might imagine a period of rest following such a massive tour – Dylan himself must have imagined or dreamed of it – but it was not to be. The need for rest was pushed aside by a greater need. The temptation is to call it a need for refuge, but life and human experience are too complex for such characterizations ever to be entirely accurate.

Dylan returned to California and almost immediately enrolled himself in the School of Discipleship at the Vineyard Fellowship, a Bible-study group and Christian church in Tarzana, not far from his home in Malibu. "At first I said, 'There's no way I can devote three months to this. I've got to be back on the road soon.'" (The classes, three and a half hours a day in a group situation with other students, four days a week, for three and a half months, were strikingly similar in outward form to the art classes Dylan had attended five years earlier, in New York, with Norman Raeben.)

And the course of study was not far advanced before Dylan found himself writing a new cycle of songs, found himself pushed once again (from within) to create, express, perform, record. He told Robert Hilburn in 1980 that he started writing the *Slow Train Coming* songs after about two months of Bible classes (although early versions of "Do Right to Me Baby" and "Slow Train" were performed at the end of the 1978 tour, apparently after his first "born again" experience but prior to his enrolling in the discipleship course). "I didn't even want to sing them. I was going to give them to Carolyn [Dennis] and have her sing them. I thought maybe I could produce her record."

In 1984 he repeated this story in a conversation with Bono Hewson of U2, who asked him, "I wondered had the songs you were writing ever frightened you in some way?"

"Oh yeah, I have written some songs that did that. The songs that I wrote for the *Slow Train* album did that. I wrote those songs — I didn't plan to write them, but I wrote them anyway. I didn't like writing them, I didn't want to write them, I didn't figure ... I just didn't want to write those songs at that period of time. But I found myself writing these songs, and after I had a certain amount of them, I thought I didn't want to sing them, so I had a girl sing them for me at the time, Carolyn Dennis, a great singer ... I wanted the songs out, but *I* didn't want to do it because I knew it wouldn't be perceived in that way. It would just mean more pressure. I just did not want that at the time."

But by March he had contacted Jerry Wexler, a New York producer famous for his work with Ray Charles, Aretha Franklin, Wilson Pickett and other great "soul" performers, and asked him to book recording sessions for a Bob Dylan album. Wexler brought in keyboardist and coproducer Barry Beckett, bass player Tim Drummond, and two musicians from the new British band Dire Straits, guitarist Mark Knopfler and drummer Pick Withers. Dylan brought along three back-up singers, Carolyn Dennis, Helena Springs, and Regina Havis, and with the help of the Muscle Shoals Horns they recorded *Slow Train Coming* in a series of sessions at the legendary

Muscle Shoals Sound Studio (in Alabama, not far from Memphis), between May 1 and May 11, 1979.

If I could keep only one performance from the *Slow Train Coming* album (strange games we play!), it would have to be the title song, "Slow Train," much as I love to listen to "Precious Angel," much as I am in awe of Dylan's vocal performance on all of "When He Returns" and pieces of "I Believe in You." But "Slow Train" is *it*, the white-hot core of the album, the one track that can and must be listened to again and again and again, inexhaustible, essential. (This finally is my simple home test for greatness in recorded performances: listen to the individual track over and over and over, and on a good night a good performance will only get better, unfolding more and more, ultimately revealing universes never visited before, no matter how many times one has listened to the same performance in the past. Real truth, real spirit, real beauty loves repetition.)

What is it about "Slow Train"? Clearly, it's the sound: the sound of the band (lead guitar, bass, drums, keyboards), together with the sound of Dylan's voice as it responds to and works with the groove the band's creating. This is not just some clever confection for the ears. The way the performance sounds is the essential quality of this work of art (just as it is for the studio recordings of "Like a Rolling Stone" and "Knockin' on Heaven's Door"), the location of its message, its power, its genius. Its truth.

What we need to remember about sound is that just as much as lyrics, melody, and rhythm, it is a form of expression. It is a vehicle for taking what's inside and putting it outside, where others can touch it.

The sound of "Slow Train," the overall texture of voice and instruments as they touch, collide with, our ears, communicates to us the truth about Bob Dylan at this moment in his life, and also the truth (or a good chunk of it) about ourselves as we listen. This is far beyond anything the lyrics of the song accomplish (though the chorus phrase is perfect); rather the lyrics, dumb as they are at times, are ennobled and given meaning by the power and intelligence of the band's music and the singer's performance.

There is a tendency to think of *Slow Train Coming* as well-produced. It is, certainly: a brilliant technical and musical realization of each song's possibilities, with an overall sound that is cleaner and brighter and more friendly to the ears of the novice listener than nine out of ten Bob Dylan albums. The contrast with *Street-Legal* is startling, and the superficial reason for this, the difference between an album self-produced in a rehearsal studio and an album professionally produced in a first-rate facility, is obvious and accurate. But we must be careful not to overlook the fact that the circumstances in each case are a reflection of the artist's will (conscious and unconscious).

If *Slow Train Coming* sounds so good because Jerry Wexler and Barry Beckett are great producers, why is the overall sound and the quality of the performances on *Saved*, recorded nine months later by the same producers in the same studio, so disappointing (a lot muddier than *Street-Legal*, in fact)? There are some plausible answers to this question, the simplest of which is to say that for whatever reason Dylan wasn't really dedicated to making a first-rate album at that particular moment. Which is the point: the primary variable is not the ability or pedigree of the producers or the musicians or the quality of the recording studio. The primary variable is the intention of the artist. *Slow Train Coming* sounds the way it does because that's what Dylan wanted. What's noteworthy is that we can tell from the way the album sounds that he wanted it with the sort of hunger and sense of purpose that resulted in the "sound" of *Bringing It All Back Home* and *Blonde on Blonde* and *Blood on the Tracks*. The producers played their part, as did the musicians, and they did a superb job. But what you hear is, finally, and for better or worse, the expression of one person's will, one person's intention, one person's state of mind at a particular (never to be repeated) moment in his personal and artistic life.

And "Slow Train" is the performance that most closely captures and shares that state of mind. We know this not by what it says. We know this by how it feels.

It feels as though Bob Dylan, the voice of a generation, voice crying in the wilderness, Old Testament prophet reborn in a changing time, has, for one brief shining instant anyway, totally regained control of his vision, his role, his sense of purpose and public identity. We can feel the cool power and trembling excitement that courses through him as he inhales the breath of this moment. The fact that his vision is tainted and his renewed sense of destiny illusory is unsettling, to say the least; but it doesn't necessarily diminish his personal artistic accomplishment here.

Like many of Dylan's finest creations, this is a song of unexpected and overwhelming release, a fierce bright penetrating howl of joy.

His vision is tainted not because he likes Jesus (that subject doesn't come up in this song), nor because he smells apocalypse around the corner (he puts it over so powerfully I start smelling it too, and that makes for good art, good rock and roll). No, the problem with his vision is that he sees through the eyes and speaks with the voice of racial prejudice and righteous nationalism. This is overt when he speaks of "sheiks walking around like kings, wearing fancy jewels and nose rings" (anti-semitism, by God!) and "foreign oil controlling American soil," but a general mean-spiritedness breaks through in other verses too, sometimes in subtle ways, as when he sneers about the absence of "brotherly love" instead of, say, lamenting it.

As for the joy, it's not in the words as such (after all he starts right off by telling us he feels disgusted) – rather it's a sort of overlay, something that comes through as he unburdens himself, perhaps a joy at finally being able to see and say these things, liberation through denunciation – in any case, it's my view that the band becomes the vehicle for expression of a feeling that transcends and indeed transforms disgust, you can hear it in the guitar burst that opens the song, you can hear it in Dylan's phrasing throughout, particularly the care he takes in the first verse and the extraordinary way his voice drops an octave as he moves into the chorus, you can hear it when the female voices first come in (end of the second verse), you can hear it in the great instrumental passage that takes us out of the song, most of all you can hear it after the fifth verse, brief incredible keyboard orgasm (just before "People starving and thirsting/Grain elevators are bursting" – dumb lyrics notwithstanding there are also some couplets here that just absolutely spit genius). That keyboard moment pulls together the entire performance, striking a note that is unmistakably from the heart of the singer (even though it's Barry Beckett's fingers pressing the keys), showering spirit down in all directions.

"Slow Train" closes the first side of the album. "When He Returns," the song that closes side two, is, regardless of what I said before, just as magnificent and every bit as essential, though hardly characteristic of the album as a whole. Originally Dylan didn't want to sing on this record; then, once he gave in and started recording it, he still had thoughts of not singing on this particular song. He was going to have the background singers perform it without him, and he recorded a demo vocal for the women to use while rehearsing, with Barry Beckett accompanying him on piano. Then, according to Jerry Wexler via Jann Wenner, "Dylan abandoned his original notion and, after practicing overnight, redid his vocal to fit the demo's spontaneous piano track."

The performance is astonishing, shattering, in its emotional power and nakedness. The other songs on the album (with the partial exception of "I Believe in You") tend to be sung from a place of certainty, even smugness at times, praising the righteous and challenging or condemning skeptics and doubters—but "When He Returns" is performed from a place of great vulnerability, and (as a result) its sincerity is unmistakable. The power of what Dylan has gone through truly comes across here, and it is frightening in its intensity, disturbing and confrontive in its undeniable authenticity. Something has happened to this man.

The words of the song, by themselves, don't tell us what happened. But his voice does. It tells us that this man has been terrified; and it suggests that he has welcomed this terror, rejoiced at it, because it has brought relief from all his fear and anticipation of it. It tells us that he has, in some fashion, surrendered, taken off his mask. It also tells us that he is aware that he will need to do so again and again. His struggle and terror will continue. And hating his own pride as he does, he is eager for the battle. Because now he has a Helper, a Guide, a Master, a sense of purpose in his life again.

What comes through most strongly for me in this performance is a landscape, a wilderness, blood-stained ground, all those beautiful piano chords spread around like so many broken crystals and Dylan standing in the middle of them, under a huge gray sky. There is a classic bit of Dylan timelessness in the lyrics, subtle but (I think) central to the impact of the song: "He unleashed His power at an unknown hour that no one knew" (reference Matthew 24:36, 24:42) is in the past tense, though it unquestionably describes the same event the title and chorus of the song refer to. The event is still in the future, yet Dylan is standing and singing from the midst of it, as though it has already happened. This, he seems to be saying, is the reality we falsify and deny, that the apocalypse has already occurred, and we are wandering in the rubble pretending otherwise. How long can we so pretend?

Slow Train Coming finds Dylan and his audience both confused about who they are to each other. Long-time listeners who are not evangelical Christians can't help but ask themselves, "Is he trying to convert me? Is he calling me a fool? Is he sharing his feelings with me, or mocking me? Am I one of the 'so-called friends' he talks about? Is he asking me to identify with what he's going through, or is he waving goodbye?" Dylan for his part seems to have made a supreme (and very successful) effort to make an album that sounds good, that will appeal to a large audience, that leads off with a hit single, that puts him forward as a mature musical artist and popular performer (all things he reached for but failed to achieve with *Street-Legal*).

But who is the album directed toward? Dylan in his early years delighted in singing to an audience of his own creation, a strongly-felt "us" always ready to challenge or make fun of or "put on" somebody—the establishment, our parents, the ruling generation—who perhaps weren't always aware that they had become "them." "Something is happening but you don't know what it is, do you, Mr. Jones?" Playing to an ever-changing and growing audience that he helped define with his presence and his songs, he greatly enjoyed ringing changes on the "us-and-them" game, including tough street-kid challenges to his audience to keep up with him (think I'm protest? think I'm folk? think I'm rock and roll? look again!). Then in the 1970s it all seemed to freeze into position; Dylan's innovations were received with enthusiasm (Rolling Thunder), hostility (*Renaldo & Clara*), or mixed reactions (the entertainer tour), but nothing ever picked up a momentum big enough to affect the audience's sense of "who we are" or to make a dent in the frozen myth of Bob Dylan the 1960s protest folk guitar "Like a Rolling Stone" famous has-been.

Turning Christian—radical, fire-breathing, "Who's not for Me is against Me" Christian—*that*'ll wake them up! That will force people to stop straddling the fence, to make some choices in their mushy lives, to either hate my guts or take a look at what fools they've become! Won't it?

The new convert is a passionate proselytizer. He's usually a little shy at the same time, since he is frequently reminded (by his teachers and seniors) of how little he knows and how green he is. *Slow Train Coming* is a glorious explosion of newly discovered positions, attitudes, insights, language, beliefs, historical and literary images (all from the Bible of course), a kitchen sink of confessions, harangues, assaults and seductions, powerfully attractive in its rediscovery of passion and of all the ways that melody and rhythm and phrasing and timing and vocal texture can be used when one really has something to say ... and irritating in its understandable ambivalence about how much the singer actually wants to say and who he wants to say it to.

Perhaps the most consistently recurring theme on the album is the singer's defensiveness towards his "friends." The hostility is overt (and the friends are very much third person) on "Precious Angel": "My so-called friends have fallen under a spell/They look me squarely in the eye and they say, 'All is well.'/Can they imagine the darkness that will fall from on high/When men will beg God to kill them and they won't be able to die?" This can be read as simple scriptural musings, but there's a vengeful side of it that comes through quite clearly in the performance. In "Slow Train" the friends are also third person (meaning he's not singing to them; they may be eavesdropping, but he's talking to someone else). "Can't help but wonder what's happening to my companions ... have they counted the cost it'll take to bring down/All their earthly principles they're gonna have to abandon?" This is milder, but still strongly edged with superiority: they're going to have to go through big humiliation, if they're lucky enough to wake up at all, and when they do they'll still be way behind me 'cause I've done it already.

In other songs these "friends" are outright enemies ("They'd like to drive me from this town ... They say don't come back no more ... Cause I don't be like they'd like me to") ("How long can I listen to the lies of prejudice?") ("Gonna ... stop being influenced by fools").

This is, on the one hand, the Dylan we've always known: "Like a Rolling Stone" and "Positively 4th Street" and "It's All Over Now, Baby Blue" are also addressed to friends or former friends or so-called friends, and God knows those songs are at least as vicious as anything on *Slow Train Coming*.

But there's something different too. On those songs he sings directly to or at his "friends." He gives them his full attention. On this album, even when he sings to the woman he loves ("Precious Angel") he's not very personal, he lectures, he complains about his so-called friends, he gives what sounds like a bitter aside aimed at his ex-wife, as though it's her fault that he didn't learn about Jesus

Probably recording session for *Blood on the Tracks*, New York, September 1974.
(This photo coutesy of Stephen M. H. Braitman, Amorous Archives, San Francisco)

Robbie Robertson, Garth Hudson, and Bob Dylan at The Last Waltz, San Francisco, November 1976. *(This photo courtesy of Stephen M. H. Braitman, Amorous Archives, San Francisco)*

In performance, 1978.
(This photo courtesy of Stephen M. H. Braitman, Amorous Archives, San Francisco)

Spring 1980. (© 1980 by Susan Wallach Fino)

Dylan and Roger McGuinn, Warfield Theater, San Francisco, November 22, 1980.
(© 1992 by Nancy Cleveland)

Regina Havis and Bob Dylan, *"Mary on the Wild Moor"*, San Francisco, November 1980. (© *1992 by Nancy Cleveland*)

Warfield Theater, November 1980. *(© 1992 by Nancy Cleveland)*

Warfield Theater, November 1980. (© 1992 by Nancy Cleveland)

Spring 1980. *(© 1980 by Susan Wallach Fino)*

In performance, 1981. *(© 1980 by Susan Wallach Fino)*

Slane Castle, Ireland, July 8, 1984. *(© 1984 by John Hume)*

Between songs. (© 1984 by John Hume)

a lot sooner—and then in the chorus he shifts and seems to be singing directly to his Lord (and the weakness of what is, in many ways, a very moving performance, is that this "Shine your light on me" chorus is beautiful but a little too cleverly contrived, it feels staged, built to communicate to us the watchers rather than you the person being sung to).

The most powerful performances are the soliloquies, "Slow Train" and "When He Returns." The songs that are addressed to "you" don't have the same punch. This is not a flaw—just an interesting shift. One can speculate that at this particular moment there is no "you" Dylan wants to sing to other than his Lord—and that he's still a little shy about addressing Him directly. We can hear this in the alternately wimpy and spine-tingling vocal-and-guitar performance on "I Believe in You," a song which comes and goes in intensity and effectiveness precisely because it shifts back and forth between being addressed to an apparently easily manipulated stage audience ("I walk out on my own/A thousand miles from home") ("I don't mind the pain/Don't mind the driving rain") and being addressed to a heartfelt, personal God (the magnificent "Don't—let me drift too far"). Dylan has a point he wants to get across, and it's not God he wants to get it across to. But in order to do it he shares a little of his actual conversation with his Saviour, and the rest of the song seems thin gruel by comparison.

On "Slow Train" and "When He Returns" the confusion about who Dylan is speaking to is resolved: both performances have the form of Shakespearean soliloquies, the actor alone on one part of the stage, addressing himself or the heavens, explicitly aware that he is after all an actor and that he and the playwright are taking this opportunity to let the audience hear the character's private thoughts. In "When He Returns" the ambiguous, careful use of the word "you" to include the listener precisely to the extent that he or she is willing to be included, brings the album as a whole to a subtle and very wonderful resolution.

Who is he speaking to? The album starts with the rhetorical "you" of "Gotta Serve Somebody," a brilliantly crafted bit of songwriting and recording, exquisitely sung, this one is a confection and a great one, with a sting in its tail. Everything about it is perfectly conceived and executed to serve one purpose: to be the opener (Dylan went on to use it as the first song of almost every concert he gave from 1979 through the end of 1981), the transition from over there (old Dylan audience or curious bystander) to here ("behold I make all things new, sayeth the Lord"), the shill, the come-on, the challenge, the seduction. "You may be an ambassador to England or France" — the message of the song is immediately evident, who you are or who you think you are doesn't matter, every "you" a set-up for the "but" of the chorus ... and yet I'm not am ambassador, so I don't feel directly assaulted, it's an entertainment and an attractive one, I'm pulled in, I listen. And then the sting in the tail, that rhetorical "you're gonna have to serve somebody" sounding more like the "you" he's speaking to is me every time I hear it. But why does he give me the choice — oh I see — he's really saying I'm *already* serving somebody, and so if it isn't the Lord it must be — Well fuck you, Bob Dylan. But he never quite says it directly, does he, never directly rubs my face in it, the title of the song is "Gotta Serve Somebody" but he never actually says "gotta" anywhere in the song —

So it's "you" meaning me, the listener, only if and when I decide to take it personally. Very tricky.

In "Precious Angel," as we've seen, "you" is sometimes his girlfriend, sometimes Jesus, but never the listener, though the listener seems to be the only one of the three he's really thinking about most of the time. In "I Believe in You" "you" is always the Lord, though the singer's only addressing Him when he speaks in the second person (most of the song's in first or third).

In "Slow Train" "you" shows up a few times, but it's a figure of speech, not a direct involvement of the listener. Singer speaks for the listener's behalf, constantly conscious of his presence, but not directly to him. In "Gonna Change My Way of Thinking" there's a nasty "you" ("You forget all about the golden rule" "Just so you know where He's coming from") who finally gets the supreme insult of being addressed as "mister." As on the first song on the first side, the listener is given a heavily manipulated choice: do you wanna be this "you" asshole I'm singing to, or will you identify with the "I" of the song and change your way of thinking too? (Great sound, though, isn't it?)

In "Do Right to Me Baby" "you" is a woman, and perhaps by extension could refer to his relationship with his audience as well. In any case it's a very stupid song — a conditional golden rule, as though it were a deal made by lawyers — real pretty to listen to as long as you don't think about it. In "When You Gonna Wake Up" "you" is America, although in this case we listeners naturally hear it or feel it as being addressed to us personally as well. "Man Gave Names to All the Animals" offers a welcome break: no you, no me.

And finally, in "When He Returns," for the very first time "you" slips in as an actual friend who's actually being spoken to directly and lovingly, in the fifth line: "Don't you cry and don't you die and don't you burn." This sets up the appropriate ambiguity in the third verse, when "how long can I?" from the second verse becomes, rhetorically, "how long can you?" and you can take it as addressed to you the listener directly if and only if you're ready and willing (and in no other performance here is Dylan such an attractive figure, someone one really does want to identify with and project onto). Working backwards, if we take it personally, "He sees your deeds" is actually comforting (listen to his voice) and "Surrender your crown" becomes a terrifying, heroic challenge. From the charming condescension of the opening track we've progressed to a point where charm is stripped away and we may, if we wish, identify with and share in the naked truth of what this man is feeling. At our own risk.

A very well-constructed album.

One outtake is available from these sessions; it's called "Trouble in Mind," and was released as the B-side of the single of "Gotta Serve Somebody."* It's a straightforward blues, very simple musically, and an outstanding performance by both singer and instrumentalists. The words of the song describe, far more directly and in more detail than any of the songs on the album, the personal factors that led Dylan to open himself to accepting Jesus and, more exactingly, the discipline of the Vineyard Fellowship.

The first verse speaks of the singer's fear of death (also referred to in "Slow Train"), and links it with his compulsive womanizing (the link is the need for self-discipline: "I got to know, Lord, when to pull back on the reins"). The common element throughout the song is mental anguish, as described in the chorus: "Trouble in mind, Lord, trouble in mind/Lord, take away this trouble in mind." The mental anguish in womanizing ("Satan whispers ... 'When you get tired of that Miss So-and-so I got another woman for ya'") is that the easy availability of new lovers makes a person a coward, keeps him or her from the risks and rewards of a deeper, more committed partnership.

---

*Another outtake, "Ye Shall Be Changed," can be heard on *The Bootleg Series*.

The second verse has to do with feelings of worthlessness, dissatisfaction with work and self—"When the deeds that you do don't add up to zero ... You think you can hide but you're never alone"—and the anguish of self-criticism. The third verse addresses the prison of vanity, and sounds to me like Dylan describing his 1978 tour: "Satan's ... gonna make you a law unto yourself, build a bird's nest in your hair/He's gonna deaden your conscience 'til you worship the work of your own hands/You'll be serving strangers in a strange and forsaken land."

He goes on to talk about adultery, excuse-making, dishonesty, and guilt ("you're all the time defending what you can never justify") and, in the last verse, pride and materialism. The last verse also states that people's pride ("they still want to be the boss") is what keeps them from surrendering to the Lord and His discipline, which is, presumably, the cure for "trouble in mind." All of this material is very private, and we can see why Dylan was reluctant to include it on the album (as he was reluctant to sing "When He Returns"). But it's also clear that since these private issues are the crux of the matter, if you're unwilling to talk about them you're not going to have much success at getting people to open themselves to the radical solution you've found.

Slow Train Coming was released in August 1979, and became one of Dylan's most successful albums. "Gotta Serve Somebody" got to #24 on the charts, Dylan's last top 40 single (as of 1990). In October Dylan put together a new band—including three people who performed on *Slow Train Coming*, Tim Drummond on bass and Regina Havis and Helena Springs on background vocals, plus Mona Lisa Young on background vocals, Fred Tackett on guitar, Jim Keltner on drums, and Spooner Oldham and Terry Young on keyboards. They began rehearsing for a new tour, including in their repertoire eight new songs that Dylan had written since the *Slow Train Coming* sessions.

On October 20 Dylan and his band performed on the U.S. television program "Saturday Night Live," offering solid, unremarkable performances of "Gotta Serve Somebody" (Dylan sings "you may call me Jimmy" rather than "Zimmy"), "I Believe in You," and "When You Gonna Wake Up." And in San Francisco tickets went on sale for two weeks of Dylan shows at a 2200-seat former movie theater called the Warfield, his first concerts as a newly awakened Christian.

VII. Evangelist

November 1979 - November 1981

*"I'm really not the right person
to tramp around the country saving souls."*
—Bob Dylan, 1966

10.

The importance of identifying Bob Dylan as a performing artist, as distinct from the popular perception that he's a songwriter and recording artist, is immediately clear when one has a chance to hear his fall 1979 concerts. "What Can I Do for You?," "Solid Rock," "Saving Grace," "Covenant Woman" and "In the Garden" as performed at these shows are some of the finest works in Dylan's oeuvre, but you'd never know that from listening to *Saved*, the 1980 studio album that features these compositions. The *Saved* performances are technically adequate, but they fail to put across the essential character of any of these songs, which I suppose tells us that that essence is not automatically present in the words and music of a song; it is possible (and in this case it happened) that these elements can be in place and yet whatever it is that makes the song meaningful can still be missing.

Which is to say, your awareness and appreciation of Dylan's greatness is incomplete until you hear these songs (and "When He Returns") as performed live in the fall of 1979, in San Francisco (fourteen shows November 1–16) and in southern California, Arizona, and New Mexico (twelve shows between November 18 and December 9).

The first thing that distinguishes these early "gospel" or "born again" shows is that Dylan performed only songs he had written in the last twelve months, that is to say the songs from the *Slow Train Coming* album plus eight newer songs (one of these, "Blessed Is the Name of the Lord Forever," is identified by Clinton Heylin as a traditional gospel song). "All old things are passed away," Dylan told the audience at one of the San Francisco shows, in response to requests for "Lay Lady Lay" and "Like a Rolling Stone." Even in 1965-66 fans got half a concert of acoustic Dylan before being confronted with his new persona of rock and roller. But in 1979 Dylan is uncompromising: new songs (i.e., Christian songs) only. No exceptions.

The second immediately striking aspect of these shows is the size of the theaters. In 1978 Dylan was playing in sports arenas, with 14,000 or 15,000 seats, and selling out most of his concerts. A year later he's playing 2000- or 3000-seat theaters. Embracing Jesus and refusing to play greatest hits has required some sacrifice on his part (more than expected – originally the Warfield shows were meant as a warm-up for a tour of larger venues, which had to be scaled down; even in the smaller theaters, some shows were canceled because ticket sales were poor). But artistically, in terms of the sound quality of the performance and the level of interaction between performer and audience, the small theaters are a tremendous leap forward. Clearly the Dylan we hear on the fall 1979 tapes is delighted to be a performing musician again after almost a year's break, and clearly he's very excited about his new music and the good news he wants to share. But it seems fair to assume that another factor in his evident joy is the opportunity to perform with a hot band in a human-size setting. The intimacy in his new music and the intimacy of the environments he finds himself working in reinforce each other very nicely.

The third thing we notice right away is that this is not the same person who recorded *Slow Train Coming*. Bob Dylan has transformed himself again. He's still singing about God (still singing the same songs, in fact), but every note he sings tells us that his God of vengeful righteousness has also turned out to be a God of restoration and love.

The first show, November 1, 1979, proved to be an exact model for the concerts that followed (the sequence and choice of songs were almost unchanged from night to night). The lights went down and a black woman walked on stage. "Regina McCrary [Havis] played with me for a while," Dylan recalls in the *Biograph* notes. "She's the daughter of Preacher Sam McCrary from Nashville who used to have the old gospel group the Fairfield Four. She would open these shows with a monologue about a woman on a train, she was so incredibly moving. I wanted to expose people to that sort of thing because I loved it and it's the real roots of all modern music..." Regina's performance is indeed riveting and sets a tone of intimacy and (as she transitions into the first song) excitement and spirited joyousness that is sustained throughout the evening. She and Mona Lisa Young and Helena Springs, with Terry Young backing them on piano, sing six glorious gospel numbers, "Let Me Ride," "The Rainbow Sign," "Do Lord, Remember Me," "Look Up and Live by Faith," "Oh Freedom," and "This Train." I attended eight of the San Francisco shows and this opening set was more of a delight each time I heard it; on that great day when a recording of one of these concerts is made available to the public (I recommend November 6, 8, or 16, but almost all of them are very good), the women's gospel set should definitely be included.

Lights down again at the end of "This Train"; when they came up a moment later the full band and Dylan had taken the stage and started right into "Gotta Serve Somebody," Dylan in a black leather jacket over a white t-shirt, the three women remaining on stage to sing back-up harmonies on almost every song. He followed with "I Believe in You," "When You Gonna Wake Up," "When He Returns" (no band, just Dylan on electric guitar and Spooner Oldham on grand piano), "Man Gave Names to All the Animals," "Precious Angel," "Slow Train," and then the first new song of the evening, "Covenant Woman."

Dylan introduced Regina Havis, who sang "Put Your Hand in the Hand" backed by the band, while Dylan took a cigarette break (other nights it would be Mona Lisa Young singing "Ordinary People" or Helena Springs singing "What Are You Doing with Your Heart?"). Without an intermission, Dylan returned to sing the two remaining *Slow Train Coming* songs, "Change My Way of Thinking" and "Do Right to Me Baby," and then launched into a string of new songs: "Solid Rock," "Saving Grace" (Dylan played lead electric guitar between verses of this one, drawing cheers from the crowd), "What Can I Do for You?" (featuring extended harmonica solos), "Saved," and, climax of the set, "In the Garden." He and the band came back and played "Blessed Is the Name of the Lord Forever" as an encore (he introduced the musicians before the song), and then, after much applause (very few people jeered or walked out, despite the reports in the newspapers), a second encore, "Pressing On," Dylan playing piano on the first verse, then walking to the front of the stage and clapping his hands, singing the second verse and chorus into a microphone with no guitar between him and the audience.

The show lasted two hours. The same script was followed for the next 25 concerts, except for a couple of nights in Arizona when one or both encores were omitted, a night in San Francisco when "Precious Angel" was omitted, and the last night in San Francisco when Dylan sang an extra song after "Covenant Woman" – "Ain't No Man Righteous, No Not One," originally recorded at the *Slow Train Coming* sessions but not included on the album.

Of the seventeen songs Dylan sings, there isn't one that isn't a rewarding performance (on a good night, and most of the nights at these November and December shows were good nights). Minor songs like "Do Right to Me Baby" and "Man Gave Names to All the Animals" become genuinely endearing (the latter is also a lot of fun, notably on November 16, when Dylan clowns around with the lyrics – "wasn't too big, think I'll call it a ... giraffe!" – and evidently clowns around on stage, maybe doing a little dance, judging from the audience's delighted response). Songs like "When You Gonna Wake Up" and "Change My Way of Thinking" that sound great musically on the album but make me uncomfortable with their lyrical belligerence, are transformed by Dylan's apparent shift in attitude (whether this is a function of the months that have gone by or, just as likely, the way it feels to be performing to a live audience instead of a dimly imagined one) into songs that, for this listener anyway, are much more available. I can identify with them now (the words haven't changed, but the emphasis certainly has), I find myself moved by them without misgivings, I like the spirit that's coming through. "When You Gonna Wake Up" can be a low-key rocker, earnest and friendly; it can also be, particularly in shows from the second week onward, keen and demanding and fiery. Both readings (and they have more in common than my description suggests) are splendid; in concert the song has an integrity and warmth that assures me that it is about what I want it to be about, which is the need for awakening. "Strengthen the things that remain"—yes, the real values. And let go of everything else.

"I Believe in You" is sincere and effective. "Precious Angel" and "Slow Train" make a fine crescendo, it sounds so good to hear them, they lend themselves to live performance, this is a mini-climax each night, and each night it turns out to be a set-up for the real climax of the first set, the new song, "Covenant Woman." There's a particularly sweet "Precious Angel" November 6, an especially invigorating "Slow Train" November 16 (with a fine rap preceding it—but I also like the quick phrase he throws in as introduction November 6: "from a hard rain to a slow train...").

But the most memorable performance from among the *Slow Train Coming* songs is, almost every night, "When He Returns." The performance on the album, vocal and instrumental, can't be recreated, so Dylan doesn't try—instead he and the piano player go off in another direction, gentler, more restrained, but equally electrifying. What a mood this song sets! And how much it has to say to its listener, once listener and pianist and singer are sharing the same mood. The live version manages to go beyond the gloriously dramatic, self-conscious vulnerability of the album track into a shared vulnerability, a welcoming (with no softening of the song's fiercely honest language), a fellowship. What results is a performance worthy of a great singer and a master creator—Dylan at his most naked and his most inspired, quite a combination. Just to hear him sing "wilderness" (long drawn-out vowel in the last syllable) makes the whole evening worthwhile, and speaks volumes about his view of the contemporary world and how it feels to live here.

And there's a lot more to come. "Covenant Woman" is extraordinarily affecting. Dylan's greatness as a songwriter is often associated in people's minds with tour de force extravaganzas like "Mr. Tambourine Man" and "Hard Rain" and "Desolation Row," with the result that he has become a sort of symbol of the modern poet as a person with a gift for fancy (and penetrating, timely, accurate) language. That's fine, but Dylan himself would be the first to say that what distinguishes most great songwriters is their gift for simplicity (he says this when he chooses the songs other than his own that he likes to sing).

True simplicity is awesome. Consider the lyrics of "Knockin' on Heaven's Door" or "Lay Lady Lay" or "Oh Sister," and the easy, graceful way these lyrics work with their respective melodies, song structures, vocal and instrumental settings. "Covenant Woman" has a lot in common with "Oh Sister," except that in "Covenant Woman" Dylan sings as though he's already found the lady he seems to be looking for in the earlier song: a woman who will make him feel at home in this great mysterious world, a woman who will make him feel at times that she is the friend he's dreamed of being with since childhood, and at other times that he and she are together in that Friend's presence.

The love in the song is overwhelming (I'm listening to the November 6 performance from San Francisco). Dylan this time has no difficulty communicating love for a woman and love for God in the same song, perhaps because this time he *is* singing directly to the woman, giving her his full attention; even when he takes a verse to tell the past, present and future of his relationship with life and the Lord, she's the one who's brought forth this confession, and he rewards her patient attention by ending the verse with a marvelous (and simple) (and very sweet) uniting of his two themes: "He must have loved me oh so much to send me someone as fine as you."

The song is in fact full of great lines, some of them clichés given dignity and emotional power by their musical settings and the way Dylan delivers them ("you know that we are strangers in a land we're passing through") and others startlingly fresh ("who sees the invisible things of Him that are hidden from the world"). "I've been broken, shattered like an empty cup" is striking in the power of its imagery, in the effectiveness of its meter and the wonderful phrasing that that meter and the rising melody lend themselves to, and in its placement within the song, opening a new verse amidst the emotional reverberations of the vocal and musical climaxes the last chorus just built to. The interplay between organ, piano, voice, and rhythm section during this eight-word phrase is extraordinary, as it is throughout the performance.

I don't know how simple a piece of music is that relies on two interwoven keyboard parts (with a vital additional percussion role for the drums-and-bass), but I know it *sounds* simple, as though the music were picked out on the piano by a student whose hands have just found a delightful and playable progression, something he can pour his half-formed rhythmic and melodic longings into. Dylan's success at getting this very basic sound from the back of his mind out to where we can hear it sitting in the audience, is again the result of his gift for music, gift for words, gift for song-creating, gift for performance. Awesome simplicity. He opens his mouth, the band plays, and suddenly our hearts are feeling what's in his heart.

Great singing at these shows.

"Solid Rock," more precisely "Hanging On to a Solid Rock Made before the Foundation of the World" as Dylan introduced it at these concerts, is a tremendous crowd-pleaser — so much so that in 1979, fresh from being part of that crowd, I wrote that the song "is sure to become one of his all-time classics." This didn't happen, partly because of what Dylan in the *Biograph* notes calls "religious backlash" (the old fans didn't want to hear this message, and the anticipated new fans never really got on board), but also I think because Dylan failed to capture the song on record. Even in live performance the song deteriorated subtly as the weeks went by, eventually losing its core of incredible power and becoming just an up-tempo noisemaker.

This points to an aspect of performing art that I find rather mysterious: the fragility of some great songs, the ease with which their seemingly indestructible power can be lost forever if they're not captured (i.e. recorded) at the right moment. "Subterranean Homesick Blues" as recorded in 1965 for *Bringing It All Back Home* is recognizably brilliant and its power seems likely to endure for many more years to come. But if we knew the song only through its later live performances (1988, 1989) I doubt that we'd pay it much attention. It sounds good, has a nice beat and some clever lyrics. On a good night, Dylan performs it quite well. But it's nothing special, which is to say, in my opinion, the greatness of the song is not apparent and, arguably, not even present. Where did it go?

To be able to answer this question, we'd have to know where it came from in the first place. It comes, I think, from a feeling, or from a gestalt of feelings; it comes (greatness comes) from having something to say, something you need to say, something that feels like it won't be communicated unless you do it right. It comes from inspiration. "Hanging On to a Solid Rock Made before the Foundation of the World" is an inspired song and, on November 6, 1979, for instance, it communicates something very real and palpable, "you can feel it, you can hear it." But you can only feel and hear it when the performer feels and hears it. Greatness goes, disappears, when that intensity of need is not present, for whatever reason. You can't fake it. Thus, performance is the most demanding of art forms, or, put differently, is at the center of all creative experiences.

The performer makes a bridge. He passes on his inspiration, re-creates it, lives it or relives it so we can live it. He needs something. His performance is an expression of that need.

"Solid Rock" is a remarkable achievement, both lyrically and musically (not that the two are separated for Dylan; but it's unusual for a songwriter to be so original and so fluid in both realms at once). Lyrically, Dylan's achievement is not unrelated to what distinguished him earlier in his career: his ability to absorb a language-of-consciousness quickly and deeply and intuitively, and then to speak things that that language had been wanting to say but hadn't found words for yet. He gave voice to a movement, in the 1960s, that only fully recognized itself once it heard him speak. This did not occur in relation to his embrace of born-again Christianity, for reasons that don't need to concern us here (basically, the movement already had plenty of voices, many of them rather jealous of their territory). What is significant is to realize that Dylan, in the new fall 1979 songs, began a process of, in effect, adding to and extending and modernizing the language of the Christian faith and of the primary work of Western literature, the Bible—not intellectually but from the heart and in the spirit, inspired, filled with *enthousiasmos*.

I do not know the Bible well enough to assert that the image and actual language of Dylan's chorus, "I'm hanging on/to a solid rock/made/before/the foundation/of/of the world" (the separations indicate the actual form in which this phrase is vocalized, with a full stop and musical embellishment after each segment), does not come whole cloth from some part of the King James or Revised Standard editions. However, Bert Cartwright (a Protestant minister whose theological degrees are from Yale) describes the phrase as "combining the imagery of the love the Father had for Jesus 'before the foundation of the world' (John 17:24) with Paul's writing about the Rock that was Christ (1 Corinthians 10:3)." Cartwright, in his booklet *The Bible in the Lyrics of Bob Dylan*, says that in this phrase and in his line from another song, "the saving grace that's over me," Dylan "although seeking to stick close to the biblical teachings he is learning ... allows his poetic mind to roam across pages of the Bible and freely express thoughts [from] his own depths." Helena Springs, recalling to Chris Cooper in 1985 the Dylan she knew when he was "exploring Christianity" in 1978 and 1979, describes him as "a very inquisitive person" trying "to learn everything he could ... You know, he's a sponge, he absorbs so much."

A sponge. We've heard this word before, but I think we perhaps forget how central it is to the riddle of "who is Bob Dylan?" In any case, what I want to point to here is the vital power of this image Dylan has come up with (he is undoubtedly drawing on his pre-conversion experience of the song "Rock of Ages" as well as on more immediate sources). This title phrase, and the rest of the chorus ("Won't let go and I can't let go/Won't let go and I can't let go/Won't let go and I can't let go no more"), and the hard rockin' gloriously melodic rhythmic netting in which words and singer and audience are suspended, articulate with phenomenal clarity and accuracy an image and a felt spiritual awareness of Jesus as funda- ment (and what that means and how it feels in one real person's life) that I suspect is not grasped (or hung onto) much of the time by most born-again Christians. The song serves both to introduce the singer's faith and attract others to it, and to articulate and reawaken the faith that may already be present in the listener. It is absolutely brilliant (referring always to the early San Francisco performances, not to the frustrating close-but-no-cigar reading on *Saved* that somehow sabotages the song's revelatory power even as it attempts to preserve it for posterity). The verses, with lines like "It's the ways of the flesh/To war against the spirit" and "Nations are angry/Cursed are some" and the extraordinary rhythmic energy of the music they contain and are contained by, are almost as effective as the choruses. Every breath, every pause, every empha- sis in the song is inspired, even though there is no single night (that I've heard) when Fred Tackett totally gives himself to the lead guitar break and lets it take on its full fierceness, or when Dylan is so committed to the song that he doesn't swallow one or more vital phrases in the course of his delivery. It's a difficult piece, Dylan is trying to invent heavy metal gospel and he and his band aren't quite adequate (technically and, in Tackett's case, emotionally) to the full realization of the song's potential. But they come close enough to leave you absolutely awestruck (crawling back the next night to hear it again). This is not a song about an idea. It is an expression of the singer's experience of a more substantial reality than this everyday world. Its words are not from the Bible so much as they are a carrying on of a conversation initiated by the Bible.

This is living literature, living art, contemporary Logos (or perhaps Logos and Eros combined).

I'm not done raving. The next song, "Saving Grace," is a good enough song to move this listener any time Dylan performs it, but it becomes a transcendent experience on those rare nights when Dylan feels the inspiration and the courage to really sing it directly to the One he loves. On November 6 in San Francisco his vocal is so sensitive and vibrant that every word of the song is infused with life and meaning and intimacy; in such a state the performer can do no wrong, so that for example when he hurries the first line of the second verse (singing the words a half-beat or more ahead of the accompanying music) the mood of the song is not broken but actually strengthened, the melody responding to his leadership and reshaping itself, improving itself, on the spot.

Dylan is writing his own spirituals. As "Solid Rock" reaches back to "Rock of Ages," "Saving Grace" is (lyrically) a cousin to "Amazing Grace." The singer describes the joy of living in a state of trust and vulnerability, living by God's will, as opposed to the hell of living in a state of cynicism where one follows nothing except the voice of one's own ego (he identifies the "search for love" as vanity, narcissism; in this sense the philosophy expressed here is opposite to—and arises naturally from—the state of mind that expressed itself on *Street-Legal*). "Trouble in Mind" from the *Slow Train Coming* sessions described the problem; "Saving Grace," which touches on many of the same issues, describes the solution, not theoretically or as taught but as experienced. Dylan is bearing witness. The song's delicacy and sweetness derive in part at least from the fact that the despair, fear of death, and sense of hopelessness he speaks of are not in the past but still here in his present; God's love has not rescued the singer from this pit but rather allows him to live in the midst of it. "Thy rod and thy staff they comfort me." In "Saving Grace" Dylan gives this comfort a name and a location, and allows us to feel (ah those rippling guitar lines) how sweet its presence can be.

"What Can I Do for You?" is the supreme achievement of this astonishing song cycle. Another elegantly simple composition, its essence is summed up in its opening lines: "You have/ Given everything to me/ What can I do for you?" This is what the singer wants to say; the rest of the song is simply an expansion of this phrase. Each of the three verse-chorus stanzas (with the chorus coming first) begins with the same words, "You have—", and ends with "What can I do for you?" In between Dylan orchestrates a glorious crescendo (lyrical and musical) of tension, release, tension, release, each phrase building on the one before, each bit of musical and vocal phrasing seemingly more powerful and startling and satisfying than the last. The song is so well-constructed, so pretty, and so wonderful to sing, it literally takes on new meanings every time he performs it. This is odd, because its essential message of humility, devotion, gratitude, and eagerness to serve never changes. The song is a story, the everchanging story of the situation and feelings and hopes and fears of the person delivering its never-changing message. Or you could say, what Dylan has to say to God here never changes, but how he feels about God, and about his audience (he's a performer, he knows they're out there), and about himself, and about his relationship with God, and about his role as prophet or artist or preacher or public truth-teller, these feelings change constantly, and in so many subtle ways you could never describe or list them. But you can hear them. This is the complexity within the simplicity. The song is a question without an answer. Surely it answers itself—surely there is no greater gift a singer could give God than to sing and play his harmonica for Him—and yet for the singer to be satisfied with this answer invites the sin of pride and the renewed blindness and self-absorption that comes with it. To stay true to Spirit, one must keep asking, without presuming as one asks that one already knows the answer. Thy will, not mine. Return always to the question.

"What can I do for you?" The second and third verses each build into what I want to call harmonica solos but they're not, they're ensemble performances, fantastic journeys, led by the harmonica but also featuring bass, drums, keyboards, and a chorus of female voices ("oooohhh, oooohhh") harmonizing with and counterpointing against Dylan's structured but unpredictable harmonica eruptions. Here, by conscious prearrangement, the performer's heart is split open and he shares as much as he's able to share.

The song scares Dylan a little, understandably, and he tends to stumble over the opening. November 6 is perhaps the most perfect performance (although November 16 is also indispensable), but the first line is all wrong—he accidentally sings "you have done" instead of "you have given," which robs the song of its cornerstone image and instead gives the impression that he thinks of God and himself as equals. The only solution is for the listener to mentally insert the proper words and let the performance go on from there, which it does, exquisitely. Indeed, there are a number of places in the song where Dylan has had trouble making the words mean what he wants them to say. ("You opened a door that couldn't be shut.") He sings them anyway, and so powerfully that the listener feels the intended meaning, and (usually unconsciously) scrambles the words to make them fit the felt truth.

The biggest problem is in the next-to-last line of the song. At early shows Dylan sings, "I don't deserve what I have come through," or "I don't deserve it, but I have come through." I'm fairly sure what he wants to say is that he has come through an amazing experience, a gift of the Lord which he feels he doesn't deserve but which he gratefully accepts. But his inability to get the words to actually say this and at the same time to have the necessary punch required of this line (the verbal climax of the final verse) causes him fairly early (by the second week of performances) to let the line alter itself to "I don't deserve it, but I sure did make it through," with vocal emphasis on "sure did," which unfortunately is a boast, at exactly the point in the verse where a well-intended boasting of how willing he is to serve is supposed to give way to heart-opening expression of humility. His heart does open, every time, in the great harmonica foray that follows, but these new words and (often) the way they're sung are false to the spirit of the song. This leaves it up to the listener to mentally alter or disregard the words that don't fit, or else perhaps be put off or distracted, consciously or unconsciously, by the prideful language that's slipped back into this song of humble supplication.

What I'm saying is the song and performance are great, are great even in their imperfection; this imperfection or awkwardness is a perfect expression of the authentic struggle going on within the artist, and it emerges here because this is not a set piece. Dylan is renewing his vows of spiritual poverty every time he sings it. It isn't easy for him. What is most astonishing and most moving about the song is that he almost always succeeds. This is a song of letting go, a song of love, a song of giving oneself away.

The harmonica makes the difference.

Almost every show Dylan performed during his overtly religious period, from November 1979 to November 1981, started (his entrance) with "Gotta Serve Somebody" and ended (end of the regular set, before the encores) with "In the Garden." Where other songs talk about the singer's relationship with Jesus, this last song is a passion play, a formal work, Dylan's way of bringing the Gospel – that is, the story of Jesus – directly into his concert, in the most honored place. It's a fascinating song, different from anything else he's written (in the *Biograph* notes he says, "'In the Garden' is actually a classical piece; I don't know how in the world I wrote it but I was playing at the piano, closed my eyes and the chords just came to me"), majestic in performance at these autumn 1979 shows, full of colors and shapes not normally encountered in whatever sort of music it is that Bob Dylan usually makes. Very deeply affecting.

And it is characteristic of Dylan that he manages to tell the story as a series of questions, questions that are more than rhetorical, questions that somehow escape our natural tendency to think we know exactly what the asker intends the answer to be. "When they came for Him in the garden, did they know? Did they know he was the son of God – ?" The primary question in each stanza is repeated four times, twice at the beginning and twice at the end, with two lines that are sometimes statements, sometimes questions, but always additional information, sandwiched in the middle. I don't know of any other narrative, poetic or otherwise, structured this way. It's hypnotic. It's impassioned.

It's Dylan attempting to yield his stage to a more worthy subject for our attention. He does it very gracefully (ironically, after beating us over the head with the cheerful – but, for the nonbeliever, very confrontive – "I've Been Saved by the Blood of the Lamb"). I don't know how you measure the success of evangelism (that is, of this sort of supportive evangelism, which doesn't actually invite people to step forth and accept Jesus right now), but in artistic terms "In the Garden" is a stunning accomplishment. It is intended to invoke wonder – like a medieval chapel – and it does. The singer is using his Voice.

And "Pressing On," the second encore, is a simple but very special gift from Dylan to his live audience. He plays the piano (a moment of conscious intimacy, like the harmonica solos but even rarer); he sings out in a stirring, full-hearted voice; and finally he stands before us and (rare moment indeed) acknowledges and accepts our love, communicating by his presence how much he does in fact appreciate it.

And then he disappears into the night.

There is one other aspect of these concerts that must be commented on, and that is the "raps" – Dylan's between-song speeches. At first he spoke to the audience very little, which is normal for him – he'd introduce the band after the encore, introduce one of the women to sing in the guest slot after "Covenant Woman," and that was it, except for a brief rap before "Solid Rock." This rap was very different from the little bantering fables he would tell before two or three of the songs on the '78 tour (which grew longer and more free-form as the tour neared its end) – instead it served as an announcement apart from the content of the songs that this is what he believes, and wants us to know: "Do you know now we're living in the last – last days of the end times? We're in the *last* days of the end times. You're gonna need something strong to hang onto. So this song *is* called, 'Hanging On to a Solid Rock Made before the Foundation of the World.' You're gonna need something *that* strong."

Notice the rhythmic, repetitive language. Dylan never just talks to his audience; there's always a self-consciousness in his comments, a flair, a twist, something to help him pull the words out of himself and deliver them – through his performer, on-stage persona – to his audience.

Clinton Heylin has made an extensive survey of Dylan's 1979–80 raps, in his three-part essay "Saved! Bob Dylan's Conversion to Christianity" (*The Telegraph*, #28–30, 1988). He notes the little declarations that start to show up in the band introductions ("I'd like to say we're presenting the show tonight under the authority of Jesus Christ"), and the news-of-the-world raps that start to show up before "Slow Train," often with comments on Iran (the taking of hostages in the American embassy in Iran had occurred just as Dylan began this series of concerts). On November 16, Dylan for the first time incorporates into this rap a direct inquiry to the audience as to how many believers there are out there:

> You know, we read in the newspaper every day what a horrible situation this world is in. [guitar chords] And how God chooses to do these things in this world to confound the wise. [guitar] Anyway, we *know* this world's gonna be destroyed; we know that. And Christ *will* set up His kingdom in Jerusalem for a thousand years, where the lion will lie down with the lamb. Have you heard that before? [pause]

Have you heard that before? [pause] I'm just curious to know, how many believe that? [positive response] All right. This is called 'Slow Train Coming.' It's been coming a long time, and it's picking up speed.

The San Francisco audience included a fair number of Christian believers, but I think was predominantly made up of skeptics, many of whom were very audibly enthusiastic about the great music Dylan and his band were making; they (we) were won over by the performances, not necessarily by the message. The next four shows were in Santa Monica, and were heavily attended by people from the Vineyard Fellowship and other evangelicals. These shows were the closest Dylan came on the tour to performing for and preaching to the faithful, and perhaps as a result Dylan tries out various different commentaries and "preachings" at different places in the various shows: a rap about Satan before "Saved," a rap about "a God that can raise the dead" before "When You Gonna Wake Up," a rap about Peter and Jesus in the garden of Gethsemane before "In the Garden," and an extended rap about Moses while introducing "Ordinary People" (sung by Mona Lisa Young).

It's worth noting that performing in a self-consciously "Christian" environment may not have been an entirely positive experience for Dylan. Helena Springs recalls, "I remember a lot of people [at the concerts] were from the Vineyard in Los Angeles. It's kinda like a cult, a Jesus-type cult. I remember a lot of them pressuring him about a lot of things. Like if he'd drink some wine ... One time he said to me, 'God, it's awfully tight, it's so tight, you know.'"

Following the "friendly" reception in Santa Monica, Dylan went to Tempe, Arizona (playing at an auditorium in or near Arizona State University) and found himself before the most hostile crowd of the tour. Five years later when he was interviewed for *Biograph* the bitter memory was still with him: "Then we'd play the so-called colleges, where my so-called fans were. And all hell would break loose: 'Take off that dress!' 'We want rock and roll!', lots of other things I don't even want to repeat, just really filthy mouth stuff. This really surprised me, that these kids didn't know any better, all from good homes and liberal-minded to boot ..."

The second night in Tempe (November 26) Dylan responded to the hecklers with two exceptional raps, spontaneous monologues filled with obvious sincerity and at times an almost intolerable preachiness; these reveal a Dylan whose thinking process is a lot further from the norm than most of his fans (who secretly believe he's "just like them") would ever care to admit. Before "When You Gonna Wake Up" he says, "Pretty rude bunch tonight, huh? ... The spirit of the Antichrist is loose right now." He tells a (frequently interrupted) story about a cassette he saw of a guru who holds huge monthly gatherings in various cities, and who claims to be God. Dylan: "There's many of these false deceivers running around these days. The Bible says, anybody who preaches anything other than the one gospel, they're gonna be accursed." He concludes by telling the audience, "There's only two kinds of people: there's saved people and there's lost people.... Remember, you heard it here, that Jesus is Lord. Every knee shall bow."

Before "Solid Rock" he talks about the end times, tells the story of "let him who is without sin cast the first stone" (in response to cries of "Everybody must get stoned!"), announces that "America will be judged" and explains ("you ask your teachers about this; I know they're gonna verify what I say") that when God comes against a country, first he attacks their economy; next he attacks their ecology; and "if that doesn't work he just brings up another nation against them." He announces that Russia and China are going to attack in the Middle East and start a war called the Battle of Armageddon. (This belief of Dylan's is an interpretation of the Book of Revelation that was popularized by a bestselling book by Hal Lindsey called *The Late Great Planet Earth*; Clinton Heylin believes many of the lyrics of the *Slow Train Coming* songs were directly influenced by Lindsey's writings.) Five months later, at a concert in Toronto, Dylan recalls his Arizona experience, and says, "I was telling this story to these people. I shouldn't have been telling it to them. I just got carried away." (He's not really apologizing; he tells the same story to the Toronto folks, and mentions the Soviet invasion of Afghanistan in December as proof of the prophecies.)

Towards the end of his second five-minute monologue in Tempe, Dylan says something that seems to apply to how he sees his own current role as evangelical performer: "When Jesus spoke His parables, He said parables to all these people. Everybody heard the same parables. Some people understood them and some people didn't, but He said the same thing to everybody. He didn't try to hide it. Those that believed it believed it and understood it, and those that didn't didn't."

And on November 28, at a San Diego show, he's quoted as saying, "People say, 'Bob, don't do that stuff.' It may be costing me a lot of fans. Maybe I'll have to start singing on street corners. Still, I'll give all praise and glory to God."

The last fall 1979 show was December 9. During the Christmas break, Helena Springs left the tour, and was replaced by Carolyn Dennis and Regina Peeples. Dylan may have lost more than a singer and friend. In 1987 Dave Kelly, who was Dylan's personal assistant during the 1979 and 1980 tours, told Chris Cooper that at one point Dylan and Springs were planning to get married, but "at the end of the first tour they had a big row and he told her to leave."

The tour started again January 11, 1980, in Portland, Oregon, and continued through Seattle, Spokane, Denver, Omaha, Kansas City, Memphis, Birmingham, Knoxville, and Charleston. The last show was February 9, and was followed by the recording sessions for *Saved* in Muscle Shoals the following week, probably February 15 to 19. *Rolling Stone* at the time reported that "while in Seattle, Dylan paid a visit to a jewelry store, Friedlander and Son, where he purchased a diamond engagement ring, which one tipster claimed cost $25,000." Later in 1980 Dylan started performing a new song called, "The Groom's Still Waiting at the Altar."

The winter 1980 tour featured the same songs in the same order as the fall 1979 shows (the last two shows, February 8 and 9, introduced a new song called "Are You Ready?"). In general, however, these 23 concerts from January and February 1980 don't generate the same excitement as the first set of concerts. Whereas on some tours Dylan's enthusiasm for the material and his degree of inspiration seem to increase as he plays more shows, this time there's a falling off, a loss of energy, maybe a subtle distance has crept in between the singer and what he's singing about. In the first shows, the power and conviction of his performance of the new songs is enough to melt all resistance on the listener's part; the covenant and the solid rock and the saving grace and even the war against the flesh are made vividly real, sweet and strong and nourishing and terrifying. The second set of shows can't quite live up to this remarkable achievement.

But, as always, there are a lot of fine performances spread here and there. The second Birmingham concert, February 3, is particularly good, and features a "What Can I Do for You?" that is absolutely amazing (indeed, a tape of performances of this song from throughout this period would be fascinating and rewarding; even on the sleepiest nights, it seems to bring Dylan to life, and it's a subtly different song every time he performs it), followed by a blockbuster rendition of "In the Garden."

The *Saved* recording sessions close out this period. Dylan hasn't often recorded with his touring band; he tried it with *Blonde on Blonde* and was dissatisfied, ultimately keeping only one track that he cut with the Band (they had not yet been touring with him when *Planet Waves* was recorded, so that doesn't count). He tried it on *Street-Legal*. In the case of *Saved* he broke his own rule in a grander fashion: where he usually comes into the studio with new songs and sits down to record them live, with musicians who often haven't met him before and who've heard the songs once if at all, this time he came in with his travelling band and recorded songs they'd been performing together for three and a half months.

It didn't work. Not only is the spark missing, that energy of hot pursuit (of the creative will o' the wisp) that seems to get Dylan through his studio shyness, but the error is compounded when Dylan either came up with or allowed someone else to suggest a batch of uninspired new arrangements for several of the best songs. On "Covenant Woman," for example, the drum part is dreadful, and the lovely keyboard-and-percussion riff on which the live performance was based is lost, which in turn leaves the vocal with nothing special to play against. "What Can I Do for You?" is given a generic intro, and the slowness and depth of the original arrangement are replaced by a hurried blandness. "Pressing On" starts off powerfully and then degenerates into an overbaked crash-and-thud I find almost unlistenable.

The only song from the fall 1979 shows that can be said to be well-performed on the album is the title track, "Saved," which is tight and full of life and actually sounds better to me on the record than it did at most of the concerts. The closing track of the album, "Are You Ready?", is also an uplifting performance; Dylan and band grab hold of a strong riff and ride it for all it's worth. The song's lyrical content is predictable, but to the point: Dylan sees himself as being in the business of saving souls, and he wants to leave you thinking about what condition yours is in.

And there's a little miracle here as well. The opening track, a country standard called "Satisfied Mind," is absolutely magnificent.

This is spontaneous Dylan, inspired Dylan, the performing artist at work; you can hear the man's genius not only in his voice but in the astonishing performance of the back-up singers and in Tim Drummond's delightful bass playing. Dylan, when the spirit moves him, breathes out great music as easily as another person laughs.

Dave Kelly says, "I think Bob himself was unhappy with that album [*Saved*]. He certainly tried to stop its release." Be that as it may, the album did come out, in June 1980. Like *Slow Train Coming* it had a painting on the cover, but where that album's art had been subtle and intriguing and attractive, the cover of *Saved*, and the very title of the record, seem carefully chosen to give the finger to any and all of Dylan's "so-called fans" who haven't already seen the light. Songs that had the potential to open some well-defended ears to a new message end up doubly buried, limp performances wrapped in repellent packaging. The desire to reach out to the world that Dylan demonstrated in the care he took with *Slow Train Coming* and in the love he poured into the Warfield shows seems to have slipped away somehow with the new year, new decade.

11.

Dylan won a Grammy award (his first) for "Gotta Serve Somebody," which was judged "Best Vocal Performance of 1979." He and his band attended the televised award ceremony (February 27, 1980) and delivered a very hot, seven-minute version of the song, complete with new lyrics and even some harmonica playing. Dylan wore formal dinner wear (white tie) and thanked the Lord and his record producers.

The next leg of Dylan's gospel tour started on April 20, 1980; he played four shows in Toronto, Canada, four shows in Montreal, and then another 21 shows in the northeastern United States, in various cities in New York, New England, Pennsylvania, and Ohio (but no shows in the biggest cities, New York, Boston, and Philadelphia). The band line-up stayed the same, but again there was a change in the back-up singers; Carolyn Dennis and Regina Peeples left, and Clydie King, Gwen Evans, and Mary Elizabeth Bridget joined the veterans Regina McCrary Havis and Mona Lisa Young. Dylan now had ten people on stage with him, one less than at his "big band" concerts in 1978.

These April-May 1980 shows are far more spirited than the January-February performances. "When He Returns," "Covenant

Woman," "Change My Way of Thinking," and "Blessed Is the Name of the Lord Forever" are gone, replaced by two new Dylan compositions, "Ain't Gonna Go to Hell for Anybody" and "Cover Down" (the fourth and fifth songs each night), with "Are You Ready?" as the first encore. "Ain't No Man Righteous, No Not One" returns at a number of shows, but usually is sung by Regina Havis (the excellent November 16, 1979 version was primarily sung by Dylan). Another new Dylan composition, "I Will Love Him, I Will Serve Him," is performed by him at a few shows, as is a gospel tune called "I Will Sing."

It's difficult to characterize the spring 1980 concerts, except to say that they're very different from the similarly structured fall 1979 shows—they don't achieve the same level of phenomenal power and grace found on the Warfield '79 tapes, but they have a personality and intensity all their own that is very much worth hearing. Dylan seems to have grown comfortable with the haphazard mix of hostility, suspended judgment, and enthusiasm that meets him each evening; these 29 shows (in 35 days) are the most self-consciously evangelical of his entire religious period, but his preaching is far from humorless, and never predictable. The musical performances are not necessarily intimate, but they're rich and vibrant and intense. Because *Saved* won't be released till June, he's now performing nine songs (out of 16, most nights) that his audience is completely unfamiliar with. And—although there are always some audience members shouting out for the old songs—he makes it work. It's a gutsy, charming, very energetic show, and it hangs together well. My favorite of the concerts I'm familiar with is Albany, New York, April 27; but one of these years the professionally shot film footage of the April 19 and 20 concerts in Toronto (commissioned by Dylan; I think Howard Alk directed the filming) will start circulating or perhaps even be released commercially, and (judging from the excerpts I've seen) it'll be riveting, and a little-known concert tour may turn into one of the best-documented and thus best-remembered.

Indeed, the more I listen to these concerts, the more I find to like. Many of the *Slow Train* songs have taken on a fresh passion, notably "When You Gonna Wake Up," "Precious Angel," and "I Believe in You." The arrangements are not really changed, but the performer, because he's in a new place in his relationship with himself, his audience, and his art, easily and naturally gives the songs new interpretations, like paintings suddenly sparkling with new colors, new highlights.

Of the new songs, "Cover Down" is the standout, a blues rock gospel sermon with a great soul riff and without the hostility of the *Slow Train Coming* songs, Dylan preaching passionately from his pulpit with the Good Book open before him:

> You heard about Pharaoh's army, trampling through the
>   mud
> Heard about the Hebrew children, redeemed by blood
> Same spirit running in you that raised Christ from the dead
> If you're quick in your mortal body, then let Him run to
>   your head.

This is followed by a great and enigmatic chorus, Dylan leaning into the riff (particularly the night of May 7 in Hartford) with all the muscle of his best rock performances:

> Cover down, cover down, breakthrough.
> Cover down, cover down, breakthrough.

Enigmatic but not really, because the moment you hear him sing it you *know* what he's saying—it's just that the words are startling and unusual, which gives the song an ambiguity and depth that add significantly to its power. He's talking about God's protection, and how great our need for it is. He's shouting out, Take cover! Take refuge in the Lord.

The verses are full of wonderful fire-breathing language, biblical in the best sense, which is the poetic:

> We all need protection
> Of the full armor of the Lord
> The word of God is quick and powerful
> Sharper than any double-sided sword
> The hammer of salvation
> The blade of righteousness
> Genesis to Revelation
> Repent and confess.

Pow! Bam! And it goes on, another great thundering chorus, then: "Wake up early in the morning, turning from side to side ...

Demands are laid upon you, burdens impossible to bear." Dylan is describing his life (and, he assumes, not unreasonably, the listener's as well). It all climaxes in the fourth verse with a promise (or threat) of liberation via ego death: "You've got an image of yourself that you built all alone/ It will come tumbling down, just like the walls of stone/You will be separated from everything you seem to be..." Marvelous song. It should be part of the basic repertoire of every Christian heavy metal band (and some of the non-Christian ones too), but in fact I believe it's still unrecorded (by anyone), just another Dylan classic that got away.

"Ain't Gonna Go to Hell for Anybody," the other new song Dylan included in every spring show, is not as effective: the choral opening and the title are striking, and the tune has some possibilities, particularly the bridge. But the lyrics and the performance are a disappointment: "I can manipulate people as well as anybody," Dylan boasts, "Frost 'em and burn 'em, twist 'em and turn 'em; I can make believe I'm in love with almost anybody, hold 'em and control 'em, tease 'em and squeeze 'em." This is obviously not a gift to be particularly proud of, but the attempt at irony falls flat as the phony boast gives way to a real (and childish) boast in the chorus.

"I ain't gonna go to hell for anybody," Dylan asserts, "Not for father, not for mother, not for sister, not for brother, no way." Dylan's former assistant Dave Kelly provided some insight into the possible inspiration for this song and for parts of "Cover Down" when he described to Chris Cooper the period between the fall 1979 and winter 1980 tours: "At the time I guess what I remember more than the business people coming and going were the rabbis that were coming. And the pressures that his mother was putting on him to submit to these very high rabbis from the orthodox Judaic. It was like a war going on. They were trying to get him to go away and do some other training. But CBS, Bill Graham, and everyone was pushing onto him. It was ridiculous. Especially when the Christian community was not always supportive of him. One record distributor responsible for putting records in about 2,000 Christian record stores refused to put Dylan's records in for a couple of years."

The Bible quote Dylan chose for the sleeve of *Saved* is from Jeremiah, referring to the Lord's promise to make "a new covenant with the house of Israel" (the issue is whether or not Jesus is the Messiah of the Jews foretold in the Old Testament). Dylan's other new song from this time, "I Will Love Him," which he performed

twice at the Canadian shows, makes reference to the formation of
the state of Israel in 1948 as a fulfillment of one of Christ's proph-
esies. The words to the song are impossible to catch, but it's a
strong hymn in a storytelling verse/singalong chorus format, with
some very nice melodic changes.

"Solid Rock" tends to be hurried and, to my tastes, unconvincing, at these spring shows. "Saving Grace" is sometimes bland,
sometimes very moving. "What Can I Do for You?" is a consistent
showstopper – the harmonica playing on April 27 must be heard to
be believed; the audience members are falling over themselves in
ecstasy throughout the two solos, and for good reason. "In the
Garden" also continues to be the occasion for a great performance
night after night (the April 27 reading is particularly fine).

But the climax of these shows comes with the first encore.
Dylan introduces the band, with the "Are You Ready?" riff pulsing
beneath his words, great sustained heat and tension (a trick he also
used in 1978, the band would play the fierce "It's Alright, Ma" riff
over and over during the introductions, exploding into the song
when Dylan finally finished talking), building up to a disarmingly
powerful bit of evangelizing and testifying when he comes to the
preacher's daughter (this particular rap is from April 27; they
changed every night):

> Over on the other side is the girl who told you about
> Jesus earlier, remember? Somebody's got to tell you about
> Jesus – if you never hear of it again, if you never hear that
> name again, remember, you have heard it. [pause, while the
> music builds] You want to be delivered? Jesus *will* deliver
> you. You need a lover? Jesus'll do that. You need a doctor?
> He'll do that too. And I know you need a lawyer! Well, he's
> all that. [pause] Manifest in the flesh. Justified in the spirit.
> Seen by angels. Leaned on in the world. Preached to the
> nations. Raised up all men to glory. From Nashville, Tennes-
> see: Regina McCrary! [he pauses for a beat, then starts
> singing] Are you ready? [girls and band echo, "rehhh
> deeee"] I said, are you ready?

And we're off into an absolutely smoking performance of the
song – justified in the spirit, indeed. If anyone in the audience is
going to be moved to speak in tongues tonight, or to come forth to
be baptized, this would be the moment.

The version of "Pressing On" that follows, April 27 and every other night of this tour, is almost equally uplifting—Dylan has taken the "big band" arrangement that doesn't work for me on *Saved* and revamped the rhythm and now it's a glorious expression of community similar to the triumphal "Like a Rolling Stone" at the end of the 1974 concerts.

Lots of raps at these shows, fascinating, complex performances; I particularly like the way he accompanies himself, tickling out notes from his electric guitar, offhandedly but with great timing, very expressive. The rap before "Solid Rock" on April 27 is a good example.

Occasionally the raps are offensive, as when he gets into the subject of "homosexual politics" in San Francisco, in Hartford, Connecticut, May 8. Often they're quite bizarre. They are always fascinating windows into the workings of a very unusual mind.

Dylan was wound up in April/May 1980; listening to the shows, he sounds like he's ready to crisscross North America three times a year for the next twenty years, singing about Jesus and preaching the Gospel. I'm sure he felt that that was the way it would be. But in fact the last show of this leg of the tour—May 21 in Dayton, Ohio—turned out to be the last Dylan show to feature religious songs only. It was the end of his overt evangelizing (the raps). It was also the last live performance (through 1990) of "Saving Grace" and "Pressing On."

Dylan took a break from performing for five and a half months. Little is known about his activities during this time, except that he wrote some exceptional songs, including "Caribbean Wind," "The Groom's Still Waiting at the Altar," "City of Gold," "Yonder Comes Sin," "Let's Keep It Between Us," and "Every Grain of Sand."* And somewhere along the way he decided the time had come to make a change in the format of his concerts; the October 1980 rehearsals (with the same basic band, except that Willie Smith replaced Terry Young and Spooner Oldham on keyboards; the back-up singers were now Regina Havis, Carolyn Dennis, and Clydie King) included songs like "Mr. Tambourine Man" and "Blowin' in the Wind." The

---

*One of the treasures of *The Bootleg Series* is an exquisite "demo tape" performance of "Every Grain of Sand," recorded September 23, 1980, with Fred Tackett and Jennifer Warnes.

period of absolutism (performances made up of nothing but newly-written songs, performances organized from start to finish with the single intention of preaching the Gospel and saving souls) had given way to a new approach.

The only known performance of "Yonder Comes Sin" is on a demo tape made during these rehearsals. It's a great song—while the band plays variations on "Jumping Jack Flash" worthy of the Rolling Stones in their prime, Dylan unleashes his best rock and roll voice (biting off the words and flinging them at the listener with sweet nasty cool uncompromising joy). Aside from the unfortunate fact that song and performance are unreleased (the 1980s were to be a decade in which the albums Dylan didn't make were for the most part better than the ones he did release), there are two more causes for regret regarding this otherwise fabulous performance: the demo tape cuts off after four verses, whereas the full song is seven verses, each stanza building on the ones before, rising to a fever pitch of intensity that could have made this one of Dylan's most effective evocations of the chaotic interaction of internal and external stimuli since "It's Alright, Ma." (The full text of the song is included in the copyright files; the circulating demo tape is the only known performance.) The other, lesser cause for regret is that Dylan chose to sing the same pre-climactic line in each chorus ("Can you take it on the chin?/Yonder comes sin") instead of letting loose with the delightful variations included in the written text: "Pour me another glass of gin," "Ain't no room tonight at the inn," "Sounding like a sweet violin," "So masculine, so feminine," "Take off that sheepish grin," and "Being pulled in all directions by the wind." He does offer one variation in the singing that doesn't show up in the written lyrics: "Enough to put you in a tailspin ..." When this singer/writer is hot, rhymes and phrases and images flock to him, like the women and pilgrims outside his hotel room door (as described by Anne Waldman in her privately-published account of a 1978 tryst with Dylan), eager to be used in any way possible.

Dylan is stimulated, repulsed, and overwhelmed by the energy that swirls around him, and he makes his experience universal in this relentless song about the assault of the senses: "Stretched and willing, ready and able/Yonder comes sin/Standing on the chair, standing on the table/Look at your feet, see where they've been to/Look at your hands, see what they've been into—" At one point he identifies himself with an Old Testament prophet, but (you have to hear him sing it) with humorous resignation rather than pride: "Jeremiah preached repentance/To those who would turn from hell/But the critics all gave him such bad reviews/Put him down into the bottom of a well/But he kept on talking anyway..."

Dylan and his band opened the next leg of their tour with 12 shows at the same San Francisco theater where he'd played a residency the year before (the other longest residencies in his career, after his early club days, were in Los Angeles and London, but never more than eight shows). These 12 Warfield shows (November 9–22, 1980), plus the seven shows that followed in Tucson, San Diego, Seattle, Salem (Oregon), and Portland, are known as the "Musical Retrospective" tour because of the advertisements Bill Graham (the San Francisco promoter) ran to try to assure fans that the "old Dylan" was back in action. The concert still began with Regina's story about the old woman and the train, followed by four gospel numbers, and Dylan's opening numbers continued to be "Gotta Serve Somebody" and "I Believe in You." "In the Garden" was still the curtain-closer. But within this basic structure Dylan presented a show comparable only to the 1975 Rolling Thunder shows for its rich variety, its clear desire to please the fans, and its touches of warm nostalgia for the singer's "folk" days combined with enthusiastic, unselfconscious offerings of newly-written material. It was also a very fluid show, with song selections changing and evolving night to night. In 78 concerts between November 1979 and April 1980, Dylan had performed a total of 23 different songs. In 19 shows in November and December 1980, he sang 40 songs. The shows that resulted cannot be said to reach the heights of greatness of the year before (except during some of the performances of the newest songs), but they are very wonderful in their own way, and certainly (because of their variety, their many surprises) a tape-collector's delight.

One of the uncharacteristic flourishes of the Warfield shows was a series of guest performances: Carlos Santana joined the band on guitar for four songs November 13, Michael Bloomfield (famous for his work on *Highway 61 Revisited*) sat in on two songs November 15, including "Like a Rolling Stone," Jerry Garcia of the Grateful Dead played guitar on four songs November 16, Maria Muldaur (whom Dylan had known since the Cambridge folk days of the early 1960s) sang a song November 19, and Roger McGuinn sang and played on "Mr. Tambourine Man" and "Knockin' on Heaven's

Door" November 22. David Grisman played mandolin on "To Ramona" at the last show of the mini-tour, December 4 in Portland.

The best overall concert of this series is November 15 (because of the high level of performance song after song—how much Dylan gives to each song, the mood he's in, and what he's inspired to give are always the most important factors in the quality of a show, though of course the inclusion of new or seldom-heard songs is of great significance to those of us who attend or listen to a lot of concerts). November 12 is a close second, and historic because it features the only live performance (so much better than the studio version!) of "Caribbean Wind." But there are some fascinating fall '80 selections that aren't included in either of these excellent concerts, and other shows (notably November 22) that are arguably as good.

Incidentally, there is a soundboard tape (presumably recorded by the sound engineer, directly from the mixing board at the show) of November 15 which, to my ears, is simply not as enjoyable as the audience tape I have from the same show. I mention this because there is a presumption among collectors that soundboards are always better, and of course they often are; but it can also happen that the mix of the soundboard tape is inappropriately skewed in some way or (especially in a small theater like this) that the overall sound of the concert comes through much better when you can hear the crowd and the ambience (acoustics? echoes?) of the room. (Of course, if I can feel so differently about two good recordings of the same show, you must recognize the unreliability of my pronouncements that a certain show of a series was the "best"—not only have I not listened carefully to all the shows, but there could well be shows I'd hear quite differently if I listened to other tapes of the same concert.)

Dylan employs an unusual structure for these concerts: he opens his part of the show with a mini-set of three songs, "Gotta Serve Somebody," "I Believe in You," and "Like a Rolling Stone." The effect is to turn all three songs into anthems, with the mini-set as a whole functioning as a statement of purpose or identity. This in turn provides a springboard for the rest of the show. Without this or some similar device there's a danger that the concert would seem (to the performer) like a watered-down version of his 1979-80 show, greatest hits added and overt evangelizing deleted by popular demand. Instead Dylan succeeds in telling himself and us that this is a new show, an evolution from and transformation of what he was doing before, a conscious and heartfelt statement of who he is and what he has to share right now.

"I Believe in You" is given a new, organ-based arrangement more suited to its anthemic role, and its performance on November 15 is particularly moving. For the first time I hear in this song the possibility that it could (also) be addressed to the singer's live audience: "I walk out on my own/A thousand miles from home/ But I don't feel alone/'Cause I believe in you." "Don't/Let me drift too far/Keep me where you are/Where I will always be renewed." This is presumably unconscious, but not inappropriate; in any case, Dylan's great affection for his audience, for this living presence that he can lean into and draw from as he performs, is unmistakable here.

An unusual openness, authentic modesty, characterizes this set of concerts, during which Dylan seemed to be in the process of rediscovering various parts of his past, in particular his identity as a musician and lover of music. This is not to suggest that he had lost these parts of himself in his Christian conversion, but rather that he had a genuine experience of being born again and letting go of old identity—a "tabula rasa" state that led in time naturally to this transitional moment, in which he is consciously and enthusiastically reclaiming parts of himself that continue to be meaningful and alive for him. His theme this season is "Who am I?" rather than the emphatic "This is who I am!" of a year earlier; but this has the feeling of a continued, committed growth process rather than a falling back or falling away from anything. He was a newborn; now he's a child (with the memories of a 39-year-old man). In his lengthy introduction to Michael Bloomfield's guest appearance on "Like a Rolling Stone," Dylan describes the first time he met Bloomfield during a club date in Chicago in 1962, recalling this young guitar player who "played all kinds of things— does the name Big Bill Broonzy ring a bell? Or Sonny Boy Williamson, that kind of thing?" Dylan's affection not so much for Bloomfield as a person but for those times and that music comes through very clearly.

The first three songs are followed by Regina Havis singing "(I'm Gonna Keep on Falling in Love) Till I Get It Right," and somehow, even though Dylan's not singing, the song and its title sound like a message from his heart.

The second set starts with the easy-going "Man Gave Names to All the Animals," followed by a truly delightful "Simple Twist of

Fate." The star of this performance, as with the equally wonderful "Girl from the North Country" a few minutes later, is Willie Smith; his light-fingered piano playing brings out new colors and textures in Dylan's voice and pushes him to make these songs brand new and sparkling.

Sandwiched between "Simple Twist" and "Girl from the North Country" is "Ain't Gonna Go to Hell for Anybody," which has been transformed into a song about a love relationship. The chorus and tune and bridge are the same, but Dylan has completely rewritten the verse lyrics—instead of making lists of things he can do, the singer is now telling a story through a series of disconnected images. The song is fast and loud, and the words are hard to catch—a close listen suggests, however, that the real reason words and story don't come clear is that these are "dummy" lyrics, as in 1967's "I'm Not There." The song is being performed midway through its metamorphosis, an experiment to see if perhaps it will find its true shape on stage, or to see if it's possible for a song to exist free of shape. Dylan seems to draw from a grab bag of phrases and couplets, spontaneously rebuilding the song each time he sings it—a particular line may be part of the first verse one night, the last verse another night, and another time its key images are transposed or it is left out altogether. Fascinating. I don't know if Dylan even wanted to arrive at a definitive version of the song, but in any case that didn't happen (as far as we know). Like so many other beloved playthings before it, the song stayed behind while the singer moved on.

The fifth and last song of the second set, November 15, is a rousing "Slow Train." "Animals," "Hell," "Girl," and "Train" were constants in this set throughout the shows; the second song varied between "Simple Twist of Fate," "To Ramona," and "Precious Angel." (Interesting the songs Dylan regards as equivalent for performance purposes.) On November 12 Dylan added "Mary from the Wild Moor" after "Ain't Gonna Go to Hell" (it later found a home in set three). Starting November 17 the second set permanently expanded to six songs minimum, ballooning to seven or eight songs at many of the later shows. Songs added included "All Along the Watchtower" and some marvelous cover versions: "We Just Disagree" (written by Jim Krueger, popularized by Dave Mason), "A Couple More Years" (by Shel Silverstein), and the great Little Willie John/Peggy Lee hit "Fever." The first two songs are clearly chosen for their lyrics, in the country & western tradition of building a song around a felt "message": "there ain't no good guys, there ain't no bad guys, there's only you and me and we just disagree"; "I've got a couple more years on you babe, and that's all." Hearing Dylan sing these phrases is an enriching experience, not because his approach to the songs is particularly unusual or original, but because the feelings contained in song and performance are so close to the surface, so warm, so full of a great singer's awareness of the way a few words and a simple tune can capture the inarticulate longings of the heart and lay bare the powerful secrets of our lives. This fall 1980 cornucopia of performances—San Diego, November 26, is another recommendable show, showcasing the wide variety of material Dylan presented on this tour—is among other things a celebration of the power of song.

Dylan's (strictly non-religious) raps on this mini-tour are unusually open and off-the-cuff, as though all his evangelizing— many of those raps were also quite extemporaneous—has loosened his tongue. In San Diego he tells a story about a newly married couple who came into his hotel room from a connecting balcony the night before (they shared their champagne with him and he gave them tickets to the show). November 22, before his performance of "Fever," he talks about how much he's enjoyed these weeks in San Francisco, acknowledges the promoter for his support despite bad reviews in the press, and then tells this story:

> I ran into a girl here on the street a while back, and she said I was a strange person, and she told me why. She said, she says, "you were born up in a certain area where the ground is metallic." And uh, actually she's right. Where I come from the ground *is* metallic. And as a matter of fact during the Second World War 90% of all the iron and steel that went into all the ships and the boats and airplanes and all kind of weaponry, 90% of all the iron and steel that went into all that came from the area where I was, uh— lived. They dug it out of the ground there, so sure, there is something to that, I'm sure.
>
> But anyway, it's back there, there's a great big lake, it's called Lake Superior ... across the lake is a town called Detroit. And I happened to go to Detroit once when I think I was about 12 or so, I was with a friend of mine who had relatives there. Anyway, I can't remember how it happened but I found myself in a Bingo parlor, there were people

coming to eat all day and they played Bingo all night and there was a dance band in the back, and that was the first time— See where I'm from I'd only hear mostly country music, you know, Hank Williams, Hank Snow, Hank Penny, all kindsa Hanks. But anyway so this was my first time face to face with the rhythm & blues, it was in Detroit, I think I was about 12 years old, there was a man there that was singing this song here, I don't think I'll do it as good as he did it but I'm going to try it anyway.

As it happens, Dylan was 12 in 1953, and Little Willie John's "Fever" didn't come out until mid-'56, by which time Dylan was well steeped in Little Richard and late night r&b radio. But the story has a ring of truth to it—it may have been a different song, maybe even a different city, but surely there was a moment when rhythm & blues first presented itself to Robert Zimmerman's amazed eyes and ears, and nothing was ever the same again. Dylan's 1980 performance of "Fever" (great back-up singing, great piano) shares with us the feeling that was put in him that day, that's still in him, still calling on him to get up on stage and let it out, still driving him to be a performer.

The third set began, almost every night of the tour, with Dylan and Clydie King dueting on Dion's 1968 hit (written by Dick Holler) "Abraham, Martin and John." This is a somewhat maudlin tune about America's assassinated martyrs, given an odd twist when Dylan sings, "Has anybody here seen my old friend Bobby?/ Can you tell me where he's gone?" The sound of Dylan and King harmonizing together is the source of the magic here ("Clydie's one of the great singers ever," Dylan said in 1985). Dylan plays piano on this and on the next song, one of the high points of the 1980 shows, "Let's Keep It Between Us." Dylan's voice takes on a different character when he accompanies himself on piano; it has a resonance which, although the tonal space it occupies is actually quite limited, seems to expand to fill the listener's universe in every direction. Intensity and intimacy. This performance, built around Dylan's voice and piano, with explosive accompaniment from Willie Smith on organ and Tim Drummond and Jim Keltner on bass and drums, always strikes me as a sort of masterpiece in black and white, so stark, so focused, so penetrating. Again a few words telegraph oceans of feeling: "Let's keep it between us; these people meddling in our affairs they're not our friends." The voice here is exhortative, and what's important is not so much what he urges as how deeply he feels it; the expression of his (our) need for privacy becomes a vehicle by which he can also express his love. Wonderful language rolls off his tongue ("before the last door closes and the whole thing breaks down and ends" "backseat drivers don't know the feel of the wheel but they sure do know how to make a fuss"), given energy and power and character by the sound of his voice as the spirit in it ebbs and flows and overflows on the tide of his piano playing. The song is so keenly felt. It is as if the moment he starts singing it, Dylan is aware of nothing but his beloved and the forces surrounding and threatening their love—paradoxically fully aware at the same time of the presence of an audience with whom he can share these feelings, whom he immediately and generously includes within this exclusive, passionately private land called "us."

The song may also be heard as having spiritual connotations. One's private relationship with the divine can be harmed or destroyed by the attention of the public or of well-meaning friends—the analysis and judgments and opinions and gossip and for-your-own-good interference of the world at large. "Let's Keep It Between Us," though unheard since 1980, has the potential to be an enduring Bob Dylan theme song (like "It Ain't Me Babe"). I wish he'd get out his piano and sing it more often.

"Mary on the Wild Moor" is extremely pretty—Dylan and Regina McCrary Havis harmonize together on this ancient ballad while he plays guitar, she plays autoharp, and Fred Tackett plays mandolin. There had been a media fuss, this first week back in San Francisco, about whether Dylan was playing as many "old songs" (code for "not that religious stuff") as the ads had seemed to promise. Dylan's response was to come up with "a song I used to sing before I even wrote any songs; this is a *real* old song.... I hope it brings you back; I know it brings me back." Typical of Dylan to come up with something radically fresh and unexpected by way of honoring his audience's request that he go back to doing the stuff he used to do.

The next two songs are ostensibly "new songs"—the Christian material that is at the heart of the controversy—but ironically sound old and tired compared to the material Dylan has just introduced into his concerts. "Covenant Woman" is performed fairly well November 15, better than at the other fall 1980 shows, but still a pale shadow of its earlier magnificence. "Solid Rock" on

November 15 doesn't deserve even such faint praise; it's downright dull. What's wrong? There's an ambivalence in the performance of the Christian material at these shows that could suggest a crisis of faith; what's also likely is that Dylan's relationship with his songs and his audience is changing quickly ... under the circumstances it's important for him to include these songs (in order not to seem to give the wrong message; the press and some fans would love to believe he's rejected Jesus already), but he hasn't yet found a way to reinvent them, to make them part of what he feels as a performer right now.

The momentum of the November 15 concert is restored by a truly inspired reading of "Just Like a Woman." It is as though some songs are closed to the singer in this moment, and others are wide open. The arrangement of the song is familiar and straightforward, but when Dylan sings it this particular evening we feel his heart leaping out of him with every phrase. The way he sings the chorus of the second verse and the "It was raining..." section that follows is riveting, so filled with a richness of human presence — what theory of art can account for the beauty of such a performance? All the words I might throw at it pale before the single spontaneous intake of breath — "oh!" — I hear gasped by someone sitting next to the person who taped the show as Dylan sings the first word of the next song. The word is "Senor," and in that gasp we understand not only the listener's surprise and delight that Dylan's singing this song, but also his absolute shock and awe at the quality of the performance he's just experienced; his "oh!" says, "My God, he's following *that* with *this*, pinch me, what an embarrassment of riches, what did I ever do to deserve to be sitting here at this moment?"

Great art is not a concept, not a technique. I suppose it isn't a sharp intake of breath either, since that could as well be the response of a teenager when her hero walks onstage in his tight pants — Oh well. In any case, Dylan goes on to sing the sweetest, most powerful "Senor" I've ever heard from him. "Oh!", indeed.

What follows is another sort of greatness: Dylan and Michael Bloomfield trading vocal and guitar licks on another newly-written song, "The Groom's Still Waiting at the Altar." This is an amazing song — like the *Highway 61* material it's so reminiscent of, it demonstrates how brilliantly a string of seemingly disconnected images can come together to make great performed poetry, great rock and roll. Dylan doesn't slur and obscure these lyrics; he spits them out with full confidence. He knows what he's singing about, and regardless of whether we could ever paraphrase, we feel and receive that knowledge. As the lyrics sink in they become more and more meaningful:

> Prayin' in the ghetto, with my face in the cement
> Heard the last moan of a boxer, seen the massacre of the
>   innocent
> Felt around for the light switch, became nauseated —

We can feel the scenario. This particular live performance is exquisite (one of five live performances of this song, all between November 13 and November 26, 1980; this is the only one with Bloomfield, and, alas, his last stage appearance before his untimely death), but the studio recording six months later is just as magical. The lyrics of the later version are different, particularly the chorus: the earlier version is more explicitly a "lost love" song. Listening to the earlier form of the chorus, we can see how it evolved into its recorded form, as much to disguise the song's meaning as to enhance it. The original is:

> Set my affection on things above
> Let nothing get in the way of that love
> Not even the rock of Gibraltar
> If you see her on Fannin' Street
> Tell her I still think she's neat
> And that the groom's still waiting at the altar.

There's a couplet in this song that I particularly relate to — it addresses the way love and sexual attraction can bring us out of ourselves, and the transitory nature of that inspiration, and also perhaps says something about the slippery art of performing:

> There's a wall between you and what you want and you've
>   got to leap it
> Tonight you've got the power to take it, tomorrow you
>   won't have the power to keep it.

So, *carpe diem*, I guess. Rip into that song while you can feel it in front of you. Shake the roofbeams. Ask questions later.

The last two songs of the third set are "When You Gonna Wake Up" and "In the Garden." This time the task of integrating the various pieces of these shows with the still-present evangelical framework is more successful: "Wake Up" is a solid, exciting performance (no match for "Groom," but what'd'you expect?) that definitely benefits from the addition of the harmonica, and the vocal on "In the Garden" is unusually sensitive, truly beautiful.

This third set, November 15, features ten songs; other nights he does as few as eight or as many as eleven. There's a lot of variation: "Abraham, Martin and John," "Let's Keep It Between Us," "Solid Rock," "Just Like a Woman," "Senor," and "In the Garden" were included almost every time; "Mary from the Wild Moor" "When You Gonna Wake Up" and "Rise Again" were performed at more than half the shows; and after that it's a grab bag — "What Can I Do for You?", "Saved," "Just Like Tom Thumb's Blues," "Do Right to Me Baby," "Caribbean Wind," "Mr. Tambourine Man," and "Knockin' on Heaven's Door" are among the songs that make occasional appearances, most of 'em only once or twice.

"Rise Again," a contemporary Christian song written by Dallas Holm, is particularly effective: it's another Bob and Clydie duet, with Dylan playing piano, and they sing it with a lot of feeling. It's a surprising song — to me, anyway — because the singer speaks in the first person as Jesus. The chorus has universal applications anyone can relate to ("I will rise again, ain't no power on Earth can tie me down!"), but the verses are subject specific: "Go ahead, drive the nails through my hand." I like the interplay of the singers' voices, and the soaring glissando when they come together on the "rise again" chorus. Good stuff.

The first encore every night of this tour was "Blowin' in the Wind," first verse sung gospel-style by the back-up singers before Dylan comes in. On November 9 this was the only encore, but thereafter he did three at most shows (in the latter part of the tour this would expand to four or even five). The second encore every night was "City of Gold," a new Dylan song with the grace and simplicity of a traditional spiritual. Another lost gem (he sang it once on tour in the summer of 1981, and never since), this is one of my favorite performances from this tour. Singing in an unusual open-voiced style (with wonderful swooping harmonies from the gospel chorus), he offers a vision of a non-sectarian Jerusalem (the name of the city is never mentioned; this is a new ecumenical Dylan, apparently working in the tradition of songs like "Twelve Gates to the City") "far from this rat race, and the bonds that hold."

He sings it as a kind of love song to his audience, an offering, benediction—and follows it each night with a further offering, what he knows we want, a solo acoustic performance, just himself with guitar and harmonica, usually "Love Minus Zero/No Limit," occasionally "It's All Over Now, Baby Blue" (with lovely long harmonica solos), "Don't Think Twice," "It Ain't Me Babe," or "It's Alright, Ma." A few nights he brought the band back after this and did a final encore of "A Hard Rain's A-Gonna Fall." Openness, sincerity, generosity—unusual words to characterize a Dylan tour, but unavoidable when talking about these shows.

Dylan made an interesting comment to Robert Hilburn in an interview conducted November 19, 1980, regarding the art of performing and the care needed in approaching one's older material: "It's a very fine line you have to walk to stay in touch with something once you've created it. A lot of artists say, 'I can't sing those old songs any more,' and I can understand it because you're no longer the same person who wrote those songs. However, you really are still that person some place deep down. You don't really get that out of your system. So you can still sing them if you can get in touch with the person you were when you wrote the songs. I don't think I could sit down now and write 'It's Alright, Ma' again. I wouldn't even know where to begin, but I can still sing it, and I'm glad I've written it."

I had some fascinating conversations with Dylan backstage during the Warfield shows. At one point he read the lyrics of a new song to me, which turned out to be "Every Grain of Sand." Another time he talked about how he'd gotten in touch consciously with some of the songwriting techniques he'd used unconsciously (and so successfully) in the mid-sixties. He spoke of one song he was particularly proud of, that he'd written "a while back," that successfully functioned on the level of complexity of his mid-sixties material, taking the listener outside of time (I don't know that he actually used these phrases; I'm just recalling my impression of what he told me). He said the song was called "Caribbean Wind," and that he'd try to play it if I'd phone his assistant some afternoon before a show and remind him of my request.

He performed the song Wednesday, November 12, towards the end of the third set, after a wonderful rap: "This is a 12-string guitar. First time I heard a 12-string guitar it was played by Leadbelly—I don't know if you've heard of him? ... He made lots of records. At first he was just doing prison songs, and stuff like that … He'd been out of prison for some time when he decided to do children's songs. And people said, 'Oh wow! Has Leadbelly changed?' Some people liked the older songs, some people liked the newer ones. But he didn't change. He was the same man."

"Caribbean Wind" is the high point of the fall 1980 shows, a sublime performance of a Dylan masterpiece that never quite came together in the studio (the *Biograph* performance, recorded in April 1981, is inferior both lyrically and musically). Dylan was dissatisfied with the band's playing on the song November 12, but that may be because he was on stage, not in the audience. Tim Drummond (de facto bandleader) and the other musicians provide superb support and hard-rock embellishment as Dylan delivers a blistering vocal performance; the net result, even though you can't hear all the words, is filled with an excitement comparable to the best of Dylan's spontaneous studio sessions. The song, through this performance, burns itself into the consciousness of every person who ever hears it. It becomes flesh; it breathes; even the mere memory of hearing it roars in the listener's blood.

The song is a dramatic narrative, whose success depends not on the conveying of information but on the conveying of a *feeling*: what it's like to be inside this moment. (The same could be said of most stage plays: the important thing is not what Stanley did to Herbert but how we feel as we watch and listen.) And what I find, as I listen to the November 12, 1980 performance of this song over and over, is that my visceral response to the song is most noticeable to me in the non-vocal passages, certain notes the band plays (particularly the bass and lead guitars) sum up everything I'm feeling at the moment, and I acknowledge this by making a fist and pounding an imaginary table in front of me in time with the music. Paradoxically, this response—my ability to feel the entire situation described in the song (as I imagine it, as it exists for me) in Dylan's tense strumming at the beginning, in Tim Drummond's nine descending bass notes between stanza and cho-rus in the last verse, and in the lead guitar flourishes that run behind and between the verses, offering punctuation, emphasis, constantly announcing the intensity of the narrator's involvement in this story he's telling—this response to the music tells me how successful the lyrics are, they've done their job, they've got my attention ("tell me a story") and directed my mind and ego to a place where I can feel and respond to the emotional truths that are the songwriter's primary focus.

The lyrics in turn are successful (and the music he writes and performs is successful) because the songwriter knows his story, feels something deeply and is able to draw on that feeling throughout the creative process. It is this *knowingness*, ultimately, that informs the live recording of the song and gives it its greatness, and that is so obviously missing from the later studio recording when one compares the two.

In the gap between the November 12, 1980 live performance and the April 11, 1981 studio recording falls a self-consciousness that would plague Dylan (as a songwriter and a maker of records; not so much as a live performer) throughout most of the 1980s. (This self-consciousness was telegraphed, as it were, when Dylan expressed doubt about how well he and the band performed the song immediately after finishing it that night at the Warfield – a doubt that seems reflected in the fact that other new songs and cover versions introduced on the fall '80 tour were played at additional shows following their debut, but "Caribbean Wind" was not attempted a second time.)

The root of this self-consciousness seems to lie in the question, "How much truth do I want to tell?" I would speculate that the very intimacy of the 1979 Warfield shows provoked an (unconscious) reaction in Dylan that obstructed his sharing that same intimacy on *Saved*, the album version of those songs – even though his entire conscious purpose in life at that moment was to move people closer to their Savior by reaching them with these songs. And a comparison of the two versions of "Caribbean Wind" that are available to us again suggests that the intimacy, the very personal nature of the song and the intensity of meaning it has for the singer, a meaningfulness he has brilliantly universalized through his skillful songwriting, this intimacy is what has provoked the doubt about the song's success (as a performance, as lyrics) and has caused songwriter-as-editor to tinker with the song, to try to obscure or even destroy its more personal elements. Alas, he is successful. The later version, while still filled with the shadow of greatness to an intriguing and frustrating degree, has lost its focus. The new opening couplet ("Rose of Sharon") is excellent. All the other substitutions (more than half the lyrics of the song) are "fake Dylan" – clever phrases with no story to tell, no purpose behind them other than holding the space formerly occupied by a more honest or revealing phrase.

Dylan confirms this, I think, in the *Biograph* notes: "That one I couldn't quite grasp what it was about after I finished it. Sometimes you'll write something to be very inspired, and you won't quite finish it for one reason or another. Then you'll go back and try and pick it up, and the inspiration is just gone ... Then it's a struggle. Frustration sets in. I think there's four different sets of lyrics to this, maybe I got it right, I don't know. I had to leave it ..."

But the November 12 version is finished, except for the second line of the first verse which is so slurred it may be "dummy lyrics," and the last couple of notes which trail off instead of crashing to the conclusion that seems to have been led up to. It's a great song — Dylan was correct to cite it as an example of his regaining his mysterious powers in this realm. It is perfectly constructed to include rather than exclude the wide range of emotions generated by the story told; its relation to its listener/observer is every bit as skillful as what Dylan accomplished in "similar" constructions like "Visions of Johanna" or "Idiot Wind."

The story told has unity of space (Miami — a hotel room, or theater, or beach, or combination of these) and time (the gay night; she's gone before dawn breaks), and as usual with Dylan the characters are himself, an attractive woman, and a shadowy third figure (male). The basic story is that he meets this beautiful brown-skinned woman, talks with her, falls in love, wonders what's really going on, does or does not make love with her (but certainly wants to), fails to ask her to marry him, and is left after she's gone with the feeling that something tremendously important has happened.

The song as printed in *Lyrics* has three verses of 12 lines each, each followed by a four-line chorus. The first line of the original ("She was from Haiti, fair brown and intense") is disarming in its directness, totally believable regardless of whether he's fictionalized the details or not. The listener is instantly captured by the undertow of this unexpected intimacy, as in the first line of a good detective novel. The fourth line in both known versions is "Told her about Jesus, told her about the rain" (which tells us very neatly who he was at that moment); as printed in *Lyrics* it is made ambiguous by the dropping of the word "her," so that it could be she doing the telling. Fifth line in the original is "She told me about the vision, told me about the pain" — which is wonderful, a quintessentially female response to his male gambit—followed by "That had risen from the ashes and divided in her memory," which is a little weak, admittedly. (I'm transcribing these lyrics from a live performance; there certainly may be errors in my transcription that could alter the quality or meaning of these lines.) But Dylan in his salad days left in a great many weak lines in order not to interfere with the process by which the songs and their great lines got out to their audience. His process was to fix up and improve what he could, often rewriting in the studio just before a recording, and then go ahead and put out the recording that resulted, warts and all, don't look back. But for the April recording he has rewritten both lines, replacing the lovely bit about vision and pain with the very clever but disingenuous "She told me about the jungle where her brothers were slain" (disingenuous because it's intended to distract us from the truth of the moment rather than include us in) which leads into the rather ludicrous line "By the man who invented iron and disappeared so mysteriously." Good meter, but something's definitely been lost here.

The next six lines in version two (and *Lyrics*) are good, except again for the bitchy bathos of the last line, which makes "gay night" into a bad pun. But compare the original:

> Was she a child or a woman? I really can't say
> Something about her said 'Trust me' anyway
> As the days turned to minutes, and the minutes turned
>   back into hours [great line!!]
> Could I've been used and played as a pawn?
> It certainly was possible, as the gay night wore on
> But victory was mine, and I held it with the help of God's
>   power.

This is the kind of narrative that gives that voice and those guitars something real to bite into.

The first lines of the second verse on November 12 are, "Shadows grew closer as we touched on the floor/Prodigal son sitting next to the door/Preaching resistance, waiting for the night to arrive." This is infinitely more powerful than the rewritten lyric, which is filler for two lines, building to a third line which is striking largely because it has this more meaningful original line lying as a shadow underneath it. The quoted lines suggest to me both the possibility of three people in a room (and so the "other" is a revolutionary?) and the possibility that the male character has been divided in two, one side flirting or perhaps rolling on the floor with the senorita, the other trying to be a good Christian, good repentant ("victory was mine, and I held it with the help of God's power").

There's more here than we can possibly discuss—let's move over everyone's favorite line about "a voice crying 'Daddy'" and go right to the extraordinary second half of the last verse (only because I can't bring up the subject of the live performance of this song without sharing this with you):

> Would I have married her? I don't know. I suppose
> She had bells on her braids and they hung to her toes
> The curtain was rising, and like they say, the ship would
>   sail at dawn
> And I felt it come over me, some kind of gloom
> I thought, 'Say, "Come home with me, girl, I've got plenty
>   of room"'
> But I knew I'd be lying, and besides she had already gone.

The man's a genius. And, sometimes, the most devious enemy of that genius, as well ("Did you ever have a dream that you couldn't explain?", indeed!). But fortunately, he has lived his creative life under compulsion to perform. And we have—some of, enough of—the performances.

12.

"I've made my statement and I don't think I could make it any better than in some of those songs. Once I've said what I need to say in a song, that's it. I don't want to repeat myself."
—Bob Dylan, November 1980

Dylan's brief fall 1980 tour ended December 4 at the Paramount in Portland, Oregon (a small downtown theater; Dylan like a barnstorming ghost would return to give another great performance here almost ten years later, August 1990). There are indications that, thrilled by his Warfield experience, the bandleader/performer wanted to take his tour east under similar conditions (a New York newspaper reported he was looking for a 2500-seat theater in the city to book for an extended appearance, possibly as much as six weeks). There can be little doubt, however, that the murder of John Lennon by a "so-called fan" in New York, December 8, 1980, forced him to reconsider.

Dylan's next public appearance was June 10, 1981. In the meantime, along with more private activities, he prepared for and recorded a new album, *Shot of Love*.

There were rumors at one point that Dylan was considering releasing a three-record album. Certainly he had enough material; 1980-81 was for him a period of prolific and very high quality songwriting. Songs he could have put on his new album (but for which there are no known 1981 recordings) include "Ain't Gonna Go to Hell for Anybody," "Cover Down," "I Will Love Him," "Yonder Comes Sin," "Let's Keep It Between Us," and "City of Gold." Known outtakes from the *Shot of Love* sessions include "The Groom's Still Waiting at the Altar" (released as the B-side of a single; it received so much praise and airplay it was actually added to the *Shot of Love* album in 1986, I believe the only time Dylan has allowed one of his albums to be altered after its initial release), "Caribbean Wind" (later included on *Biograph*), two "cover" songs, "Let It Be Me" (released as the B-side of a European single) and "Mystery Train," and two new Dylan compositions, "Need a Woman" and "Angelina." It seems likely that there are other songs and recordings from this period that have never been heard at all.*

"Caribbean Wind," the studio version, was recorded at the Muscle Shoals Studio in Alabama on April 7, 1981. Dylan was backed by the core of his live band, Tim Drummond, Jim Keltner, Fred Tackett, and Clydie King, plus Benmont Tench on organ and Carl Pickhardt on piano. The producers were Chuck Plotkin and Bob Dylan; *Shot of Love* was the first album other than *Hard Rain* on which Dylan listed himself as producer or coproducer, though he'd certainly played that role on *Planet Waves* and *Blood on the Tracks*.

This same crew moved west, and the other recordings from this period, April and May 1981, were made at Clover Recorders in Los Angeles (with the exception of the song "Shot of Love," recorded at Dylan's rehearsal studio in Santa Monica). The basic band was joined by additional musicians including Steve Ripley and Danny Kortchmar on guitar, Madelyn Quebec, Regina Havis and Carolyn Dennis on backing vocals, and Steve Douglas on saxophone. One song, the final version of "Heart of Mine," featured Ron Wood on guitar, Willie Smith on organ, Donald Dunn on bass, and Ringo Starr on drums. Clydie King sang harmony or

---

The Bootleg Series includes three performances from the *Shot of Love* sessions: "Angelina," "Need a Woman," and a previously-unheard song, "You Changed My Life."

second vocal on many of the songs from these sessions (notably "Every Grain of Sand"), and Dylan played piano on "Lenny Bruce" and "Heart of Mine."

"Well it's always been my nature/To take chances/My right hand drawing back/While my left hand advances." 1981, a long and very productive year for Bob Dylan, is in my imagination dominated, haunted, by these revelatory lines, the opening of one of his most disturbing and rewarding performances. "Angelina," which starts with piano playing and Dylan's naked voice, later joined by background voices and the rest of the band, didn't make it onto the *Shot of Love* album, and stayed unreleased for ten years. The words of the song are so powerful, punching the listener in the gut at two or three different places in every verse, spinning his mind off in a dozen new directions each time he listens, that it is possible to forget momentarily that what one is hearing is not a song, not a set of words, but a *performance*, a man's voice, accompanied by the voices and instruments of other men and women, singing these words at a particular moment with a set of feelings unique to that moment, song every bit as mysterious and intriguing to performer as it is to listener. (Yeah, even if he is the same guy who scratched these words on paper at some other moment.)

That voice!! Elsewhere in the song, one of a score of vignettes that are never detached from but can never quite be connected to each other, Dylan sings, "His eyes were two slits/make any snake proud/With a face that any painter would paint/As he walked through the crowd." This way of describing a face (and, therefore, a man) is perhaps also the only way to approach describing Dylan's voice throughout this extraordinary performance: to hear it is to become a poet or painter or searcher after God, its fiber and depth and the flickers of light/sound that resonate from it awaken or reawaken in every listener an unresolvable hunger. Any painter would paint it. Any preacher would scream from his pulpit in vain hopes of releasing its hold on him. Any lover would listen for and respond to slight echoes of that voice in whatever man presented himself to her, praying to somehow embrace just enough of the mystery to scratch her itch without propelling herself into the abyss.

"Angelina" is the voice of a man singing about a woman, singing in the conscious presence of all his revulsion and desire and awe, and singing also from the heart of his confusion regarding the conflict between his love for this woman and his love for God. It's the biggest subject in Dylan's or probably any man's life, and in a bizarre way he does it justice. Bizarre because he constructs his song as a riddle that compels solution and can't be solved. The answer exists only in the expressiveness of the singer's voice. (Exists at that moment when one *feels* one's own presence in the situation that's being sung about.) And, compelling and satisfying and inspiring as that voice-sound is, still the problem with the answer it offers is very simply this: it's not the answer we want to hear.

(Here is a performance so troubling one wonders if it will ever take its place among Dylan's recognized major works. And yet, how can it possibly be ignored or overlooked?)

The surprises in the text of the song, the way it twists and twists again while making every line strong enough to stand as a song on its own (the technique Dylan once suggested he was using when he wrote "A Hard Rain's A-Gonna Fall"), are well illustrated by the lines that follow the "his eyes were two slits" segment quoted above:

> Worshipping a God with the body of a woman
>   well-endowed
> And the head of a hyena.

This says one thing, but very powerfully, viscerally, evokes three or four other matters that are also central to the song's concerns. If we follow the lyrics literally, we are disturbed by a slight grammatical discontinuity (typical of Dylan, and to dismiss this as accident or carelessness is to misunderstand the essential nature of his technique): surely he was not worshipping *as* he walked through the crowd. Rather, the "worshipping" line is meant as a further description of this man—he's an infidel, indeed from the singer's point of view a particularly scary, distasteful, intriguing sort of infidel—and in context also suggests that this is meant to give us a further picture of what he looks like (i.e., it's a racial comment). But among the other things I believe reach the listener's ear is a vague or not-so-vague impression that the description "with the body of a woman well-endowed and the head of a hyena" is somehow a characterization of the song's title character, or of how the narrator sometimes feels about her. It's a violent, shocking image, neatly yoked to the snake and the crowd and the implied purposefulness of the man's movement.

In each of these five verses, a mini-climax is reached at the halfway point, when, after singing three long rhymed lines (the first and second lines each broken in half by a full breath), Dylan sings a short line of three to six words, ending in a word that will rhyme with "Angelina" (always the last word of each full verse). These words themselves are invariably surprising ("concertina," "hyena," "subpoena," "Argentina," "the arena"), and then the verse restarts (music never stopping, though somehow a great mental pause has taken place) with a forceful shift of gears, each time leaving the listener uncertain whether the new line is meant as a continuation of what was just being said, or not. The line following "hyena" is, "Do I need your permission/to turn the other cheek?" This for me is easily as memorable and quotable as any line on *Blonde on Blonde*, and Dylan immediately croaks out another: "If you can read my mind, why must I speak?" It is difficult to know if he is being nasty or loving here; no doubt the listener is correct to hear it as sometimes one, sometimes the other, and always a little of both. Third line of the triplet makes another subtle shift—still talking to the same person, he now pulls back from her, cold, disinterested, covering his earlier vulnerability: "No I have heard nothing about the man that you seek/Angelina." Actually the disinterest masks anger, and barely masks it. Feelings shift moment to moment here, and threaten constantly to burst the bonds of language and performance.

Feeling is everything. Even Dylan's Christian conversion must be understood as a visceral thing ("I had this feeling, this vision and feeling... There was a presence in the room that couldn't have been anybody but Jesus"). Seeking to "understand" the song, we must be wary of trying to "figure out" the meaning of Dylan's various references to Revelation, particularly in the last verse ("I see pieces of men marching/trying to take heaven by force/I can see the unknown rider/I can see the pale white horse"). The *feeling* of the Book of Revelation is what's important here; Dylan sprinkles his song with images from Revelation because the situation he's both in and describing has the smell of Revelation to him, it feels like those Bible verses feel when he reads them. "I can see the pale white horse." He can see it. Lines like this set a scene (perfectly expressed by the weary elegance—*fin de siecle*, last verse of an epic—of the music and the singer's phrasing). What bursts forth from the scene (though the scene itself is fascinating and pulls at our attention) is an abrupt return of singer talking directly to his beloved, his tormentor: "In God's truth babe tell me what you want/And you'll have it of course." This line jumps out blazing into the listener's thoughts, but though we hear it as complete Dylan drowns out our meditations as he insists on finishing the sentence: "Just step into the arena." Oh Jesus. Love is war.

And how do we feel about this? It depends, probably, on the emotional situation that we're in as we're listening. A song like this is a Rorschach test. The joint presence of deep affection and of hostility, of sexual and religious and (occasionally) political imagery, of storytelling (*who* was stolen from her mother?) and of me-to-you direct address, creates an environment in which many different realities can be mirrored. This ambiguity allows the song to bond with the listener's own thoughts and feelings and circumstances (precisely the technique which leant such power to performances like "It's Alright, Ma" and "Desolation Row"). The singer is now speaking to the listener's private reality, and may therefore have the opportunity to give expression to feelings that had not previously been able to take on form.

He does it with his voice. The lyrics are brilliant, but they only take on meaning as he sings them. In the third verse, listen to the seductive wistfulness of "The peaches they were sweet/And the milk and honey flowed." It would be easy to hear in this Biblical history, American history, personal history (his, yours), but always you'll hear the longing and the affectionate sadness. Listen to the singer's timing on "I was only following instructions/When the judge sent me down the road/With your subpoena." Listen to the beat of your own heart when he says, "When you cease to exist/Then who will you blame?" And when he reengages your mind with the last line, and you start to think again about Satan's presence in these verses ("Your best friend and my worst enemy/Are one and the same"), his voice will let you feel the pain and horror of the trap he's in, and the lack of conviction with which he dismisses her will eat at you, and finally his plaintive, rooftop-rattling cries of "Ohhh ... Angelina!" will leave you with an aloneness more real and immediate than any ideas you might have about the song.

If you wish to know the most private secrets of Dylan's relationship with God, with Woman, with his art and his audience, listen to the sound of his voice during this performance. (You might also learn something about your own secrets.) An artist is a person who takes chances. Did his right hand draw this recording back, keep it from the public? Perhaps. But he threw all the courage of his sinister side into writing and performing it in the first place.

"Angelina" is not included on *Shot of Love*, perhaps because it is such a revealing piece of work, but probably also because the artist was told a double or triple album was out of the question, and placing both "Angelina" and "Every Grain of Sand" on a single record would have unbalanced Dylan's concept of the album, which was I think (taking a cue from the cover) to create a bright, simple, forceful work of pop art.

Dylan succeeded and failed, both at once. The album *is* simple, forceful and bright, and it's a lot better than its reviews (Paul Nelson in *Rolling Stone* dismissed it as being "filled with hatred, confusion and egoism") and its sales (one of Dylan's poorest-selling studio albums) would suggest. Public and critical reaction to the record was badly skewed by the hostility Dylan's righteous "born again" stance had already stirred up — if the album had come out at some other period in Dylan's career, and if the song "Property of Jesus" had been left off, *Shot of Love* would hardly be identifiable as a Christian album. Dylan clearly wanted the record to be heard and judged on its own merits, but he was trapped by his (understandable) resentment of people pressuring him to alter or obscure or renounce his beliefs in order to be accepted by the marketplace. He "showed" them by singing "Property of Jesus" (apparently a response to some snide remarks of Mick Jagger's regarding Dylan's conversion, as quoted in a newspaper), and "they" in turn "showed" him by ignoring or reviling his album.

But *Shot of Love*, even when heard apart from the tug-of-war between Dylan and his fans regarding who "Bob Dylan" really belongs to (assuming that it's possible for any of us to listen even now without unconsciously taking sides), is not, in my opinion, as good as Dylan says it is. This is an interesting phenomenon, Dylan's professed love for this album — he seldom has anything to say about a record once he finishes recording and mixing it, but *Shot of Love* is an exception. A month after recording it, he called it "the most explosive album I've ever done," and told interviewer Paul Gambaccini, "I feel that same way about this album as I did when we recorded *Bringing It All Back Home*. It was like a breakthrough point; it's the kind of music I've been striving to make, and I believe that in time people will see that."

Listening to this interview, one can feel Dylan sincerely believes this new album might have the kind of revolutionary impact on a mass audience that his mid-sixties records achieved. He was very eager for it to be released, and during his July concerts in Europe he expressed frustration with his record company for not getting it out faster (the album finally hit the stores on August 12).

Two years later, July 1983, Dylan was still beating the drum: "To those who care now where Bob Dylan is at," he told interviewer Martin Keller, "they should listen to 'Shot of Love' off the *Shot of Love* album. It's my most perfect song. It defines where I am at spiritually, musically, romantically and whatever else. It shows where my sympathies lie. No need to wonder if I'm this or that. I'm not hiding anything. It's all there in that one song."

And four years on, summer 1985, in the *Biograph* notes: "People didn't listen to that album in a realistic way. 'Shot of Love' was one of the last songs Bumps Blackwell produced and even though he only produced one song I gotta say that of all the producers I ever used, he was the best, the most knowledgeable and he had the best instincts ... Clydie King and I sound pretty close to what's all the best of every traditional style so how could anybody complain about that? The record had something that, I don't know, could have been made in the '40s or maybe the '50s ... there was a cross element of songs on it ... the critics wouldn't allow people to make up their own minds, all they talked about was Jesus this and Jesus that ... *Shot of Love* didn't fit into the current formula. It probably never will. Anyway people were always looking for some excuse to write me off ... I can't say if being 'non-commercial' is a put down or a compliment."

(Dylan had boasted about the great commercial success of *Slow Train Coming*. He expected *Shot of Love* to be perceived as a breakthrough, maybe in aesthetic terms, or as a return of his powers as a popular, hit-making songwriter, man of the people — when the record failed to make a splash on radio, or in sales, or in terms of public or critical response, anything, he expressed his disappointment by becoming quite bitter and confused about the whole process of making records, a state of mind that lingered for most of the 1980s.)

What is it about the song "Shot of Love" that led Dylan to claim "it defines where I am at spiritually, musically, romantically and whatever else"? (Not uncharacteristically, he contradicted this in spring 1985, telling Bill Flanagan, "Certainly nothing that I've written defines me as a total person. There's no one song that does that.") I truly don't know. I like the feel of the song, its energy, its rhythms, its riff, its edgy, insistent tension. It's fun to listen to. The sound of the performance is assertive and friendly, effectively overruling the lyrics, which are mostly bitchy and passive (inject me, please). It's an appealing recording, but it doesn't quite have the charm (or, really, the content) to put it up there with Dylan's best work.

The success of *Shot of Love* (aside from its one obviously great track, "Every Grain of Sand," and one other very special performance, the underrated "In the Summertime") lies in its freshness, its variety, its determination to be different from any earlier Dylan album (why repeat yourself?). With "Shot of Love," "Dead Man, Dead Man," and "Watered-Down Love" Dylan is reaching for a new form (for him), something archetypal, maybe a white r&b, punchy and rhythmic and lyrically uncomplicated. The idea of he and Clydie King singing together is very important to his concept. He's following a sound he hears in his mind's ear, usually a very good way for Dylan to make records.

And, clearly, he's satisfied that he achieved that sound (in the 1983 Keller interview he refers to *Shot of Love* as his "favorite" album). But what I hear on the album are some songs that are half-baked ("Lenny Bruce" drags, despite some moving moments; "Property of Jesus" has an appealing sound but the lyrics, intended to be clever, drip with resentment and self-pity; "Trouble" starts well, with a terrific riff, but the lyrics are inane, the concept's a cliché, and even the riff becomes tiresome), and others that could be excellent but are merely good due to lack of effort by band and vocalist ("Dead Man, Dead Man" — fabulous lyrics! — and "Watered-Down Love").

"Heart of Mine" is a delight, the best uptempo song on the album, wonderfully performed with Dylan wailing away at the piano and Donald "Duck" Dunn holding things together with a really inspired bass line. The looseness of the track, and the expressiveness of Dylan's vocal (Clydie King's harmonies are particularly effective here), give some hint of how good the album might have been if Dylan's touring band had been less self-conscious in the studio.

"In the Summertime" sneaks up on you. Dylan has often said he writes songs by following the first line, and this is a classic example: "I was in your presence for an hour or so." That's the whole story, that's everything he wants and needs to say, and it becomes a song when he succeeds in fleshing out a verse with the same subtle rhythms and musical flavor, building to the inspired melodic hook in the chorus, the words ("In the summertime/Ah ah in the summertime/In the summertime/When you were with me") as rich in melody as the music, great open-voiced singing, followed (each time) by a restatement of the chorus in Dylan's other voice, the harmonica. The harmonica solo after the first chorus, in particular, is one of Dylan's finer moments on that instrument. The whole song is framed by harmonica, starting and ending in the middle of something (endless loop technique, like the lyrics of "All Along the Watchtower"), and when Dylan lets loose after the first chorus, he takes that opening sentence and actually recreates (as convincingly as on "What Can I Do for You?", only this time he caught it on record) the moment, that particular and most powerful interval, when he was in "your" presence. Fifteen seconds of harmonica, and most of the action is in the first eight seconds or so, and it just lays the artist naked. This is sharing with your listener. This is fellowship.

On the strength of this unbreakable bond between the song's suspension point (opening line) and its chorus (arc of the pendulum), every phrase in the song and every moment of the singer's and musicians' phrasing resonates, full of colors and sounds and feelings unique to this particular track, recording, performance. Simple statements become luminous: "I'm still carrying the gift you gave/It's a part of me now, it's been cherished and saved." "Where the sun never set, where the trees hung low/By that soft and shining sea."

"Every Grain of Sand" is the other harmonica song on the record, and indeed "In the Summertime" is the only (even subtle) link between this memorable hymn and the rest of the *Shot of Love* album. Perhaps we can also say that "Every Grain of Sand" is the shot of love that the title track cries out for. The juxtaposition of styles is peculiar and clearly intentional. "Shot of Love" and the songs that follow set up a tension; "Every Grain of Sand" provides the release.

The love in "Every Grain of Sand," though firmly rooted in Dylan's conversion experience and his Bible studies, immediately and obviously reaches beyond its context to communicate a deeply-felt devotional spirit based on universal experiences: pain of self-awareness, and sense of wonder or awe at the beauty of the natural world. The key to the performance is its motion: it moves like the sea, forth and back and forth and back, filled with a quality of restfulness but never resting.

The song is about the moment(s) in which we accept our pain and vulnerability and bow down before (and are lifted up by) the will of God. Bert Cartwright says, "In 'Every Grain of Sand' Dylan expresses the solace of God's caring presence in the face of life's treacheries and sorrows." Dylan does this, of course, through music, as well as through the words. Jonathan Cott notes that the song "elicits from Dylan one of the most ethereal, healing harmonica solos he has ever presented on record." "Healing" is an appropriate word. The song is intensely personal, for listener and singer both; the intimacy of confession, the honest sharing of a sense of sinfulness and despair, creates a possibility of genuine reassurance. "Every Grain of Sand" cuts through doctrine and proselytizing and speaks directly to the listener's need.

Dylan in 1985 described the writing of "Every Grain of Sand": "That was an inspired song that came to me. I felt like I was just putting down words that were coming from somewhere else, and I just stuck it out." (*Biograph* notes) "You're not *conscious* of it. In a song like that, there's no consciousness of any of this stuff having been said before. 'What's this like?' Well, it's not like anything. 'What does it represent?' Well, you don't even know. All you know is that it's a mood piece, and you try to hold onto the mood and finish." (Flanagan interview)

A few thoughts on the use of the Bible in Dylan's songwriting: he has drawn from it extensively throughout his career, as we know, for example on *John Wesley Harding*. When he composed the *Shot of Love* songs he had been involved in intense study and discussion of the Bible for more than two years, and so naturally the language of the Bible must have influenced his writing, his choice of words and images, even when he wasn't consciously alluding to specific passages.

It's difficult for someone not well versed in the Bible to know how these songs might sound to an initiate. Bert Cartwright's booklet *The Bible in the Lyrics of Bob Dylan* includes a line-by-line list of biblical references for most of Dylan's songs through 1983;

looking up the references Cartwright found in "Every Grain of Sand" I am surprised to find that the only places where I would say Dylan is using the actual language of the Bible in this song are the ends of verses two and three: "every hair is numbered" and "every sparrow falling." Both are from Matthew 10:29-30.

The other 13 possible references Cartwright lists are instances where Dylan uses an image or word that *could* be said to have a biblical counterpart. In these cases the allusion to the Bible may be conscious, or unconscious, or merely inferred. For example, Dylan sings, "I have gone from rags to riches in the sorrow of the night." Cartwright says, "The persona exclaims he has gone from the 'rags' of righteousness (Isaiah 64:6) to the 'riches' of the grace of God (Ephesians 1:7, 2:7) in the 'sorrow of the night' — that dark night of the soul known to the psalmist, as in Psalms 6:6." I like this. Certainly I can imagine Dylan saying here that he has gone from righteousness to grace, and playing that against the literal meaning of the line (which is that he made a lot of money quickly and hasn't necessarily enjoyed it). But since the biblical passages do not use the phrase "rags to riches" — rather Cartwright has found a reference to "rags," and elsewhere a reference to "riches" — I cannot judge from the Bible alone whether this is likely to be Dylan's conscious meaning. It is if in fact it is common for preachers or commentators whom Dylan may have encountered to speak of "rags to riches" as meaning the process of spiritual uplift, righteousness to grace. Then he could be making conscious reference to the Bible by way of a body of commentary on the Bible, aware that this phrase would have a special meaning for some of his listeners.

This is important because Dylan's evident fascination with the literal word of the Old and New Testaments confronts us with difficult questions regarding the literalness or precision of his own use of language. His quoted comments above suggest strongly that he wrote "Every Grain of Sand," for instance, in a sustained session, focusing only on holding his mood and letting the words come through; this suggests to me that he didn't stop to look up biblical phrases as he went along. Cartwright's annotations are consistent with this impression.

The words and images from the Bible play the same role in most of Dylan's songs that all words and images play in his writing: they have a musical or auditory/visual or "dream" logic, they sound right to the artist, they contain the smell or rhythm of truth and at best are a good representation of the mood and inspiration in which the original composition took place. Like images in dreams, they should not be taken too literally; rather they exist in the context of a whole: a flow of language, a rhythmic/melodic/linguistic palette. Interpretation is better left to intuition than to logic. For example, in "In the Summertime" Dylan sings, "Then came the warning that was before the flood/That set everybody free." But there was no warning before the flood, except to Noah; that in fact is the point of Jesus's line from Matthew (24:38) that Cartwright cites as a source for this Dylan line.

I think Cartwright has it exactly right here. What is striking is that this section of Matthew 24 is clearly one of Dylan's favorite Bible passages; it is the source of "Jesus said, 'Be ready, for you know not the hour in which I come'" and "Like a thief in the night, He'll replace wrong with right." What this means to me, then (I hear "I got the heart and you got the blood" as meaning, 'Your spirit circulates in me, I'm Your vessel'; and "we cut through iron and we cut through mud" as meaning, 'we've been through a lot of shit together'), is that Dylan thinks (intuitively, not consciously; writing too fast to think about it) of the warning before the flood in terms of this passage from Matthew, and thinks of the passage from Matthew as having set him (and therefore everybody, when and if they open themselves) free.

This cannot be considered a literal interpretation. It depends not on the language of the Bible but on my sense of the person reading that language. To a large extent, it reflects the way the song and its words and the sound of the singer's voice *feel* to me. It requires a leap of faith, dream logic.

But there may be some truth in it.

And there's more fascinating oddball music from these sessions, outtakes and B-sides. The two "covers" are ragged, and both go on a little too long, but both offer some spine-tingling moments of Dylan singing full out, utterly unselfconscious. These are also in some ways better examples of Dylan singing with Clydie King than anything on *Shot* except for their amazing collaboration on "Every Grain of Sand." "Mystery Train," a song associated with Elvis Presley's first Sun sessions, is a thrilling fragment, spontaneous and authentic (with a very hot guitar solo by Danny Kortchmar). Dylan flashes us another glimpse of where he comes from on "Let It Be Me," a pop/country ballad originally done by the Everly Brothers.

The musicians are sleepwalking on this one, but the vocals more than make up for it.

"Need a Woman" is not a great song (or performance) but I'm quite fond of it. Its beat, again different from anything else done at these sessions, is unusual and charming, and Dylan has fun performing it. What holds the song back is it doesn't have a lot to say, other than the sentiment expressed in the title, but one still can't help being tickled by many of the couplets and phrases Dylan tosses out here: "Lately I've been having evil dreams, I wake up in a cold blue glare/I run the tape back in my mind, wondering if I took the wrong road somewhere." (That's the opening of the circulating version; the song as published in *Lyrics* has very different words, and in this case it would seem there's another recorded version.) Dylan says he needs a woman "to be with me and know me as I am," which is certainly a common wish, but the next line sounds more specific to his situation (dilemma?): "to show me the kind of love that don't have to be condemned." What kind of love is that, exactly? Listening to the songs one gets the feeling that in the spring of 1981 Bob Dylan was not too sure. As he tells us elsewhere in the song, he's "Searching for the truth the way God designed it/But the real truth is that I may be afraid to find it." Amen. I can identify.

"The Groom's Still Waiting at the Altar" *is* great, just as fine on record as it was on stage. The May 1981 recording seems a kind of tribute to Michael Bloomfield, and it comes off well, all shuffle and hot licks. Dylan's singing is superb, the raw energy of "Mystery Train" honed and focused without losing any of that fierce spirit. Great texture, great grain. The rewrite of the song is masterful, like a new painting laid over an earlier one: "I see the turning of the page/Curtain rising on a new age/See the groom still waiting at the altar." Nice how the personal becomes universal. Performances like this almost make the world make sense sometimes, and that's saying something.

13.

Dylan went on the road again in June. He played a total of 54 concerts in 1981, 27 in the summer, mostly in Europe, and another 27 in North America in the fall. His band was an evolution of the band that backed him in 1979 and 1980: Tackett, Drummond and Keltner on guitar, bass, and drums, plus Steve Ripley, also on guitar. Willie Smith continued on keyboards in the summer segment, but was replaced by Al Kooper (back in Bob's band after 16 years!) for the fall leg. The back-up singers in summer were Clydie King, Regina Havis, Madelyn Quebec, and Carolyn Dennis; Dennis was not present at the fall shows. The other change for fall was the addition of Arthur Rosato as a second drummer. The summer tour started June 10, in Chicago; after four "warm-up" shows in the U.S. the tour proceeded to France, England, Scandinavia, Germany, Austria, Switzerland, and ended July 25 in Avignon, France. The fall tour began October 16 in Milwaukee, Wisconsin, and wandered through Indiana, Massachusetts, Pennsylvania, New Jersey, Ontario, Quebec, Ohio, Michigan, Louisiana, Texas, Tennessee, and Georgia, ending November 21 in Lakeland, Florida.

This date marks the end of Dylan's publicly evangelical period, in the sense that these shows are an extension of his overtly Christian presentations in late 1979 and early 1980. By 1981, however, the character of the concerts had evolved. Dylan did not preach to his audience in 1981; the songs with specifically Christian content usually made up about a third of his nightly songlist; the segment of gospel songs that had opened the shows was dropped in mid-July; and Dylan no longer seemed at all self-conscious about mixing together his old and new material.

Indeed, what characterizes the 1981 shows is a charming lack of self-consciousness. These shows have no special concept to drive them (as compared to the Rolling Thunder Revue, or the "all new, all Christian" 1979 concerts), not even in the sense of the grand retrospectives put together for the stadium tours in 1974 (defensive; I am who I am) and 1978 (aggressive; I am who I choose to be). Instead they are "just concerts," building on the structural model of the 1979-80 shows ("Gotta Serve Somebody" and "I Believe in You" at the start, followed by "Like a Rolling Stone"; "In the Garden" as the finale, followed by encores starting with "Blowin' in the Wind"). Three or four songs from *Shot of Love* are performed at each concert. Not many cover songs are offered (unlike the fall '80 shows); instead it's Bob Dylan singing songs from his last three albums, plus a generous sprinkling of old chestnuts from his many delightful past lives.

We get "Man Gave Names to All the Animals," "Gotta Serve Somebody," "I Believe in You," and "When You Gonna Wake Up" from *Slow Train Coming* at almost all the shows, plus "Slow Train" maybe half the time; "In the Garden" and "Solid Rock" from *Saved*, plus the occasional "What Can I Do for You?" or "Saved"; "Watered-Down Love" and "Heart of Mine" from *Shot of Love*, plus "Lenny Bruce" at all the summer shows and "Dead Man, Dead Man," "Shot of Love," and "In the Summertime" turning up here and there. Basic oldies (almost every show) are "Maggie's Farm," "Girl from the North Country," "Ballad of a Thin Man," "Just Like a Woman," "Forever Young," "Blowin' in the Wind," "Like a Rolling Stone," and "Knockin' on Heaven's Door." Other frequent choices are "All Along the Watchtower," "Masters of War," "Simple Twist of Fate," "The Times They Are A-Changin'," and "Mr. Tambourine Man." "Hard Rain," "It's Alright, Ma," "I'll Be Your Baby Tonight," and "I Want You" are sung a lot at the autumn shows.

It all adds up to a couple of hours (Dylan typically sings 25 or 26 songs) of solid entertainment. And as with most of Dylan's tours, there are individual concerts, and particular moments in other concerts, that are exceptional; the muse descends and suddenly singer and band are wide awake. It still amazes me that such moments can be captured on tape, and no doubt there are limits on the extent to which such an experience can be communicated through a recording. There is no doubt in my mind, however, that what *is* on these tapes is capable of enduring the way a great painting endures: as a work of art, portrait and product of a moment, an encoding of personal experience that puts us inside the bodies and hearts of other humans across space and culture and time.

What constitutes a memorable performance? This is an extremely difficult question, but unavoidable. My criteria are necessarily subjective: on tape, I look for performances that catch my attention, that nurture and reward me in some deep way, and that continue to please and intrigue me on repeated listenings. Sometimes it is fairly evident to me what attracts me to a particular performance (for example, idiosyncratic diction is often a turn-on, especially when it seems filled with purpose and personality, for example in "I Want You" from November 10, 1981, New Orleans); other times I just notice that a performance gives me pleasure, that I can listen to it again and again with ever-increasing interest and satisfaction. Sometimes it feels as though it's the mood in which the song was sung that makes it so special, that gives it its particular appeal. How can this sort of criterion ("I again placed the canvas upon my easel and told Picasso it was the saddest painting I had ever seen" – David Douglas Duncan, *Picasso's Picassos*) be objectified?

Clinton Heylin calls Dylan's July 1, 1981 concert at Earl's Court in London "one of his finest shows," and makes specific reference to the power of Dylan's singing. I respect Heylin; our tastes in Dylan and in music coincide surprisingly often, and in writing this book I have often gained comfort and guidance from his pathbreaking efforts in this odd task of trying to annotate, describe, and identify individual great performances from among the more than 800 shows Dylan has performed so far. But we do differ on the 1981 tours; he raves about the July 1 show whereas I, after repeated listenings, can only say it doesn't excite me much (a big difference, of course, is he was there and I wasn't). My own favorite summer 1981 concert, of the ones I've heard, is Drammen, Norway (near Oslo), July 10—a soundboard tape that's painfully treble-y and is missing one and a half songs, but that showcases an extraordinarily heartfelt and creative performance. But my difference with Heylin is not really about which of these shows is the true *tour de force*. Rather it's his assertion, in his book *Stolent Moments* and again in his survey of concert tapes published in *The Telegraph*, that Dylan's "vocal gymnastics" at the Earl's Court shows "took their toll on his voice" to such an extent that Heylin's description of the rest of the European tour and of the fall concerts in America is quite dismissive: "The 1981 American tour proved that Dylan had badly damaged his voice in Europe."

I disagree, and since history is ultimately made up of nothing more or less than the opinions of Heylin and me and the newspaper reviewers etc. and Dylan (and you, if you'd like to participate), I think this is worth making a fuss over. It may be true that Dylan hurt his vocal cords (his manner of singing makes it hard, for me at least, to say for sure), but if so he compensates gloriously (sings better without them?), and anyone who appreciates Dylan's art will be missing out if they stop listening to his 1981 shows as of July 1. For the rest of this chapter I intend to focus primarily on three concerts that I think prove this point extremely well (ultimately you must listen to the performances and decide for yourself): Drammen July 10, New Orleans November 10, and Houston November 12.

A concert is a canvas. It is also a kind of drama, in the classical Greek sense: a presentation (often outdoors) before a public gathering. The difference between a painting and a dramatic performance is, if you'll bear with me for a moment, that the painting is a unit of space, whereas the performance is a unit of time. If you think of a movie camera recording the painter's every brush stroke from the moment and place where s/he starts on the canvas to the place and moment where s/he finishes, you will understand that every painting is a kind of straight line, a movement, a performance, compressed upon itself. All those moments are seen at once (time becomes no time), laid atop each other on a surface.

A painting is measured in square feet and inches; dramatic performances are measured in minutes and hours. There is unity of experience in a performance, in a temporal sense: artist performs for two hours, audience is present with him (her) (them) for two hours. But, as with painting, there is also a transformation here; as the painting compresses time into something that can be felt all at once, so the performance takes human experience and stretches it out so that instead of just feeling it altogether (as we do in life) we feel it a morsel at a time, in a sequence. We go with the artist on his temporal journey.

A painting is seen all at once, and it begins wherever the eye happens to fall, with whatever aspect first catches the viewer's attention. (This is very important: all objects of art are created by the observer's attention.) A play, on the other hand, begins with a particular entrance and statement. A concert begins with a specific song. Bob Dylan's concert at the Drammenhalle on July 10, 1981 begins with "The Times They Are A-Changin'," performed solo with some of the band coming in near the end of the song. It begins also with how the singer and the musicians felt at that moment, that evening; and it continues through a sequence of feelings, a journey, made up of both deliberate, Apollonian elements—a list of songs to be played, preexisting lyrics and tunes and previously rehearsed arrangements—and spontaneous, Dionysian elements—the *presence* of the performers, the way they move, apart and together, the way they play their instruments, the way the singer sings and what he sings, not the words or basic tune but what else he sings.

What else he sings. July 10, 1981, Dylan puts something into "The Times They Are A-Changin'" that is unique to the evening. It's not the way he sings the song, in any technical sense, but rather the feelings he manages to communicate. There's a sincerity in his singing, an unusual degree of conviction (the song has tended to be more of a set piece over the years), a fresh, bright enthusiasm often associated with springtime. This does not seem consistent with Dylan's view of the state of the world as expressed in other songs and interviews and concerts during 1981. My tentative explanation for this is that the song is not about the general political/cultural situation, as it was when it was written, but instead expresses the performer's personal reality at this moment, the way he feels about being here. He sounds like he's feeling a new enthusiasm for performing, for being this man singing these songs in this place for these people. The song comes out of him like a rediscovery and invocation and celebration of creative freedom.

This feeling is communicated, I think, in equal parts by the texture of the singer's voice, and by the tempo of the song, a groove created (or discovered) by Dylan's fingers on his guitar, which the voice in turn responds to and becomes part of. Voice and guitar and harmonica work out a spontaneous, complex, wonderfully expressive dance, and the rhythm of this dance (along with the color of the voice) is the feeling that lifts my heart as I listen.

A concert's a canvas, and Dylan is trying a little experiment. July 4, in Birmingham, he started with "Saved" instead of "Gotta Serve Somebody," the first time he opened with a different song in 20 months of touring. July 8, Stockholm, he started with an acoustic "She Belongs to Me" (the song with which he opened all his concerts on the 1965–66 tour) and followed that with "The Times They Are A-Changin'" (his opener from 1963 to 1965), and then launched into "Serve Somebody." July 9, Drammen, he tried "Times" again, this time with full band and near the middle of the concert (before "Slow Train"). Next night, same town, he's starting his concert with "Times," and as inspiring as the performance itself is, it also works as a great springboard for "Serve Somebody" (Dylan and the band hit a fantastic groove, reaching epiphany as the girls sing "serve somebody oooh—") which in turn sets up (the excitement of the band, the strong feelings aroused in the singer) a performance of "I Believe in You" that is extraordinary, unforgettable.

"I Believe in You" has become, for this particular month in the man's lifetime, his declaration of existence. Everything is contained in this one song. We are reminded of the intensity of "Like a Rolling Stone" when it was first recorded, and again when it climaxed his European shows in May 1966. If you wish to meet Dylan, if you would like to spend some time with the private man and really find out what he's feeling, what's going on with him, listen to this performance of "I Believe in You." It is straightforward, honest, enormous, filled with the exuberance of a Walt Whitman, Dylan singing in his best North American voice. He's sharing his soul, and he knows it.

This is followed by a wonderfully anti-climactic "Like a Rolling Stone." The performance is rousing and passionate yet somehow modest, it isn't just a statement about past glories still having currency, instead the song's message has been brought into the present. Dylan's voice on "…and say, 'Would you like to make a deal?'" ties "Rolling Stone" directly to "Gotta Serve Somebody" in a way I've never noticed before. Suddenly the entire four-song opening set (Dylan takes a break after "Like a Rolling Stone")

hangs together with a fierce unity of purpose, and now I begin to
get in touch with a deeper explanation of the impact of the opening song. This night, in this position (something very vulnerable
and therefore very powerful about opening a concert with an
acoustic song, especially when you haven't been doing that), it is
clearly intended to convey a deeply felt, personal and universal,
spiritual message:

> Come gather round people wherever you roam
> And admit that the waters around you have grown...
> If your time to you is worth saving
> Then you'd better start swimming or you'll sink like a
>   stone
> Cause the times they are a-changin'.

This is sung not with the "I've got the answer" arrogance of his
1980 evangelism, but with a warmth and sense of purpose that is
remarkable, effectively integrating the idealistic Dylan of 1963 with
the mature 40-year-old performer of 1981, who seeks to share
himself with his listeners not necessarily with the intention of bringing them to Christ this evening but with the certain knowledge that
the best way to express his love is through service, and the service
that is available to him in his life is testifying through music, telling
the truth in public about what he hears and sees and feels.

So what has the experiment purchased? For this evening,
anyway, it has made all things new. The harmonica on "The Times
They Are A-Changin'" cuts through all thinking, blowing a hymn
of devotion, love of music, love of God. "Serve Somebody," as I said
before, gets into a groove, which is to say a miraculously tight and
self-sustaining rhythmic riff that pulses through every bloodstream
(on stage and in the audience), the musical equivalent of speaking
in tongues, natural high, ecstatic possession. Hot stuff. And "I
Believe in You," though only the third song, is the untoppable
climax of the concert. Where to go from here? Well, you could get
overexcited, try too hard. Or you could lose interest, fall asleep.
Dylan does neither. He and his band follow the playlist, fill up the
canvas, joyfully, playfully, inspiring each other, delighting the audience, finding new possibilities and rediscovering old truths in
almost every song. They take us on a journey across the evening,
and when we arrive at the end we are not the same people who
departed the beginning just two short hours ago.

The intensity dissipates a little at the start of Dylan's next set: "Man Gave Names to All the Animals" and "Maggie's Farm" (which Dylan frequently introduced at the 1981 shows by saying, "Here's the first animal song I ever wrote") are less challenging, less demanding for singer, band, and audience, than the opening songs, and I think part of their purpose each night is simply to loosen things up. I like the sound of Dylan's voice on "Animals," but the contrast with "I Believe in You" is striking: the incredible power of that performance is centered in the sound of the singer's voice, yet here's more or less the same voice and the performance that results is pleasant but forgettable. The difference is content — what the singer has to say at the moment that he's performing, what he's putting into the song. In other words, what we hear on "I Believe in You" that is so electrifying seems to be (and is) the sound of Dylan's voice; what we're really hearing, however, is the sound of his heart. Or you could say (and he probably would) that we're not hearing Dylan at all: spirit is speaking through his voice, spirit is alive in the room.

That spirit begins to stir again on "Girl from the North Country" (a very pretty performance, with moments in the vocal that are spine-tingling) and "Ballad of a Thin Man" (the first verse is glorious; after that the singing is still splendid but the song is weighed down by the slickness of the arrangement). "In the Summertime" is wonderful, again thanks to the richness of Dylan's voice, but again the arrangement's just a little too clean, metronomic rhythm putting the band to sleep, you can hear spirit pacing around ready to burst forth with fiery power, but it just can't find an opening.

"Slow Train" is the breakthrough. Tackett, Drummond and Keltner wake up and find the groove, and to my ears and bloodstream the shift is obvious and extraordinary. Spirit uncoils and (through Dylan's voice and Ripley's lead guitar and Smith's organ and the girls' chanting drone) crackles across the stage. We're talking information here. A slow train *is* coming. This band, singer included, is working as a unit now, living and breathing only to get this message across. The rest of the set has been entertainment. This is art. This is greatness.

After the mid-concert break (Carolyn Dennis singing "Walk Around Heaven All Day"), Dylan and Clydie King share vocals on "Let's Begin," a song of courtship written by Jim Webb. They stand together on stage, gesturing with their hands (no guitar), she looks at him during certain phrases (you can hear some of this interplay on the audio recording as well, voices weaving apart and together), he looks boyish, she looks confident, mysterious, sultry (in Avignon, anyway; I haven't seen video footage of Drammen). The reading they give the song is catchy (appropriate for a pop song) and quite original. It's an intimate, playful send-off for the second half of the concert, and only the third love song of the evening (I count "In the Summertime" as a love song, and of course the other is "Girl from the North Country").

"Lenny Bruce" follows, and somewhat dampens things, in spite of Clydie's harmonies. It's an ill-conceived song, lyrically and musically, and even a relatively good performance of it can seem like it takes a couple of months, at least in the 1981 arrangement.

No matter. Dylan's enjoying himself, and he proves it with a truly spectacular "Mr. Tambourine Man." Unselfconsciously (the most difficult part of the trick), he turns the song inside out—the new rhythm introduced in this arrangement, and carried off especially well in this particular performance, provides the inspiration, the jumping-off place, but the real genius of this "version" (as Shakespearean scholar Christopher Ricks pointed out when some mutual friends played him this tape) is the way Dylan alters his inflection throughout, his voice rising on a word or phrase where we would expect it to fall, and vice versa. The effect is to invite and require us to experience the song as something new (our old sense of its language has been annulled, destroyed). And what matters in the end is not the experiment (which is natural, easy, like leaning forward into the wind instead of letting it blow you back), but the result, which is utterly delightful. Again, it couldn't be half so good (probably couldn't be at all) were it not for the very special dynamic between Dylan and his band on this particular Norway evening.

Exuberance again, very different in style and flavor from what he expressed in "I Believe in You," yet identifiably the same spirit. The man is happy. The world makes sense to him, for this one night anyway. He wants to share what he's feeling. And he does.

"Solid Rock," alas, is missing from the Drammen soundboard; if you have it on an audience tape, please send me a copy. After an eclipse that lasted through all of 1980, the song was reborn at the summer 1981 shows—Bad Segeberg, Germany, July 14, is one notable example. I can't imagine a true rock and roll fan listening to this performance and not gaining an understanding, on a visceral level anyway, of Bob Dylan's Christian experience. And at last the guitar playing is as ferociously emphatic as the singing. Wow. Play it loud.

"Just Like a Woman" at Drammen is yet another wonderfully moving reading of this amazingly durable song, which so lends itself to Dylan's gift for inventive phrasing. Essentially it's the fall 1980 version, which in turn is based to a significant degree on Dylan's 1978 arrangement of the song, and yet it sounds so fresh; what lovely little twists it takes (the female voice gently echoing "just like a woman" during the chorus, Dylan's voice when he says "fog" and "she even makes love," and most of all the landscape Dylan and band create during the break ("and I was dying there of thirst so ... I ... came in here"), new rhythms, new punctuations, new realities. Beautiful stuff.

And still the night's not over. Dylan's 16th song is an unusually warm and affectionate arrangement of "Forever Young" (other years the song in concert has been too anthemic for me). Spirit is definitely present: you can hear it in his voice, and in the things the lead guitar player does, but mostly it's in the two harmonica solos, an extended one in the middle of the song, full of Dylan's feelings about all sorts of unnameables, and a brief brilliant one that ends the performance.

The next song, "Jesus Is the One," is a new Dylan composition (first performed July 9); he sang it eight times during the summer tour and twice during the fall 1981 tour. It's a minor composition, not much to say besides what the title expresses; the lyrics resemble an advertising jingle ("It ain't Mr. Rockefeller/That can raise the dead/Jesus, He's the one"). But as a performance it's well worth while, particularly the taut reading given at Drammen, with a wild intro that features among other things a lovely taste of Chuck Berry guitar and flashes of Motown from the rhythm section. Bob and Clydie both play cowbells as they sing, and the band plays hot rock and roll behind the girls' gospel vocalizing. Everybody's showing off, and it all hangs together splendidly. Fun. Evidently Dylan (remember he'd also recently started singing "Saved" again) felt the need to remove any ambiguities about his position vis-a-vis the Jesus issue. (Once you start proclaiming your faith publicly and loudly, you're stuck with the fact that failure to do so may be interpreted as a change of heart.)

Dylan sits down at the piano for "Heart of Mine," and he and Willie Smith on organ absolutely romp through the performance (duelling keyboards). How Dylan loves to sing this song, and what a good song it is for him! In these live performances of the *Shot of Love* songs it is easier to understand what Dylan aspired to and felt he'd achieved in the album: a new kind of Dylan song, simpler and in some sense more universal (he had a similar feeling about *Nashville Skyline*, I think, at least at first). There's a pretension in this idea, some kind of reverse snobbery maybe, but certainly no pretension in this song or this gorgeously loose, wonderfully sincere performance. This is not the Dylan-voice that gives us chills on "I Believe in You" or "Girl from the North Country," but it is in its own way a great Dylan-voice (spirit in it, yeah you bet), and how useful, when what you're creating is a two-hour concert (not just a song), to have so many different parts of yourself to bring forward at different times in the evening. (I love how Jim Keltner on drums gets into the mood of what those keyboard guys are doing.)

"When You Gonna Wake Up" features a terrific two-part introduction: first a long rambling not quite tune-up session between organ and bass and guitar, and then Dylan singing the first verse and chorus very slow and powerful over a sort of crystallization of that warm-up stuff, adventurous and brilliant music, transitioning abruptly into the fierce staccato rhythm the song is normally performed in. Nice guitar solo in the middle of the song, nice ensemble work, a real hot performance overall which must have been fabulous to experience in person. (I don't get the feeling from Dylan's vocal, however, that he felt strongly connected to this song on this particular evening.)

The rest of the concert is anticlimactic. "In the Garden" offers some excellent vocals, from Carolyn Dennis and the other singers as well as from Dylan, but it meanders a little. I find it jarring that Dylan chooses this song to do his band introductions in, but he does, and they're entertaining as usual ("On the bass guitar tonight, one of the last bass guitar players left in the world, ladies and gentlemen, Tim Drummond! (heh heh) He's got one of the last bass guitars around, that's why"). The encores are performed on automatic pilot – this arrangement of "Blowin' in the Wind" is dreadful, all thud and crash, and Dylan's singing this particular evening doesn't improve matters. "It Ain't Me Babe" is superficially pretty, but lifeless – a striking contrast to the other acoustic performance this evening, the opening song. I do like the 1981 calypso arrangement of "Knockin' on Heaven's Door," it's fun, a good curtain-closer, but the Drammen rendition of it is merely adequate. Sometimes Dylan seems to leave his body during a concert several songs before he actually leaves the stage. No matter. It's been a great evening.

There are lots of other fine performances from the summer 1981 tour, of course, some of which I've heard, some I haven't, some I've heard but haven't properly appreciated (peace, Clinton) — a rich playground for the serious tape collector, Dylan scholar, music lover, whatever. Dylan performed a fiery "Shot of Love" at Avignon, July 25, which at first was scheduled to be included on the 1991 *Bootleg Series* album set; I'm also especially fond of "What Can I Do for You?" and "Heart of Mine" as performed at Basel, July 23.

In addition to the concerts, there's another fascinating Dylan performance from summer 1981, a lengthy interview conducted in London July 2 by American disc jockey Dave Herman, and later released by CBS as a promotional album for use by radio stations. Dylan is relaxed and very forthcoming, but what really makes this recording special is that he sits and strums a steel-string guitar throughout the interview (despite the interviewer's objections), treating us to something like the sound of his thought process as he parries his interrogator's gentle thrusts. For the receptive listener, what Dylan shares of himself via his guitar noodling is even more revealing and rewarding than what he says in words (and quite interesting in terms of insight into how he "thinks" on the guitar, as a performer and songwriter). A marvelous document.

Evidence that the fall 1981 tour of America may hold some special place in Dylan's heart surfaced late in 1989 when "Dead Man, Dead Man" — recorded live in New Orleans, November 10, 1981 — was released as the "B-side" or extra track of a Dylan single (the A-side was "Everything Is Broken" from *Oh Mercy*). This was precisely the third time in Dylan's career that he had chosen to share an otherwise unavailable live recording with his listeners via the B-side of a single; the others were "Just Like Tom Thumb's Blues" from Liverpool 1966, and "Isis" from Montreal 1975. If one were to consciously select one live track per decade to sum up what Dylan was reaching for as a performer in that era, one could hardly improve on this short list.

"Dead Man, Dead Man," like its two listmates, is the work of a brilliant rock and roll singer performing with a band that is right out there on the edge trying to push him over at every moment (can't have great rock singing without that).The sheer intensity of the performance ennobles and breathes new significance into the lyrics: "The race of the engine which overrules your heart/Oooh I can't stand it, I can't stand it, pretending that you're so smart!" When rock and roll is really sung right, for example on the Rolling Stones' best singles, the listener's attention is not even on the singer; it's deflected onto a *gestalt*, a tension, a riff, created by and between the rhythm section and the lead instrument, Keith Richards' guitar or, in this case, Al Kooper's piano. Pounding through, becoming, illuminating, transforming the listener's sympathetic nervous system. "Dead man, dead man/When will you arise...?" Such a sad, angry, and ultimately hopeful question. Such a joyous, spontaneous work of art.

The complete soundboard of the 11/10/81 concert, from Dylan's private collection (same show that earlier provided the live "Heart of Mine" included on *Biograph*), was remixed by producer Daniel Lanois at the time of the *Oh Mercy* sessions, which took place in New Orleans (one can imagine Dylan saying, 'Hey, I did a great concert here once...'). The sound quality of the resultant tape, which is in circulation and which one hopes will be released in its entirety to an appreciative public someday, is absolutely brilliant, and I know it's given a number of fans a very different perspective on Dylan's 1981 performances. This is a concert to listen to for the pure joy of the music. The recent songs are particularly exciting: outstanding versions of "Shot of Love" and "Watered-Down Love," plus an extraordinary, blazing performance of a brand new song, never heard before or since, called "Thief on the Cross."

The Chinese book of wisdom called the *I Ching* describes music as having "the power to ease tension within the heart and to loosen the grip of obscure emotions." It is the peculiar genius of rock and roll to achieve this by first heightening that tension, and by tightening the grip of those odd emotions, yanking them forward into consciousness, filling the listener's heart and mind with their mysterious shapes and colors, their ferocious, invigorating screams. Tension is eased, in other words, not by suppression but by *expression*. You can hear this in Dylan favorites like Elvis Presley's "Mystery Train" and Little Willie John's "Fever." Something wants to get out, something large and nameless and vitally important, and this type of music calls it forward with a simple repeating rhythmic phrase that builds on itself so insistently that the webbing of the universe becomes visible and the inner creature sees it vibrating, grabs at it, inflamed with the possibility of creating a wider opening, escaping, breaking through. There is a paradoxically ecstatic experience to be found in this musical tension that builds and builds mercilessly, with no overt release during the actual duration of the performance. The lyrics of such a song should be evocative, simple, and inexplicable, a koan, a riddle capable of engaging hidden feelings and bringing them to the forefront:

> There's a thief on the cross
> His chances are slim
> There's a thief on the cross
> I wanna talk with him.

The rhythm of the language is as important as its literal content. Rhythm of music and language pulses through the listener, creating waves of feelings, while the mind flounders, seeing Jesus and the two robbers, not certain which of the three the singer is referring to, but feeling the urgency of the need for information. This refusal of a song's lyrics to resolve themselves complements the relentlessness (rising tension, no overt release) of the musical performance. The words of the verses are only partially decipherable, but that doesn't hurt either, and what does come through is perfect: "Everybody's been diverted/Everybody's looking the other way" "Wanna ask about his mother/Wanna ask about his – –" "… it's rising in his *eyes*…"

The song is a cry from deep in the soul. It only needed to be sung once. But I could listen to it a thousand times.

The New Orleans concert (actually the first of two, November 10 and 11, at the Saenger Performing Arts Center) is magnificent, 29 songs from every period of Dylan's career, superbly articulated by both singer and band, climaxing with the usual string of firecrackers: "Shot of Love," "Masters of War," "Just Like a Woman," and then this very pointed sequence, Dylan's own passion play: "Thief on the Cross," "Dead Man, Dead Man," "When You Gonna Wake Up" and "In the Garden." In talking about how great the band sounds I want to specifically include the back-up singers; their voices and the ways they use them (and their timing!) are central to the sound and the success of these performances. This, as much as the "wild mercury" of the mid-60s albums, is the sound the performer has always heard somewhere inside him. His achievement as an artist is that sometimes, with the help of his companions, in a particular town and on a particular evening, he makes it possible for others to hear it as well.

And what is almost monstrous about the recording and preserving of performances is the overwhelming quantity of original, memorable work that can result. In Houston two days later, November 12, Dylan gave an equally fine and very different performance—and then another very good one in Nashville, November 14. Dylan sounds well-oiled with alcohol on the Houston tape, his voice very low and rich, his commentary between songs (and his pacing, when he talks) bizarre and rather charming. That voice! If you love Dylan's work, then you must somehow get hold of copies of "Simple Twist of Fate" and "A Hard Rain's A-Gonna Fall" from Houston, 11/12/81. And "Solid Rock." The new, "slow version" of "Solid Rock" performed at the fall 1981 shows is one of the highlights of a year of astonishing creativity and expressiveness for Dylan, right up there with "Angelina" and "I Believe in You" and "Every Grain of Sand."

Of course what you really want is a copy of the entire Houston concert; there are high points aplenty, and a fascinating sense of momentum from song to song, as the strange mood he's in ebbs and flows, clashing with a song occasionally, more often discovering and magnifying itself in the folds and twists of the song's lyrics and chord changes and rhythms and most of all in the accumulating composite message that the song exists to express—not a message that can be restated in flat words but a kind of living entity, a possibility that becomes real, becomes flesh, at the moment when it is sung and performed and brought to life, in planned/spontaneous collaboration between singer and musicians, a message inspired by and delivered to a living audience, itself a tangible entity, a collective, a great immediate Ear.

The excitement of this entire process, this two-hour drama, coalesces and focuses itself in the perfection of the individual songs, segments-of-performance, mentioned above. In the case of Houston 1981, it seems to me this is a voice of his that is unique to this show, a voice and a side of Dylan's personality consistent with but identifiably distinct from what is heard and expressed in all the rest of his oeuvre. It is this infinite variety to be found in a single human soul that makes the love of another person (and specifically long-term love, marriage, relationship) such an endlessly involving and rewarding undertaking. And this is captured and summed up (voice and insight both) in the November 12, 1981 performance of "Simple Twist of Fate."

How to describe that voice? I cannot. There's so much in it. It is full of detail, full of flavor, bursting with life. I suppose it is my job to explain how this is done, but I can't begin to guess. I can only gesture awkwardly and enthusiastically at the result. And listen, and take it in, and listen again, with enduring pleasure and awe. I want this released on an album, I want to be able to say to people, "Here, *this* is Bob Dylan. This is what all the fuss is about." And they'd be able to hear it or not, but at least I'd have shared my secret. It's the voice, the sensuousness of it, its inexhaustible richness of content, its humanness, word by word and breath by breath, its immediacy, its nakedness. The sound of that voice *inside*, inhabiting, the unique narrative of *this* song: "She looked at him and felt a spark/Tingle to her bone/Twas then she felt alone/And wished that she'd gone straight/And watched out for a simple twist of fate." Oh God.

I'm not sure how I feel about the damned wrong-key harmonica that interrupts the fine organ solo after the last verse and breaks the mood, waking this dreamer and ending the song. I guess I find it jarring but appropriate. It separates me from perfection. It leaves me uncertain, insecure. "How long must he wait?" I want to rewind the tape, re-find that specialness, listen to the singer's voice again.

"Hard Rain" from Houston is quite simply one of the all-time great performances of this great song. One of the gifts that is essential to what Dylan has achieved is his genius for *arrangement*. On the fall 1981 tour he is working again with one of his finest collaborators in this realm—Al Kooper—and indeed this brilliant re-framing of "A Hard Rain's A-Gonna Fall" rests squarely on the little piano figures that follow each phrase of the chorus ("it's a hard...") and the bass & keyboard figure that repeats throughout the verses, unique bits of music, as memorable and as successful as, for example, Kooper's bouncing electric organ embellishments that contribute so hugely to the *Blonde on Blonde* performance of "Memphis Blues Again."

This arrangement (substantively different from the original, yet underspoken, subtle, not arrestingly and obviously different like the wild 1975 Rolling Thunder arrangement) creates a frame that is absolutely perfect for this singer (Dylan 1981) in relation to this song. The freshness with which Dylan attacks each and every one of the 37 descriptive lines (one great poem made up of 37 separate-but-related poems) is thrilling. In Houston he is totally present with each verse, leaving off or adding the personal pronoun at the start of each line as the mood strikes him, entering each line as if he were singing it, pressing it out of himself, for the very first time. Line for line the performance is extraordinary, but what is most moving is the cumulative effect of these passionate one-line performances, strung out one upon another, verse after verse, always introduced by the repeating question ("What did you see?" "Who did you meet?"), then this procession of descriptions, followed by the exquisite drama of the chorus with its relentless, unchanging spiritual weather report—the hook of the song—inescapable, irresistible release.

It is a tribute to this performance, the effectiveness of the new arrangement and the strength of character in the singing, that one is newly dazzled by the depth and richness of the song's structure. Suddenly I notice the mathematics, number magic, that permeates it: five verses, exactly five repetitions of the word "hard" in the chorus, never more, never less, five basic verse lines (the descriptive phrases that answer the opening question) in the first stanza, then seven in the second, seven in the third, six in the fourth, and a climactic twelve in the fifth. And listen to him *speak* numbers—once a line in the first verse ("twelve" "six" "seven" "dozen" "ten thousand"), then once ("ten thousand") in the second, thrice ("one hundred" "ten thousand" "one") in the third, once ("one") in the fourth, and once in the fifth, very explicitly ("where black is the color and none is the number"). What does this all mean? Ah. It doesn't mean. It sparkles. It affects. It's poetry. It sings.

And as these old chestnuts ("Twist," "Rain") are made marvelously new by the performer's art, so is that relatively recent and equally worthy addition to the repertoire (alas that Dylan has not—yet—performed it since 1981), "Solid Rock."

The fall version of "Solid Rock" demonstrates again how closely Dylan's genius for rearrangement, and his ability to be reinspired in the act of performance, work together. Both the Nashville (11/14) and the Houston performances of this song are outstanding, exemplary works of religious art—like medieval paintings of the crucifixion, filled with the painter's own feelings about mortality and faith and despair and about the human condition at the time of painting as well as at the time of the crucifying. Time is collapsed in such art, if anything the Savior is much more present Here in the visions of the painter and the person looking at the painting than There in his historical moment. "Solid Rock," more than ever in its amazing fall '81 incarnation, is an arrow of performance that pierces time, spilling and mingling the blood of performer, audience, and subject. Time stands still, suspended, in this new version, as it did in the best of the fall 1979 performances of the song, via slightly different musical devices this time (one has the feeling that the change of tempo has produced an entirely new song, which is not actually true—words, message, even the melody and some aspects of the rhythm are unchanged; what's different besides the tempo is the mood, the entire flavor of the presentation).

This is Dylan at his most prophetic, and, in a strange sense, his most personal, both at once. Not everyone can relate to the vision of Christ as a solid rock ("made before the foundation of the world") that he's presenting here, nor even perhaps to the collateral, implied vision of the non-solidity of the material world. That's an obstacle. But there's a rare beauty here, in these performances of this song, that is well worth putting aside all considerations for; if the listener can suspend judgment while the performer suspends time, both may be rewarded in the greatest coin, which is the language beyond beliefs, the intimate language (more musical than verbal) of the human heart.

There's more, of course. A particularly moving "Let It Be Me" sung with Clydie King in Toronto, 10/29/81; jolly versions of "I'll Be Your Baby Tonight" and "It's All in the Game" (pop song from 1958) at many of the fall concerts; a surprise live unveiling of "Every Grain of Sand" (no harmonica, but still a striking performance) at Lakeland, 11/21/81, the last show of the tour. All in all, a very rewarding tour in terms of musical accomplishment. Dylan's relationship with his band—on stage, at the moment of performance—was particularly good in the fall of 1981, and the music that resulted was exceptional. After years of striving to blend the old and the new, the spiritual and the worldly, Dylan and companions seemed to have found the right recipe. One could easily imagine them continuing this tour for several more years, crisscrossing the continents, playing for skeptics, believers, whoever wants to show up.

In fact, however, the evangelical tours were over. Dylan beat a retreat. His next concert was not until May 1984, two and a half years later. It would be a full two years before he even released another album.

VIII: Loner

December 1981 - April 1984

"My work is understood in the blood of the heart."
— Bob Dylan, July 1983

14.

After two years of almost continuous touring, Dylan stepped out of the spotlight for a while. In 1982 his only public performance consisted of three songs sung with Joan Baez at a large nuclear disarmament rally (Peace Sunday) in Pasadena, California, June 6. It's a sloppy performance, consisting of "With God on Our Side," "Blowin' in the Wind," and a Jimmy Buffet song (Dylan's choice) called "A Pirate Looks at Forty." Dylan's only other public appearance in 1982 was in March, when he was inducted into the Songwriters Hall of Fame. (During the summer, in Minneapolis, he attended a number of concerts and club appearances by contemporary performers, often accompanied by his teenage son Jesse.)

Other information about Dylan's life and work in 1982 is hard to come by. The year began with the suicide of his close friend Howard Alk, his collaborator on *Renaldo & Clara*. Clinton Heylin identifies early summer, 1982, as a likely date for Dylan's unreleased, uncirculated recording sessions with Clydie King ("I've got a record of just me and Clydie King singing together," he told Mikal Gilmore in 1985, "and it's great, but it doesn't fall into any category that the record company knows how to deal with. It's something like the Delmore Brothers; it's very simple and the harmonies are great"). Heylin also speculates that a mysterious tape of unfinished Dylan studio tracks, some of them quite striking, dates from late summer or fall 1982. (Michael Krogsgaard dates this tape as May/June 1980.)

1983 again saw only one public Dylan performance, on February 16 at the Lone Star Cafe in New York City; he got on stage during a set by his former accompanists Levon Helm and Rick Danko and sang clumsy back-up vocals and played guitar with them for fifteen minutes.

Between April 11 and May 8, 1983, Dylan recorded at Power Station Studios in New York (with Dire Straits guitarist Mark Knopfler as his co-producer). Later, Dylan came back by himself and remixed or rerecorded some of the songs. This process was completed in early July. The album Dylan put together from these sessions, *Infidels*, contains some very good and some very bad performances side by side. The album title is suggestive and ambiguous in the best Dylan tradition; I hear it as a comment on the unholiness and corruption of the world. In the end, some of the better songs and performances from the sessions were left off of the album, including an unmistakable masterpiece, one of the true high points of Dylan's astonishing career as composer and performer, "Blind Willie McTell."

"Blind Willie McTell" is a song about *seeing*. Dylan sees something—a vision, if you will, of America, of the history of black Americans and the American south—and communicates what he sees through his voice. This seeing is done not with the eyes but with the heart. It is a form of perception that includes hearing (hoot owl, tribes a-moaning, undertaker's bell—notice how "visual" these auditory images are) and seeing and smelling and also an information source not sensory but simply felt within, monstrously and unerringly, communicated by the verb "seem": "Power and greed and corruptible seed/seem to be all that there is." The window Dylan says he's gazing out of is, certainly, a real window— the song is exquisitely concrete from start to finish, you can see, hear and smell everything—but (as is the case when we gaze out windows) it is also, and in a truer sense, the window of memory, of awareness, of feeling, where everything one has ever heard and sensed in relation to some particular subject is suddenly conjured up in a moment of pure feeling, like Proust's sweetcake epiphany.

Dylan glances out the window and *sees* this historical tableau, as though he were sitting in Minnesota's fabulous old St. James Hotel (a real place, although the hotel's name also acknowledges the source of the song's melody, for this is Dylan's loving tribute to and jazz improvisation on "St. James Infirmary"), gazing with some third or fifth eye all the way down the Mississippi River to the historical vista that lay at the other end decades and centuries — time and space both telescoped — ago. Sees it, feels it, and cries out in pain and despair and a kind of joy which is the liberation inherent in the blues, the liberation of being able to express and release the "oppression of knowledge" (as John Bauldie calls it), a declaration of freedom and personal power. "Blind Willie McTell" is, not paradoxically, one of the saddest and most uplifting songs this listener has ever heard.

It's a painting. It's the painting Dylan has wanted to paint all his life, his "tall oak tree," his "picture of what goes on around here sometimes," his "painting where you can see the different parts but then you also see the whole of it." It is in a real sense the culmination of his artistic aspirations, and I do not find it surprising that he hesitated (in 1983, and for years afterward, until the release of the piano/guitar version of "Blind Willie McTell" on *The Bootleg Series* in 1991) to cast this particular pearl before the swine who had for so long howled at him from the critics' gallery and, sadly, from the audience's pit as well. Of course he expected us to love the song. And he also knew, from bitter experience over the past decade or more, that we would most probably ignore it, or damn it with faint praise. In such a circumstance the pride of the artist, and his vulnerable love for what he's created, urge him towards silence.

But only after the fact. First there is the need to express, and the inspiration (both at once; how could we ever say which comes first?), and the resultant expression of need is the key to the mystery of the performing artist, because while "Blind Willie McTell" is a stunningly brilliant composition that we could analyze needlessly and ecstatically for hours, the heart of this masterpiece is its performance. All the effort of composition is mere preparation for this moment. This is the antithesis of silence. This is that human act so linked with and perhaps even more courageous than *seeing*; this is the holiness that Dylan perceives in the old blues singer, and by extension perhaps in all of humanity, though we most of us or all of us fall short; this is *speaking*.

And what speaks in "Blind Willie McTell" (the *Bootleg Series* version), what arises out of and caresses and calls attention to and finally separates itself from the silence, is the piano. Dylan's voice follows. The beauty and expressiveness of his voice send shivers through us, immediately and repeatedly, every time we listen; he is so present it scares us, and yet this presence is so sweet we can't pull ourselves away. This is his following. The piano is guiding him across a vast and mighty landscape, the land of his vision, full of images and sounds and smells, and his voice follows, bringing words and tune and the deep keening of his heart along with it. Every phrase is a voyage, filled with awareness and need and life. And finally the voice stops, and the piano continues (ably supported throughout by Knopfler's understated guitar accompaniment), allowing and requiring the listener to gaze out of (and into) the window of his or her own heart.

There are eight songs on *Infidels*; five more tracks from the same sessions are included on *The Bootleg Series*. One song from these sessions, "Death Is Not the End," turned up on Dylan's 1988 album *Down in the Groove*; another, "Clean Cut Kid," was rerecorded for 1985's *Empire Burlesque*. The other known Dylan composition from these sessions (there are 16 in all), "Julius and Ethel," is still unreleased. There are also said to be fourteen "cover" songs recorded at this time, one of which, "Angel Flying Too Close to the Ground" (written by Willie Nelson), was released as the B-side of a single in Europe in 1983. One other "cover" performance, "This Was My Love" (by Jim Harbert), is in circulation. Circulating material from the *Infidels* sessions also includes alternate takes of seven of the released songs, plus some alternate mixes of official takes that are sometimes better than the released versions.

Given all this, the temptation to put together one's own version of *Infidels* is considerable. However you do it, it's not hard to come up with an album vastly better than what was released. My choice is to put the four epics (ambitious, big-screen numbers) on side one: "Foot of Pride," "Blind Willie McTell," "I and I," and "Jokerman." Side two could lead off with "License to Kill" (the alternate mix; I find the drum sound on the released version intolerable) as a transition into a suite of love songs: "Don't Fall Apart on Me Tonight," "Sweetheart Like You," "Tell Me," and "Someone's Got a Hold of My Heart."

The inclusion of "Blind Willie McTell" and "Foot of Pride" improves the album immeasurably, but the exclusions are almost as important. "Neighborhood Bully" to me is a dreadful song; "Man of Peace" and "Union Sundown," at least as performed here, are not much better. I don't like the *sound* of these songs—they're smug, they thud and plod, they condescend. They irritate. And they're full of muddy thinking. "Good intentions can be evil," says Dylan; "Sometimes Satan comes as a man of peace." I can't argue with either of these statements, but the juxtaposition is intriguing. Does Dylan think Satan has good intentions? Of course not, but when you've got the "sweet gift of gab" you don't always pay attention to what your words are saying. "Neighborhood Bully" with a few changes could be a defense of the activities of any nation-state at any time in history, even Hitler's Germany. "Union Sundown" seems to want to be an attack on capitalism and corporate greed, but the only thought that comes through clearly is: buying things that are made in other countries is stupid and bad.

I don't like hate songs. But I love "Idiot Wind" and "Like a Rolling Stone." Why? Because they're not shallow. Because they gaze honestly and empathetically and courageously into the pit of real human feelings, including anger and hatred. The man who sings them cares about what he's saying. He's not out to manipulate his listeners; instead he's pouring all of himself into the effort to find and express the truth.

"Foot of Pride" is in a sense written from the same place of hostility and anguish and self-righteousness as "Man of Peace" and "Neighborhood Bully" and "Union Sundown," but I like it, I can listen to it over and over again, I intuitively put it in a class with Dylan's better work rather than with his clunkers. Why? Because of its intelligence, its sincerity, its originality, its great sound and superb vocal performance. Most of all I think what sets it apart from "Man of Peace" etc. (and what makes the intelligence and sincerity possible) is that it acknowledges and shares the anguish the speaker is feeling. It moves beyond smug righteousness into the wild uncharted land of self-doubt, and disappointment, and honest confusion, anger, despair.

"Foot of Pride" is in fact, in the words Dylan used to describe the composition of "Like a Rolling Stone," "a long piece of vomit." And it rings with conviction. What is it about? It's about how pride destroys us and turns us into monsters. The four middle verses are in fact a gallery of monsters, and the song could be taken as another parade of devils (like "Man of Peace") except for the subtle but crucial difference that in this song Dylan gets across the true horror: that these devils not only confront us, they *are* us. We become them, with our stupidity, cupidity, vanity, lust, self-import- ance, timidity ... we not only are menaced by them, we cross the line and are transformed by them (and our own weaknesses) into "anything that they want" us to be.

I find in the first and last verses a suggestion of structure, in that the song seems to be about, or anyway inspired by, a funeral. The "he" in the first verse seems to be the same person as the "he" in the last verse ("He reached too high and was thrown back to the ground" / "Did he make it to the top? Well he probably did and dropped"). This is helpful because it points ever so subtly towards a solution to the extremely recalcitrant problem of identity that is central to the songs recorded at these sessions.

This problem can be summed up (switching songs for a mo- ment) in a simple but baffling question: Who is Jokerman?

I have been reading commentaries on the song, and none of the ones I've seen has an answer that satisfies me. Many people assume that he's Dylan; some see him as Christ, or Satan; and one or two seem to perceive that he could be all three. Yes, but how? Nick de Somogyi is most insightful on this subject, in his essay "Jokermen & Thieves," noting the connection between Jokerman and the joker in "All Along the Watchtower." De Somogyi sees both these figures as deriving from the Holy Fool (wise innocent) por- trayed in the zero card of the Tarot, and notes the further connec- tion of this character with the fool in *King Lear*, with Dionysus and other tricksters, with Everyman, and with Christ. Dylan is certainly conscious at the very least of the Tarot connection, as he acknowl- edges in the line (from the earlier take of "Jokerman"), "So drunk, standing in the middle of the street/Directing traffic with a small dog at your feet." The small dog is from the picture on the Waite deck Tarot card of The Fool, a picture which also resonates in my opinion with the chorus of "Jokerman" (dancing high and free).

So what? Good question. If the song is specifically about Dylan, it's insufferably vain – I don't think there's any other in- stance of him describing himself in such pukingly romantic terms, nor does this seem consistent with his 1983 mood as revealed in almost all these songs. If it's specifically about Christ, why is this strict by-the-book Christian and/or Jew now describing him as "born with a snake in both your fists" like Hercules or some God with the head of a hyena? And so forth. The prince in the last verse is almost certainly the Prince of Darkness, and whoever the Jokerman is, one is left wondering why he doesn't show any response to the Prince's evil acts.

Fascinating, baffling song. Of course interpretation is not often the best way to penetrate Dylan's art, but some songs aggressively confront us with riddles. It is possible of course that the song is just more muddy thinking – we have some familiarity at this point with the unconscious aspects of Dylan's technique, we know he doesn't always pay attention to what he might be saying. But while there are aspects of both composition and performance that make "Jokerman" annoying, even grating at times, it still has a grace and power about it that takes it out of the realm of "imitation Dylan" (a realm it superficially belongs in, to be sure; newspaper critics predictably greeted the album as a return of the good old boy, thanks largely to the sound of this song and their first impressions of its language, its imagery).

Consciously or unconsciously, Dylan *is* saying something here, something that is quite important to him. We can feel that as we listen (I have a preference for the earlier vocal take, which is less contrived and therefore warmer and easier to listen to over and over; but I must admit that the beauty of the later vocal, though I mistrust it, is also quite moving at times). But what?

I don't know. But the funeral in "Foot of Pride" is helpful. The man who has died is certainly human; is not Christ (though his death inspires the preacher to talk about Christ betrayed); is certainly not Satan. He could be Dylan, I suppose. When Dylan sings, "Yes I guess I loved him too, I can still see him in my mind climbing that hill," I can't help thinking of Christ (I also think of Mercer in Philip K. Dick's *Do Androids Dream of Electric Sheep?*, but never mind). It would probably be a fair reading to say that the singer is thinking of a dead friend who at times reminds him of himself, at times also reminds him of Christ, and who also confronts him with the horror of our human failings and the inevitability of retribution. Regarding the old question of "Who is Queen Jane?" (in "Queen Jane Approximately"), I like to think it's Dylan seeing himself (his ambition, his indifference to others) in his friend Joan, and using his hostile feelings towards her as a horse to ride as he releases his self-judgment, his deep feelings of self-dissatisfaction. In the same way, Dylan can be moved simultaneously in "Foot of Pride" by feelings of love and by feelings of repugnance and castigation, feelings that can seem to him to be directed outward but which as he lets them out take on the full fury of his own self-hatred — and serve also as a covert expression of his dissatisfaction with God as well. If the world is shit, as Dylan tells us it is in these songs, it is, according to Dylan's sincere beliefs, the fault of the corruptibility of men; it is we who have betrayed Christ. Unspoken however beneath the surface feelings of anyone undergoing a crisis of faith (as most of us do at least once a year) is the firm, ego-based conviction that it's just the other way around: *He* has betrayed us, betrayed me.

These feelings stir around inside a person, and sometimes pour out, as at the *Infidels* sessions, in a tempest, a cavalcade, of hostile ambivalence. Nothing makes any sense. I don't want to talk about it (though I can't stop talking). And all of you are to blame.

So who is the Jokerman? He's a clown. A hero, a fool, a devil, a saint, a joke, a mockery. He's me (the person singing) in the pathetic absurdity of my self-idealization. He's the projection of my own confusion. I don't know if he's Christ or an imitation of Christ. If the latter, is he a holy fool, or a foolish infidel, or the Devil incarnate? He's a superstar, ha ha. The thoughts whirl around. The chorus attempts to idealize him gently as a dancer, to connect him with that reliable old identity, the devotee of the tambourine man. But it doesn't quite work. Freedom is no longer enough of an answer. "With truth so far off, what good will it do?" The speaker is too full of dread. Nighttime means aliveness in the chorus. In the fourth verse it means peace. But in the fifth verse it surely means death. Not death like release, or liberation; there *is* a little taste of good old vengeance in it, but mostly it just seems to signify that soon the jig will be up.

I'm babbling. I don't always like this song, and I suspect those who do like it of not always listening past the surface. And yet I acknowledge it as a powerful and probably very accurate expression of the singer's inner turmoil. His efforts at oversimplifying his identity beautifully betray and reveal the true complexity of his situation.

(And for his sins, he will be forced to release this self-portrait on an album, and sing it at concerts at which he'll be greeted like a king. Afterwards they'll write reviews in which he'll be dismissed as a fool. All part of the ongoing joke.)

"I and I," the other epic from these sessions, is a beautiful song, powerfully sung, with a wonderfully moody and evocative instrumental setting that is marred (especially on the final, released mix) by a melodramatic, heavily-echoed bass drum part that starts crashing away during the first chorus and gets worse throughout the rest of the song. This flaw is, I think, another manifestation of Dylan's ambivalence while making this record: ambivalence towards the world, towards his beliefs (feels them deeply, questions them deeply, mocks himself for giving a damn), towards his audience, towards his work, and towards the whole idea of recording and releasing an "album," a commercial product, a fragmentary and necessarily distorted representation of his creative (and personal, spiritual) process. One part of him probably thinks this drum part sounds terrific. Another part, in my opinion, cynically feels like he's giving the record company and the public what they want. And what results, as he sits at the mixing board, is a level of distraction: he *isn't* "listening only to my heart." The artistic sureness that is so awe-inspiring so often in Dylan's career winks on and off at these sessions.

When it's on it's as devastating as ever. The picture painted in the first verse of "I and I" is unforgettable. Notice the gentleness and strength in the singer's voice; each word is simply and directly spoken, none of the complex, layered phrasing of 1974's "Simple Twist of Fate," yet the voice is equally expressive, perfectly yoking melody and rhythm and language. What a marvelous image, the speaker alone with a sleeping woman, studying her, moved by her body language, suddenly travelling as if on the vehicle of her dreams across space and time to another reality, feeling (through his response to her) a momentary connection with Solomon, lord of a purer moment, idealized monarch, poet, lover. And what is communicated most of all, as in a Matisse nude, is the dignity of woman, and the possibility of redemption (letting go of the world and its defilements) through her grace.

Her unconscious grace, because "if she wakes up she'll just want me to talk," she'll reverse her role, become a force pulling me away from simple presence with myself and with God, and back to the self-conscious or interpreted universe.

The transition into the first chorus is particularly striking: psalms (songs praising God) and moonlight streams bring us suddenly, starkly, and very gracefully to the thought of me and God, alone, in nature ("creation"). Suddenly the presence is here, and it is atavistic, the Old Testament God, terrifying rather than comforting, uncompromising, not human, not a denial of Christ but if you will an absence, no son or holy ghost. "No man sees my face and lives." This is a very specific Bible passage, Exodus 33:20—God's response to Moses when Moses asks God to show him His glory.

In the third verse I believe Dylan tells us directly and honestly of something that has happened to him since the last batch of songs he wrote and that has brought about a shift in his perception of what is. "Took a stranger to teach me to look into justice's beautiful face/And to see an eye for an eye and a tooth for a tooth." Clearly he has received instruction in the Books of Leviticus and Deuteronomy, as he tells us in "Jokerman," and has received an awakening related to old Babylon king Hammurabi's code of justice (also attributed to Moses). These "eye for an eye" lyrics seem to carry much more conviction than Dylan's explication of the golden rule (a radically different concept of man's relationship with justice), "Do Right to Me Baby." But at this point I must say that while I hear his conviction, I do not know what he's driving at. In "Foot of Pride" he tells us scathingly, "They don't believe in mercy/Judgment on them is something that you'll never see." Because justice takes place in the next world, not this one? But that's not what "an eye for an eye" is about. Ah well. I don't think this is a case of Dylan being careless in his language. Rather, I think he has gotten back in touch with an intrinsically vengeful ("Something's gotta be evened up," he told that reporter in 1967) part of his nature, has found agreement for it in the Holy Book, and is just letting fly. He is who he is. Sometimes I identify fiercely with his expression of who he is. Other times it just seems utterly alien.

Alien but sincere. And deeply moving. "I and I"'s a fine performance. I like it when he says, "She should still be there sleeping." I like the illuminated quality of the first four verses, which take place at night, contrasted with the narrow darkness of the last verse, which takes place at noon. I don't like the way he complains "I still go barefoot," but I love the ambiguity of the line. He could even be singing to Jesus. Kind of brash, but then God's not the only one whose nature "neither honors nor forgives." Dylan's petulance here is unattractive to me, but his honesty is almost holy.

Honesty and cynicism are at war in these performances. In some ways the *Infidels* album seems to have been manufactured by Dylan with an eye towards muddying the issue of his religious stance, presumably for commercial as well as personal reasons. The photo of him on the inner sleeve kneeling on a hill overlooking Jerusalem, and his song defending Israel ("Neighborhood Bully"), combined with the absence of any overtly Christian material on the album, have the effect of suggesting that the Jewish singer has returned to the religion of his childhood. Certainly there is other evidence that Dylan had turned his focus back towards his Judaic roots. Always interested in the literal word of the Bible, he now was seen spending time with the Lubbavitchers, a sect of Jewish fundamentalists. But what comes across in *Infidels* is not so much a redirecting of Dylan's beliefs—and certainly not the straightforward rejection of his Christian beliefs that many of his fans wished for—but rather a loss of sureness. The album snarls its hostility towards a culture in which "power and greed and corruptible seed seem to be all that there is," and stridently or sorrowfully wonders how to defend innocence (children, women-as-angels) in "a world that's been raped and defiled." This is not inconsistent with the Dylan we've always known, the Dylan of "It's Alright, Ma." But what comes through under the surface is not the revolutionary strength and self-reliance (reliance on the power of one's own perception) communicated by "It's Alright, Ma." Instead the underlying feeling in the *Infidels* performances as a whole is one of uncertainty—a painful, defensive self-doubt.

This undermines the topical songs—"License to Kill," the best of them, can't resolve the brilliance of its chorus with the muddy pretentiousness of most of its verses—but it helps give the session's love songs a redeeming modesty and grace. In the private space of woman and man ("the only place open is a thousand miles away"—a *very* private space), Dylan expresses his uncertainty with tenderness and passion: "Tell me, I've got to know"; "Don't fall apart on me tonight/I just don't think that I could handle it"; "I once knew a woman who looked like you/She wanted a whole man, not just a half"; "Everything looks a little far away to me." The singer is not sure of himself, not even sure enough to pull this woman to him. But he certainly doesn't want her to go away.

So he serenades her. And the songs that result are truly charming—even the confrontive "Sweetheart Like You," or the jealousy-tinged "Tell Me" — as opposed to for example "Lord Protect My Child," which I find skillful and occasionally brilliant, in both lyric and performance, with a message I relate to keenly, but which still somehow adds up to something unappealing, charmless, a song I can admire from a distance but which I don't enjoy listening to.

The man-woman songs I enjoy very much. I particularly like the way they run together, Dylan's different voices and stances and the seemingly different women and relationships referred to all becoming one voice, one relationship with a thousand aspects and a single presence. "I need you, yeah." This is real. There are other moments in "Don't Fall Apart on Me Tonight" that are condescending or too clever by half, but Dylan's singing in the good parts cuts through the bullshit. It's like the compassion and vulnerability in his voice drowns out the cockiness and equivocation in his words. Spirit triumphs over mind one more time.

"Sweetheart Like You" is puzzling. The verse "A woman like you should be at home/That's where you belong/Taking care of somebody nice/Who don't know how to do you wrong" is deliberately provocative, but at the same time full of heart — the sincerity is evident — not at all a reprise of 1978's "Can you cook and sew, make flowers grow/Do you understand my pain?" What's going on here? I think the subject of the song is a woman whom the singer perceives as someone trying to make it in the corporate world; he is not speaking of "a woman's place" but rather lamenting the loss of female values when a woman is pressured or seduced into trying to "make it" as a man in a corrupt and evil reality. The clue to this, again, is not in the lyrics as such (they fit my interpretation but they certainly don't make much effort to point to it) but in the astonishing beauty of the vocal and instrumental performance. Dylan and the other musicians have captured a mood here. The musicians are following Dylan, and he's following his inspiration — but the magical success of the finished product demonstrates unequivocally that this is not a conflicted or contradictory inspiration, such as I perceive in "Jokerman." Confronted with such a pleasing and powerful work of art, we are forced I think to suspend our doubts about what it seems to be saying and instead work to find the real source of its light, its beauty, its harmony and fierce visionary strength. What's a sweetheart like this song doing in this dump of reactionary, politically offensive ideas? That's the puzzle. I don't know if my solution is the correct one. But I do know that beauty like this cannot be lightly dismissed.

"Tell Me" is pretty rather than beautiful, but its waltz-time sweetness and rich easygoing vocal contribute generously to the cumulative impact of this set of love songs. Dylan's language here is graceful and subtle and humourous ("Is that the heat and the beat of your pulse that I feel?/If it's not that then what is it you're trying to conceal?"). John Bauldie writes that this song's about the beginning of a relationship, but there's a contradictory thread here ("old acquaintance of ours") that suggests a long-time relationship possibly facing its end. Dylan's not above trying to have it both ways; some love affairs are like that. End or beginning? Tell me...

And the summation, my favorite of these love songs I think although "Sweetheart" is exquisite, "Someone's Got a Hold of My Heart." Every one of these four songs is distinguished by an attractive and very communicative melody; in this case melody and arrangement and vocal and lyrics work together so intelligently and so naturally that the result is breathtaking in its understated elegance. It's the musical equivalent of a shrug—but what a shrug, involving not just shoulders but eyebrows, lips, tilt of the head, spread of the fingers, even a small but unmistakable swivel of hips. The lyrics go by almost unnoticed, worming their way in on repeated listenings until the phrases ring in the mind like so many classic Dylan coinages before them:

> It's getting harder and harder to recognize the trap
> Too much information about nothing, too much educated rap
>
> Never could learn to drink that blood, and call it wine
>
> What looks large from a distance, close up is never that big

... all sung in a voice that melts in the listener's heart almost before it's out of the singer's mouth. This is Dylan at home with his gift, sorting through all the fancy expectations and getting down to what's real for him, with an incredible efficiency of image and language. When we hear him say, "You're the one I've been waiting for, you're the one that I desire/But you must realize first I'm not another man you can hire," it comes through so clear: You have won me with your beauty, your power. But if all you can see is the effect of your power, you're not seeing me. And so you'll lose me again. And I don't want you to.

This is not the jokerman. This is someone whose heart can be got ahold of. And in a real sense this person is more vulnerable, and even more in need of a place to hide, than the genius who could write and perform "Blind Willie McTell."

On July 5, 1983, as he was completing the mixing of *Infidels*, Dylan did an interview with Martin Keller for the Minneapolis *City Pages*. Words flow out of him easily, passionately. When asked about his Jewish roots, he sounds like a man who could ad lib "Foot of Pride." He's quick, eloquent, rhythmic, poetic, Biblical, sarcastic: "Roots, man — we're talking about Jewish roots, you want to know more? Check up on Elijah the prophet. He could make rain. Isaiah the prophet, even Jeremiah, see if their brethren didn't want to bust their brains for telling it right like it is, yeah — these are my roots I suppose. Am I looking for them? Well, I don't know. I ain't looking for them in synagogues with six-pointed Egyptian stars shining down from every window, I can tell you that much. But you know, it's sleepy time down South." Sounds like cocaine talking, to me. Eloquent and very edgy. And quite characteristic of Dylan's public statements in the 1980s. Sometimes the inner man is revealed, perhaps inadvertently, as in this comment from a guy who has spent the last three months recording and then making choices about his album: "The sound of my own voice ... I can't get used to it, never have gotten used to it. Makes you wanna *hide*."

In October 1983 Dylan filmed a video — his first, unless you count the brilliant film clip he did in 1965 with D. A. Pennebaker for "Subterranean Homesick Blues" — to promote "Sweetheart Like You." It's utterly uninteresting. Dylan's role in it is passive — he had no creative input into the script or concept (could have had, but chose not to), and he is not performing — instead, like everyone else on MTV, he is pretending to sing while the studio recording of his song plays on the soundtrack.

Dylan's next video — for "Jokerman," filmed in March 1984 — is well-liked by most of the Dylan fans I've talked to. I find it pretentious and dumb; it consists of a series of images, mostly taken from famous paintings and sculptures, superimposed over the lyrics of the song, with shots of Dylan pretending to sing (actually he's writhing in pain) on the choruses. None of the marriages of word and image strike me as having any poetry in them, any genuine magic or grace. In any case, this is not a Bob Dylan creation we're discussing—again, he offered no input at all into the process; the producers came up with the concept and chose all the images.

Dylan's submissiveness here is surprising—one imagines that at another time in his life he either would have refused to make any videos, or he would have seized control and come up with something as improbable and iconoclastic as *Eat the Document*. Instead, throughout the 1980s, he chose to show up and go through the motions, gritting his teeth. His next video ("Tight Connection to My Heart," 1985, made by movie director Paul Schrader) is the most obnoxious of all. After that Dylan tried as director a fellow musician with a strongly individualistic bent, Dave Stewart, but the two videos they produced together (also from *Empire Burlesque*), though less embarrassing, are just as boring and empty. Eventually, in 1991, a Dylan video was released that is actually worth watching—"Series of Dreams." In fact, it's quite marvelous ... but again it's not a Dylan creation. He made himself available for a new photo or two, and that apparently was the extent of his involvement.

Dylan did however manage one performance before a video camera in this period that is absolutely electrifying. On March 22, 1984, he appeared on the American television program "Late Night with David Letterman" and performed three songs with a put-together band. Television is not usually his forte, but on this night he was magnificent. Backed by three young rock and rollers, Justin Jesting on lead guitar, Tony Marisco on bass, and Charlie Quintana on drums, Dylan ripped into Sonny Boy Williamson's "Don't Start Me to Talking," a witty comment on the fact that Dylan had agreed to sing on the show, but was refusing to be interviewed. This is followed by "License to Kill" and "Jokerman," both songs transformed, all freshness and immediacy and fire.

One has only to watch this set—shot in loving, unselfconscious close-up—to see what it is that puts Dylan in that very small pantheon of great singer/performers that includes Billie Holiday, Om Khalsoum, Otis Redding ... It is the strength of his will. Like Picasso, he can take the simplest of elements and, without apparent forethought, meld them together into an utterly original and inescapably powerful articulation of, of ... of something never expressed before in this medium yet immediately recognizable to the observer. This is raw creation, making the unknowable knowable, manufacturing excitement out of empty air—and watching this ten-minute television appearance one can see that it is done not by skill or talent, though both are certainly involved, but by pure will power.

Dylan rehearsed his new band extensively the night before and at an afternoon soundcheck, but at the last moment decided to start with a song they hadn't rehearsed, perhaps because he knew this would be the best way to push the band (and himself) past their nervousness into the white heat of performance, or perhaps because the title of the song just came into his head as he stood there watching the TV host walk towards him. The only words he can remember from Sonny Boy's verses are "two dollars" and "beauty shop," but he manages to spit out dummy lyrics with fabulous conviction, diving headlong into the performance, whipping the band to an intensity of frenzied musicianship worthy of the Velvet Underground or John Coltrane with Elvin Jones or Junior Wells and Buddy Guy on a hot (Chicago) night.

And these lyrics *mean something* to the listener, because the song, the performance, means something, and we as observers fill in the missing or implied parts. That is why all the words to "License to Kill," even the ones that make me grimace on the album version, sound great when Dylan sings them in his "Letterman Show" voice, duetting with Jesting's astonishing guitar fills, leaning into the song with the self-confidence born of a sense of destiny, born of his absolute faith in this moment, this rhythm section.

Dylan's ability to "lean into" his art reaches a startling climax when the quartet plays "Jokerman." Watching the tapes of the afternoon soundcheck (those rascally collectors get their hands on all sorts of things), we see a fine performance of the song with its hot new rock and roll arrangement (slimmed down to just the first three verses), quite marvelous, but something further happens when Dylan takes off his dark glasses and changes into his slim-look new suit and gets his hair slicked back by the make-up person and feels himself actually standing in front of that huge invisible skeptical television audience, and it's something rhythmic, the song has been moving towards this re-conception but now it *arrives*, clicks into place and it's a place Dylan's never been before and you can hear and see his excitement:

> Jo ker man DANCE
> to the night ing gale TUNE
> Bird fly high by the-light-of-the-MOON

Listening to the album version and watching the rehearsal and then watching/hearing the TV performance is like confronting the absolute mystery of how the *Bootleg Series* version of "Like a Rolling Stone" turned into the perfect final released performance of "Like a Rolling Stone" out of blue sky, out of a moment's breath, out of one man's intuition and will power. The creation of the new. Makes you sweat, even as you sit in front of the TV tube, and that doesn't happen often.

With this band, one thinks, Dylan could have set the world on fire again. But that thought, if it occurred to him, did not instill in him a sense of obligation.

IX: Survivor

"Remember that picture of Dylan inside the back page of the last issue of The Telegraph? *With that hat on, looking like a tramp? He might not look the same as he once did, but he's remained faithful to himself. He's still the same as he always was, he has the same soul, the wanderer, the hobo—remember? He was exactly the same when he was 20, when he first came to New York. Being true to yourself is the most important thing ..."*
—Hugues Aufray, 1991

"To me it's not a business. It's never been a business and never will be a business. It just is a way of surviving ..."
—Bob Dylan, July 1984

15.

Dylan played 27 concerts in a mini-tour of Europe between May 28 and July 8, 1984. This tour stands as a little island in the middle of a four-year absence from regular performing, the second-longest such stretch in Dylan's career. Originally Dylan's wish was to do a South American tour, but that failed to come together and the European tour was a last-minute substitution ("I had sort of set my mind mentally to do something so I did this 'cause the other one didn't come off").

All of the 1984 shows were in outdoor stadiums or arenas, with audiences ranging in size from 30,000 to 100,000 people. It was a package tour, with the rock band Santana as the second headliner (Joan Baez was the opening act at five of the early shows). The tour started in Verona, Italy, and travelled through twelve countries, including Dylan's first appearances in Belgium, Italy, and Spain. The last shows of the tour, in Newcastle and London, England, and Slane, Ireland, were professionally recorded, and an album called *Real Live* was later released featuring performances from these three concerts.

It would be fair to say Dylan played it safe with his choice of songs for these shows. The only songs from his controversial "religious" period performed on the tour are "Every Grain of Sand," "Heart of Mine" twice, and a secularized rewrite of "When You Gonna Wake Up" (performed during the first third of the tour). "I and I," "Jokerman" and "License to Kill" from *Infidels* are performed at every show ("Man of Peace" turns up a few times), there's a Willie Nelson song ("Why Do I Have to Choose?") included occasionally in the encores, and one new song (with dummy lyrics), "Enough Is Enough," is included in the later shows. Otherwise the program is strictly greatest hits, the songs that made Bob Dylan famous, with a strong emphasis on 1963-65 (half of the songs performed are from three albums: *Freewheelin'*, *Bringing It All Back Home*, and *Highway 61 Revisited*).

Dylan also pleases the crowd by including more solo acoustic performances (five or six per show) than on any tour since 1974. This is fortunate, because Dylan's band this time – Mick Taylor on lead guitar, Ian MacLagan on keyboards, Gregg Sutton on bass, and Colin Allen on drums – is extremely wooden. The rhythm section has no imagination and displays minimal talent; the lead guitar player is flashy with a great sound but little ability to respond to what the singer is singing, expressing, feeling; the keyboard player is competent and reveals no personality of his own. Together they produce acceptable generic stadium rock and roll, but give Dylan almost nothing to work with as a springboard for his spontaneous artistry as singer and performer. If Dylan gets credit for what he brings forth from musicians on other occasions, he must also be held accountable for the mediocrity of his accompanists this time out. The evidence is that for once Dylan did not want (consciously or unconsciously) musicians he could interact with. He is satisfied with or has actively chosen predictability instead.

With these ingredients – huge arena shows, over-familiar songs, uninspired accompaniment, a Dylan committed to "playing it safe" – one could reasonably expect a set of lackluster and unrewarding performances. Instead we find Dylan in very good voice, evidently deeply committed to sharing himself with his audience and to staying present with his material. This is intriguing. Paddy Moloney of the Chieftains says of Van Morrison, "He only really gets that [emerges from his shell] when he's onstage and there's that magic that comes out of improvising and interplay and reaching some kind of state." One could say the same of Dylan, certainly; in fact his *modus operandi* throughout his career, on stage and in the

recording studio, has been to keep the other musicians unin-
formed and off-guard, on edge, and then to lean into that edge to
bring the best possible performances out of himself and his accompanists. Dylan's method is entirely based on improvisation and
interplay as tools for overcoming his own shyness and reluctance –
it is a technique for producing great art through a sort of spontaneous combustion.

But in 1984 Dylan achieves a significant degree of presence as
singer and as performer without forcing his band to improvise,
without setting up a charged creative environment in which to
work. The European tour in this sense is the polar opposite of the
Letterman Show performances ... Dylan is still using will power,
but in an uncharacteristic way. His normal (and transcendent) role
is that of rebel. For the 1984 tour he seems to have made a
tremendous effort to win back his live audience, setting out to give
them what they want, not cynically (had his mood been cynical,
these shows would have been truly awful) but with real enthusiasm
and generosity. He uses his will power to find that place in himself
where he can and does love his audience, and his old familiar
songs, that place where he can be inspired not by the urge to create
or to break new ground but simply by the impulse to give.

These concerts cannot stand comparison with Dylan's finest
work. And yet to have been present at the best of the 1984 shows
(Paris, Barcelona, Vienna, Offenbach), particularly if one was somewhere towards the front of that sea of humanity, able to see the
man and hear him, must have been an unforgettable experience.
Here is Dylan offering himself – through his singing; he does almost no talking between songs – openly and enthusiastically and
warmly. He *is* something like those old favorite recordings brought
to life. It's a role he's always avoided, but for this moment he wears
it with real grace.

An example of this can be found on the otherwise unsatisfactory *Real Live* – unsatisfactory because it's too short to get across
any of the true dignity or character of these shows, and because it
includes at least two tracks, "Ballad of a Thin Man" and "Maggie's
Farm," that confront the listener with the chug-chug-chug quality
of the tour at its worst – a lovely, grace-filled acoustic performance
of "Girl from the North Country," from the July 8 concert at Slane.
This is sweet, naked, and very affecting. It is not, I might argue,
great art, because although it is heartfelt it does not go down to the

deep place where new and unexpected feelings burst through. Perhaps it is Dylan's very concentration on opening and sharing himself that, paradoxically, keeps this from happening. No matter. It's still a wonderfully intimate performance.

The 1984 shows are structured somewhat differently from any of Dylan's past retrospectives. After some experimentation the first two nights of the tour, Dylan settled on a first set that would stay the same for all the rest of the shows: "Highway 61 Revisited," "Jokerman," "All Along the Watchtower," "Just Like a Woman," "Maggie's Farm," "I and I," and "License to Kill." Gregg Sutton would then sing a song while Dylan took a short break.

The second set began each night with three solo acoustic performances. "It's Alright, Ma" was the first song the first night; it moved to second song for the next few nights, and then settled into the third acoustic slot for the rest of the tour. Other songs that made regular or occasional appearances in this acoustic mini-set include "It Ain't Me Babe," "Don't Think Twice," "A Hard Rain's A-Gonna Fall," a newly-rewritten "Tangled Up in Blue" (introduced at the sixth show, in Rotterdam), "Mr. Tambourine Man," "Girl from the North Country," "To Ramona," and "Desolation Row."

The rest of the second set consisted of six songs with the band (or five, or seven), starting with "It's All Over Now, Baby Blue" or "Simple Twist of Fate," then "Masters of War," "Ballad of a Thin Man," "When You Gonna Wake Up" or "Man of Peace" or "Enough Is Enough," "Every Grain of Sand," and "Like a Rolling Stone." "Every Grain of Sand" was typically the dramatic climax, and "Like a Rolling Stone" more of an anticlimax, complete with introducing the band. (Other songs that found their way into this part of the set were "Love Minus Zero/No Limit," "Shelter from the Storm," "The Times They Are A-Changin'," "Heart of Mine," and "Lay Lady Lay.")

The encores to these concerts actually make up a third set, usually seven or eight songs (but varying between three and ten). Lots of encores is presumably a good way to make a stadium crowd feel like they got their money's worth—which they certainly did; these two and a quarter hour shows, with Dylan singing between 19 and 27 songs, are huge, particularly considering that Dylan is the second of two headliners. The "encore set" would start with two or three solo acoustic numbers, followed by five or six songs with the band, usually with Carlos Santana sitting in on lead guitar. The acoustic songs were chosen from the list given earlier (with "The Lonesome Death of Hattie Carroll" and "With God on Our Side" also making rare appearances). The other songs would almost always include "Tombstone Blues," "Blowin' in the Wind" and "The Times They Are A-Changin'"; less regular selections included "Leopard-Skin Pill-Box Hat," "Knockin' on Heaven's Door," "Why Do I Have to Choose?," "I Shall Be Released," "It Takes a Lot to Laugh," "Senor," "Just Like Tom Thumb's Blues," "Forever Young," and occasional displaced songs from the list for the second set. In Offenbach, June 11, the show-closer was "All Along the Watchtower," enthusiastically performed for the second time that evening, this time with the able help of three of the percussion players from the Santana band.

Other "special guests"—an unusual touch for a Dylan concert—included Hugues Aufray in Paris and Grenoble, joining Dylan to sing "The Times They Are A-Changin'" in French; Van Morrison duetting with Dylan in Paris, London, and Slane; Joan Baez duetting with Dylan at Hamburg and Munich; Eric Clapton sitting in on guitar in London; and Bono of U2 duetting with Dylan in Slane. Of these, the Paris collaborations are the most successful.

Paris (July 1) is my favorite show of the tour (based on the tapes). Dylan is in front of a huge crowd (100,000 people) in a city he has always loved to perform in; he is probably still feeling the glow from his wonderful reception in Spain earlier in the week; in any case, his voice sounds great—rich in musical texture and full of aliveness and personality—throughout the concert.

In the first set, even such tired chestnuts as "All Along the Watchtower" and "Maggie's Farm" are exciting to listen to, at least when Dylan's singing. "I and I," always a high point at these concerts, is full of vocal fire, stepped on somewhat by insensitive accompaniment and overly long guitar solos, but a thrilling performance nonetheless.

"Tangled Up in Blue" in Paris, July 1, 1984, second song of the second set, marks perfectly that mysterious transition into work filled with spirit, art capable of reaching deep into the soul of both performer and listener. The version on *Real Live* (from London, July 7) is so similar I'm not sure I can articulate what makes the two performances different; yet the difference is as unmistakable as that between an ordinary starry night and the same night the instant after a lightning bolt has shattered the sky.

The key to the differentness may possibly be found (and in this search for the source of greatness I am also listening to the transition from a well-sung but uninspired and uninspiring "Hard Rain," opener of the acoustic set in Paris, to this astonishing performance of "Tangled") in the way Dylan plays the guitar. On *Real Live*'s "Tangled Up in Blue" the guitar seems to me to follow the vocal, dutifully doing its part, whereas in Paris the guitar from the first moment seems pulled by some great unknowable relentless force. The surprising punch in the vocal phrasing in the Paris version is, I suggest, a response to the tempo set by the guitar — a very specific rhythm that in itself gives the song a whole new meaning, one that the phrasing must instinctively find a way to express.

Close attention to these similar-but-different concerts and individual songs forces us to notice that, in the act of performance, there's a "click!" sometimes and then greatness happens. To say that in this case the click may have occurred when heart and brain found a tempo with which fingers could express new and necessary feeling — or, equally likely, that it occurred when fingers happened upon that tempo, and heart and brain responded and reinforced — is helpful I think if it calls our attention to felt rhythm as a key to the emotions music calls forth, both from the performer of the music and from the person listening to the performance. We feel a rhythm, and parts of us that we have no name for respond. And the greatness of vocal music lies very often in the relationship between the singing and the rhythmic accompaniment, a meta-rhythm if you will (the pulse of rhythm and voice dancing together).

Whatever. This performance ("Tangled Up in Blue," Paris, 1984) gets to me. It makes me scream. And its impact as far as I can tell has nothing to do with the new words, except in the not insignificant fact that the new words change the singer's relationship with the song: it is new for him, filled with the excitement of discovery, freshness, new creation. On the other hand I don't mean to suggest that the impact of the performance stems mainly from the guitar playing. Its impact is in Dylan's diction this particular evening, and in the sound of his voice as he tells the story. The importance of the guitar playing is that it creates the environment in which this diction and this voice are drawn forth.

Dylan in a 1985 conversation with Bill Flanagan, included in Flanagan's collection of interviews with songwriters, *Written in My Soul*, says of this version of "Tangled Up in Blue": "I always wanted it to be the way I recorded it on *Real Live*... The old [words] were never quite filled in. I rewrote it in a hotel room somewhere. I wanted to sing that song so I looked at it again, and I changed it. When I sang it the next day I knew it was right. It was right enough so that I wanted to put it down and wipe the old one out."

Fortunately, of course, new versions of already-performed songs don't wipe out the old ones; if they did Dylan's body of great work would be much smaller. If I had to choose, I'd say the earlier lyrics are more effective at what Dylan says in this interview he wanted to do in the song, which is "defy time, so that the story took place in the present and the past at the same time." But it doesn't matter. I love the line "I could feel the heat and the pulse of her" in the 1984 version. And I think it's ironic that if "the old one" *had* been wiped out, Flanagan wouldn't have had a title for his book (such a perfect title, such a classic line) – that whole verse disappeared when Dylan did his hotel room update.

"Tangled Up in Blue" was followed in Paris by the single best live version of "It's Alright, Ma" that I've ever heard. This time the transition (greatness to greatness) doesn't seem so strange. It makes sense for fine performances to come in bunches, one ricocheting off another till entropy and friction have their way. Again the flawless tempo seems at the heart of the matter (so easy to be too fast or too machine-like with this one), but this time it's more apparent what force it is that impels those flying fingers (tongue, lips, vocal cords) forward. It's conviction. I don't think I've heard a performance of this song since the original album version in which the singer is so able to inhabit every phrase, see every image, feel every expressed feeling. Nothing is thrown away, no part of the song is sung on automatic pilot. The performer is awake. The result is frightening, and beautiful.

And awakening.

But these moments of breakthrough are rare. For the most part, Tour '84 adds to our understanding of Dylan's artistry by demonstrating what it isn't. It isn't these huge long wonderfully entertaining shows sung in rich, emotive voice that send the crowds home fulfilled and happy. You and I might really enjoy attending such a show, once or twice anyway – but I say this is not an example of Dylan's artistry simply because, to my own ears, very little new ground is broken. Dylan either is choosing not to take risks, or else is unable to take risks because of the limitations of the band he's working with. On July 30, just after returning from this tour, Dylan told interviewer Bert Kleinman:

> I'm usually in a numb state of mind before my shows, and I have to kick in at some place along the line, usually it takes me one or two songs, or sometimes now it takes much longer. Sometimes it takes me to the encore! [laughter]
>
> *Kleinman:* The band I would imagine has an effect on that.
>
> Oh, absolutely. I've played with some bands that have gotten in my way so much that it's just been a struggle to get through the show.

Dylan is quick to add that he thought his last band was "pretty good," but maybe he's just being polite.

So if we make a distinction between performer and performing artist – and admittedly this is a difficult, subjective, dangerous, judgmental activity – I think we can say, on the evidence of the tapes, that in the spring of 1984 that artist was biding his time. He was, let's say, allowing "the performer" to take care of business, the rather important business of reestablishing both a career and a positive relationship with an audience. Dylan's recalcitrant, unpredictable side is unusually restrained at these shows (he did allow it to do a few press conferences). What this suggests is how very vital Dylan's recalcitrance, his orneriness, his refusal to do what's expected of him, is to his body of work. If he were a nicer guy, we might have nothing.

Nothing but fragments. "Every Grain of Sand" recast as a rock anthem is the other major innovation at these shows (alongside the rewritten "Tangled Up in Blue"; "Simple Twist of Fate" also gets a whole new rewrite, and it can be delightfully outrageous, as in Paris, or surprisingly tender, as in Barcelona, but it isn't innovative, just one more variant on a now-familiar theme ... the dummy lyrics and shifting verses add to the fun, especially if you listen to more than one concert, but this is a song Dylan plays with in 1984 – he never gets challenged by it). The first verse of "Every Grain of Sand" in Paris strikes me as a great fragment, a moment of truly powerful singing and self-expression (the guitar playing on this song – and Paris is more restrained than many of the other concerts—is Taylor at his most misguided). The last twenty seconds of singing on the Barcelona version (to get really picky) are also quite amazing.

An Italian television station filmed three and a half songs from the Barcelona (Spain) concert. The footage of the last encore, "Blowin' in the Wind," is priceless. Dylan had been encouraging the fans to sing along on the choruses to this song for about two weeks, but on this evening the crowd—who had been wonderful all through the performance, despite the fact that it didn't start till after midnight—caught Dylan by surprise. They start singing—loudly and in fine harmony—at the start of the first chorus (no doubt they all saw newspaper or TV coverage of the Madrid concert two days earlier), and Dylan is visibly and audibly startled, and then deeply moved. He sings the next verse in his best "big and earnest" voice, and choreographs the singalong with a verve that would make Pete Seeger proud—and then, inspired by the beauty of the sea of people in front of him, all waving their hands above their heads, he suddenly really wakes up and sings the third verse (and harmonizes on the chorus) as though he just wrote the song five minutes earlier. It's a lovely moment.

The one other fragment that must be mentioned is from a rehearsal tape (Beverly Theater, Los Angeles, May 23) just before the tour started. Dylan's singing on the tape is quite lifeless for the most part, as if he's sort of forcing himself to sing so the band can work out arrangements, but doesn't want to spoil his relationships with these songs by getting involved in them too early. The exception is late in the tape, when he sings a brief fragment of an unknown song with a gorgeous melody, possibly a Dylan original, probably called "Almost Done," followed by a few attempts at singing and arranging Willie Nelson's "Always on My Mind." Dylan performs these song fragments with tremendous spirit and commitment. Suddenly his voice is filled with passion. He's let down his guard. We see/hear a glimpse of who this man really is.

16.

Dylan came back from Europe and started working on a new album. Somewhere along the long road of his career, however, he had lost his fierce intuitive sense of album as performance, quick slice of fresh music and feeling served up on plastic and on to the next gig. The man who'd come back from Europe in summer 1964 and laid down *Another Side of Bob Dylan* in one sloppy exuberant evening now found himself uncharacteristically intimidated by the medium he had to work through.

"When I started to record, back in the sixties, they just turned the microphones on and you recorded," he told Bill Flanagan in March 1985. "Whatever you got on one side of the glass was what came in on the controls on the other side of the glass. The problem is, you can't record that way anymore. If you go into a studio now, the technology is so different that you might have a live sound that you want and you'll put that live sound down, but it won't sound that way on the other side of the glass. So then you have to contrive the sound to make it sound the way you really want. In other words, if you want to sound a certain way, whatever that way is, it'll never happen in the studio."

Dylan goes on to tell Flanagan how he's dealing with the problem ("What I do now is just record all the time"). In other interviews from this period he drops hints that he's been tempted to give up making records altogether. He hates the recording studio ("you could be indoors for months—it's like working in a coal mine"). But he feels that writing songs and making albums is the price he has to pay for the privilege of getting to perform live. "I'm just thankful I can play on stage and people come and see me," he told Bert Kleinman in July 1984. "Because I couldn't make it otherwise, I mean if I went out to play and nobody showed up that would be the end of me. I wouldn't be making records, I'll tell you that. I only make records because people see me live. As long as they're coming along to see me live I'll just make more records."

Dylan's solution in 1984-85 is to do what he says "everybody does"—to go in and lay down a rough track for a song, often a purely instrumental track, sometimes with a rough or reference vocal, and then listen to it and come back to it at subsequent sessions, possibly many months later. In an interview with Bob Brown of ABC-TV in September 1985, Dylan describes this process, and I think poignantly communicates his deep ambivalence: at one moment he's saying he had to become his own producer because he couldn't trust anyone else to get him the sound he wants, and the next moment he's talking about how helpless he feels with this technology and how he needs to work with somebody who's more familiar with the studio. Dylan's friend Ron Wood, who played guitar on Dylan's July 1984 recording sessions, told John Bauldie that "the weak side of [Dylan] would come out" during the playbacks. "The way he's let producers just take his stuff and bury it has surprised me. They'd say, 'Hey Bob, we don't need this,' and he'd say, 'Oh. OK.' They'd make a mix to *their* ears and he'd just stand outside and let them do it. There'd be something going on in the back of his head which didn't allow him to interfere. And yet if he'd gone into the control room with the dominance that he had while we were cutting the stuff, it could have been mind-bending."

Dylan's sessions in July and December 1984 (there could well have been other, undocumented sessions in the intervening months), and in January, February, March and April of 1985, resulted in ten songs that were released in June 1985 as the album *Empire Burlesque*, plus three songs that later had additional instrumental and vocal tracks added to them for release as part of the 1986 album *Knocked Out Loaded*, and a handful of outtakes, some of them instrumental tracks and others actual songs with reference vocals. There is one significant alternate take available – the early version of "When the Night Comes Falling from the Sky," released in 1991 on *The Bootleg Series*.

The unreleased songs from these sessions ("Waiting to Get Beat," "Who Loves You More?", "The Very Thought of You," "Straight A's in Love," and "Go Away Little Boy") are of very little interest, either as songs or performances. "Maybe Someday," which was overdubbed in '86 and included on *Knocked Out Loaded*, has a similar dreariness of sound and content. "Drifting Too Far from Shore," another song that ended up on *Knocked Out Loaded*, is more promising: it's based on a fine riff, which mysteriously is lost between the July 1984 rough track and the spring 1986 spruce-up. One gets the feeling there's the basis for a powerful song here, but that Dylan never found the energy (or inspiration) to write it.

The other *Knocked Out Loaded* song that dates in part from these *Empire Burlesque* sessions is the epic "Brownsville Girl," originally called "Danville Girl" or "New Danville Girl." The (minimal) music is by Dylan; the lyrics are the result of a collaboration between Dylan and playwright Sam Shepard (although the lyric changes in the 1986 re-recording are presumably the work of Dylan alone). The December 1984 version, which circulates on an unreleased tape, features a different vocal than the released version – and of the two, it is somewhat more enjoyable, because Dylan's interesting half-sung, half-spoken vocal performance is more audible (the vocal mannerisms on the later take are equally entertaining, but they tend to be obscured by the background singers and additional instruments).

Both "Danville Girl" and "Brownsville Girl" are impressive on first listen, due to the ambitiousness and originality of the undertaking. But the excitement diminishes rather than builds on multiple listenings, largely I think because the song doesn't have much to say. The "trying to remember a movie" frame is clever, but the love story contained within the frame is unconvincing, rich in style but meager in content. The girl, and the singer's feelings for her, just don't seem very real. This makes it hard for the singer to break through; he gives a solid and inventive performance that lacks transcendence – and unfortunately transcendence is what the song's length and construction require. The repetitive tune is probably not the big problem here; look how wonderfully "Lily, Rosemary & the Jack of Hearts" turned out. But the spontaneity of the released performance of "Lily" does suggest that laying down a track first, and attempting a series of vocals on top of that track, may possibly have kept "Danville Girl" from evolving into the great song and performance it obviously wanted to be.

I do like *Empire Burlesque*. I think in fact that it has more to offer as an album than the released versions of *Infidels* or *Shot of Love* (although the overall quality of work done at the sessions for those albums far surpasses what Dylan achieved at his 1984–85 sessions). *Empire Burlesque* hangs together. Dylan worked quite consciously to create something here, a specific sort of assemblage (in sound and in subject matter), and I think he succeeded. Like *Planet Waves*, *Empire Burlesque* is an album where the songs support each other and the end result is a satisfying, unique, and moving statement about who the singer is at this particular moment in his life. If it's also a contradictory statement, so much the better in terms of reflecting the true nature of what goes on around here sometimes.

Although sessions for *Empire Burlesque* began in July '84, the only track from that month that ended up on the album is "Clean-Cut Kid," a song Dylan first recorded during the *Infidels* sessions. "Something's Burning, Baby" dates from December; the other eight tracks were all recorded between January and March of 1985 (some in Los Angeles, some in New York City). Dylan supervised overdubbings (synthesizers, other keyboards, horns, percussion, bass, backing vocals) in March and April, and then took the tapes to "remix master" Arthur Baker, who did a final remix, also in April. Baker, a producer of rap and dance records, was known for his innovative and assertive techniques of adding sounds to records (echoes, percussion, sound effects) to make them "hotter," more exciting, more danceable. Dylan's choice of Baker was unusual and daring; my own assessment is that it was also successful, and that the sound the album ended up with is something closely related to what Dylan was hearing in his head as the album began to come together for him in January.

Empire Burlesque tends to be a misunderstood album because, as so many times in the past, Dylan is choosing to go in his own direction. We his listeners admire him for this, but — perhaps understandably—we have difficulty distinguishing between his sloppiness ("Union Sundown," "Maybe Someday") and his willfulness. The songs from *Empire Burlesque* that get the most criticism, "Never Gonna Be the Same Again," "Trust Yourself," "I'll Remember You," and "Emotionally Yours" all strike me as good examples of Dylan achieving exactly what he is reaching for, artfully in every case and masterfully in the case of "Emotionally Yours." But because what he is reaching for is new—for him and his listeners, though not necessarily for the world of music and song in general—it can be quite difficult to recognize. The listener is required, in effect, to drop preconceptions and, out of faith in the artist (or, hopefully, out of attraction to the new work even though it does not fit past models), to listen over and over until he begins to hear and appreciate what it is that the artist's will and sincerity has brought into existence.

New language. "Emotionally Yours" is new language. This will not be apparent to the Dylan listener who expects a certain complexity of imagery and verbal cleverness in every "significant" Dylan song. Nor will it be apparent to many of us that Dylan is sincere in his 1985 profession of admiration for Bing Crosby, and that a song and performance like this is an expression of Dylan's search for a way to incorporate into his own work what he has learned from Crosby and others as a singer and as an interpreter of songs. I don't mean it's a homage to Crosby. I mean it's the work of a singer and songwriter who has been genuinely inspired to explore new ground, in his phrasing, in his notions of what a song is, and particularly in his relationship (as a singer) with melody.

The clue that we are hearing new language lies in the song's charm. "Gates of Eden" could easily strike an unsuspecting listener as ridiculous nonsense. If additional listenings cause him or her to start to reclassify the work as "charming nonsense," then recognition and appreciation of the new language this singer is speaking are probably not far behind.

The one song on *Empire Burlesque* that I personally find charmless is "Clean-Cut Kid." It's clever, well-written, well-performed, makes a number of political and social points that I tend to agree with. But it irritates me. I don't like the riff. I don't like the, uh, tone of voice. I guess I question the song's sincerity. It seems manufactured. By contrast, "Never Gonna Be the Same Again," though simplistic in its form and lyrics, seems to me an honest and deeply felt expression of personal experience. The song is alive, it grows on me, and there turn out to be aspects of its musical structure and even of its cliché-ridden lyrics that are far more subtle and inventive than I realized on first hearing. "Never Gonna Be the Same Again" is an open door to an emotional and musical space I'm still exploring. "Clean-Cut Kid," on the other hand, for me at least, goes nowhere. It seems superimposed onto an album where all the other songs are connected by blood, by spirit, by intention, by living tissue.

Like *Blonde on Blonde* and *Planet Waves*, *Empire Burlesque* is dominated by love songs. All of the songs except "Clean-Cut Kid" and "Dark Eyes" are "I-you" songs (sung in the first person, to a person referred to in the song as "you"); all except these two and "Trust Yourself" are primarily or exclusively concerned with the state of a romantic, man-woman relationship ("Are you still my friend?" "Show me you know me." "Sorry if I hurt you." "I'm just glad it's over." "Didn't I try to love you?" "You're the one I've been looking for." "Stick around baby, we're not through"). The songs are interconnected but are hardly interchangeable; in fact each one seems to carve out a slightly different emotional position, almost as if Dylan were consciously setting out to portray the many different sides one person can show in the same relationship at the same time.

What time? The manipulation of subjective time as implicitly expressed in song narrative is central to Dylan's compositional technique throughout his career, a trick as obvious and as innovative and as far-reaching in its impact as Picasso's habit of putting both eyes on the visible side of his subject's profile. In *Empire Burlesque* the issue is relationship time: present relationship, recently over, about-to-be-over, future relationship, long-finished but not forgotten, just begun, etc. And the question is, where are we? When Dylan sings, "I will always be emotionally yours," can he be speaking about the same relationship (and at the same approximate moment) as when he sings "I'll remember you"? "Never Gonna Be the Same Again" should be unambiguous, since it starts "Now you're here beside me." But it *sounds* like the relationship is in the past. This is the trick, and like Picasso's eyes, the intention is simply to give a more accurate representation of human perception than that offered by conventional methodology. We do actually see both sides of the person. We do actually experience the relationship as present and not-present at the same time.

John Lindley, writing in *The Telegraph* in 1986, reported an interesting discovery about *Empire Burlesque*: some of the song lyrics are borrowed directly from films, particularly Humphrey Bogart films, particularly *The Maltese Falcon*. The first lines of the album, "I had to move fast/And I couldn't with you around my neck," closely echo Bogart's comment in his 1951 movie *Sirocco* (to an actress who says, "I'm coming with you"): "I've got to move fast—I can't with you around my neck." Later in the film Bogart tells her, "I don't know whether I'm too good for you, or you're too good for me," one of my favorite lines from the album, also from the opening song, "Tight Connection to my Heart." Other lines from this song have been tracked down to *The Maltese Falcon* ("You want to talk to me, go ahead and talk") and to an episode of the TV series *Star Trek*.

Edward G. Robinson, in his 1948 film (costarring Humphrey Bogart) *Key Largo*, mutters, "Think this rain would cool things off, but it don't"; Dylan transmutes this into the opening lines of "Seeing the Real You at Last," a song which gives some indication of being almost entirely composed of film dialogue, a veritable tour de force of imaginative borrowing. Our detectives have identified another line from *Key Largo*, two sets of lines from *The Maltese Falcon* (Bogart: "I don't mind a reasonable amount of trouble" and, to Mary Astor, "I'll have some rotten nights after I've sent you over, but that'll pass"), two bits of Bogart/Lauren Bacall dialog (one from *To Have and Have Not*, the other the closing lines of *The Big Sleep*), plus lines from *The Hustler* and from a Clint Eastwood film called *Bronco Billy* ... all in "Seeing the Real You at Last."

So, if Dylan didn't exactly write these lyrics, is there something ironic about the song's title (reminiscent of the album called *Self Portrait*)? Dylan, who has successfully used "ready-mades" (a term coined by painter Marcel Duchamp circa 1913) in his compositions throughout his career, notably clichés ("Why wait any longer for the world to begin?/You can have your cake and eat it too" is a triumphant example, from "Lay Lady Lay"; later, 1989, he would actually build a very good verse around "Roses are red, violets are blue") and lines from the Bible, offers some keen insights into his writing philosophy in his interview with Bill Flanagan, conducted during the mixing of *Empire Burlesque*:

> A lot of times you'll just hear things and you'll know that these are the things that you want to put in your song.

Whether you say them or not. They don't have to be your
particular thoughts. They just sound good, and *somebody*
thinks them. Half my stuff falls along those lines. ...I didn't
originate those kinds of thoughts. I've felt them, but I didn't
originate them. They're out there, so I just use them.... It's
more or less remembering things and taking it down.

Flanagan: Do all your songs have a literal reality to you?

Dylan: Well, songs are just thoughts. For the moment they
stop time. To hear a song is to hear someone's thought, no
matter what they're describing. ...You have to have seen
something or have heard something for you to dream it. It
becomes *your* dream then. Whereas a fantasy is just your
imagination wandering around. I don't really look at my
stuff like that. It's happened, it's been said, I've heard it: I
have proof of it. I'm a messenger. I get it. It comes to me so
I give it back in my particular style.

So who is the real you? It could be the person who responds,
who feels something private and personal, when listening to a Bob
Dylan song or watching a Humphrey Bogart film. The important
thing, in a love relationship, is not the things we say; maybe in fact
we say what we say because we're remembering some song or some
movie. The important thing is what happens to us, the moments
when we break through our stubborn habits and illusions. Thus
the pivotal moment on this album is the bridge in "Emotionally
Yours":

> It's as if my whole life never happened
> When I see you it's as if I never had a thought.

Reality is reconstructed from here, and it starts with calling you to
me. Songs, according to Dylan, are thoughts that stop time; love is
what gets us in trouble and gets us out again; and trouble is what
makes life worth living. "Every time you get this close it makes me
want to scream." "There is no more/you cut to the core/quicker
than anyone I knew." "I'm just trying to get used to/seeing the real
you at last."

Dylan's gift is his ability to organize (or perhaps disorganize)
the babble of our all-powerful unconscious minds. He doesn't just
do this with lyrics, though the lyrics are easiest to point to. He does
it with music: melody, rhythm, sounds, lyrics, a melange of all these

elements that adds up (on a good day) to something fresh, appealing, confrontive, liberating.

This is a very playful album. We don't necessarily know, as we
listen to it, that Dylan is playing with cutting up movie scenes and
turning them into songs, or that he's playing with the melody and
lyrics and sound of a song he recorded a few years ago, "Someone's
Got A Hold of My Heart" and turning it into a pastiche of itself, so
that aesthetically and emotionally it's both the same and the opposite of what it was before. He is, in fact, adapting it into a movie of
itself. We don't have to know this; the playfulness is still there,
ready to be enjoyed directly. "Tight Connection to My Heart" is a
comic song, from its opening images of escape to its last plaintive
cries ("You've got a tight connection — ow! ow! ow!"). It's the song
of a guy who's being guilt-tripped. And, um, he does at times seem
to be enjoying it.

Dylan's command of sound on "Tight Connection" is impressive. For all its baroque complexity, every element of the song's
sound seems perfectly realized and placed (once the listener relin-
quishes his or her expectations, and starts listening to what's here
instead). The timing of the background vocals, and the triangle
formed between Dylan's sly vocal and the back-up voices and the
rhythm section, is a pure delight, full of wit and intelligence and
warmth. What after all is the (famous, enduring) attraction of the
sound on Dylan's *Highway 61 Revisited* album, say for example on
the title track, if not precisely this sort of loose-but-flawlessly-real-
ized ensemble performance full of rare musical humor, perfectly
tuned to the sound and personality of the singer, who in turn is
creating with his voice a world and an attitude toward the world
both instantly recognizable and yet never before heard anywhere?
But humor and personality, and audience receptivity thereto, are
very much a matter of context; *Empire Burlesque*'s cover (and choice
of clothing) would probably have seemed brilliantly witty and
eccentric from Dylan in 1965, just as *Highway 61 Revisited*'s cover, if
first released in 1985, would probably have been dismissed as an
unfortunate lapse of taste. The point is (look at the two covers
together), it's the same guy, expressing the same sensibility, the
same odd perspective on reality, the same sense of humor. The only
big difference is that he's no longer the new kid in town.

The sound of "Seeing the Real You at Last" isn't perfect (it has
the potential to sound as ferociously glorious as the Stones doing

"Live With Me" or "Bitch" and Dylan doesn't pull that off, he's not the rock singer Jagger was at his peak), but it's still quite wonderful thank you, and oh that riff. Wish Otis Redding was alive to perform this one! Nice chuckle after "sailed through the storm." And what splendid lyrics, assembled or remembered or whatever they be: "Whatever you gonna do/Please do it fast/I'm still trying to get used to/Seeing the real you at last." In concert in 1986 this became a (playful) song to Dylan's audience, a companion piece to "It Ain't Me Babe." "I'm just thankful and grateful..."

"I'll Remember You" and "Emotionally Yours" are both piano-based ballads (Dylan on piano), with a taste of Dylan's old ambition (circa *Nashville Skyline*) to write the great American love song, something straightforward and timeless, free of "rock and roll" and his other idiosyncracies. Asked by Bob Brown (9/85) to cite a favorite song from his new album, Dylan said "I'll Remember You" stands out for him. Why? "Because I still feel exactly the same way as I did when I wrote it, and I figure I said what I had to say and I said it, um, in a way that was very concise and very brief and then it was over, you know ..."

But to my taste "Emotionally Yours" is far and away the more satisfying song and performance. "I'll Remember You" is sweet but a little insipid, musically as well as lyrically. It reaches for something, but keeps veering back towards the ordinary. "Emotionally Yours," on the other hand, is melodically stunning from first note to last, very unusual, some kind of pop hymn born out of "Pomp and Circumstance," and Dylan sings it (the tune and pacing are particularly well-suited to his voice) with tremendous commitment. There's an excitement of discovery here that overflows the grooves of the record. Despite all the talk about laying down tracks first, I find it hard to believe that the beautiful closing passage (an instrumental verse, the equivalent of Dylan's harmonica solos on earlier ballads) isn't a response (particularly Mike Campbell's lyrical guitar playing) to the power and beauty of Dylan's vocal.

This is not Dylan trying to be something or someone he's not. This is Dylan having the courage to follow his heart into a new realm of who he's capable of being.

(Piano for Dylan means percussion as much as melody. Feel the fatness of the rhythm as Dylan's voice gets into the push of fingers leaning into keys. Oceanic. And then on the bridge he's pounding up from the depths, trying to break through and drown in the air.)

As I think the album title suggests, *Empire Burlesque* is a show, an eccentric, diversified, funny entertainment, some kind of extravaganza. Its eccentricities—the strange rhythms and sounds of "Never Gonna Be the Same Again" and "Something's Burning, Baby," the latter a song with no chorus or tag line, that finds its only release in an unexpected repetition of the bridging verse (I love Dylan's performance of the song's two best lines: "You can't roll away the stone if your hands are tied" and "I've had the Mexico City blues since the last hairpin curve")—are in fact its unifying force. Each song gains support for its own individuality by being in the presence of all these other off-the-wall love songs (always excepting "Clean-Cut Kid"). "Trust Yourself," then, with its crude, comic rhythm and its odd exhortative quality, is not so much the moral of the album as its theme song—Dylan the producer and MC of this show is trusting himself (tonight and always) not because he's so full of self-confidence but because he knows of no other way to pull together and harness all his doubts.

And the thing to notice about "Trust Yourself" is that it's spoken in the context of a relationship, one person to one other person (or singer speaking to audience), and it has a secondary message of "don't trust me." This is not cynical nor arrogant; rather it describes the basis of the relationship that Dylan is examining and pursuing and surrendering to throughout the album. He doesn't want the woman to depend on him; he loves her because her power is equal to and resonant with his own. The song is about beauty, truth, and love—and the singer is explicitly denying that he has any knowledge of these things that can be relied on in any way by anyone but himself.

And somehow this fits with the strange tension underlying "I'll Remember You": that you could be the person I'll remember when I've forgotten all the rest, and yet this song says nothing about wanting to see you again.

Elsewhere in the album—the climactic song, pièce de résis-tance, I always expect it to be the next-to-last song but for some reason Dylan didn't sequence it that way—the two lovers are (according to the narrator) about to have their reunion. "About to" is the key to the song; the subject of "When the Night Comes Falling from the Sky" is anticipation, the incredible feeling of being present here in this time that is so full of everything that's happened before and so trembling with what (I assert, I dream, I pray, I fear) is about to happen now. You and me. In this time space, nothing has ever happened in my life but you and me – and nothing else is happening or is about to happen or matters to me now.

This song is one of Dylan's greatest forays into the world of stopped time. It takes place both when the night comes falling (a timeless space, or the door to a timeless space) and also in the moment prior to that event, a breath drawn but not yet released. Anticipation. Foreboding. "This time tomorrow I'll know you better." Amen. More heartfelt words (true or false, who's to say?) were never spoken.

"When the Night Comes Falling from the Sky" presents the lover as stalker. Worthy opponents. Love as a heroic (or anyway courageous) confrontation; a challenge; an act of will. In this respect the song is connected to "Isis" and "I Don't Believe You" and "Angelina" and "Simple Twist of Fate" ("maybe she'll pick me out again," lover as prey) and "Idiot Wind." And "Visions of Johanna," because Dylan in so many of his finest songs portrays love as a landscape. You can see it. You can walk through it. And as weather. You can feel it coming.

"Look out across the fields, see me returning." Dylan talks in 1985 as so many times before of how songs come to him in the form of opening lines, usually words and music together, and everything unfolds from there. In this case, once he had this line (lyric rhythm melody) and the title the song was Dylan's to screw up, I mean only serious malfeasance could have kept it from being a classic. The line sets the scene (night falling from the sky has to be outdoors, and this line takes care of that, doesn't matter if the rest of the action is interiors), sets the mood, evokes both Christian and classical mythology, sets the pace (accelerating tension), sets the story in motion. The story is all inference and dissociated images, but it's real, "it's happened, it's been said, I've heard it," and so a picture forms and a feeling is communicated, "it becomes *your* dream then – whereas a fantasy ["Changing of the Guards," for example?] is just your imagination wandering around."

Real dream. Tangible story. Dylan's craft is apparent in the wonderful image of "the fireplace where my letters to you are burning," establishing immediately that she has power too, and also placing her as home and hearth and he as the wanderer/

outcast. The sloppiness of his technique is also apparent ("you draw a smile" is awkward), and (more importantly) how he makes it work, singing the words so that they mean much more than what is written, phrasing and rhyme and the rightness of tempo combining to build images in our minds even in those places where the right phrase hasn't quite been found.

Great images. "I've walked two hundred miles, look me over/ It's the end of the chase, and the moon is high." He didn't screw up. "I can hear your trembling heart beat like a river." "I saw thousands who could have overcome the darkness/For the love of a lousy buck, I've watched them die." This is inspired songwriting. Dylan is writing and singing like he does in fact want to win you, like he knows his poetry and his delivery and his guitar playing and his total attentiveness at every moment may make the difference.

His singing. Dylan, with Madelyn Quebec almost inaudibly and very effectively present on every phrase ("I" am not solely male, I am a soul voice beyond male and female), sings his heart out here. I know there are those who prefer the early take of this song included on *The Bootleg Series*, but to me it's just a crude handsome gesture in the right direction, a shadow of what the song was fated to become. I love the way Arthur Baker has brought together the sound of this track, finding and drawing in bold strokes the exoskeleton of the performance, physically grabbing the music and making it dance to the singer's lead. The percussion overdubs (by Bashiri Johnson) are perfect, and precisely placed to highlight all the grace notes of Dylan's inspired vocal. I like the rhyme structure, two-syllable rhymes on A (hurting, flirting) and mostly monosyllables on B, ABAB four-line verses followed by near-limericks, CDEED. I like the way the rhythmic structure emphasizes individual words and phrases. I like the way he sings "Yoooouuu-hoooo." And I like most of all the way the time sense moves from present ("I can hear your trembling heart") to remembered past ("You must have been protecting someone") to asserted past ("I never asked you for nothing") to promised or threatened future ("Don't look for me, I'll see you/When the night...").

I like, finally, the closing lines of the song: "This time, I'm asking for freedom/Freedom from a world which you deny" (somewhere here is the heart of the conflict between man and woman) "You'll give it to me now/Or I'll take it anyhow" (this would be the language of rape, were it not that the "it" has been so clearly identified as freedom—and perhaps this is a truth about the rapist, that his pathology is an obsession with the power women have over him) (anyway the violence Dylan is threatening is that of the death of his own ego) "When the night comes falling/When the night comes falling/When the night comes falling from the sky...."

And then there's "Dark Eyes." Such grace. That lilting (haunting) Irish melody, that extraordinary voice, oh so conscious simple rhythm (the brains of songs are in their rhythms), and the wild Yeatsian language, mystery mystery mystery. Beauty and mystery. Dylan reasserts the purity of his power. And what a great riddle to end on: who is this speaker? The singer, of course, always some persona of the singer, but— Here are the clues: "I live in another world." "I can hear another drum, beating for the dead that rise." "All I feel is heat and flame." "A million faces at my feet but all I see are dark eyes."

I don't know. I don't want to know; I like the question too much to be distracted by answers. On this album about me speaking to you, here is the only song that is I with no you, a soliloquy, from another world, or rather from a persona that lives in another world and only visits this one. And still love is a subject, something observed if not participated in, observed and apparently appreciated: "the earth is strung with lovers' pearls" "passion rules the arrow that flies" "I care nothing for their game where beauty goes unrecognized." This is extremely charming. That extraordinary voice. And how can we help but believe—though of course we can't know—that this spirit *does* love, that the dark eyes he sees are of his loved one, may even be what keeps him coming back to this world of gentlemen and cocks and soldiers and children and mothers and falling gods. Question mark. Dylan's harmonica and guitar and little melodic pattern sound like a question mark. I like this song, and this well-thought-out album, very much.

1985 was a year of high visibility for Dylan, although he didn't tour. Dylan normally says no to almost all requests made of him—or rather, he says nothing, shows no response, a "no" by default—but for whatever reason or reasons 1985 found him saying yes quite often to interview requests and offers to participate in special projects. Furthermore, he approached the interviews in particular with genuine openness and modesty, demonstrating a willingness to cooperate (most of the time) without buying in to the preconceptions of the interviewers or otherwise compromising his own standards of self-honesty. The result is a series of conversations that are genuinely revealing, that give the sensitive reader and viewer a real opportunity to get to know this man a little better, to momentarily see the world from his unusual perspective.

The interview barrage started in 1984 with the Westwood One "Dylan on Dylan" radio show, a 50-minute interview with Bert Kleinman and Artie Mogull taped in July 1984, augmented with a great many Dylan songs and released to radio stations in November. Dylan is relaxed and has a lot to say, about his work and how he sees things. It's a very quotable session: "The easiest way to do something is to just not ask anybody's opinion." "I never think in terms of growth. I tell you what I do think, though, that you never stop anywhere." "Anybody who expects anything from me is just a borderline case." "I've always played live since I started out, and that's where it's always counted for me."

March 1985: Dylan spoke for several hours with Bill Flanagan, for his collection of interviews with songwriters, *Written in My Soul*. The 20-page conversation that appears in the book includes Dylan talking about how he writes, with comments on specific songs ("Every Grain of Sand," "Idiot Wind," "Ballad in Plain D" and "Hurricane" among others). A vital document. "People seem to think they know all about me. Maybe they don't. Maybe everything I've done has been one side of something. Certainly nothing I've written defines me as a total person. There's no one song that does that."

In June 1985, Dylan made himself available to answer listeners' questions on a national radio show called "Rockline." Dumb show, dumb questions, and Dylan responds with dumb, weary answers. But then August and September brought three extraordinary interview sessions, all apparently at Dylan's home in Malibu: long conversations with Scott Cohen, for *Spin* magazine; with Cameron Crowe, for the sleeve notes and special booklet that accompany the *Biograph* album; and with Bob Brown for ABC-TV's "20/20" program. (The interview as seen on TV is very good; the unedited footage, which I've been fortunate enough to watch, is much longer and tremendously moving, simply because Dylan is so present, so careful and generous and vulnerable and conscientious. He knows from long experience how truth is triply distorted, first by the inadequacy of the speaker, then by the medium, and finally by the listener, and with a kind of passionate modesty very relevant to his identity as performer and artist, does his best anyway to speak simply and from the heart in relation to whatever he's been asked.)

Interviews with MTV, *Time*, *Rolling Stone*, a journalist from Boston, and two Los Angeles newspapers complete this rare stretch of public talkiness. Meanwhile Dylan's perceived role as a sort of elder statesman of rock and roll, particularly insofar as the music seems to have any social or political relevance, put him high on the list of those asked to take part in the storm of superstar fundraising (and consciousness-raising) events that took place during 1985. Dylan said yes to singing a line on the "We Are the World" famine relief song (recorded in January, released in March) and was therefore seen with Michael Jackson et al on the covers of *Life* and *People* and in "The Making of 'We Are the World'" video, etc. He said yes again to appearing at one of the two huge Live Aid concerts (again for African famine relief) that were broadcast to an estimated world audience of one and a half billion people, July 13, 1985. He was invited to appear at an international Youth Poetry Festival in Moscow, where he sang "Hard Rain" and "Blowin' in the Wind" and "The Times They Are A-Changin'" (July 25). He sang a line on another collaborative record called "Sun City," intended to call attention to continuing racial injustice in South Africa. And he appeared at a large fund-raiser for American farmers, Farm Aid, September 22, 1985, which was organized by Willie Nelson in response to a comment or suggestion Dylan had made onstage during his Live Aid appearance.

This whole busy year (he also made three undistinguished videos in an earnest but ineffectual attempt to promote *Empire Burlesque*) was capped by the release in November of *Biograph*, the first (in the U.S.) of what would later become a flood of boxed sets by well-known recording artists. *Biograph*, a package of five albums or three cassettes or compact discs, plus sleeve notes and booklet (interview, many photographs), was a retrospective of Dylan's musical career: 53 recordings, 18 of which had not been released before. The boxed set, which had been in preparation since 1981 (and therefore does not include any material recorded since then), was not Dylan's idea—it was put together, very skillfully, by Jeff Rosen, an employee of Dylan's song publishing company. Song selection was by Rosen; Dylan's only input, apparently, was to ask that the original recording of "Like a Rolling Stone" be used rather than a later live version.

Biograph was much more successful than the record company or anyone else had anticipated; it got tremendous press coverage and phenomenal reviews, and sold very very well. The quality of the previously unheard material was astonishingly high (tracks like "Abandoned Love," "Lay Down Your Weary Tune," "I'll Keep It With Mine," "Caribbean Wind," "Up to Me," "Visions of Johanna" live from 1966, the alternate take of "You're a Big Girl Now," and "Isis" live from 1975 were a revelation for listeners who were not part of the in-crowd of Dylan tape collectors). And the impact of all this material from throughout Dylan's career collected side by side in non-chronological fashion was extremely powerful in making the case for Dylan not as the representative of a particular moment in pop music but rather as a major twentieth century artist.

But to the extent that Dylan had a motive in his willingness to go public during 1985, it was definitely not to promote *Biograph*, a project he felt distant from at best and resentful of at worst ("I haven't been very excited about this thing," he told Mikal Gilmore; "All it is is repackaging, really, and it'll just cost a lot of money"). Rather, what Dylan was interested in (appropriately) was that people notice his current work, *Empire Burlesque*. And in this he was to be disappointed. All of his high profile in 1985, and all of his careful work coming to terms with 1985 recording techniques, and all of the creative enthusiasm and playfulness he poured into the album, meant nothing when measured in sales — not the best measure of success, perhaps, but what is one to think when *Empire Burlesque* gets to number 33 on the American top album charts and disappears a few weeks later? *Infidels* had peaked at number 20 and sold somewhat better; *Shot of Love* got to number 33; *Saved* got to number 24. Mikal Gilmore asked Dylan if he was disappointed that *Empire Burlesque* didn't attain the commercial prominence that was expected. "'Yeah,' he said without hesitation. 'In fact it concerns me to the point where I was thinking about regrouping my whole thought on making records. If the records I make are only going to sell a certain amount, then why do I have to spend a lot of time putting them together?'"

Or as he confesses in the *Biograph* notes: "Sometimes you feel like a club fighter who gets off the bus in the middle of nowhere, no cheers, no admiration, punches his way through ten rounds or whatever, always making someone else look good, vomits up the pain in the back room, picks up his check and gets back on the bus heading out for another nowhere."

Live Aid was something like that for Dylan. The biggest concert ever, for the largest (broadcast) audience, all for the worthiest of causes, and he'd been chosen to be the closing act. One gets the feeling he'd rather have been kicked by a mule, but anyway he convinced his friends Ron Wood and Keith Richards, of the Rolling Stones, to be his backing band, and they actually started rehearsing two days ahead of time—a tape of one of the rehearsals shows the three of them conferring seriously on what songs to do, what keys to play them in, trying out different arrangements and so forth.

And then the moment finally arrived, after a very long day of hanging out backstage and drinking and either being nice to people or not being nice to people (it's about equally stressful whichever way you choose to go), and as it turns out they're pushed in front of the curtain, a grand finale production number of "We Are the World" is being rehearsed noisily behind them while they perform, the stage monitors don't work or are behind the curtain so the musicians can't hear themselves or each other, and though Dylan looks determined to rise to the occasion no matter what, Keith Richards is obviously on some other planet. Jack Nicholson comes on to tell people that Dylan is doubtless the greatest historical figure since King Solomon, and then here we go, showtime.

It didn't work. Dylan's choice of songs was daring and appropriate: "Ballad of Hollis Brown" (first public performance in 11 years, song about a farmer driven mad by being unable to feed his family), "When the Ship Comes In" (first public performance in 22 years), and, predictable but to the point, "Blowin' in the Wind." He was in good voice (judging from the beginnings of the songs, before his inability to hear himself made it impossible for him to stay on pitch), and his approach to the songs was fresh and full of potential. But he was mightily distracted. As he told Bob Brown, "We were sabotaged, in some kind of way. There was no way we could really perform there. It's difficult to play if you can't hear." By the time Dylan got to the line that presumably caused him to select "When the Ship Comes In"—"the whole wide world is watching"—he was screeching tunelessly. An embarrassing moment.

No tape of Dylan's performance in Moscow has yet turned up on the collectors' circuit. But after suggesting at Live Aid that maybe just a little bit of the money raised for the people in Africa could be used to pay the mortgages "that the farmers here owe to the banks" — not as jingoistic a statement as it might seem at first hearing; as Clive Wilshin rightly observed in *The Telegraph*, "How typical of Dylan that he should be so uncomfortable while other stars were cooing smug, glib clichés about world peace" — Dylan could hardly refuse to take part in Farm Aid. This time he chose to perform with Tom Petty & the Heartbreakers (three of the band members had played on *Empire Burlesque* sessions); rehearsals began at least four days before the concert. Dylan was also joined, at the Los Angeles rehearsals and at the soundcheck and concert in Champaign, Illinois, by four black back-up singers, three of whom had sung with him on *Empire Burlesque*.

The Farm Aid performance is magnificent. ("Sometimes" — *Biograph* notes again — "you feel like a troubadour out of the dark ages, singing for your supper and rambling the land or singing to the girl in the window, you know, the one with the long flowing hair who's combing it in the candlelight, maybe she invites you up.") Dylan and entourage perform six songs, three from *Empire Burlesque* ("Clean-Cut Kid," "I'll Remember You," and "Trust Yourself"), one cover ("That Lucky Old Sun," a song associated with Ray Charles), one semi-original ("Shake," improvised lyrics over a classic Chicago blues riff), and only one song Dylan has ever performed publicly before, the ever-timely "Maggie's Farm." Four of the songs were televised. But it's obvious from the music, even without seeing Dylan's grinning face or his forefingers jabbing the air at the end of "Trust Yourself," that the man is enjoying himself thoroughly. He's at home. This is what he lives for.

"Maggie's Farm," despite having been totally used up and left for dead the year before, is fresh and perky and a lot of fun. I even like "Clean-Cut Kid" — Dylan and his singers and the Petty band have a groove going here that makes any song they choose to play worth listening to. (At the Los Angeles rehearsals, parts of which were captured on videotape by the ABC-TV crew, they do a sparkling version of "Louie, Louie.")

"Trust Yourself" is a great kick-ass r&b number live that makes good use of the talents of the assembled musicians (on the TV footage you can hear this wall of sound and watch it being built before your eyes and ears). But it's the two ballads that make this set exceptional.

"I'll Remember You" at Farm Aid is proof positive that when we talk about the meaning and quality of a Dylan song, we're really talking about the performance. My comments on the song as it is heard on *Empire Burlesque* have no relevance here; this new song, which has exactly the same lyrics and essentially the same tune as that other one, is in no way insipid, and Dylan when singing it attains everything he's reaching for and more. He, um, transcends the lyrics (maybe when Jack Nicholson called him "the transcendent Bob Dylan" he knew what he was talking about) and makes them speak volumes about man and woman and the human condition. After you hear this particular version (about which there is nothing extraordinary except the depth of *feeling*, and the tonal quality in the voice, which perhaps is the same thing), the song can never be the same again. I mean, "All of Me" and "I Cover the Waterfront" could have been dumb songs before Billie Holiday performed them into works of genius — how would we know? Sometimes the performer creates the song more than the writer does. And forever after we hear, not just words and melody, but his or her performance.

That tonal quality is not achieved by Dylan alone. It emanates from him, and is reflected, amplified, modified, punctuated and counterbalanced by a family of singers and instrumentalists working with him to produce the collective sound that we the listeners hear. The TV footage from Farm Aid gives us a rare and wonderful opportunity to spy on this process in all its intimacy and raw power — in the smiles on the faces of Mike Campbell and Benmont Tench and Stan Lynch, and the gestures and movements that pass between them and Dylan and the other musicians, but most particularly in the interaction between Dylan and Madelyn Quebec, who sings a supporting or second vocal with Dylan on "I'll Remember You," sharing the same microphone.

Dylan and Quebec do a dance together that involves bodies and eyes as well as voices. Quebec only sings on every other line of the verses, but she moves in as if to sing on every line, supporting the singer by keeping him always on edge. She glances at him constantly — she looks frightened, lusty, motherly, deferential, assertive, in awe, playful — he in turn acknowledges her by constantly pretending not to notice her, even as his every movement is in response to hers. The effect of her presence and participation on his voice and on the aliveness of his vocal is unmistakable. (The pitch and volume of her voice also have a great impact on the pitch and tone of what he sings and what we hear.) She looks as though he's told her to let spirit guide her as to when to sing a line full-voiced and aggressive and when to whisper or sing half-voice or slide around or hold back, and she's constantly struggling to live up to his instructions, with all the uncertainty all of us have as to whether we dare do this or not.

This dance, which is ultimately auditory and which involves him confronting a living embodiment (both fleshly and ghostlike) of all the feelings that live for him in the song, is sublime. Being able to see it this once gives us some clue, if we can imagine Dylan's voice doing a similar dance with a rhythm guitar riff or with the pitch and tone and changing rhythm and volume of a piano, as to the value Dylan gets, aesthetically and in terms of personal satisfaction, out of working with other musicians.

The other triumph from the Farm Aid mini-set, not captured on video, is "That Lucky Old Sun." That voice! The song is a prayer, sung by a farm laborer or farmer or any working man, requesting freedom in the form of immediate release from this earthly prison. Dylan sings it with great love and empathy; presumably it serves as a kind of oblique explanation of why he is here at this benefit concert today. The sound of his voice is beautiful, astonishing. "When I do whatever it is I'm doing there is rhythm involved and there is phrasing involved … it's in the phrasing and the dynamics and the rhythm," he said in the Westwood One interview, and this performance serves as splendid example. The rhythm of the song is what ignites Dylan's singing, that's where his passion comes from and how it expresses itself. That's what gives the vocal such fullness and life. And his phrasing is the vehicle by which he articulates the strong and very specific feelings that the words of the song arouse in him. When we try to point to the beauty we hear in the performance, we find ourselves pointing to his phrasing. That extra something. The spin on the ball.

Farm Aid was easily Dylan's most exciting experience of performing with a band since his last American concerts, four years earlier. The Heartbreakers were pretty jazzed by the experience too. It's not surprising that Dylan and Petty et al. were soon looking into the possibility of collaborating on a joint tour through those parts of the world Dylan hadn't played in for a while: the Far East and the United States.

17.

Rehearsals for the 1986 True Confessions Tour ("Bob Dylan with Tom Petty and the Heartbreakers, alone and together," according to the posters) took place in Los Angeles in December 1985 and January 1986. On January 20, 1986, Dylan flew to Washington, D.C., to take part in a stage-and-television tribute to Martin Luther King; in addition to joining Stevie Wonder and Peter, Paul and Mary in an uncomfortable ensemble rendering of "Blowin' in the Wind," he performed a surprisingly different version of "I Shall Be Released" (backed by Wonder's band and his own back-up singers) — new words, new arrangement — a marvelous throwaway, never to be heard again.

On February 5, in Wellington, New Zealand, the tour began. Petty and his group were a popular, well-established rock and roll band in the U.S., and the idea of them going out on tour essentially as supporting musicians was unusual, an indication of a modesty and an adventurousness not common in rock stars. At first only the Far East dates — two shows in New Zealand, 14 in Australia, and four in Japan — were planned: a five-week excursion. But it was understood that if the shows went well, and if the experience was a positive one for both Dylan and the Petty group, an American tour might follow.

Dylan's performances were broken into three sets plus an encore, with Tom Petty and the Heartbreakers performing by themselves in the breaks between sets. On a typical night they did only four songs alone, and backed Dylan on 23 or 24 songs; Dylan would also do three solo acoustic songs, at the start of his second set. Later, on the American leg of the tour (June 9 to August 6, 41 shows in 59 days), Petty and band did eight songs of their own, while Dylan usually did 21 with the band and three alone.

Dylan's set list, which stayed fairly constant throughout the 61 "True Confessions" gigs, was significantly different from 1984: typically only 8 or 10 "greatest hits" out of 24 or 26 songs. The other songs included 4 or 5 from *Empire Burlesque*, 4 from Dylan's other "recent" albums (1980-1983), and 6 or 7 covers, most of them rockabilly or country or country/pop. At the U.S. (one was in Canada, so perhaps we should say North American) shows Dylan usually added a new song, "Band of the Hand," recorded by Dylan and Petty and the Heartbreakers and the Queens of Rhythm (Dylan's 1986 name for his back-up singers) in Australia in February. This was written and recorded as the theme song for a Hollywood movie about cops and dope dealers.

The covers and the *Empire Burlesque* songs give the 1986 tour its special character. For Dylan a tour is a construct, a composition to be performed. The set list is the score; as we know, Dylan most years likes to stick with his set list (with variations and evolutions). The score is arranged for certain instruments (this year piano/organ, three guitars, four female voices, bass, drums, very occasional harmonica, and a touch of slide guitar or mandolin); these arrangements take place not on paper but in the act, usually in rehearsals, and often are not verbalized — they exist in the leader's mind, and no one else can be sure he or she knows what the songs should sound like.

A small insight into Dylan's creative method (spontaneity and stubbornness; very similar to Kerouac's) can be had by observing the origins of the 1986 shows in the Farm Aid set. Farm Aid of course is what brought Dylan and TP & the HBs together (I believe Petty & co. were also the band Bill Graham had wanted Dylan to use at Live Aid). First night in New Zealand, three of the songs in the first set were songs Dylan and the Petty band had done at Farm Aid; by the second night, five songs out of the eight in the opening set were the songs they'd done at Farm Aid, and in the same order (the only one missing was "Maggie's Farm"). Four of these stayed in place more or less throughout the Far East shows; two or sometimes three can be heard at most of the North American shows. More significantly, the personality of the 1986 shows follows a blueprint arrived at in the selection of the 9/85 Farm Aid set: covers (one a generic blues/rockabilly rave-up, one a soulful country ballad), *Empire Burlesque* songs, and a reliable "greatest hit" as anchor and/or encore. It's a musical flavor; Dylan happened on it serendipitously and went ahead and built a year of performances around it.

The sets go roughly like this: #1: introductory song/ "Positively Fourth Street" ("All Along the Watchtower" in this slot for 11 of the last 15 U.S. shows)/"Clean-Cut Kid"/"I'll Remember You" (alternated with "Emotionally Yours" every fourth time or so)/ "Trust Yourself" in Asia, "Shot of Love" most nights in the U.S./"That Lucky Old Sun" in Asia, "We Had It All" at most shows in the U.S./"Masters of War." The introductory song was most frequently "Justine" in the Far East; in the U.S. it was either "So Long, Good Luck and Goodbye" (a good joke, and typical Dylan "set list" humor) or "Shake A Hand" or occasionally "Unchain My Heart."

The three-song acoustic mini-set that begins set two is by tradition a "singer's choice" spot, but Dylan's choices did not range too widely in 1986. The Far East shows (keeping in mind that there are no circulating recordings, and therefore no set lists, for four of the Australian shows) feature "It's Alright, Ma" every night, plus "Girl from the North Country" 8 times, "Hard Rain" 8 times, "To Ramona" 5 times, and an occasional "Times They Are A-Changin'," "Mr. Tambourine Man," and "Don't Think Twice." (Dylan attempted "Dark Eyes" one night but gave up after less than a verse, uncertain of both words and tune.)

In North America, 41 shows saw "One Too Many Mornings" 31 times, "Ramona" 28 times, "Hard Rain" 24 times, "It Ain't Me Babe" 18 times, "Times They Are A-Changin'" 8 times, "Mr. Tambourine Man" 5 times, occasional appearances for "Girl from the North Country," "Lonesome Death of Hattie Carroll," "Song to Woody," "Don't Think Twice," and "I Want You," and zero performances of "It's Alright, Ma" (when you're out, you're out).

The acoustic set was followed, at all but 2 of the 61 True Confessions shows, with a classic country & western song called "I Forgot More Than You'll Ever Know" (about her). This is sung by Dylan and Petty together, both slashing away at acoustic guitars, Heartbreakers subdued in the background except for lovely mandolin solos by bass-player Howie Epstein. (Time to introduce the band, perhaps; in addition to Epstein on bass and Petty on rhythm guitar and vocals, there's Mike Campbell on lead guitar, Benmont Tench on keyboards, and Stan Lynch on drums. The Queens of Rhythm are Queen Esther Marrow and Madelyn Quebec, plus Elisecia Wright and Debra Byrd on the Far East leg, Carolyn Dennis and Louise Mathoon on the U.S. leg.) The rest of the second set: "Just Like a Woman" (all Far East shows, a few U.S. ones) or "Band of the Hand" (U.S., except for "Lenny Bruce" 4 times/"I'm Moving On" (Far East)/"Lenny Bruce" (Far East)/ "When the Night Comes Falling" (all Far East shows and 34 U.S. shows)/ "Lonesome Town" (all but three 1986 shows)/"Ballad of a Thin Man." The second set is 10 or 11 songs in the Far East (the extra is "Seeing the Real You at Last," which moved to the third set partway through the tour), but only 8 songs most of the time in the U.S.

Set #3: "Rainy Day Women"/"Seeing the Real You at Last"/ "Across the Borderline"/"I and I"/"Like a Rolling Stone"/"In the Garden." (very consistent, both legs of the tour)

The encores begin with "Blowin' in the Wind" and end with "Knockin' On Heaven's Door" at almost all the 1986 shows. Three encores is the standard, though occasionally there are four. The middle song is usually "Uranium Rock" (an obscure rockabilly number; Dylan delights in coming up with these) in the Far East and a third of the time in the U.S. "Rock With Me, Baby" and "Unchain My Heart" and "Shake A Hand" each make six appearances as encores, and there are a number of songs that turn up once or twice, most of them covers (a notable exception is "Got My Mind Made Up," sung on the first night in the U.S., the only song from Dylan's new album *Knocked Out Loaded* that he performs at any of the 1986 shows, unless you count his performing the chorus of "Brownsville Girl" at the last show of the summer).

But what does he do with these songs, besides sing them? He creates, shares, explores and conveys a mood. That is the purpose of his score, his composition, his show. It contains all sorts of things:

words, music, performance. But its general purpose is to make an emotional connection—not necessarily between singer and audience, but certainly between singer and song, and between song and audience. This concert is about the relationship between "Seeing the Real You at Last" and "Positively Fourth Street," between "We Had It All" and "Lonesome Town" and "Across the Borderline." Some nights or afternoons it's all summed up in "One Too Many Mornings." It isn't an idea. It's a mood. A place.

1986, the U.S. leg, is Dylan's most consciously geographical tour. Maybe I just say this because it's the one tour I've followed coast to coast—twelve and a half thousand miles in my wife's Toyota, 29 shows in a row (I skipped 11 of the last 12). But leaving my personal experience out of it, I believe this is the only Dylan tour that, in the space of a couple of months, moves across the entire width of the U.S. and back again, California to Texas to Minnesota to New York to Washington D.C. to Kansas to Colorado and back to California, ending up (Dylan himself pointed this out) in Paso Robles, not far from where James Dean breathed his last. Sense of place. And in every city, Dylan preached to us about "Lonesome Town," and "Across the Borderline," and the garden, and the night that comes falling from the sky.

The Far East leg of the tour is hard to evaluate, partly because the sound quality of many of the existing tapes is not first-rate, but also because the shows lack something that is hard to define until you hear it in (many of) the later shows. The opening night show, Wellington February 5, is rough-edged and loose and very appealing. It has spirit. You can feel that this tour is going to turn into something quite wonderful. But in subsequent shows it sometimes seems Dylan and the band put so much attention on tightening up their act that they lose the looseness and freedom that is their greatest asset (listen to and look at the "Farm Aid" footage again).

There are of course many wonderful moments—a few that have caught my attention are "Lonesome Town" much of the time, notably in Sydney February 12 (the sweetness of the melody really comes through in this performance, as though a certain sublime pitch of voice and instruments has been stumbled upon and clung to tenaciously, thrillingly), "To Ramona" in Sydney February 25 (so vulnerable), and "Lenny Bruce" in Osaka March 6 (wonderful strange rhythm on this one, Dylan responds with a deeply felt vocal, edgy and inventive and penetrating). The last concert, March 10 in Tokyo, has many high points including the surprise inclusion of an old Ink Spots song, "We Three" (my echo, my shadow, and me), which Dylan performs with real affection. Dylan's spoken introduction to "Lenny Bruce" is particularly moving on March 10; he is quite talkative during the Far East tour, and here he throws all of his performer's magic into a brief recitation (spoken over a piano backing) of a quote from Tennessee Williams that hovers between conversation and poem and prayer, intimately and tellingly focused on the relationship between artist and audience (if someone's putting together another Dylan compilation album, this bit of dramatic reading would be on my list of recommended inclusions): "There's a great American playwright named Tennesee Williams. He said, 'I'm not looking for your pity. I just want your understanding. And no, not even that, but just your recognition – of me in you – and time, the enemy in us all.'"

Dylan's only commercially released performance video, *Hard to Handle*, was shot in Sydney at the February 24 and 25 concerts. It's a disappointment. The performances (ten songs, six of which are "greatest hits," none of which are covers) have no spark – they display Dylan's routine power as a performer, but not his transcendent power, his moments of real communication. The photography is self-conscious and soulless – one gets no sense of the relationship between singer and audience, and even the relationship between musicians is poorly presented, too stylized. Part of the problem, clearly, is that awareness of the filming has made Dylan himself very self-conscious. Ordinarily he sings on stage with little awareness that anyone can see him, and his gestures while performing are spontaneous and full of idiosyncratic grace; but in this film he looks almost as inauthentic as he does when he's lipsynching at a video shoot. It's subtle – since at the same time he *is* performing for a live audience, and he works hard at it – but disheartening. *Hard to Handle*, which was broadcast on the Home Box Office cable channel before it was released as a home video, includes a fine harmonica introduction to "Knockin' on Heaven's Door," but other than that the film offers little clue (visually or musically) as to who Dylan can be in concert, what it is that makes him – now as much as at any time in the past – such a vital artist.

The subject of this book is performed art, art that is written in the air rather than on paper or canvas. The history of performed art is necessarily distorted by the fact that the text of Shakespeare's plays survives, but not his directing of the plays or the performances he gave as an actor. We cannot see or hear Mozart's operas as his contemporaries did; in fact we cannot even hear Beethoven's music as it was played by him — we can only hear re-creations of that music, performed by people who never experienced the original performances. The endurance of these artists' works under these circumstances is a great testament to their power; however this does not mean that the only measure of performed art is its ability to endure via transcript. Quite the contrary: we must admit that in many ways we know nothing of the great performed art of past eras. Performance is by nature ephemeral. It arrives and departs with its moment.

The extent to which audio and videotape recordings of performed art alter this situation is open to argument. What is certainly so is that these recordings do alter the nature of criticism or discussion of performed art, simply because now there is something that can be taken as a common reference point. You and I can both take out our copies of the soundboard recordings of Dylan's July 7, 1986 concert at RFK Stadium in Washington, D.C. and play them on our home audio systems, and though we will hear them differently we can feel fairly certain that what comes out of the speakers and enters our ears is the same for both of us and for everyone else who has these tapes — there is something "objective" here, an object of art if you will, that is common between us and that makes our discussion of the subjective differences we hear somewhat meaningful.

Art criticism depends on this assumption that there is an accessible common object that can be discussed. We may not, and probably will not, agree, but at least we have the illusion that we're talking about the same thing. As a result, art history and critical literature have been tremendously biased towards painting, sculpture, writing, composed music, recorded music, film etc., and against dance, theater, oral poetry, live music — the performing arts. This bias will presumably shift somewhat, or has already begun shifting, in our current era, as a result of the availability of video and audio recordings of live performances.

In a serious study of the work of a performing artist, such as this book purports to be, we must therefore address the issue of the acceptability of recordings as representations or accurate archives of the artist's work. In this sense, the opportunity presented by my having "followed the tour" in 1986 to experience 29 consecutive live performances by Bob Dylan is that this at least allows me to make some observations of myself as observer in the two realms (member of the live audience versus listening to or watching the show on tape) ... and, if you still follow me, of myself as a recorder of observations.

And the first thing I must report is that great cliché of the Twentieth Century: the act of observing a thing alters its nature. This applies of course to Dylan's self-consciousness when he knows his February 25 and 26 concerts are being filmed for television — but it also applies to the problem of a "critic" attending a concert or a play he knows he's going to be writing about. If you take notes, you are taking your attention away from the performance. Even if you do not take notes, if you are human you are likely to have all sorts of chatter going on in your head: judgments, evaluations, clever phrases in which to express those judgments and evaluations, interesting bits of information or insight you want to be sure to remember, etc. etc. All this thinking necessarily comes between you and your experience of the performance. How come all those other people are laughing? What did you just miss?

Feeling a responsibility to report what one is observing alters the experience of observation (and, therefore, alters the data received). And there are other problems. At a show in Boston I couldn't get a decent seat (standing in the back of a large outdoor arena alters one's experience of a performance a hell of a lot, believe me), so I used my ticket from the night before to sneak into the front section. All evening I was tense and distracted, expecting to be accosted at any moment. The concert seemed to me much less passionate than the wonderful show the night before. But afterwards, the people I spoke to all loved the show, and felt it was a great improvement over the previous night. I can't be sure that their assessment was "correct" — but neither can I trust my own impressions under such circumstances. If I listen to a tape while I'm in a bad mood (or, conversely, an unusually receptive and enthusiastic mood), I can always listen again another day and compare my responses. But a live performance only goes by once.

My solution to the problem of worrying about the observations I should be making, as I followed the 1986 tour, was to forget all that and be there as a fan. The one thing I did do was write down the songs Dylan performed, on a folded sheet of paper I kept in my back pocket, and if I was particularly impressed by a performance of a song I'd put a checkmark beside it, or two or even three checkmarks, sometimes with a brief note scribbled during the applause between songs. Minimal stuff. Certainly not enough to write a chapter about Dylan's 1986 tour, five years after the fact. In truth, I found it difficult to say much about my experience of the tour even immediately after I returned (I was asked to do an article for *The Telegraph*).

I mention this to call attention to what I think is a startling fact: that without the crutch of taped recordings there are significant barriers to writing critically, or anyway intelligently, or in depth, about specific works of performed art.

One can say what one felt, of course, or what one remembers feeling. But to look more deeply into the various aspects of the performance, unless one has an extraordinary memory, the sort that can replay events accurately in the mind's eye and ear, is to risk not having been present at the performance in the first place. To be a good listener and viewer, I suggest, requires a degree of abandon. One must surrender judgment and other critical faculties, suspend disbelief, and be (as much as possible) completely present with the performance. This is the responsibility of the listener, and it is just as holy as the performer's responsibility. We create this art together.

The audience creates the performance by experiencing it. Dylan can only do in the recording studio that which he does so well on stage at those moments (rarer as the years go by) when he truly feels the presence of an audience out there beyond the studio that is (or will be) listening. But the listener not only provides the performer with a reason to sing and a direction to sing in; he or she also creates something for himself or herself. What we create is our own experience. We give our attention to another person or group of people for a period of time, with the expectation that something will happen in that time-space. We actively solicit a work of art by going to some effort to create a two-hour stretch of time in which we are properly located (physically, emotionally) to receive it. We offer up our emptiness, our innocence. On a good night, hopefully, we do not get repaid with scorn.

The best nights (and afternoons) of Dylan's 1986 North American tour were—according to my notes, my memories, and my experiences listening to the tapes (and keeping in mind, as always, that I haven't seen all the shows or listened to all the tapes): Berkeley June 13 and 14, Buffalo July 4, Washington July 7, Boston July 8 and 9, Saratoga Springs (New York) July 13, and New York City July 17. If I had the thankless job of choosing one of these to be released as a double compact disc, I suppose I'd end up choosing June 13, for the beauty of Dylan's voice on so many of the songs and because it strikes me as a good representation or expression of "the 1986 show" as Dylan conceived it—but then I'd want another 2-CD set to show the wonderful directions in which the show evolved, and that one would have to be a composite: 1st four songs from July 9, balance of 1st set from July 7, and then second set, third set, and encores from July 17. Plus "Hard Rain" from July 8, "Union Sundown" from July 13, "All Along the Watchtower" from July 19, "Gotta Serve Somebody" from August 5, and the list goes on.

To the heart of the beast: "Shot of Love," "We Had It All," and "Masters of War," Washington, D.C., July 7, 1986. It's a hot, hot day, and 50,000 people are out there watching (most of the American shows were in the 8000–16,000 range, but there were five shows double-billed with the Grateful Dead, played in football stadiums, that attracted huge crowds). Dylan has things off to a good start, with a rousing sequence of "Unchain My Heart," "Positively Fourth Street," "Clean-Cut Kid" (lots of Chuck Berry guitar licks), and an extremely ambitious and successful version of a difficult song, "Emotionally Yours." And then suddenly with a rush of adrenaline that can be heard surging through each musician and singer separately (and together), Dylan and crew let loose with "Shot of Love" the way it's always wanted to sound, pure unadulterated 130% take-no-prisoners raucous rock and roll.

The Heartbreakers have never sounded better—or looser—and what's driving them is a simply incomparable uptempo vocal performance. My notes from the show say, "Dylan is a *leader*." He does here what he did with the Band in the spring of 1966: requires the bass player and drummer to be a world-class rhythm section so that the other musicians (and the singer) can just totally forget themselves and fly into the musical ozone. Tench and Campbell sound like they've died and gone to heaven. Dylan, on the other hand, sounds like he's just found something to live for. The strength and freedom in his voice are extraordinary, and suddenly after all these years I understand perfectly: it's a song about trans-formation. Hate into love. The frenzied music breathes fire into the vocal, and the vocal in turn inspires and dances on top of the music's wildness. Bass and drums sustain a genius tempo. The "positively subterranean" music that Mikal Gilmore (in *Rolling Stone*) reported hearing at a May 1986 Dylan recording session has yet to surface, but this'll fill the bill just fine. 45 years old and he hasn't lost a bit of his power. Performances like this suggest he might still be picking up steam.

The first verse of the song offers a brilliant, mystifying exam-ple of Dylan's technique. He sings "hurricane" instead of "heroin," apparently deliberately because he does the same thing at other shows, and then sings the nonsense word "whorley" in the second line (I think he started to say "whiskey" a line early and caught himself), and instead of backing off he seizes on the power of these strange words and just lets them come through, speaking in tongues, pure spirit at the end of the third line, propelling the song forward into unknown realms, fourth line more nonsense but dummy lyric technique takes over from holy babble, maintaining momentum while holding song structure in place. Conscious/unconscious, acci-dent/intention, skill/sloppiness/inspiration. What is amazing is the demonstration (again) of how will power can be more effective than language at communicating meaning through sounds. And how such moments inspire singer and band to ever greater levels of penetration into the mystery.

"We Had It All" sustains the energy of the previous perfor-mance while moving it into a different musical realm. Dylan is pure primal power here, the beauty of his voice in the first verse ("I can hear that wind blowing in my mind") before full band and back-up singers come in, the grace of Madelyn Quebec's timing and the rich textures created by the interaction of voices, the authority of Dylan's rapping (spirit talk again) during the bridge, and then the unbe-lievable summation of the first half, the swirling of the music, the way he sings "good," the way he repeats that word, and then the way he illuminates and ennobles and clings to and lets go of the entire experience in the one word "man"… The band lives up to Dylan's trust in them on the instrumental break, and then he comes back with the piercing intensity of the coda, totally in com-mand of his art, utterly inspired, demonstrating now and forever why it is one goes on the road and sings and plays these songs to whoever shows up, night after night: because there is no other way to keep this appointment. Tonight could be the night...

"Masters of War" follows, and serves as a kind of release: a wonderful performance, fabulous groove, nothing specifically transcendent about it, just Dylan and the band totally tuned to performing together. In a real sense it's a Mike Campbell/Stan Lynch duet, and Dylan as vocalist just does his job as a bandmember to support and further their riff. This song's supposed to be angry, we all know that, but today what it sounds like is a straight-out expression of joy.

The July 9 concert at Boston (actually an amphitheater in a far suburb, Mansfield) offers exceptional performances of the first four songs of the show: "Unchain My Heart" (a Ray Charles hit from 1962) makes me think of Dylan in high school, wanting to stand up before a crowd of people and scream music at them for the rest of his life. He made it. "Clean-Cut Kid" is so spirited and fresh it overcomes my prejudice and (the July 9 version only) I like it a lot. "I'll Remember You" is a glorious rendition, Dylan's voice is vibrant and warm and fills every corner of the song, and the band is right there for him. Wow. And "Positively Fourth Street," when I was listening to it last night, seemed to me the best performance of the song I'd ever heard. Today I'm not so convinced — this song was a great vehicle for Dylan in 1986, if I were to go through the tapes carefully I'd probably find half a dozen performances of this caliber, all different, each of which would sound like the best ever while I was listening to it. What's remarkable here is the expressiveness of Dylan's idiosyncratic phrasing ("No I do not feel that good" is slurred together into one quick word, while "thief" is emphasized and stretched with a very similar slur, one slow word, both sung in a voice that sounds like it's bumping down stairs), set against the nervous pace and rich musical texture of the Heartbreakers' accompaniment. Nothing else sounds like this, and it's not some arbitrary experiment but a specific feeling, one that's never found a way to express itself before. When Dylan sings, "I know the reason," and "I used to be" and "among the crowd" and "such a fool" and "one who tries to hide what he don't know," each phrase is a statement that can't be written down, must be heard, and when it is heard is instantly recognized and deeply felt. He rolls these words like dice, but not randomly — rather like he has the power to make them come up exactly how he wants them. New patterns. New meanings. Unique truth.

Sweet music.

I'm listening to tapes, you see, and not because they give me a chance to remember what I loved in the performances; rather, they *are* the performances, for better or worse—like the score for Beethoven's Fifth Symphony, they are what survives. This book is not really about history at all. It's about music/art that is in existence now, a body of work that survives the touring and the amphitheaters and the dreams and ambitions and intentions and obstacles of that particular moment in the performer's life. This body of work, these tapes, are not equivalent to the live performances—but they are what we have, to listen to, to talk about, and it is my firm conviction and primary argument that, imperfect as they are, they are worthwhile. Indeed, they are something more than that; they are works of performed art. They stand on their own. They offer direct (and continuing) access to the mystery.

I have here audience tapes of Dylan's two concerts at the Greek Theater in Berkeley, California, June 13 and 14, 1986. My wife and I attended these concerts, more than five years ago; we had good seats, and enjoyed both shows a great deal. We discussed the shows at the time with other friends who attended them, and of course heard a variety of opinions and reactions. For example, some people who attended the concert with the idea that Dylan had lost his vitality as an artist sometime in the past, changed their minds as a result of what they heard and felt; others remained unimpressed. My wife Donna and I had a suprisingly similar experience listening to Dylan sing "Hard Rain" on Friday night (June 13): we heard the song, or parts of it, as if for the first time. In my case I *saw* the image of "reflect from the mountain so all souls can see it" in a way that made me feel I'd never really listened to that line before. I also remember listening to "Lenny Bruce" and thinking what a beautiful performance Dylan was giving and then noticing that I was thinking so hard about something else I was missing the performance—it seemed to me then, as it has on other occasions since, that my mind was scared by the strength of my feelings, and intervened to distract and protect me.

The tapes are long—two hours each—and therefore unwieldy. When I write about a piece of recorded music I like to listen to it over and over, become familiar with it, let it hit me in different ways—but how can I do that with a two-hour concert (one which I conceive of as a unified work of art)? Problems of attention span become significant. I have listened to these shows quite a few times, but not enough to be completely confident of my evaluations. Tentatively, what I have to report is this: there are great differences between these two concerts performed an evening apart in the same theater, differences not only of playlist (nine songs are played the second night that weren't played the first night) but in the way the performances sound and feel. To articulate this, I have to characterize the shows, and that gets into dangerously subjective territory. But okay. Both shows benefit greatly from Dylan's affection and respect for his perceived audience – the last time he actually performed in Berkeley was December 1965, and in some ways it is as though Dylan has entered a timewarp, welcoming the opportunity to try to reach his cutting edge radical politics folk music smart college student 1965 audience with this show that expresses his current aesthetic and political vision, one he feels could be appreciated by this imagined group. He is clearly *excited* to be playing here (the old friends backstage and in the audience also add to this).

The first night (listening to the tape) Dylan is humble, earnest, vulnerable, he is actively courting the audience, and the performance that results is astonishing. In particular the acoustic set ("To Ramona," "Hattie Carroll," "Hard Rain") and the songs that follow it ("I Forgot More," "Lenny Bruce," "When the Night Comes Falling," "Lonesome Town," and "Ballad of a Thin Man") are sung in a heartbreakingly beautiful voice, sung as though he is opening his life to us and truly wants us to receive what he's saying and feeling. Every line is enunciated clearly so we know its content matters, each song's melody is a bouquet of flowers lovingly arranged and handed over with big eyes and boyishly proud expectation.

Saturday night, on the other hand, clearly follows a Friday night in which (from the point of view of the suitor) the courtship was successful. The songs are loud and brassy and full of joyous confidence. Occasionally ("Hard Rain") they're a bit overdone, but mostly they're just filled with life and energy, not as sensitive and pretty as the night before but overflowing with contagious enthusiasm. "Lucky Old Sun" is a stunning *tour de force*. Dylan sings it like a conquering warrior. "Don't Think Twice" starts off totally tangled in mixed-up lyrics, but Dylan is unfazed, and his performance – vocal, guitar, harmonica – is masterful, a treasure. The second half of the concert trails off somewhat, with bombast masquerading as conviction at times. But Dylan's sense of place stays with him to the end: in the pause before the final words of the final encore ("Knockin' on Heaven's Door"), he shouts out, "I'm gonna dedicate this concert tonight to the memory of Malvina Reynolds!" Reynolds was a respected writer of topical songs and a contemporary of Dylan's in his "protest period" – "I'm still in that period," he joked at Berkeley, a line he'd also used at the Far East concerts before singing "Masters of War."

New York City was another "return of the homeboy" celebration for Dylan, on and off stage, and the third and final NYC show, July 17, 1986, finds him again in a very expansive, "conquering hero" mood. It's a terrific concert. I loved watching it and listening to it from the 20th row in Madison Square Garden, and I love it now, listening to the superb circulating tape (made by the German master, "CB"). The first set includes some unusual offerings – "We Three" and "Union Sundown" – but it's the second set where the magic really starts to happen.

Dylan opens his acoustic set with "Mr. Tambourine Man" – nine days before this he'd announced to his Boston fans, "I'll tell you right now, I'm not playing 'Mr. Tambourine Man' tonight. If you'd played it a thousand times you wouldn't want to." Maybe that comment dissolved his resistance, because a few days later he played the song in Saratoga Springs, and now New York City gets a turn. Dylan sings the old classic in a voice calculated to melt hearts and bring grins to faces all over Madison Square Garden. And at the same time he contrives quite cleverly and successfully to escape the straightjacket of his audience's expectations by toying lightly with the phrasing of the song, mostly at the ends of lines, letting his voice rise when a falling intonation is expected, stretching out words by their vowels. Words that end in vowel sounds lend themselves particularly well to this sort of play, because the singer can ride them out into the middle of nowhere, "you-ooh-ahh," "sorrow-woe-oh-oh." Dylan does this, and by the last verse he's really having fun – in the early verses he sings the song like a beautiful object he's pleased to show off, but the last verse finds him almost as excited as the crowd, delighted by the song's willingness to interact with him, its elasticity, its joy at being performed.

The second acoustic song (again, Dylan alone playing guitar and harmonica) is "One Too Many Mornings." After playing this the first night of the summer tour, Dylan dropped it until the 11th show (Dallas, June 22). Thereafter he played it at every concert, and though it was always good to hear it, something happened around the time of the first outdoor afternoon concerts, Akron and Buffalo, and suddenly Dylan was singing and (particularly) playing the guitar like he'd fallen in love with this song, it became for him (for a week or two) a personal anthem, seemingly the central moment of his whole two-hour extravaganza. My notes show that I was ecstatic about the July 17 performance of the song at the time (three checkmarks); listening to it now I still admire it greatly, for its elegance and grace and evocative power and for all of Dylan's outrageously inventive flourishes of phrasing, but I don't think it's as heartfelt as it was in Buffalo. Dylan's performance has reached an apex of skill and inventiveness, but familiarity is starting to take its toll; the artist is copying something that a few weeks ago he was still in the midst of discovering, recognizing, embracing.

This is borne out for me in the next performance, one unique to the entire tour: "I Want You" as an acoustic duet, Benmont Tench on piano and Dylan on guitar and vocals. Now the muse descends in fact, and makes a mockery of all brilliant celebrations of her memory. Dylan leads off assertively on guitar, and Tench responds in kind, adding the rich colors of the song's melody to Dylan's strummed chords, immediately they find a rhythmic groove together and Dylan launches into a sheer masterpiece of a vocal performance, uniting 1966 and 1986 like they were born twins and then bursting beyond any re-creations of the song into an astonishing cry of urgency (end of the second verse): "I want you! I want you! I want you, so bad ... Honey I want you!" He is totally in the present now, there is no possibility any more of clever phrasing, instead the phrasing (which is more daring and imaginative and delightful than ever) is entirely a direct transmission of feeling, with no hint of thought intervening. He is performing like it's a matter of life and death. He is inspired. He's alive.

This, obviously, is my idea of great art. It may not be yours. But I'm fairly confident—based on his comments to interviewers and his behavior on stage—that Dylan's sense of aesthetic value is not too different from my own (except in the huge difference that he's the performer, and I'm a listener). He lives for moments like these. You can hear it throughout this performance. He is ecstatic. And rightly so.

It helps for him not to be alone with the song. He likes the interactive quality of working with other musicians. My idea of the perfect gift for Dylan would be for Benmont Tench to be instantly available to play duets with him whenever the mood might strike him. Or G. E. Smith (Dylan's bandleader from 1988 to 1990). Or some stranger, chance met, beautiful (like Scarlet) or brilliant or merely endowed with the same sort of musical curiosity. And love for song.

Dylan loves songs. It is interesting to compare "Band of the Hand" (July 17, 1986) with "Lonesome Town." "Band of the Hand" is the only new (1986) Dylan song he includes in this show, and it's topical and pithy and energetic but it's not a song. Dylan has fun performing it as a wall of sound, and as such it contributes to the variety and the pacing of the total show, but it never becomes a great wall of sound for the same reason the clever lyrics don't become a great pointed commentary on the state of our streets and our souls: there's no shape here. Not one the performer can find, anyway. So what we get is a shapeless performance.

"Lonesome Town," on the other hand, simple pop ballad that it is (in a way Dylan's unvarying introduction of the song as a tribute to Ricky Nelson, who didn't write the song but did have a hit with it, serves to distract the audience from the fact that Dylan is crossing over into pure pop for a moment), is for Dylan this year a great song, a wonderful vehicle — because he believes in it it's full of shape for him, it's a song with a purpose, an identity. It gives him somewhere to go. Not always somewhere exciting, in terms of inventiveness or elasticity of performance. But always somewhere real, a place he as performer can relate to, a place he cares about.

"I wanted just to sing ... a song to sing. And there came a point where I couldn't sing anything. I had to write what I wanted to say because ... I couldn't find it anywhere. If I could have, I probably would never have started writing." Dylan in 1984 is talking about himself in 1962. By 1986 the situation was reversed: Dylan was quite able to find songs that expressed what he wanted to say. What he had trouble with was writing them himself.

When the decision was made after the Far East tour that Dylan and Petty would tour the United States in the summer, it was pointed out to Dylan, probably by his record company, that he should have a new album out to capitalize on the visibility and publicity the tour would bring ("The summer's hottest ticket" according to a cover story in the Summer Double Issue of *Rolling Stone*). So he went into the studio with the idea of recording something quick like in the old days, but soon got bogged down, perhaps partly because he had all these unfinished tracks (instrumental backing only) and incomplete songs he'd recorded or written over the past couple of years. He spent the month of May, 1986, in recording studios, partly with Petty and the Heartbreakers, partly with a variety of musicians including Al Kooper, Steve Douglas, T-Bone Burnett, Cesar Rosas and less familiar names. We have the testimony of at least two fairly reliable sources that "There were some really wonderful things cut at those sessions" (Al Kooper) and "Dylan has been turning out spur-of-the-moment, blues-infused rock and roll with a startling force and imagination ... this music sounds surprisingly like the riotous, dense music of *Highway 61 Revisited*" (Mikal Gilmore, writing about the sessions in *Rolling Stone*). ·

If this is true, however, the recordings have yet to surface. Instead Dylan – who just might have been still angry at his record company over their failure to push *Empire Burlesque* – put together an album called *Knocked Out Loaded*, including four tracks from the spring 1986 sessions, and four overdubs of songs recorded at earlier sessions. The two weakest tracks are written by Dylan alone; three others are written by Dylan in collaboration with other writers (specifically writers of lyrics); and three songs are covers. I like the opening track, an obscure rockin' blues called "You Wanna Ramble." At times I quite enjoy Dylan's performances of "Precious Memories," "Under Your Spell," "They Killed Him" (an absurd but rather charming production number, complete with children's choir), and of course "Brownsville Girl," the overdubbed version of "Danville Girl," which serves as the centerpiece of and excuse for the album. Unfortunately, none of this material hangs together with the other tracks in the slightest; Dylan cannot have been surprised when the album (which was released shortly before the end of the tour; I bought a copy July 18) "peaked" on the U.S. charts at #55 (*Empire Burlesque* at least got to #33) and disappeared from sight shortly thereafter.

Dylan on stage in summer 1986 looked muscular and healthy, a relaxed, confident performer who had prepared carefully for this tour, this set of shows. It is as if a year earlier he watched the footage of himself at Live Aid and resolved to do whatever he had to to regain his power and dignity. Among other things, one could speculate that his renewed confidence in himself as a performer (the chemistry with the Petty band helped a lot, and on the other hand that chemistry was partly a function of Dylan's willing himself to have a good working relationship with a band again) gave him the freedom to do an arena tour without concentrating on "greatest hits." Possibly the sloppiness of *Knocked Out Loaded* is the other side of the coin, an assertion that Dylan remains a person who cannot be owned by the world's expectations of him. He likes to sell records and fill arenas, but he doesn't *have to* do any of that stuff. When he catches himself feeling entrapped by any such obligations, he finds some way to thumb his nose at his own self-importance.

One way or another what he does, what he's always done, is he goes on making music. In concert, he performs a song, and then he goes on to the next one. July 17, New York City, "Band of the Hand" is followed by "When the Night Comes Falling from the Sky." The first verse, sung very slow and deliberate, stretched out, no back beat, is spine-tingling, electrifying, incredibly dramatic, as is the release when the full band comes in and the tempo suddenly revs up. Unfortunately singer and musicians both lose focus once the song gets into its rock and roll stage; they perform energetically but mechanically. I want to say the song's arrangement is brilliant because I love the first part of it so much—but in fact it's flawed, it gives Dylan no freedom in the later verses to do anything with his phrasing but bellow, and allows the band no choice but to gallop till they get to the ending, at which point the drama is reclaimed and the customers are left almost satisfied.

On to the next song. The girls, who got in the way on "When the Night" by singing "falling, falling, falling" a few too many times (Dylan's fault; he's in charge of the signals), are the key to the aliveness of "Lonesome Town," not just because they set the mood so poignantly, but because their presence singing the chorus gives Dylan the freedom to sing/talk/rap against the main melody/rhythm/lyric line in a delightful improvisation reminiscent of some of the Basement Tapes performances. Girls sing, "Going down to Lonesome Town/Where the broken hearts stay"; Dylan sings, "Going down— he can stay there, let him stay there/ Where the— go on back, get that boy, let him stay there." One of the many delights here is that Dylan in this bit of scat singing has created a character (that boy) who exists only implicitly in the rest of the song. The boy is the person singing, who switches from the impersonal ("there's a place where lovers go") to the universal ("you can buy a dream or two") to the personal ("I can learn to forget") without ever directly placing himself before us except as a voice. Dylan when he sings "he" suddenly forces still another perspective shift, actually separating himself as singer from the voice of the narrator of the song. The presence of the girls (voice of the beehive, the unconscious mind) allows him to do this. The point is not just the pleasure of this particular bit of business this particular night, but what it reveals about the role of these back-up voices: they are the soundtrack to the singer's movie, the chorus he hears (we hear) as he lives and breathes and plays out these dramas, these stories, these songs.

The second set ends with a splendid "Ballad of a Thin Man," band milking it for all its worth and Dylan full of fire and creative energy, reinventing every moment and every word of the song as he sings it—at least for the first few verses, after which he coasts a little. On the one hand the sound of Dylan's voice here and the freshness of his approach to the song are a function of his great mood (he obviously likes having Ron Wood on stage with him, even when the guy's only pretending to play guitar) this final evening in New York City ... and on the other hand the contrast between "Ballad of a Thin Man" on this tour versus the tired 1984 version is unmistakable. The Heartbreakers deserve a lot of the credit. But it also seems as though "Ballad" fits in this show, it works for the performer, it sparks him, whereas in 1984 it was just something he felt he had to do.

Taking a quick look at the rest of the show: "Rainy Day Women" is filler, bounce bounce bounce, but a definite crowd-pleaser and an effective way to transition from second Petty set to third Dylan set (Petty and the Heartbreakers never leave the stage except for the acoustic set; a long night). "Seeing the Real You at Last" is very satisfying, especially live. On July 17 he fools with the timing of the vocal on the first verse, looking to stir something up, but the song ignores him (it's not very elastic) and goes on about its business. He doesn't mind—there's a wonderful presence in his voice throughout the performance. At the end of this one, most nights, he hunches his shoulders and points at the audience, some-times with a little grin.

"Across the Borderline" is a high point in a great evening. The band, led by Benmont, are absolutely inspired, and Dylan's open-throat vocal overflows with enthusiasm and love. This song was written in the early '80s by Jim Dickinson, Ry Cooder and John Hiatt for a movie soundtrack (it was a country hit for Freddy Fender), and lyrically it's a sort of twin to "Lonesome Town," even starting with the same three words ("There's a place ..."). Indeed, one song is like a dream of the other, as key words and images recur: "broken" "street" "dream" "price you pay." This is fascinating, because it's not obvious—I don't know how many times I heard these songs before I noticed—and because the connections extend outward to other songs in the show: "street" is also a central word and image in "One Too Many Mornings," followed by the phrase "As the night comes in a-fallin'." "When the Night Comes Falling from the Sky" has a line about "It was on the northern border of Texas where I crossed the line" (an earlier version read, "Luck was with me when I crossed the borderline"), which resonates not only with the title phrase of "Across the Borderline" but also with the line "Up and down the Rio Grande" (contradiction between north and south just makes the resonance more powerful). The line in "Night" about "the love of a lousy buck" ties in with the dreams of gold in "Borderline." The punch line in "Lonesome Town," "I can learn to forget," obviously connects to "I Forgot More than You'll Ever Know," which is not unrelated to "I'll Remember You." You can take it from here.

Anyway, you may think you know the music of Bob Dylan, but if you haven't heard "Across the Borderline" from the 1986 tour (and this July 17 version is as good as it gets), you may be missing the heart of the man. For sure you're missing a truly rewarding performance.

"I and I" is another song Dylan really enjoyed performing in 1986, and again July 17 is a marvelously relaxed, intense, inventive case in point. Also another good example of how Dylan sings with and against the Queens of Rhythm, allowing them to be him (sing his melody line) when he feels like standing aside and watching or commenting or creating new harmonies and counterpoints. Again, the band is great—the song fits into the total show just perfectly—and the arrangement, the construction of the performance, is terrific. Comments on this song from my tour notebook: (July 8) "having so much fun" (the reference is to Dylan, though I'm sure I was too). (July 9) "pushing it— walking, testing edge." Amazing how on some of these songs that edge is there to be found, night after night after night.

Other songs, some years, just don't have it. This was a ho-hum year for "Like a Rolling Stone." My notes on this song from the July 17 show say, "best of tour! incredible vocals, gtrs, *keyboards*!", all of which I still agree with, though I can't imagine why I left out the most important element: Stan Lynch's drumming. The interaction between drums and vocals is what brings the song to passionate life, this particular night, and indeed it's great to hear Dylan enjoying it so much. But most nights in '86 "Like a Rolling Stone" was interesting only if you (like most of the audience) were seeing Dylan for the first time in five years or ever and the hope of watching him do *this song* was what brought you to the concert in the first place. He does it pretty good. But it just doesn't take on a life of its own most nights, doesn't fit into the show in a way that would allow it to grow beyond its own reputation. July 17 it does become something very remarkable and entertaining—not exactly a song, however. More like a festival.

"In the Garden"—okay, we have a concept here. Make "Like a Rolling Stone" the next-to-last song of the (regular) show, and follow it with "In the Garden." Lest anyone miss the point, Dylan on the Far East tour introduced "In the Garden" with a rap about heroes, offering current examples and then announcing, "I don't care nothing about those people. I have my own hero; I'm going to sing about Him right now." He even arranged for this comment to open the HBO special (or maybe the director just felt that was the most dramatic moment of the evening; but one suspects Dylan had a hand in this). So: nothing remotely "religious" about the concert as a whole, but it was important for Dylan, probably for reasons of orneriness as much as for reasons of faith, that his audience know that he still has very special feelings for Jesus of Nazareth.

As for the performance—like the previous song, it's a little discombobulated, but it has some fine moments. Not quite the equal of the fantastic Buffalo performance of "In the Garden," but a suitably powerful end to an unforgettable show.

Not really the end, of course—encores are practically obligatory at any modern rock concert, although Dylan has been known to break that rule a few times. The first encore July 17 is the inevitable "Blowin' in the Wind," a song that Dylan and Petty and band experimented with quite a bit earlier in the U.S. tour, but which still just sits there sounding feeble. Not its year. "Shake a Hand," in the "rockabilly oldie" spot (second encore), is good fun, though the message of the song still escapes me (it does include the rather classically Dylanish line, "Be truthful to me/I'll be truthful to you").

And then a surprise—since "Knockin' on Heaven's Door" was the final encore just about every other night of the tour—and a very pleasant one: "House of the Rising Sun" with the full band. It's a classic performance, a slice of greatness, Dylan drawing on those same reserves of enormous creative power he's been reaching into at times all evening, and the Heartbreakers and the Queens of Rhythm matching him in intensity and incandescence, great surges of melodic sound pulsing between the verses while Dylan sings and screams the story of the narrator's life with a passion and immediacy and dignity that remind us why songs like this one endure as long as they do, and why performers live their lives for the chance to get out on stage at an inspired moment and sing them.

As Dylan put it at the first New York show, two nights earlier: "New York City baby! We celebrate tonight."

And I can't leave this chapter without mentioning again the extraordinary slow arrangement of "All Along the Watchtower" (girls oooohing throughout) Dylan introduced for the last part of the tour, an outstanding example of which can be heard on the July 19, 1986 tape from Philadelphia. It would be absurd to think of Dylan's body of creative work being reduced to a shelf of songbooks, words and music on a printed page—but it is almost as unsatisfactory to think of his legacy as the set of his studio recordings. The songs are excellent, and many of the records are masterpieces, but they still add up to a very limited picture of the true life work and accomplishment of this prolific artist.

No one—not me, not you, not Dylan himself—will ever see the whole picture, except insofar as it is captured in a moment, the whole of the artist's identity transmitted in one transcendent moment of listening to and actually *hearing* a performance like the just-mentioned versions of "House of the Rising Sun" or "All Along the Watchtower." Or "I Want You" or "Shot of Love" or "Lenny Bruce." At that moment, everything can be known—but then, in a real sense, it must be forgotten again. No memory of the moment of contact can be as intense as the moment itself, which is ephemeral. And somehow we try to grasp how moments add up to songs, and songs add up to concerts, and a set of concerts and tours and songs and recordings becomes a lifetime of creative work ... We try and, necessarily, we fail. Like God, like love, art is bigger than we are—and somehow at the same time it's only a part of our total experience, one aspect of our lives, however important. How can we sum it up?

We can't. But if we could, it wouldn't be in the form of writing. It would have to be a performance—live, in front of an audience, even if it's one other person—a moment in which we have at least the illusion that everything is expressed; a moment that comes, and then is gone again.

Who was that masked man? "Bob Dylan" isn't even his real name. But we thank the stranger.

("Okay. We'd like to play 'em all for you, but we're into overtime now, so we can't do it." And he turns and walks away, towards the back of the stage and the darkness.)

Discography

I. Albums by Bob Dylan

All of the following (except *Masterpieces*) are available in the United States from Columbia Records. All were originally released by Columbia Records except *Planet Waves* and *Before the Flood*, which were first released by Asylum Records. All of the albums are available at present in lp and cassette formats (except *The Bootleg Series*, which is cassette and cd only), and most are also available as compact discs. For the purposes of this volume, it seems unnecessary to provide catalog numbers for the different formats. Date of first release is given, and the sequence of songs is the order in which they appeared on the original lp release. "A" indicates side one, "B" indicates side two.

1.　*Bob Dylan*, released 3/19/62. A: You're No Good/Talkin' New York/In My Time of Dyin'/Man of Constant Sorrow/Fixin' to Die/Pretty Peggy-O/Highway 51. B: Gospel Plow/Baby, Let Me Follow You Down/House of the Risin' Sun/Freight Train Blues/Song to Woody/See That My Grave Is Kept Clean.

2.　*The Freewheelin' Bob Dylan*, released 5/27/63. A: Blowin' in the Wind/Girl from the North Country/Masters of War/Down the Highway/Bob Dylan's Blues/A Hard Rain's A-Gonna Fall. B: Don't Think Twice, It's All Right/Bob Dylan's Dream/Oxford Town/Talking World War III Blues/Corrina, Corrina/Honey, Just Allow Me One More Chance/I Shall Be Free.

3.　*The Times They Are A-Changin'*, released 1/13/64. A: The Times They Are A-Changin'/Ballad of Hollis Brown/With God on Our Side/One Too Many Mornings/North Country Blues. B: Only a Pawn in Their Game/Boots of Spanish Leather/When the Ship Comes In/The Lonesome Death of Hattie Carroll/Restless Farewell.

4. *Another Side of Bob Dylan*, released 8/8/64. A: All I Really Want to Do/Black Crow Blues/Spanish Harlem Incident/Chimes of Freedom/I Shall Be Free No. 10/To Ramona. B: Motorpsycho Nightmare/My Back Pages/I Don't Believe You/Ballad in Plain D/It Ain't Me Babe.

5. *Bringing It All Back Home*, released 3/22/65. A: Subterranean Homesick Blues/She Belongs to Me/Maggie's Farm/Love Minus Zero-No Limit/Outlaw Blues/On the Road Again/Bob Dylan's 115th Dream. B: Mr. Tambourine Man/Gates of Eden/It's Alright, Ma (I'm Only Bleeding)/It's All Over Now, Baby Blue.

6. *Highway 61 Revisited*, released 8/30/65. A: Like a Rolling Stone/Tombstone Blues/It Takes a Lot to Laugh, It Takes a Train to Cry/From a Buick 6/Ballad of a Thin Man. B: Queen Jane Approximately/Highway 61 Revisited/Just Like Tom Thumb's Blues/Desolation Row.

7. *Blonde on Blonde*, released 5/16/66. 1A: Rainy Day Women #12 & 35/Pledging My Time/Visions of Johanna/One of Us Must Know (Sooner or Later). 1B: I Want You/Stuck Inside of Mobile with the Memphis Blues Again/Leopard-Skin Pill-Box Hat/Just Like a Woman. 2A: Most Likely You Go Your Way and I'll Go Mine/Temporary Like Achilles/Absolutely Sweet Marie/4th Time Around/Obviously 5 Believers. 2B: Sad Eyed Lady of the Lowlands.

8. *Bob Dylan's Greatest Hits*, released 3/27/67. A: Rainy Day Women #12 & 35/Blowin' in the Wind/The Times They Are A-Changin'/It Ain't Me Babe/Like a Rolling Stone. B: Mr. Tambourine Man/Subterranean Homesick Blues/I Want You/Positively 4th Street/Just Like a Woman.

9. *John Wesley Harding*, released 12/27/67. A: John Wesley Harding/As I Went Out One Morning/I Dreamed I Saw St. Augustine/All Along the Watchtower/The Ballad of Frankie Lee and Judas Priest/Drifter's Escape. B: Dear Landlord/I Am a Lonesome Hobo/I Pity the Poor Immigrant/The Wicked Messenger/Down Along the Cove/I'll Be Your Baby Tonight.

10. *Nashville Skyline*, released 4/9/69. A: Girl from the North Country/Nashville Skyline Rag/To Be Alone with You/I Threw It All Away/Peggy Day. B: Lay Lady Lay/One More Night/Tell Me That It Isn't True/Country Pie/Tonight I'll Be Staying Here with You.

11. *Self Portrait*, released 6/8/70. 1A: All the Tired Horses/Alberta #1/I Forgot More Than You'll Ever Know/Days of 49/Early Mornin' Rain/In Search of Little Sadie. 1B: Let It Be Me/Little Sadie/Woogie Boogie/Belle Isle/Living the Blues/Like a Rolling Stone. 2A: Copper Kettle (the Pale Moonlight)/Gotta Travel On/Blue Moon/The Boxer/The Mighty Quinn (Quinn the Eskimo)/Take Me as I Am (or Let Me Go). 2B: Take a Message to Mary/It Hurts Me Too/Minstrel Boy/She Belongs to Me/Wigwam/Alberta #2.

12.   *New Morning*, released 10/21/70. A: If Not for You/Day of the Locusts/Time Passes Slowly/Went to See the Gypsy/Winterlude/If Dogs Run Free. B: New Morning/Sign on the Window/One More Weekend/The Man in Me/Three Angels/ Father of Night.

13.   *Bob Dylan's Greatest Hits, Volume II*, released 11/17/71. 1A: Watching the River Flow/Don't Think Twice, It's All Right/Lay Lady Lay/Stuck Inside of Mobile with the Memphis Blues Again. 1B: I'll Be Your Baby Tonight/All I Really Want to Do/My Back Pages/Maggie's Farm/Tonight I'll Be Staying Here with You. 2A: She Belongs to Me/All Along the Watchtower/The Mighty Quinn (Quinn the Eskimo) /Just Like Tom Thumb's Blues/A Hard Rain's A-Gonna Fall. 2B: If Not for You/It's All Over Now, Baby Blue/Tomorrow Is a Long Time/When I Paint My Master-piece/I Shall Be Released/You Ain't Goin' Nowhere/Down in the Flood.

14.   *Pat Garrett & Billy the Kid*, released 7/13/73. A: Main Title Theme (Billy)/ Cantina Theme (Workin' for the Law)/Billy 1/Bunkhouse Theme/River Theme. B: Turkey Chase/Knockin' on Heaven's Door/Final Theme/Billy 4/Billy 7.

15.   *Dylan*, released 11/16/73. A: Lily of the West/Can't Help Falling in Love/ Sarah Jane/The Ballad of Ira Hayes. B: Mr. Bojangles/Mary Ann/Big Yellow Taxi/A Fool Such as I/Spanish Is the Loving Tongue.

16.   *Planet Waves*, released 1/17/74. A: On a Night Like This/Going Going Gone/Tough Mama/Hazel/Something There Is About You/Forever Young. B: Forever Young/Dirge/You Angel You/Never Say Goodbye/Wedding Song.

17.   *Before the Flood*, released 6/20/74. 1A: Most Likely You Go Your Way and I'll Go Mine/Lay Lady Lay/Rainy Day Women #12 & 35/Knockin' on Heaven's Door/It Ain't Me Babe/Ballad of a Thin Man. 1B: five songs by the Band. 2A: Don't Think Twice, It's All Right/Just Like a Woman/It's Alright, Ma (I'm Only Bleeding)/three songs by the Band. 2B: All Along the Watchtower/Highway 61 Revisited/Like a Rolling Stone/Blowin' in the Wind. (live album)

18.   *Blood on the Tracks*, released 1/17/75. A: Tangled Up in Blue/Simple Twist of Fate/You're a Big Girl Now/Idiot Wind/You're Gonna Make Me Lonesome When You Go. B: Meet Me in the Morning/Lily, Rosemary and the Jack of Hearts/If You See Her, Say Hello/Shelter from the Storm/Buckets of Rain.

19.   *The Basement Tapes*, released 6/26/75. 1A: Odds and Ends/*Orange Juice Blues (Blues for Breakfast)/Million Dollar Bash/*Yazoo Street Scandal/Goin' to Acapulco/*Katie's Been Gone. 1B: Lo and Behold!/*Bessie Smith/Clothes Line Saga/Apple Suckling Tree/Please, Mrs. Henry/Tears of Rage. 2A: Too Much of Nothing/Yea! Heavy and a Bottle of Bread/*Ain't No More Cane/Crash on the Levee (Down in the Flood)/*Ruben Remus/Tiny Montgomery. 2B: You Ain't Goin' Nowhere/*Don't Ya Tell Henry/Nothing Was Delivered/Open the Door Homer/ *Long Distance Operator/This Wheel's on Fire. (songs marked * are performed by the Band without Dylan)

20.   *Desire*, released 1/16/76. A: Hurricane/Isis/Mozambique/One More Cup of Coffee/Oh Sister. B: Joey/Romance in Durango/Black Diamond Bay/Sara.

21.   *Hard Rain*, released 9/10/76. A: Maggie's Farm/One Too Many Mornings/Stuck Inside of Mobile with the Memphis Blues Again/Oh Sister/Lay Lady Lay. B: Shelter from the Storm/You're a Big Girl Now/I Threw It All Away/Idiot Wind. (live album)

22.   *Masterpieces*, released 2/25/78 in Japan, Australia, and New Zealand only. 1A: Knockin' on Heaven's Door/Mr. Tambourine Man/Just Like a Woman/I Shall Be Released/Tears of Rage/All Along the Watchtower/One More Cup of Coffee. 1B: Like a Rolling Stone (from *Self Portrait*)/The Mighty Quinn (Quinn the Eskimo) (from *Self Portrait*)/Tomorrow Is a Long Time/Lay Lady Lay (from *Hard Rain*)/Idiot Wind (from *Hard Rain*). 2A: Mixed Up Confusion/Positively 4th Street/Can You Please Crawl Out Your Window?/*Just Like Tom Thumb's Blues/*Spanish Is the Loving Tongue/*George Jackson (big band version)/*Rita May. 2B: Blowin' in the Wind/A Hard Rain's A-Gonna Fall/The Times They Are A-Changin'/Masters of War/Hurricane. 3A: Maggie's Farm (from *Hard Rain*)/Subterranean Homesick Blues/Ballad of a Thin Man/Mozambique/This Wheel's on Fire/I Want You/Rainy Day Women #12 & 35. 3B: Don't Think Twice, It's All Right/Song to Woody/It Ain't Me Babe/Love Minus Zero-No Limit/I'll Be Your Baby Tonight/If Not for You/If You See Her, Say Hello/Sara. (performances marked * are not available on any American album)

23.   *Street-Legal*, released 6/15/78. A: Changing of the Guards/New Pony/No Time to Think/Baby Stop Crying. B: Is Your Love in Vain?/Senor (Tales of Yankee Power)/True Love Tends to Forget/We Better Talk This Over/Where Are You Tonight? (Journey through Dark Heat).

24.   *Bob Dylan at Budokan*, released in the U.S. 4/23/79. 1A: Mr. Tambourine Man/Shelter from the Storm/Love Minus Zero-No Limit/Ballad of a Thin Man/Don't Think Twice, It's All Right. 1B: Maggie's Farm/One More Cup of Coffee (Valley Below)/Like a Rolling Stone/I Shall Be Released/Is Your Love in Vain?/Going Going Gone. 2A: Blowin' in the Wind/Just Like a Woman/Oh Sister/Simple Twist of Fate/All Along the Watchtower/I Want You. 2B: All I Really Want to Do/Knockin' on Heaven's Door/It's Alright, Ma (I'm Only Bleeding)/Forever Young/The Times They Are A-Changin'. (live album)

25.   *Slow Train Coming*, released 8/18/79. A: Gotta Serve Somebody/Precious Angel/I Believe in You/Slow Train. B: Gonna Change My Way of Thinking/Do Right to Me, Baby (Do Unto Others)/When You Gonna Wake Up/Man Gave Names to All the Animals/When He Returns.

26.   *Saved*, released 6/20/80. A: A Satisfied Mind/Saved/Covenant Woman/What Can I Do for You?/Solid Rock. B: Pressing On/In the Garden/Saving Grace/Are You Ready?

27. *Shot of Love*, released 8/12/81. A: Shot of Love/Heart of Mine/Property of Jesus/Lenny Bruce/Watered-Down Love. B: Dead Man, Dead Man/In the Summertime/Trouble/Every Grain of Sand. (Later pressings include The Groom's Still Waiting at the Altar at the start of side two.)

28. *Infidels*, released 11/1/83. A: Jokerman/Sweetheart Like You/Neighborhood Bully/License to Kill. B: Man of Peace/Union Sundown/I and I/Don't Fall Apart on Me Tonight.

29. *Real Live*, released 11/29/84. A: Highway 61 Revisited/Maggie's Farm/I and I/License to Kill/It Ain't Me Babe. B: Tangled Up in Blue/Masters of War/Ballad of a Thin Man/Girl from the North Country/Tombstone Blues. (live album)

30. *Empire Burlesque*, released 5/27/85. A: Tight Connection to My Heart (Has Anybody Seen My Love?)/Seeing the Real You at Last/I'll Remember You/Clean-Cut Kid/Never Gonna Be the Same Again. B: Trust Yourself/Emotionally Yours/ When the Night Comes Falling from the Sky/Something's Burning, Baby/ Dark Eyes.

31. *Biograph*, released 11/4/85. 1A: Lay Lady Lay/Baby, Let Me Follow You Down/If Not for You/I'll Be Your Baby Tonight/*I'll Keep It with Mine. 1B: The Times They Are A-Changin'/Blowin' in the Wind/Masters of War/The Lonesome Death of Hattie Carroll/*Percy's Song. 2A: *Mixed-Up Confusion/Tombstone Blues/*The Groom's Still Waiting at the Altar/Most Likely You Go Your Way and I'll Go Mine (from *Before the Flood*)/Like a Rolling Stone/*Jet Pilot. 2B: *Lay Down Your Weary Tune/Subterranean Homesick Blues/*I Don't Believe You (She Acts Like We Never Have Met)/*Visions of Johanna/Every Grain of Sand. 3A: *Quinn the Eskimo/Mr. Tambourine Man/Dear Landlord/It Ain't Me Babe/You Angel You/Million Dollar Bash. 3B: To Ramona/*You're a Big Girl Now/*Abandoned Love/Tangled Up in Blue/*It's All Over Now, Baby Blue. 4A: *Can You Please Crawl out Your Window?/Positively 4th Street/*Isis/*Caribbean Wind/*Up to Me. 4B: *Baby, I'm in the Mood for You/*I Wanna Be Your Lover/I Want You/*Heart of Mine/On a Night Like This/Just Like a Woman. 5A: *Romance in Durango/ Senor (Tales of Yankee Power)/Gotta Serve Somebody/I Believe in You/Time Passes Slowly. 5B: I Shall Be Released/Knockin' on Heaven's Door/All Along the Watchtower/Solid Rock/*Forever Young. (Performances marked * are not available on any other American album.)

32. *Knocked Out Loaded*, released 7/14/86. A: You Wanna Ramble/They Killed Him/Driftin' Too Far from Shore/Precious Memories/Maybe Someday. B: Brownsville Girl/Got My Mind Made Up/Under Your Spell.

33. *Down in the Groove*, released 5/31/88. A: Let's Stick Together/When Did You Leave Heaven?/Sally Sue Brown/Death Is Not the End/Had a Dream About You, Baby. B: Ugliest Girl in the World/Silvio/Ninety Miles an Hour (Down a Dead End Street)/Shenandoah/Rank Strangers to Me.

34. *Dylan & the Dead*, released 2/6/89. A: Slow Train/I Want You/Gotta Serve Somebody/Queen Jane Approximately. B: Joey/All Along the Watchtower/ Knockin' on Heaven's Door. (live album)

35. *Oh Mercy*, released 9/19/89. A: Political World/Where Teardrops Fall/Everything Is Broken/Ring Them Bells/Man in the Long Black Coat. B: Most of the Time/What Good Am I?/Disease of Conceit/What Was It You Wanted/Shooting Star.

36. *Under the Red Sky*, released 9/11/90. A: Wiggle Wiggle/Under the Red Sky/Unbelievable/Born in Time/T.V. Talkin' Song. B: 10,000 Men/2 x 2/God Knows/Handy Dandy/Cat's in the Well.

37. *The Bootleg Series, Volumes 1–3 [Rare and Unreleased], 1961–1991*, released 3/26/91. Disc one: Hard Times in New York Town/He Was a Friend of Mine/Man on the Street/No More Auction Block/House Carpenter/Talkin' Bear Mountain Picnic Massacre Blues/Let Me Die in My Footsteps/Rambling, Gambling Willie/Talkin' Hava Negeilah Blues/Quit Your Low Down Ways/Worried Blues/Kingsport Town/Walkin' Down the Line/Walls of Red Wing/Paths of Victory/Talkin' John Birch Paranoid Blues/Who Killed Davey Moore?/Only a Hobo/Moonshiner/ When the Ship Comes In/The Times They Are A-Changin'/Last Thoughts on Woody Guthrie. Disc two: Seven Curses/Eternal Circle/Suze (the Cough Song)/Mama, You Been on My Mind/Farewell, Angelina/Subterranean Homesick Blues/If You Gotta Go, Go Now/Sitting on a Barbed Wire Fence/Like a Rolling Stone/It Takes a Lot to Laugh, It Takes a Train to Cry/I'll Keep It with Mine/She's Your Lover Now/I Shall Be Released/Santa-Fe/If Not for You/Wallflower/Nobody 'cept You/Tangled Up in Blue/Call Letter Blues/Idiot Wind. Disc three: If You See Her, Say Hello/Golden Loom/Catfish/Seven Days/Ye Shall Be Changed/Every Grain of Sand/You Changed my Life/Need a Woman/Angelina/Someone's Got a Hold of My Heart/ Tell Me/Lord Protect My Child/Foot of Pride/Blind Willie McTell/When the Night Comes Falling from the Sky/Series of Dreams.

II. Singles by Bob Dylan

The intention is to list all U.S. 7-inch singles except reissues, plus overseas singles that include performances not otherwise available. Cd singles for radio stations have been omitted except when unique material is included. All singles are on Columbia Records unless otherwise indicated. An * indicates performances not available on any of Dylan's American albums. Date is date of first release.

Mixed Up Confusion/*Corrina, Corrina	12/14/62
Blowin' in the Wind/Don't Think Twice, It's All Right	8/63
Subterranean Homesick Blues/She Belongs to Me	3/65
Like a Rolling Stone/Gates of Eden	7/20/65
Positively 4th Street/From a Buick 6	9/7/65
Can You Please Crawl out Your Window?/Highway 61 Revisited	11/30/65

One of Us Must Know (Sooner or Later)/Queen Jane Approximately	2/66
Rainy Day Women #12 & 35/Pledging My Time	4/66
I Want You/*Just Like Tom Thumb's Blues	6/66
Just Like a Woman/Obviously 5 Believers	8/66
Leopard-Skin Pill-Box Hat/Most Likely You Go Your Way (and I'll Go Mine)	3/67
*If You Gotta Go, Go Now/To Ramona (released in the Netherlands only)	9/67
I Threw It All Away/Drifter's Escape	4/69
Lay Lady Lay/Peggy Day	7/69
Tonight I'll Be Staying Here with You/Country Pie	10/69
Wigwam/Copper Kettle	7/70
Watching the River Flow/*Spanish Is the Loving Tongue	6/3/71
*George Jackson (big band version)/*George Jackson (acoustic version)	11/12/71
Knockin' on Heaven's Door/Turkey Chase	8/73
A Fool Such as I/Lily of the West	11/73
On a Night Like This/You Angel You (Asylum Records)	2/74
Something There Is About You/Going Going Gone (Asylum)	3/74
Most Likely You Go Your Way (and I'll Go Mine)/Stage Fright (by the Band) (Asylum)	7/74
It Ain't Me Babe/All Along the Watchtower (Asylum)	9/74
Tangled Up in Blue/If You See Her, Say Hello	2/75
Million Dollar Bash/Tears of Rage	7/75
Hurricane (part 1)/Hurricane (part 2)	11/75
Mozambique/Oh Sister	2/76
*Rita May/Stuck Inside of Mobile with the Memphis Blues Again	11/30/76
Baby Stop Crying/New Pony	7/31/78
Changing of the Guards/Senor	9/78
Gotta Serve Somebody/*Trouble in Mind	8/79
Man Gave Names to All the Animals/When You Gonna Wake Up	11/79
Slow Train/Do Right to Me Baby	2/80
Solid Rock/Covenant Woman	6/80
Saved/Are You Ready?	8/80
Heart of Mine/*Let It Be Me (Europe only)	9/1/81
Heart of Mine/The Groom's Still Waiting at the Altar	9/11/81
Union Sundown/*Angel Flying Too Close to the Ground (Europe only)	10/28/83
Sweetheart Like You/Union Sundown	11/83
Jokerman/Isis	2/20/84
Tight Connection to My Heart/We Better Talk This Over	5/85

Emotionally Yours/When the Night Comes Falling from the Sky	9/85
*Band of the Hand (Dylan is not on B-side) (MCA Records)	4/86
Silvio/Driftin' Too Far from Shore	6/88
Everything Is Broken/*Dead Man, Dead Man (cassette single only)	10/89
*Most of the Time (promotional cd single, includes 1990 alternate performance)	4/90

III. Other Officially Released
Recordings by Bob Dylan

This list attempts to include all officially released recordings on which Dylan is the primary singer. Recordings on which he only plays guitar or harmonica or sings back-up vocals have been omitted, with a few exceptions. Unauthorized recordings (i.e. bootleg records or collectors' tapes) are not included in this discography. The list starts with song names, followed by the album on which they appear, name of record company, and month of release.

Midnight Special (Dylan on harmonica), on Harry Belafonte: *Midnight Special*, RCA, 3/62.

I'll Fly Away/Swing and Turn Jubilee/Come Back, Baby (all Dylan on harmonica), on Carolyn Hester: *Carolyn Hester*, Columbia, summer 1962.

Rocks and Gravel/Let Me Die in My Footsteps/Rambling, Gambling Willie/Talking John Birch Paranoid Blues, on *The Freewheelin' Bob Dylan* (early promotional edition), Columbia, 4/63.

John Brown/Only A Hobo/Talkin' Devil (under the pseudonym Blind Boy Grunt), on *Broadside Ballads, Volume I*, Broadside/Folkways, 9/63.

Only a Pawn in Their Game (live from the March on Washington, 8/63), on *We Shall Overcome*, Folkways, winter 1964.

Blowin' in the Wind/We Shall Overcome (ensemble performances from Newport Folk Festival, 7/63), on *Evening Concerts at Newport, Volume I*, Vanguard, May 1964.

Playboys and Playgirls (sung with Pete Seeger)/With God on Our Side (sung with Joan Baez) (from Newport 7/63), on *Newport Broadside*, Vanguard, May 1964.

Sitting on Top of the World/Wichita (Dylan on harmonica and background vocals, backing Big Joe Williams, late 1961), on Victoria Spivey: *Three Kings and a Queen*, Spivey, 10/64.

A Hard Rain's A-Gonna Fall/It Takes a Lot to Laugh, It Takes a Train to Cry/Blowin' in the Wind/Mr. Tambourine Man/Just Like a Woman, on *The Concert for Bangladesh*, Apple, 12/71.

Grand Coulee Dam/Dear Mrs. Roosevelt/I Ain't Got No Home (in This World Anymore) (from Carnegie Hall, 1/68), on *A Tribute to Woody Guthrie, Part One*, Columbia, 1/72.

Train A-Travelin'/I'd Hate to Be You on That Dreadful Day/The Death of Emmett Till/Ballad of Donald White (as Blind Boy Grunt) (recorded 1962), on *Broadside Reunion*, Folkways, 1972.

Big Joe, Dylan and Victoria/It's Dangerous (Dylan on harmonica, backing Big
  Joe Williams and Victoria Spivey, late 1961), on Victoria Spivey: *Three
  Kings and a Queen, Volume 2*, Spivey, 7/72.
Wallflower/Blues Stay Away from Me/(Is Anybody Going to) San Antone
  (shared vocals), on Doug Sahm: *Doug Sahm and Band*, Atlantic, 12/72.
Buckets of Rain (shared vocal), on Bette Midler: *Songs for the New Depression*,
  Atlantic, 1/76.
Sign Language (shared vocal), on Eric Clapton: *No Reason to Cry*, Polydor,
  9/76.
People Get Ready/Never Let Me Go/Isis/It Ain't Me Babe (live from fall 1975),
  on *4 Songs from Renaldo and Clara*, Columbia (promotional disc), 1/78.
Baby Let Me Follow You Down (two versions)/I Don't Believe You/Forever
  Young/I Shall Be Released (live from 11/76), on The Band: *The Last
  Waltz*, Warner, 4/78.
interview with occasional guitar accompaniment, on *Dylan London Interview
  July 1981*, Columbia (promotional disc), 9/81.
We Are the World (shared vocal; Dylan's role is small), released as single and
  on USA for Africa: *We Are the World*, Columbia, 3/85.
Sun City (shared vocal; Dylan's role is small), released as single and on Artists
  United Against Apartheid: *Sun City*, Manhattan, 12/85.
The Usual/Had a Dream About You, Baby/Night after Night, on Fiona, Bob
  Dylan, Rupert Everett: *Hearts of Fire*, Columbia (soundtrack album),
  10/87.
Pretty Boy Floyd, on *Folkways: A Vision Shared*, Columbia, 8/88.
Dirty World/Congratulations/Tweeter and the Monkey Man (lead vocals;
  other tracks on the album also feature Dylan on shared vocals and
  guitar and keyboards), on *Traveling Wilburys, Volume One*, Warner, 10/88.
People Get Ready, on *Flashback*, WTG (soundtrack album), 1/90.
Nobody's Child (shared vocal with the Traveling Wilburys), on *Nobody's Child:
  Romanian Angel Appeal*, Warner, 7/90.
She's My Baby/If You Belonged to Me/7 Deadly Sins/Where Were You Last
  Night? (lead vocals; other tracks on album also feature Dylan on shared
  vocals and guitar), on *Traveling Wilburys: Vol. 3*, Warner, 10/90.
This Old Man, on *For Our Children*, Disney, 5/91.

Filmography

I. Films by Bob Dylan

Eat the Document. Filmed 5/66 by D. A. Pennebaker, edited 1967 by Bob Dylan, Howard Alk, and Robbie Robertson. First shown publicly 2/8/71. Not currently available. Circa one hour.

Renaldo & Clara. Directed by Bob Dylan. Filmed fall 1975, edited 1977 by Dylan with Howard Alk. First shown publicly 1/25/78. Not currently available. Original is close to four hours with an intermission. A second, two-hour edited version was released in fall 1978.

II. Films about Bob Dylan

Don't Look Back. Directed by D. A. Pennebaker. Filmed 4-5/65. First shown publicly 5/17/67. Circa 90 minutes. Available on videocassette.

"Hard Rain." Live concert footage shot 5/23/76 in Fort Collins, Colorado, by TVTV (Top Value Television); edited by TVTV. Broadcast on NBC 9/14/76. Circa 55 minutes. Not currently available.

Hard to Handle. Live concert footage filmed by Gillian Armstrong in Sydney, Australia, 2/24 and 2/25/86. Edited by Armstrong. Broadcast by HBO 6/20/86. Circa one hour. Available on videocassette.

"Getting to Dylan." A one-hour segment of the BBC program "Omnibus." Directed by Christopher Sykes. Broadcast 9/18/87. Not currently available.

III. Films in which Bob Dylan appears as an actor

"The Madhouse on Castle Street." Dylan acted and sang in this British television drama, made and shown by the BBC, 1/63.

Pat Garrett & Billy the Kid. Directed by Sam Peckinpah. Released 5/73. Circa
106 minutes. Available on videocassette (director's original version has
now been released).
Hearts of Fire. Directed by Richard Marquand. Released 10/9/87, UK only.
Circa 90 minutes. Available on videocassette.

IV. Films that include
performances by Bob Dylan

Festival. Directed by Murray Lerner. Released 1967. Footage from Newport
Folk Festival, 7/64 and 7/65, including All I Really Want to Do/Maggie's
Farm/Mr. Tambourine Man. Available in film format.
The Concert for Bangladesh. Edited by George Harrison, with help from Dylan.
Released 3/72. Includes If Not for You (partial)/A Hard Rain's A-Gonna
Fall/It Takes a Lot to Laugh/Blowin' in the Wind/Just Like a Woman.
Available on videocassette.
The Last Waltz. Directed by Martin Scorsese. Released 4/78. Includes Forever
Young/Baby, Let Me Follow You Down/I Shall Be Released. Available on
videocassette.

V. Major television appearances

"The Madhouse on Castle Street." 1/63. (see above)
"The Times They Are A-Changin'", half-hour segment of the Canadian
Broadcasting Company program "Quest," recorded 2/1/64 and broad-
cast by CBC 3/10/64. Includes Restless Farewell and five other songs.
Archived in video form. Prior to this, Dylan made three known televi-
sion appearances in the U.S. in 1963, including one song on Johnny
Carson's "Tonight" show.
"The Steve Allen Show," live, 2/25/64. "The Lonesome Death of Hattie Carroll" and conversation with host. Archived in video form.
"Les Crane Show," live, WABC, New York, 2/17/65. Dylan sings two songs
accompanied by Bruce Langhorne and is witty and cutting in conversation. Archived in audio only.
BBC programmes recorded in BBC studios, 6/1/65, and broadcast in two
parts in 6/65: 12 songs, approximately 70 minutes. Archived in audio
only, apparently.
San Francisco Press Conference, KQED Studios, 12/3/65, broadcast by KQED
later that day. Circa one hour. Archived in video form.
"The Johnny Cash Show." Three songs, taped 5/1/69, broadcast on ABC
6/7/69. All items from here forward are archived in video form.
"The World of John Hammond," part of the National Educational Television
"Soundstage" series. Includes three songs by Dylan. Recorded 9/10/75,
first broadcast 12/13/75.
"Hard Rain." Broadcast 9/10/76. (see above)
"Saturday Night Live." Three songs. NBC, 10/20/79.
"Grammy Award Show." CBS, 2/27/80. One song: Gotta Serve Somebody.

"Late Night with David Letterman." NBC, 3/22/84. Three songs, including Don't Start Me to Talkin'.

Live Aid Concert. Three songs. 7/14/85. Broadcast live by satellite around the world.

Farm Aid Concert. 9/22/85. Four songs were broadcast live by the Nashville Network.

"20-20," ABC, 10/10/85. Interview.

"Hard to Handle." HBO, 6/20/86. (see above)

Farm Aid 2 broadcast. 7/4/86. Three songs from Dylan's concert in Buffalo, New York were broadcast live by VH-1 TV; much of the concert was shot and transmitted live by satellite in preparation for the broadcast.

"Getting to Dylan." BBC, 9/18/87. (see above)

"Grammy Award Show," 2/20/91. "Masters of War" with his touring band, introduction by Jack Nicholson, short speech in acceptance of his Lifetime Achievement Award.

"One Irish Rover — Van Morrison in performance," Arena, BBC-TV, 3/16/91. Dylan and Morrison sing three songs together (taped in Greece, probably June 1989).

VI. Promotional Videos

Between 1983 and 1991 Dylan participated to some degree in the making of promotional videotapes to accompany the following songs. All of these are studio recordings attached to footage shot later, so there are no actual new performances on these tapes, with one exception: Dylan performs live in the studio on the video of "Most of the Time."

Jokerman
Sweetheart Like You
Tight Connection To My Heart
Emotionally Yours
When the Night Comes Falling from the Sky
Handle with Care (Traveling Wilburys)
End of the Line (Traveling Wilburys)
Political World
Most of the Time
She's My Baby (Traveling Wilburys)
Unbelievable
Wilbury Twist (Traveling Wilburys)
Series of Dreams (the best Dylan video by far)

Bibliography

I. Books by Bob Dylan

Tarantula. New York: Macmillan, 1971.
Writings and Drawings. New York: Alfred A. Knopf, 1973.
Lyrics, 1962-1985. New York: Alfred A. Knopf, 1985. (Expansion of *Writings and Drawings*.)

II. Key references used in preparing this text

Krogsgaard, Michael. *Positively Bob Dylan*, Ann Arbor: Popular Culture, Ink., 1991. Lists all known recorded performances, including audience tapes of concerts, studio outtakes, etc., with full song lists for each performance. This edition is an update of his earlier books, *Twenty Years of Recording* and *Master of the Tracks*. For information about ordering, call Popular Culture, Ink. at 800-678-8828.

Heylin, Clinton. *Bob Dylan — Stolen Moments*, Romford, England: Wanted Man, 1988. A detailed, highly reliable chronology of Dylan's personal and professional life.

Heylin, Clinton. *Bob Dylan — Behind the Shades*, New York: Summit, 1991. The best biography so far, particularly for its accuracy and its coverage of Dylan's last two decades.

Cartwright, Bert. *The Bible in the Lyrics of Bob Dylan*, Bury, England: Wanted Man, 1985.

Bauldie, John, ed. *Wanted Man: In Search of Bob Dylan*, London: Black Spring Press, 1990. Interviews and essays from *The Telegraph*, including "The Mysterious Norman Raeben" by Bert Cartwright, Allen Ginsberg's interview with Bob Dylan about *Renaldo & Clara*, "Saved!" by Clinton Heylin, and interviews with Ron Wood, Eric Clapton, and Helena Springs.

The Telegraph, issues #1 (1981) - #41 (1991). Edited by John Bauldie. A phenomenal amount of Dylan information, insight, and entertainment is contained in these pages; most of the back issues are out of print, alas. Currently publishing three 100-page issues a year. For subscription information, contact Wanted Man, PO Box 22, Romford, Essex RM1 2RF, U.K., or Rolling Tomes (see below).

The Wicked Messenger, issues #1 (1980) - #757 (1991). Dylan newsletter, written by Ian Woodward. Consistent, obsessive, indispensable. Now available only as a supplement to *Isis* (see below).

III. Other sources used in preparing this text

Isis, bimonthly UK Dylan magazine, 40 issues through 1991, lots of news and information, oriented towards collectors. Edited by Derek Barker. For subscription information (includes TWM supplement), contact Isis, PO Box 132, Coventry, West Midlands, CV3 5RE, U.K., or U.S. agent Rolling Tomes, PO Box 1943, Grand Junction, CO 81502.

Look Back, quarterly Dylan magazine, 29 issues through 1991, unpretentious, fun to read, *the* central meeting place for American Dylan fans. Edited by Tim Dunn and Rob Whitehouse. For subscription information, contact Look Back, PO Box 857, Chardon, OH 44024, or Rolling Tomes.

Homer, the slut, quarterly Dylan magazine, 4 issues through 1991, lively, informal, analytical, lots of press clippings. Edited by Andrew Muir. For subscription information, contact Andrew Muir, 24A Inglethorpe Street, Fulham, London, SW6 6NT, U.K., or Rolling Tomes.

Anderson, Dennis. *The Hollow Horn, Bob Dylan's Reception in the United States and Germany*, Munich: Hobo Press, 1981.

Bauldie, John. *The Ghost of Electricity*, no publisher, 1988. Bob Dylan's 1966 World Tour.

Bauldie, John. *The Bootleg Series, Volumes 1-3* booklet/liner notes, included with album, 1991.

Bicker, Stewart P., ed. *Friends & Other Strangers, Bob Dylan in Other People's Words*, no publisher, 1985.

Bicker, Stewart P., ed. *Talkin' Bob Dylan 1984 & 1985*, no publisher, 1986.

Bowden, Betsy. *Performed Literature*, Bloomington: Indiana University Press, 1982.

Cable, Paul. *Bob Dylan, His Unreleased Recordings*, New York: Schirmer, 1980.

Cohen, Scott. "Don't Ask Me Nothin' about Nothin'" (interview), in *Spin*, December 1985.

Cott, Jonathan. "The *Rolling Stone* Interview with Bob Dylan," in *Rolling Stone*, 1/25/78 and 11/16/78.

Cott, Jonathan. *Dylan*, New York: Rolling Stone Press, 1984.

Crowe, Cameron. *Biograph* booklet and liner notes, included with album, 1985.

De Somogyi, Nick. *Jokermen & Thieves—Bob Dylan and the Ballad Tradition*, Bury: Wanted Man, 1986.

Dergoth, Jonas. *A Concise Synopsis of Bob Dylan's Masterpiece*, no publisher or date. Scene-by-scene description of *Renaldo & Clara*.

Diddle, Gavin. *Images and Assorted Facts*, Manchester, England: The Print Centre, 1983.

Diddle, Gavin, ed. *Talkin' Bob Dylan....1978*, Pink Elephant, 1984.

Dundas, Glen. *Tangled Up in Tapes Revisited*, Thunder Bay, Canada: SMA Services, 1990. Another guide to all of Dylan's performances, organized in a different fashion than Krogsgaard's. The tables showing which songs were performed on each tour are particularly useful.

Dunn, Tim. *I Just Write 'Em As They Come*, Painesville: Not-A-Ces, 1990. An annotated index to songs and other writings by Bob Dylan.

Dylan, Bob. *In His Own Write*, the bob dylan archive unltd. Unauthorized collection of hard-to-find writings from 1962-65; no city or date.

Dylan, Bob. *Positively Tie Dream*, Forban, England: Ashes and Sand, 1979. Unauthorized collection of interviews and fictions.

Dylan, Bob. *Some Other Kinds of Songs... I'm Not There (1986)*, Knaff, 1986. Unauthorized collection of lyrics to Dylan songs not included in *Lyrics*.

Dylan, Bob. *Saved! The Gospel Speeches*, Madras & New York: Hanuman, 1990. Unauthorized collection of concert raps, edited by Clinton Heylin.

Flanagan, Bill. *Written in My Soul*, Chicago: Contemporary, 1985. Interviews with songwriters, including Dylan.

Gans, Terry. *What's Real and What Is Not*, Munich: Hobo Press, 1983.

Gilmore, Mikal. "Positively Dylan," in *Rolling Stone*, 7/17/86.

Gray, Michael and Bauldie, John, editors. *All Across the Telegraph*, London: Sidgwick & Jackson, 1987. Anthology from the magazine.

Gross, Michael. *Dylan, An Illustrated History*, New York: Grosset & Dunlap, 1978.

Herdman, John. *Voice Without Restraint, Bob Dylan's Lyrics and Their Background*, New York: Delilah, 1982.

Heylin, Clinton. *Rain Unravelled Tales*, Ashes and Sand, 1985.

Heylin, Clinton. *To Live Outside the Law*, A Guide to Bob Dylan Bootlegs, Sale: Labour of Love, 1989.

Hilburn, Robert. "Dylan: 'I learned that Jesus is real and I wanted that'," *Los Angeles Times*, November 23, 1990.

Humphries, Patrick and Bauldie, John. *Oh No! Not Another Bob Dylan Book*, Essex: Square One, 1991.

Jansen, Gerhard, ed. *Bob Dylan—Pressing On*, Lelystad, Holland: no publisher, 1980.

Keller, Martin. Interview with Bob Dylan in *Minneapolis City Pages*, July 1983.

Kooper, Al. *Backstage Passes: Rock 'n' Roll Life in the Sixties*, New York: Stein & Day, 1977.

Kramer, Daniel. *Bob Dylan*, New York: Citadel Press, 1967.

Landy, Elliott. *Woodstock Vision*, Hamburg: Rowohlt, 1984.

Lawlan, Val and Brian, editors. *Steppin' Out*, Linfield, England: Steppin' Out Productions, 1987.

McGregor, Craig, ed. *Bob Dylan, A Retrospective*, New York: William Morrow, 1972. Includes 1966 *Playboy* interview, 1968 *Sing Out!* interview, 1969 *Rolling Stone* interview, plus watershed pieces by Robert Shelton, Nat Hentoff, Ralph Gleason, Irwin Silber, Jules Siegel and Jon Landau.

Miles. *Bob Dylan*, London: Big O, 1978.

Miles, ed. *Bob Dylan in His Own Words*, New York: Quick Fox, 1978.

Pennebaker, D. A. *Don't Look Back*, New York: Ballantine, 1968.

Pennebaker, D. A. "Looking Back on *Don't Look Back*," in *Fourth Time Around*, #1, August 1982.

324   PERFORMING ARTIST: *The Music of Bob Dylan*

Penrose, Roland. *Picasso, His Life and Work, Third Edition*, Berkeley: University of California Press, 1981.

Percival, Dave. *The Concert Charts*, X-asity, 1990.

Pickering, Stephen. *Bob Dylan Approximately, A Portrait of the Jewish Poet in Search of God; A Midrash*, New York: David McKay, 1975.

Ribakove, Sy and Barbara. *Folk-Rock: the Bob Dylan Story*, New York: Dell, 1966.

Rinzler, Alan. *Bob Dylan, The Illustrated Record*, New York: Harmony, 1978.

Roques, Dominique. *The Great White Answers*, Salindres, France: Southern Live Oak Productions, 1980. Guide to bootlegs.

Rosenbaum, Ron. "*Playboy* Interview: Bob Dylan," in *Playboy*, March 1978.

Rubin, William, ed. *Pablo Picasso: A Retrospective*, New York: The Museum of Modern Art, 1980.

Scaduto, Anthony. *Bob Dylan*, New York: Grosset & Dunlap, 1971 (updated, 1973). Biography.

Scobie, Stephen. *Alias Bob Dylan*, Alberta: Red Deer, 1991.

Shelton, Robert. *No Direction Home, The Life and Music of Bob Dylan*, New York: William Morrow, 1986. Biography.

Sloman, Larry. *On the Road with Bob Dylan*, New York: Bantam, 1978.

Spitz, Bob. *Dylan: A Biography*, New York: McGraw-Hill, 1989.

Thompson, Toby. *Positively Main Street*, New York: Coward-McCann, 1971.

Thomson, Elizabeth M., ed. *Conclusions on the Wall*, Manchester: Thin Man, 1980.

Thomson, Elizabeth and Gutman, David, eds. *The Dylan Companion*, London: Macmillan, 1990.

Van Estrik, Robert. *Bob Dylan: Concerted Efforts*, Netherlands: no publisher, 1982.

Von Schmidt, Eric and Rooney, Jim. *Baby Let Me Follow You Down: the Illustrated Story of the Cambridge Folk Years*, New York: Anchor, 1979.

Weasel, Verily E. "*Eat the Document*," in *Endless Road*, #5, 1984.

Wilhelm, Richard and Baynes, Cary, translators. *The I Ching or Book of Changes*, New York: Bollingen, 1950.

Wissolik, Richard David, ed. *Bob Dylan—American Poet and Singer, An Annotated Bibliography and Study Guide of Sources and Background Materials 1961-1991*, Greensburg: Eadmer Press, 1991.

Woodward, Ian. "*Planet Waves*—Dates of Recording," in *Occasionally Bob Dylan*, #4, January 1984.

Woodward, Ian. *Back of the Tapestry*, Carlisle: My Back Pages, 1991. Notes on *The Bootleg Series*.

Zollo, Paul. "Bob Dylan, the *SongTalk* Interview," in *SongTalk*, Vol. 2, Issue 16, Winter 1991.

*For assistance in locating and obtaining particular books, you may wish to contact one of the long-established mail order companies specializing in books about Bob Dylan:

My Back Pages, P.O. Box 117,
Carlisle CA1 2UL, England.

Rolling Tomes, P.O. Box 1943,
Grand Junction, CO 81502.
(303) 245-4315.

Photo Credits, Copyright Citations, and Acknowledgments

Photographs

Frontispiece: by Susan Wallach Fino. Bob Dylan in concert, spring 1980. Copyright © 1980 by Susan Wallach Fino.

Section I: On the cover of *Newsweek*, January 1974. Photograph by Barry Feinstein. Courtesy of Stephen M. H. Braitman, Amorous Archives, San Francisco.

Section II: Dylan at the television salute to John Hammond, September 1975. Courtesy of Stephen M. H. Braitman, Amorous Archives, San Francisco.

Section III: Dylan at the microphone, Rolling Thunder Revue, fall 1975. Courtesy of Stephen M. H. Braitman, Amorous Archives, San Francisco.

Section IV: Sara Dylan as Clara in *Renaldo & Clara*. Courtesy of Stephen M. H. Braitman, Amorous Archives, San Francisco.

Section V: by Greg Savalin. Dylan on Tour '78 (probably Oakland, November 13 or 14, 1978). Copyright © 1978 by Greg Savalin.

Section VI: Dylan at the recording sessions for *Slow Train Coming*, May 1979. Courtesy of Stephen M. H. Braitman, Amorous Archives, San Francisco.

Section VII: by Susan Wallach Fino. Clydie King and Bob Dylan, fall 1981. Copyright © 1981 by Susan Wallach Fino.

Section VIII: Dylan on the David Letterman Show, March 1984. Thanks to Steve Michel for the video transfer.

Section IX: by Susan Wallach Fino. Tour '86. Copyright © 1986 by Susan Wallach Fino.

(see special photo section for credits for photographs in that section)

Copyright Citations

Acknowledgments

A great many people have helped and supported me during the research and writing of these volumes. (I want to apologize in advance to those whose names are not mentioned here but should be.) My heartfelt thanks, then, to Gunter Amendt, Kiyoshi Asano, John Bauldie, Christian Behrens, Stephen Braitman, Randal Churchill, Nancy Cleveland, Dave Dingle, Glen Dundas, Carlo Feltrinelli, Bob & Susan Fino, Frank Gironda, Bill Graham, Richard Glyn Jones, Kirk Gustafson, Dieter and Asti Hagenbach, David G. Hartwell, Dave Heath, Clinton Heylin, John Hume, Jon Kanis, Jay Kerley, Jeff Kramer, Michael Krogsgaard, Jonathan Lethem, Paul Loeber, Bev Martin, Mick & Laurie McCuistion, Jim McLaren, Steve Michel, Blair Miller, Chuck Miller, Marleen Mulder, John Pateros, Michael Pietsch, Pat Reday, Elliott Roberts, Jeff Rosen, Robin Rule, Gerhard Schinzel, Gary & Mary Schulstad, Shasta, Jan Simmons, Heckel & Akiko Sugano, Brian Stibal, Clyde Taylor, Cooky Tribelhorn, Jerry Weddle, Markus Wittman, Sachiko Williams, and Ian Woodward.

Special thanks are due to my editor, Tim Underwood; my children, Erik Ansell, Heather Ansell, Taiyo Williams, and Kenta Williams; and my wife, Donna Nassar, whose patience, love, and enthusiasm have kept me going through the most challenging writing task I've ever undertaken.

And of course a word of acknowledgment is also due to the subject of this book, who, although a determinedly private person, has courageously and energetically shared himself through his music for thirty-two years now. "No one else could play that tune, you knew it was up to me." Thank you.

Index

327

Paul Williams was the founder of *Crawdaddy!*, the first American rock music magazine; he is the author of 18 books, one of which, *Das Energi*, is in its 21st printing. He is well known to Dylan appreciators as a respected scholar and writer in the field; in 1988 he was the featured guest speaker at an international gathering of Dylan fans in Manchester, England.

Williams's other books include *Nation of Lawyers*, *Remember Your Essence*, *The International Bill of Human Rights* (as editor), *The Map, or Rediscovering Rock and Roll*, and *Only Apparenly Real: The World of Philip K. Dick*.